Democracy in Canada

Democracy in Canada

The Disintegration of Our Institutions

Donald J. Savoie

McGill-Queen's University Press
Montreal & Kingston • London • Chicago

© McGill-Queen's University Press 2019

ISBN 978-0-7735-5902-8 (cloth)
ISBN 978-0-2280-0040-2 (ePDF)
ISBN 978-0-2280-0041-9 (ePUB)

Legal deposit third quarter 2019
Bibliothèque nationale du Québec

Printed in Canada on acid-free paper that is 100% ancient forest free
(100% post-consumer recycled), processed chlorine free

This book has been published with the help of a grant from the Canadian Federation
for the Humanities and Social Sciences, through the Awards to Scholarly Publications
Program, using funds provided by the Social Sciences and Humanities Research
Council of Canada. Funding was also received from the Donald J. Savoie Institute.

Funded by the   Financé par le
Government   gouvernement   Canada   Canada Council   Conseil des arts
of Canada   du Canada   for the Arts   du Canada

We acknowledge the support of the Canada Council for the Arts.
Nous remercions le Conseil des arts du Canada de son soutien.

Library and Archives Canada Cataloguing in Publication

Title: Democracy in Canada : the disintegration of our institutions / Donald J. Savoie.
Names: Savoie, Donald J., 1947– author.
Description: Includes bibliographical references and index.
Identifiers: Canadiana (print) 20190117028 | Canadiana (ebook) 20190117052
    | ISBN 9780773559028 (hardcover) | ISBN 9780228000402 (ePDF) | ISBN
    9780228000419 (ePUB)
Subjects: LCSH: Democracy—Canada. | LCSH: Canada—Politics and government.
Classification: LCC JL186.5 .S35 2019 | DDC 320.971—dc23

This book was typeset in 10.5/13 Sabon.

Contents

Preface

Alexis de Tocqueville (1805–1859), more than any other political theorist, captured my interest as a student of political science. I was fascinated that an aristocrat from France would return from an extended visit to the United States with fresh insights on the workings of democracy in America and how it contrasted with what he saw in Europe. The last thing an aristocrat would wish to do, I thought, was to explore the structure of democracy and report back to Europe on its strengths. I decided in the summer of 2015 to reread his classic *Democracy in America*.

Tocqueville's work resonates still. He explored issues that matter as much today as they did in the 1830s: the relationship between self-interest and collective action, why central governments adore uniformity, what the meaning of equality is, and how career politicians approach their work. He made the point that democracy is not satisfied with existing equality but tries to equalize everything. He wrote about the importance of a free press and the sovereignty of the people but warned against an ill-informed public opinion. He also tied democracy to equality of condition and warned against the tyranny of the majority.

What struck me in rereading Tocqueville was how much representative democracy had evolved since I was an undergraduate student. Few would have foreseen forty years ago that democracy, however broadly defined, would sweep aside communism in the Soviet Union and Eastern Europe. C.B. Macpherson, one of Canada's leading political scientists in the 1960s and '70s, wrote that "most of Eastern Europe has been brought into the Soviet orbit, and is no longer regarded as likely to move into the liberal-democratic pattern."[1] He misread the situation. He was hardly alone. No one could have predicted that we would witness the Arab Spring, that China would embrace a form of a market economy, that access to information legislation would become the norm for democratic states, that government bureaucracy would lose standing to the extent that it has, and the list goes on. One of the preoccupations of political science students in the late 1960s and early '70s was how best to promote "participatory democracy." But that was then. Howard Doughty summed it up well when he wrote, "It has been some time since the phrase participatory democracy was uttered in polite company. For many people of a certain age, however, the term evokes fond memories."[2]

I decided to take stock of the health of Canada's democracy. Canada's political institutions appear in good health, at least when compared with those of many other countries. The Arab Spring remains a work in progress; Russian oligarchs and the country's political leaders have hampered the development of the country's democratic institutions; and virtually all western liberal democracies are confronting important challenges, including declining voter turnout and low morale in government bureaucracies.[3]

We Canadians can be proud of how our national political and administrative institutions operate, at least when compared to those of other countries. Canadian democracy, however, is not without problems. A survey of Canadians reveals that they have little trust in their Members of Parliament, that politics repels more Canadians than it attracts, and that "the legitimacy of our entire democracy is at risk."[4] Robertson Davies wrote: "Canada is not a country you love. It is a country you worry about."[5] I decided to write this book because Canada is well worth worrying about.

I also take to heart then president Obama's call to action in his farewell address that applies as much to Canada as it does to the United States: "Our democracy is threatened whenever we take it for granted. All of us should be throwing ourselves into the task of rebuilding our democratic institutions."[6] This is my contribution to Canadian institutions.

At the risk of sounding Olympian, I consider this book my magnum opus. The book deals with the two issues that have dominated my work since I published my first book on Canadian federalism in 1981. I have since published extensively on regionalism, economic development, federal-provincial relations, on Canada's political-administrative institutions, particularly on how the prime minister and Cabinet work with Parliament, and on relations between politicians and public servants. In this book, I seek to bring the various questions raised in my earlier work to pose – and hopefully start to answer – a much broader question: how healthy is Canadian democracy?

I hasten to add, however, that I do not borrow sections from my earlier books. This book is not a second edition of any of my work on federalism, regionalism, or the machinery of government. It is a treatise on some of the most pressing questions for Canadians: who holds political power, how does one secure power, how do we hold accountable those who wield power, and how do our national political and administrative institutions decide and why.

This book hardly constitutes a definitive, or even the only, answer. I doubt that such a book could ever be written. I am certainly not the only student of government exploring issues that continue to shape our political and administrative institutions. My hope is that this book will encourage others to focus their interest on the structure of our democratic institutions and on how and why they can and should be improved.

I recognize that this is an ambitious book, one that addresses a broad theme and the workings of several institutions. The specialists, many of whom I quote in this book, will very likely be left *sur leur faim*, thinking that some issues are unattended while others are not fully explored. To be sure, working from a narrow perspective holds important advantages. One can explore completely the details of an issue from several angles. I was not able to do this, particularly when reviewing certain issues. But the price is well worth paying, given the current state of Canadian democracy.

My career has given me an excellent vantage point to review the health of Canada's democracy. I have published extensively on the role of the prime minister, bureaucracy, and regionalism. But these tell only part of the story. I have had the good fortune of preparing a report for Prime Minister Brian Mulroney on economic development in Atlantic Canada, of having several one-on-one discussions with four prime ministers in office: Pierre Trudeau, Brian Mulroney, Jean Chrétien, and Paul Martin. I have had many lengthy discussions with several former federal Cabinet ministers including, among others, Roméo LeBlanc (a Liberal) and Elmer MacKay (a Conservative). I also had numerous one-on-one discussions with several clerks of the Privy Council, notably Gordon Robertson, Paul Tellier, Jocelyne Bourgon, Mel Cappe, and Wayne Wouters, and a number of line department deputy ministers, among others, Peter Harder (at Foreign Affairs and later as government representative in the Senate), Richard Dicerni (at Industry Canada), and Michael Horgan (at Finance). I always came away from these discussions with a deeper understanding of the workings of government. I also worked for two of the leading senior public servants of the day, Gérard Veilleux and John (Jack) Manion. I served at the assistant deputy minister level in the Treasury Board Secretariat in Ottawa in 1987–88.

If I have a message for the next generation of political scientists and students of public administration and public policy, it is to go out and meet those who are in the thick of things trying to make the policy-making process and the machinery of government work. I could not have produced the bulk of my publications without seeking the views and advice of practitioners. For example, when I set out to write a book on the work of central agencies, I envisaged something different than the final product, *Governing from the Centre*. I had a breakfast interview with a senior Cabinet minister in the Chrétien government, who told me, "You academics have it all wrong – Cabinet is not a decision-making body, it is a focus group for the prime minister." Later interviews substantiated this view.

I also owe a special thank you to those who have travelled the territory before me, and I acknowledge many of my intellectual debts in the endnotes. Others, however, are not so formally acknowledged. I owe a very special thank you to my wife, Linda, for putting up once again with my insatiable appetite for work. I am very fortunate that she has, over the years, always supported me despite my desire to work long hours and to sacrifice too many weekends for my research.

Gabriel Arsenault, a bright young scholar full of promise at my university, read the manuscript and never hesitated to identify its shortcomings. B. Guy Peters, a friend of many years and a co-author, read parts of the manuscript that I was struggling with and provided invaluable advice. I owe a special thank you to two anonymous reviewers. Both did their homework, both presented a detailed assessment of the manuscript, and both did more than one can possibly expect from a reviewer. Their comments and suggestions made for a much-improved book. Finally, I owe a heartfelt thank you to Philip Cercone who has always supported my work from my very first book to this one. No author could be better

served. I remain, however, answerable, responsible, and accountable for all the book's defects.

I also want to thank my long-time assistant Ginette Benoit for
her good cheer in the face of my constant demands, and Céline
Basque for helping me to bring the manuscript into final form. Paula
Sarson made numerous editorial suggestions, and the book is greatly
improved as a result.

Donald J. Savoie
Canada Research Chair in Public Administration and Governance
Université de Moncton

Democracy in Canada

Introduction

Democracy is one of the most maligned and misunderstood words in the dictionary. It means different things to different people, it continues to serve different purposes and interests, and it has taken on vastly different meanings at different times in history. Democracy serves as a noun (as in "a democrat"), an adjective (as in "democratic"), and a verb (as in "to democratize").[1] All political systems, from the Nazi Party (the National Socialist German Worker's Party) to the former Communist Party of the Soviet Union, insisted on describing themselves as democratic. Joseph Stalin's 1936 constitution for the Soviet Union enshrined freedom of speech, freedom of assembly, and universal suffrage by secret ballot. We now know that it was all a sham.[2]

Ancient Greece gave the word *democracy* to the world and a democratic process to strike decisions, large and small, that involved all citizens (albeit narrowly defined) – no small contribution to be sure. The process did away with kings, politicians, and even, to some extent, bureaucrats. More is said later about Greece's experience with direct democracy. Suffice to note here that the experience with direct democracy was short-lived. Indeed, democracy became a bad word in many quarters until the twentieth century. The great political philosophers of Ancient Greece – Socrates, Plato, and Aristotle – all saw little merit in democracy. As recently as 1867, when Canada's national political institutions were established, democracy was not to be fully trusted.

Canada has had precious few attempts at using direct democracy over the years. At the federal level, we have had only three referendums – one on prohibition in 1898, another on conscription in

1942, and the third one on a proposed constitutional arrangement in 1992. All three were launched by the federal government, given that there is no provision for citizens to launch a plebiscite on any issue.[3]

Direct democracy gave way to monarchs with absolute power and then to representative democracy. The march toward representative democracy, however, was slow and uncertain. The monarchs in the Middle Ages only turned to representatives of certain segments of the population when they had to, and in order to gain a degree of political legitimacy. It was only over time and with considerable efforts that, for example, the House of Commons in Britain gained the upper hand over the monarch and became representative of the broader public.

Citizens were not to be fully trusted until fairly recently. James Madison, one of the main architects of the American representative democracy, warned against pure democracy. He wrote that "such democracies have ever been spectacles of turbulence and contention; have ever been found incompatible with personal security or the rights of property; and have in general been as short in their lives as they have been violent in their deaths."[4] Madison and his fellow architects of the American system of government concluded that the will of the people needed to be "tempered by acute awareness of the potentially negative effects of citizen power, particularly citizens who were not of the 'chosen body.'" They were concerned that the "masses" would simply "vote themselves free beer and pull down the churches and country houses."[5] Thus, democracy was, for a long time, a pejorative word. Canada's Fathers of Confederation had misgivings about democracy, too, and they sought safeguards against it, as I explain later.

The French Revolution simultaneously gave new meaning and life to democracy but, given its excesses, it led many to argue that democracy had to be constrained. The French Revolution redefined the word democracy to include "liberty, fraternity, and equality," a seminal development. It violently swept aside the monarchy and aristocracy but, at the same time, gave rise – at least for a while – to mob rule.[6] Britain's aristocracy would point to the excesses of the French Revolution to underline the perils of democracy. That view found its way to Canada and explains, in large measure, Britain's reluctance to embrace responsible government for its colonies and the 1837 rebellions in Upper and Lower Canada.[7]

Revolutions in the United States, France, and Britain eventually paved the way for representative democracy to take root throughout the Western world. Britain's revolution was not as violent or as well known as the American and French revolutions, but it did alter in a fundamental fashion the relationship between the Crown and Parliament. Indeed, the history of the Westminster parliamentary system is a story of the struggle between the king or queen and Parliament, then between Parliament and the executive.

Monarchs enjoyed a divine right to rule and kings and queens made the case that they were accountable only to God. This was true in the case of England until 1701.[8] European monarchs, at least those who remained in power, were able to cling to this notion much longer – until the early years of the twentieth century or until the Great War wiped them out in Germany, Russia, and Austria-Hungary.

By the end of the Great War, the tide had turned completely in favour of representative democracy. Democracy is now held to be the best form of government because it speaks to the interest of the many, not the few, and because it provides for citizens to be equal before the law, at least in their private disputes.[9] At a minimum, a liberal democratic society calls for free speech, competitive political parties, due process of law, privacy, a free media, protecting individuals from the tyranny of the majority, a representative and transparent government, and a professional bureaucracy.

Today, many countries and virtually all political systems claim to be democratic as a badge of honour. And yet, countries do many things in the name of democracy. A coalition of countries, including the United States, Canada, Australia, the United Kingdom, and France destroyed Baghdad in its name.[10] John Dunn maintains that, whenever a modern state argues it is democratic, "it necessarily misdescribes itself."[11] Canadian political scientist Stephen Brooks makes the point that in "the final analysis about the only thing that everyone can agree on is that democracy is based on equality."[12] That is, every adult in a representative democracy should enjoy the same political rights regardless of race, religion, gender, wealth or social class, and sexual orientation.

Democracy, however, remains an ever-elusive word. Three concepts underpin it: representation, accountability, and equality. Representation is fundamental to making representative democracy work. Accountability speaks to the requirement that all participants need to be responsible for their decisions and actions. Equality speaks to the requirement that all adults enjoy the same political rights. Democracy speaks as well to a popular control of government and participation in shaping the public interest.[13] Federalism adds – or should add – another requirement: a capacity in national institutions to accommodate regional circumstances in shaping policies.

Today, however, not all is well with democracy. An article appearing in *The Economist* argues that "democracy is going through its worst crisis since the 1930s. The number of countries that can plausibly be described as democracies is shrinking." It adds that "the United States – the engine room of democratisation for most of the postwar period – has a president who refused to say if he would accept the result of the election if it went against him."[14] Indeed, voter turnout is trending down in western democracies, national political institutions are under attack even by members who serve in them, and morale in government bureaucracies has been trending down for years.

Canada is no different. Marc Mayrand, Canada's chief electoral officer, urged Canadians not to be complacent about the state of Canadian democracy. He identified "two areas where the health of our democracy is increasingly under pressure. One of these is citizens' engagement; the other is citizens' trust in their electoral institutions."[15] Thomas Axworthy, principal secretary to former prime minister Pierre E. Trudeau, writes that "Canada's democratic deficit goes much beyond the role of Parliament. Literally every institution in our system of democratic governance – the electoral system, parties, Parliament, federalism, and the public service – as they operate presently, contribute to the democratic deficit."[16]

The book's central purpose is to take stock of these institutions, their health, and the challenges they are facing. It makes the case that various forces continue to conspire to weaken our national political and administrative institutions. Canada's Fathers of Confederation set out to build institutions to fix problems plaguing the old Canadas – now Ontario and Quebec. They have not been, and are still not, designed to accommodate the outer Canadas. National institutions, designed by and for a unitary state, have been particularly adroit at accommodating the interests of the heavily populated regions but less so in dealing with the requirements of the smaller provinces.

Though Canadian representative democracy fares well when compared to other democracies, I, too, argue that Canada has a democratic deficit. Canada's democratic deficit has a particular bent: it lacks a capacity in its national institutions to accommodate regional circumstances and to promote regional equality. Evidence of this deficit is found in the constitution, in political institutions, in the executive, and in the bureaucracy. I maintain that this constitutes Canada's most significant democratic deficit.

But there are other challenges. New forces continue to emerge that are buffeting our national political and administrative institutions. Globalization, an activist judiciary, incessant calls for greater transparency and accountability, fiscal challenges tied to the perception that government is wasteful, and a widely held view that government bureaucracies are not up to the task are making things very difficult for our institutions. The media, a key requirement in making representative democracy work, are playing their part in the delegitimization of our institutions.

A public opinion survey revealed that the proportion of Canadians who trust their government to do the right thing fell sharply from nearly 60 percent in 1968 to 28 percent in 2012. Frank Graves, the pollster, explained that the "paucity of trust in politicians is almost cartoonishly low," much lower than is the case for permanent officials. He added that another survey sought to establish trust in various professions and discovered that nurses and doctors rank very high (about 80 percent of respondents reporting a high level of trust in these professionals), while politicians were at the bottom with only 10 percent of the respondents professing a high degree of trust in them.[17] I note that since the events of 11 September 2001, first responders now rank at the top of public trust surveys, while politicians still rank at the bottom, faring only one percentage point better than car salespeople.[18]

Canadian representative democracy needs to be on guard against mediocrity, complacency, poor journalism, low regard for politicians, a debased public service, a sense that citizens have no control over their government, and that the country's national political institutions are unable to reflect Canadian society and its regions. People instinctively sense a problem with the state of Canadian democracy.[19]

Other public opinion surveys consistently reveal a growing dissatisfaction with the work of Canada's political and administrative institutions. Samara, a non-partisan, not-for-profit think tank, regularly surveys Canadians on the state of Canadian democracy and recently concluded, "Quite simply our democracy is not doing as well as a country as rich as Canada deserves. Canadians are not participating in politics as much as they could, they don't believe it affects them, and they don't see their leaders as influential or efficacious."[20] It is revealing that the public institutions now enjoying some credibility with Canadians, such as the Supreme Court and the Bank of Canada, are non-democratic in that members are appointed, not elected.

This is far from a Canada-only phenomenon. Throughout the Western world, there is a low regard for politicians, political party membership is trending down, political parties are reflecting their leaders rather than leaders reflecting their parties, and political parties are essentially running on empty in shaping policy proposals. Furthermore, there is a decline in trust in democratic institutions, with citizens increasingly believing that they have little control over government and that even their politicians have little control over events as they take shape.[21] As noted, Canada's democratic deficit has an additional challenge when compared with other western democracies: Canada's national institutions lack the capacity to articulate and incorporate Canada's regional perspective in shaping Ottawa's policy and decision-making processes. The book's central argument is that Canada is doing poorly when it comes to regional equality when compared with other federations.[22]

No one who cherishes the values and advantages of a liberal democracy should assume the inevitability of its survival.[23] Representative democracy, as we know it, is a relatively recent development. In a representative democracy, elections are to be regularly held, they are to be fair, and losers must accept their outcome as legitimate.[24] It is not sufficient, however, to rely solely on democratic elections to ensure a healthy democracy. For instance, Russia now has democratic elections, but it is weak in applying the rule of law – it follows that if rulers can change laws to suit their interest, then the country does not have the rule of law. Russian political and administrative institutions show little respect "for the individual and his and her rights."[25] The rule of law, an important prerequisite for a democratic state, has to be binding on everyone from the weak to the most powerful. Political and administrative institutions must be seen to be fair, effective, and able to manage relations between individuals, groups, and regions.

The state having a monopoly on violence is another important requirement for true democracy. A well-functioning modern democratic state must be able to go beyond family, friends, and political partisans in the way it recruits officials to administrative positions.[26] Representative democracy has many requirements, and the holding of periodic elections is only one, albeit a very important one.

Though well-functioning representative democracies share similar requirements, from a free press to holding free and open elections, they have their own defining characteristics: the United States and its emphasis on personal liberty and separation of powers, France and its revolution, and Britain and its historical ties to the monarchy. Canada's political history has been defined by a profound desire to promote an identity different from our neighbours to the south.

To take stock of Canadian democracy, we need to look to history, review the work of leading students of democracy, and understand how political parties have evolved in recent years. In addition, we need to understand how the media have changed given the rise of social media, how bureaucracy operates today, who today's elites are, and where political and economic power now reside. We know that Canada's political institutions "point toward a strong executive, a weak legislature, a few powerful people and many nobodies all working in a system where representation is accomplished far more through party leaders and appointments than through mass election."[27]

Canada, like other western representative democracies, has to deal with an information explosion. The world has created more information in the last five years than in all preceding history. And yet, as Daniel Levitin points out, the internet and the new media have "no central authority to prevent people from making claims that are untrue."[28] The traditional print media, which, for the most part, have a higher level of ethics and fact-checking, are struggling to survive. "I read it somewhere" enables citizens and even politicians to make outlandish claims that are patently untrue, forcing governments to deal, as best they can, with a "wild west media landscape in which retweetable quotes take precedence over verifiable facts."[29]

The rise of social media has in turn given rise to what former White House official Cass R. Sunstein calls the "Daily Me." There is now a media for everyone when individuals see what they want to see and hear what they want to hear. The social media have become echo chambers. If you like certain political views but not others, it is easy to only dial into media that confirm your views and to isolate yourself from uncomfortable truths. Representative democracy works better, however, if voters are exposed to material not chosen in advance and to the clash of competing perspectives. In other words, we need to hear something that is more than an echo of our own voice.[30]

There are still other powerful forces at play challenging our national democratic institutions. We live in an era where the prevalent question among many voters is, "What's in it for me?" *Time* magazine devoted an issue in 2013 to the "Me, Me, Me Generation." It reported that scientific data revealed the incidence of "narcissistic personality disorder" is three times as high among people in their twenties than people sixty-five or older.[31] "What's in it for me?" makes it more difficult for a government to define and pursue the broader public interest. In an earlier publication, I wrote about the death of the collective "we," and I made a link between the rise of "me, me, me" in Canadian politics and the fast-dwindling membership in organized religion.[32] At the same time, we are seeing an excessive level of partisanship. Bob Rae pointed to excessive partisanship as one of the most challenging problems confronting Canadian politics: "Parliament should be the place where real debate and give-and-take happens, alas, it is not ... An excessive partisanship is what Canadians see. And they don't like it."[33]

But again, that hardly tells the whole story. I maintain that one of the keys to understanding Canadian democracy is history, how Canada adopted British political institutions, how Canada's written constitution (circa 1867 and 1982) was formulated, and what forces influenced its development. I argue that to understand Canada's democratic woes, we need to return to the day the country was born and assess how today's democratic requirements square with decisions struck at the Charlottetown and Quebec conferences in 1864. Leaving aside the Canadian Charter of Rights and Freedoms (circa 1982), both the broad contours of Canadian federalism and the country's political institutions continue to operate within the confines established in 1867. We have seen, however, structural changes in Canada's socio-economic circumstances – changes largely inspired by government. I maintain that both the changes and the lack of changes in certain areas have been, for the most part, in response to decisions struck in 1867.

In Canada's first century, the country stuck with imported political institutions from Britain, unwilling or unable to introduce institutional change. This even though British and Canadian socio-political conditions were vastly different: a unitary state versus a federation, a highly class-conscious society versus a pioneer society, and a linguistic divide in Canada non-existent in Britain. Designed for a unitary state, Canada's national political institutions past and present continue to deny the country's geography. Our political institutions were imported from Britain and imposed by a handful of politicians and the British Colonial Office. As Richard Simeon writes, "Some of the most important institutions characteristic of Canadian government did not evolve out of pressures from the society below."[34]

Britain has had no difficulty in embracing a national identity. Canada is a different story. Politicians, from John A. Macdonald to Justin Trudeau, have lamented Canada's inability to find unity and purpose.[35] Prime Minister Justin Trudeau argues that "there is no core identity, no mainstream in Canada."[36] Margaret Atwood suggests that "there is no new Canadian identity ready for him [the immigrant] to step into."[37] Marshall McLuhan observed that "Canada is the only country in the world that knows how to live without an identity."[38] Ramsay Cook summed it up best when he wrote, "the question of Canadian identity is not a Canadian question at all but a regional question."[39] If Canadian identity is a regional question rather than a Canadian national question, how are Canada's political institutions dealing with it?

National political institutions, as conceived by John A. Macdonald, George Brown, and George-Étienne Cartier, largely denied the regional factor other than that found in what is now Ontario and Quebec. Those Fathers of Confederation came up with a treaty to unite two nations, *deux nations*, to forge a compact between two peoples and then imported British political institutions lock, stock, and barrel to make the treaty work. These British-inspired institutions have little capacity to deal with territorial divisions or people's attachment to their territory or space. The point is that geographic location, sense of place, and regionalism matter in shaping Canadian identity, but the country's institutions have limited capacity to accommodate regional considerations, except those flowing from the treaty that united the *deux nations*. In short, though we define ourselves by our dividedness, our national political institutions are ill-equipped to deal with that very dividedness.

John A. Macdonald, the main architect of Canada's national political institutions, defined a role for the Senate that does not square easily with the requirements of federalism or even representative democracy. He saw the role of the Senate as providing a "sober second thought," a phrase he borrowed, to keep a check on the work of an elected House of Commons, or on democracy.[40] Members of the Canadian Senate are appointed, not elected. The work of the Senate has not mattered much over the years because appointed members of Parliament do not enjoy the level of political legitimacy that their colleagues in the Commons do. The House of Commons decides who holds power, not the Senate. The Canadian Senate continues to search for a proper role, thus far with limited success.[41]

The key architects of the Confederation deal came from Canada West (Ontario) and Canada East (Quebec). They set out to solve their intractable political problems. They, with the assistance of the British Colonial Office, had a firm control of the agenda. It has led many to see Confederation as a treaty between two founding nations. One nation set out to protect its linguistic and cultural identity. It could point to several provisions in the British North America Act that protected its cultural, linguistic, and religious interests. The other, Canada West (Ontario), saw Confederation as a way out of the crippling impasse resulting from the 1841 Act of Union that brought Canada West and East together. Guy Laforest writes: "In Quebec, Confederation has always been perceived as a solemn pact between two nations."[42] Gregory Mahler reports that public opinion surveys reveal 49 percent of Canadians view Canada as a pact between two founding peoples while 46 percent see Canada as a pact among ten equal provinces.[43] Famed historian Arthur Lower wrote: "There are, as yet, two Canadas, inhibited by two peoples. In the strictest sense, there can be no History of Canada. There can be histories of French Canada. There can be histories of English Canada."[44]

The Maritime provinces and, later, the Western provinces became appendages to the *deux nations* bargain. It explains why Gordon T. Stewart can write: "The Maritime and Western provinces, while they had an impact on post-1867 government formation and parliamentary alignments and while they certainly forced attention to particular issues, did not make a fundamental alteration in the political culture already established in the pre-1867 Canadas."[45] Therein lies the problem.

Political scientists, historians, and economists have been making the case that Canada is deeply divided along regional lines. There are sharp regional differences in voting behaviour,[46] in economic performance,[47] in public opinion,[48] in language,[49] and in political culture.[50] Canada, unlike other federations, has largely relied on provincial governments to give voice to its regional differences. Politicians who are able to exploit regional differences by focusing on issues that favour heavily populated regions are rewarded with more seats in the House of Commons. The political party that wins more seats in the Commons is rewarded with political power.

In the 2016 US presidential election, the two main candidates were from New York. The fact that both came from the country's largest city was a non-issue. Things would be different in Canada if two or three leaders of the main political parties all came from Toronto, Montreal, Calgary, or Halifax. It is highly unlikely that this could ever happen. The regional factor is much too important a factor in Canadian politics and one political party would very quickly see a strategic advantage in selecting its leader from another region. Yet, regional differences in Canada lack an institutional focus in national political institutions unless they are anchored in vote-rich Ontario and Quebec.

The United States has a Senate that is a credible voice for the regions, both large and small, and an Electoral College that can act as a check against complete reliance on representation by population in deciding who becomes president. It will be recalled that Hillary Clinton lost the election though she won the popular vote by a healthy margin – 65,844,954 to 62,979,879, a difference of 2,865,075 voters. Though it was an emotionally charged and divisive election campaign, Americans accepted the outcome and nothing much was said about either the Electoral College or the fact that the two leading candidates came from the country's most populated city.

Canada does not have the same kind of safeguard for smaller regions as other federations have. Starting with J.A. Macdonald and George Brown to this day, Canada does not attach much importance to the regional factor in the operations of our national institutions. We follow in the British tradition of tying democracy to one citizen, one vote. Andrew Coyne, a high-profile columnist with the *National Post*, put it this way: "The very principle of democracy is in need of some defence. So here it is. At heart, democracy is based on a belief in the equal worth and equal rights of every citizen. That is why everyone gets one vote; it is also the principle underpinning the doctrine of majority rule. It is why we talk of governments governing only with the consent of the governed, why Winston Churchill said that in a democracy, governments are our servants and not our masters."[51] Coyne makes no provision for the regional representation requirements of federalism. The United States, Germany, Russia, and Australia – like Canada with a Westminster-inspired parliamentary system – do.

Regionalism is hardly the only challenge confronting Canada's national political institutions. Students of government are making the case that we live in a "post-democratic" world. The culprits include globalization, global financial markets, social media, and citizens withdrawing from political participation. The argument is that formal representative institutions remain in place while the locus of political decision-making has moved elsewhere.[52]

The government's ability to govern while demonstrating a level of responsiveness to secure public faith in politics is being tested.[53] If Canadians wish to locate political power, they should not look to Parliament, political parties, Cabinet, or bureaucracy. Rather, they should look to the prime minister, his immediate advisers, key lobbyists, and economic elites. Yet, formal political and administrative institutions continue to operate essentially like they always have. Put differently, we have not been able to reform our formal institutions to deal with changing circumstances. Canada's formal institutions have developed a well-honed capacity to give the appearance of change while standing still. To the extent that change has occurred, it has continued to concentrate power in fewer and fewer hands.

What is the number one challenge to representative democracy? In the United States, Ganesh Sitaraman argues that it is the collapse of the middle class and growing economic inequality.[54] What about in Canada? We have an expanding list to consider for an answer: at the top we see the inability of national political institutions to define and accommodate regional circumstances, the growing power of the prime minister, the inability of Parliament to carry out its more important responsibilities, a fast-changing role for the media, a shrinking global economy, Canadians thinking that they are not properly represented, and a federal government bureaucracy losing both its way and its standing with Canadians.[55]

Canada's two-nation concept is increasingly challenged. Stéphane Paquin labels the two founding peoples concept a "myth" that has little historical basis and was invented by politicians to bring voters to their way of thinking.[56] Peter Russell, who once saw merit in the two-nation concept, now sees three Canadas: English Canada, French Canada, and Indigenous Canada.[57] Social, economic, and political changes in Canada since the 1960s have led many Canadians to be less willing to see Canada as two nations defined by two founding people. They see Quebec as one element, albeit an important one, of Canadian diversity. Through it all, strong regional grievances persist. A public opinion survey reveals that a majority of respondents in eight out of ten provinces do not believe that their province receives its fair share in striking important national decisions. Only in Ontario and Quebec is there a majority of respondents who believe that their province has a fair share in such decisions and is treated by the federal government "with the respect it deserves."[58]

LOOKING TO HISTORICAL
INSTITUTIONALISM FOR ANSWERS

History matters in all things. Nowhere is this more evident than in politics and government. I maintain that Canadian democracy is path-dependent even more so than other western democracies for several reasons. We have a particularly rigid constitution that is designed for a unitary state, not a federation, and national political institutions that serve the economic interests of certain regions over others.

I recognize that socio-economic circumstances are never static and that partisan political considerations, wars, economic depressions or recessions, the workings of the global economy, and advances in communications will invariably force the hand of any government to react, change course, or launch a new policy. Politicians are motivated by electoral considerations and pursue the kind of change that they think will get their party elected. Governments in Canada have embraced change but they have done so largely by working outside political institutions, notably its constitution. This, in turn, has created new forms of path-dependency, guiding developments in virtually all of the country's key policy fields.

Historical institutionalism makes the point that institutions and individuals who operate in them are embedded in relationships beyond their control. As B. Guy Peters explains, choices are made "at the inception of the institution and will have a persistent influence over its behaviour for the remainder of its existence."[59] Though historical institutionalism is not without shortcomings, it offers promise in gaining a more thorough understanding of the workings of Canada's political institutions.[60] Certainly, individualistic explanations or the work, views, and biases of individuals matter in explaining political and policy developments. However, I argue that historically embedded institutional arrangements matter more in the Canadian setting than in other jurisdictions and that they account for much of Canada's political conflicts and even for incremental changes in policy. The form and character of Canada's national political and administrative institutions continue to have a determining impact on the country's policy- and decision-making processes and on the behaviour of our politicians and public servants.[61] This book explores how and why.

Historical institutionalism has been challenged on the ground that, while it is good at explaining persistence once a policy has been implemented, it falls short in explaining the initial adoption of a policy or program.[62] I maintain that, in Canada, historical institutionalism goes a long way not only in explaining the initial adoption of a new approach but also the persistence in policy direction. Canada is an excellent laboratory for applying historical institutionalism to gain insights. As noted, the country's constitution is rigid, and its main political and administrative institutions were imported from a country that remains different from Canada in both important and unimportant ways.

* * *

Geography explains virtually everything Canadian, and it is central to understanding the workings of Canadian democracy. Canadians think in spatial terms. We have English and two or three French Canadas, Indigenous peoples, the Laurentian Consensus, western alienation, the Maritime Rights Movement, the North, the Prairies, and the country's industrial heartland. Yet, the 1867 British North America Act makes no reference to space or territory. The focus is on language and denominational rights – revealing code words for the two-nation concept or a compact between two peoples.[63]

Canada imported a constitution and political institutions from a country where geography never dominated politics to the extent that it always has in Canada. British-inspired political institutions are spatially blind because it suits England's history and national character, because England is a unitary state – though on shaky grounds of late – and because its main political cleavages have not been around geography. Being spatially blind in England is one thing. Being spatially blind in Canada is quite another. We know that our Fathers of Confederation had very little to say about how to make a Westminster-style parliamentary system and federalism work.[64] Richard Simeon summed it up well when he observed, "National political institutions are unable to serve as the central arena for reconciling regional and national interests ... these failures ... are built into the system."[65]

Failures were built into the system from the first day Canada was born, starting with the Senate. Prime ministers have looked to Cabinet to provide regional voices or perspectives in Ottawa. However, Cabinet requires a fair regional distribution in the membership for it to play a meaningful role in providing regional perspectives and shaping policies, programs, and initiatives. If Cabinet has become little more than a "focus group" for the prime minister, then we need to answer fundamental questions, notably: "Can Cabinet still provide regional voices? Does Cabinet still merit 'immunity from the disclosure of its proceedings?'"[66] If the answer is no, the implications for a fundamental building block for a Westminster-inspired parliamentary system operating in a federation are clear.

Canadian politics has sought to tailor some public policies and programs along spatial lines – the equalization program is a case in point. But the offsets have never been able to get to the heart of the matter. They have rather given rise to what March and Olsen call a "logic of appropriateness."[67] Other attempts to tailor programs to fit regional economic circumstances have been short-lived or highly controversial.[68] Again, leaving aside the Charter of Rights and Freedoms, reforms in Canada have been technocratic rather than structural.

What about the public service? J.E. Hodgetts, the father of Canadian public administration, argued that the public service has had to respond to "conditions" imposed by geography in setting "goals" and delivering "programs."[69] Yet, the Canadian public service, like the national political institutions it serves, was patterned after the British public service in its design and structure. The Canadian public service is organized around the principle of technocratic efficiency and along sectoral lines which, as Alan Cairns pointed out, makes it "inherently hostile to representative criteria" with a resultant bias toward uniformity where regional considerations are largely irrelevant to departmental organizations.[70]

Indeed, Canada's public service is confronting a series of challenges. I have argued elsewhere that the traditional bargain that guided relations between politicians and public servants has broken down.[71] Public servants themselves are asking fundamental questions about their role in shaping policy, advising ministers, and delivering programs and services.[72]

This book makes the case that Canadian democracy is confronting four major challenges. First, the country's national political institutions remain unable to both address the regional factor in shaping

policy and to operate under constitutional conventions that underpin Westminster parliamentary government. Second, government
bureaucracy has lost its way, and it is no longer able to meet the
expectations of politicians and citizens. Third, the average citizen
believes that national political institutions cater to those who serve
in them, to economic elites, and to interest groups at their expense.
Fourth, accountability in government no longer meets present-day
requirements given the rise of the new media, the work of lobbyists,
and incessant calls for greater transparency.

OUTLINE OF STUDY

To answer questions outlined earlier, we need to look to history to
consider how Canadian federalism was born, and we need to review
the work of western philosophers who have had a profound impact
on democratic institutions. We need to explore how Westminster-
inspired political and administrative institutions took form and how
Canada sought to adapt them to the country's social, political, and
economic circumstances.

Canada's population factor is important in understanding the workings of Canadian democracy. Canada has long rejected the melting pot
approach to forge a national identity. Canada is home to two official
languages, regional diversity, multicultural policies, and Indigenous
communities that are, more recently, turning to the courts rather than
political institutions to be heard. This in turn has profound implications for our national political and administrative institutions.

Canada has evolved over its 150-plus years. New provinces were
added, the scope and size of government expanded, and federalism
took on new forms largely outside the constitution. The Fathers
of Confederation defined a very restricted role for provincial governments, which they saw as subservient to the federal government. However, the rise of modern society and the welfare state
have reshaped Canadian federalism to the point that the Fathers
of Confederation would not recognize it today. Leaving aside the
1982 amendments, Canada's written constitution has stood on the
sideline, largely frozen in time, as the modern state has taken shape.

Parliament and, in more recent years, Cabinet have been pushed to
the side. A prime ministerial–centric government, working with carefully selected partisan political advisers and senior public servants, is
at the centre of all important political decisions. Prime ministers and

a handful of carefully selected courtiers have full access to the levers of political power. Rank and file members of political parties and members of Parliament are left on the outside looking in at the same time as they are being asked to toe the line. Toeing the party line, however, is made more difficult for a variety of reasons. We need to explore all these issues to gain a full understanding of the challenges confronting Canadian representative democracy today.

Bureaucracy is asked to reinvent itself at the same time as it is asked to leave well enough alone in its dealings with politicians, the media, and Parliament. Surveys among federal public servants reveal that the public service is now plagued with serious morale problems. It is no exaggeration to write that the federal public service is an institution under siege. In my earlier work, I described the federal public service as a big whale that can't swim. I was struck by how many former politicians and senior public servants told me that I had it right. The more important question is why. We need to explore in some detail this question and the state of Canada's most important national administrative institutions.

Both politicians and public servants now have to deal with media different than they were as recently as twenty years ago. The media have a critical role to play in making representative democracy work. Important segments of the media have become mere echo chambers, which one consults to hear what one wants to hear. How do politicians and senior public servants deal with media that are fragmented to the point that everyone with a mobile phone is a journalist? How then can our political and administrative institutions deal with the traditional media, the new media, and social media?

The courts are shaping public policies and even program implementation to an extent that was unimaginable to politicians less than forty years ago. Canada's former chief justice Beverley McLachlin maintains that Canadians can "now go to court to challenge laws and government acts not only on the grounds that they exceeded the grants of power, but also on the grounds that they violate fundamental rights."[73] Canadians, through the courts, are now able to challenge the wisdom of their political leaders. Peter Russell explains that Canadians are growing disillusioned with the workings of representative democracy and fast losing patience with government by debate and discussion and thus turning to the courts.[74]

Lobbyists have become important actors in shaping public policy and in striking decisions in government. Lobbyists are hired by economic elites to sell truth to government policy-makers – truth as their customers see it. In a post-truth world, politicians can turn to paid lobbyists to get a second opinion about any policy issue – there are even lobbyists working on behalf of the tobacco industry. There is always a lobbyist available in Ottawa to speak the kind of truth that a politician wants to hear.[75]

The central theme of this book is framed around a combined historical, institutional, and path-dependency framework. The argument is that change in Canada is difficult because our political and administrative institutions were constructed from a British historical and cultural experience with no effort or desire to bring into the mix Canadian realities. The book traces the evolution of these inherited dysfunctional institutions and traditions in the Canadian setting. I conclude by asking – how healthy is Canadian democracy? I look at how our national political institutions have evolved over time and how they have adjusted in some areas but not in others.

PART ONE

The Context

1

Understanding Democracy

The study of democracy is as old as the study of philosophy and almost as old as the written word in Western literature. The work of political philosophers down through the ages has had a profound impact on how representative democracy has evolved, including Canadian democracy. These renowned thinkers have pushed monarchs and political leaders to shape or reform political institutions, all the while providing ammunition to others in their call for change. If they have not always been the source of change, their work has often been employed to justify change.

Plato's work on ethics, justice, and how best to organize a community's political leadership resonates to this day.[1] He explored moral dimensions, warned against "the infection of wicked coveting and the pride of power," and sought to explain the instability of Athens's direct democracy.[2] Plato laid the foundation for others to follow.

After Plato and Aristotle, the work of Cicero, Thomas Hobbes, John Locke, Thomas Paine, Alexis de Tocqueville, John Stuart Mill, and Walter Bagehot, among others, came to shape how we view democracy, how the various forms of representative democracy developed over the years, and how political institutions should operate. Their work, very often, came at a critical moment in the evolution of political institutions – including Hobbes during England's Civil War, Locke and the Glorious Revolution, Bagehot when the workings of Britain's constitutional monarchy was taking shape, and Paine when the American Revolution was in its early stages. The authors of the American Constitution – James Madison, Alexander Hamilton, and John Jay – readily admitted that they relied on "celebrated" thinkers of the past in their work.[3]

One can appreciate why contemporary students of government and practitioners may well argue that Plato's or Cicero's work, for example, has little to offer to representative democracies. Plato was hardly a democrat. However, liberal democracies and our political institutions are the product of many rivulets of thought, with some dating back to Ancient Greece. And yet, Western liberal democracy, as we know it, is a relatively recent development. As noted, it requires much more than simply voting for political leaders – it involves the rule of law, protection of rights and liberties, competitive political parties, a free press, the protection of minorities, and administrative stability.

Canadian democracy was not born in a vacuum. British institutions from the monarchy, Parliament, and common law to the nation's bureaucracy influenced greatly how representative democracy took form in Canada and how Canadian institutions operate to this day. British institutions, in turn, were shaped by developments at home, by history, and by the ideas of political philosophers. We need a brief survey of the significant developments that shaped Westminster-style parliamentary governments to gain a better understanding of how Canadian democracy was born and how it operates today.

WHERE DEMOCRACY BEGAN

Students of democracy frequently return to where it all began – Ancient Greece in 500 BC – to answer the age-old questions, Who should hold power over others, and how should they be held accountable? We can trace some elements of Canadian representative democracy to Athenian democracy, which attempted to do away with the privileges and political power aristocrats enjoyed over others. In this sense, Athenian democracy introduced the notion of equality that has stood the test of time to become the most important component of representative democracy. As Josiah Ober observed, for "the first time in the recorded history of a complex society, all native freeborn males, irrespective of their ability, family connections, or wealth were political equals, with equal rights to determine state policy."[4]

This is not to suggest, however, that equality has held a single meaning that transcends time. Equality, in Athenian democracy, was narrowly defined – only male citizens over eighteen years of age were elevated to the "equality" level. They numbered 40,000 from a population of 260,000, consisting of 100,000 citizens, 150,000 slaves, and 10,000 foreign residents.[5]

However, Athenian direct democracy laid the groundwork for the political institutions that followed, including our own in Canada. One institution was an assembly (i.e., today's Parliament) that was home to those 40,000 male citizens over age eighteen. All could attend, though only about 5,000 attended sessions held about forty times a year. At these meetings, the assembly struck all key decisions related to war and made all laws. A second institution was a body that consisted of 500 adult males who served on a council (i.e., although somewhat of a stretch, one could associate it with today's Cabinet and bureaucracy) for one year. They were chosen by chance or at random, not by election, from the assembly. They met often and ran things down to the details of the day. The random selection process guaranteed that a permanent bureaucracy could not emerge and all members had to account directly to the assembly for their decisions and their spending. A third institution – the popular courts – played an important constitutional role, dealing with the laws and injured parties. One had to be a member of the assembly and at least thirty years old to serve. The courts had the power to strike any decision its members deemed appropriate.[6]

The Greek polis, then, provided important lessons for students of government and those charged with designing political institutions. One was that a society did not have to be ruled by kings – alternative forms of government existed. The other was that the Greek polis could provide the broad contours of how democracy may operate in the future: a Parliament or an assembly, an executive, and the courts.

Athenian direct democracy was short-lived, and Athenian society drifted once again into an aristocracy or oligarchy. The reasons for the decline of the Greek polis have been the subject of numerous debates over the centuries. Military conflicts were, of course, one reason. There were structural deficiencies as well that would not only spell the end of direct democracy but also give democracy itself a bad reputation that would endure for centuries, even to the day Canada was born in 1867.

Democracy's shady reputation explains why some of history's leading political philosophers did not always see merit in it. Plato, for one, did not. He argues in the *Republic* that the running of government is too complex and too demanding to be turned over to everyone or to ordinary people. Plato compares the ships of state to any ship that requires a competent captain. The ship of state, he asserts, requires competent governors at the helm, officials who have the knowledge of laws, ethics, and military matters.

Moreover, Plato maintains that ordinary people lack the judgment to make informed decisions not only about how to navigate the ship of state but also about who should navigate the ship. Many Americans who voted against Donald Trump would likely agree with Plato, whose point is that the people are not always interested in securing the knowledge to make enlightened decisions on who is best to govern. Plato warns, however, against turning matters over to the moneyed class or the military. Rather, he envisions a group of philosopher kings charged with managing the affairs of the state.[7]

Several short paragraphs cannot possibly do justice to Plato's invaluable contributions. The important point is that Plato's *Republic* can hardly be described as a pro-democracy treatise, yet, it has had a profound influence on both practitioners and the literature through the ages. Plato identified problems in his own time that persist to this day throughout the Western world, including Canada. For instance, difficulties remain in equipping voters with the education and knowledge required to make enlightened decisions, and there is the tendency for power to flow to those with the loudest voices, at times resulting in irrational decisions. Plato's work has provided ammunition to those who saw important shortcomings in democracy.

DEMOCRACY GOES DORMANT

Democracy became a pejorative word for more than two thousand years. Before Thomas Paine published his *Rights of Man* in 1791, there were precious few voices among practitioners or even political philosophers supporting democracy in any form.[8] Democracy was not to be trusted.

Rome, for instance, was ruled by aristocrats. It did, however, introduce checks and balances in its system of government, a development that would influence future government systems, particularly in the United States, but also in Canada. Though the Roman Republic never produced a written constitution, its form of government provided for the three branches of government that we see today: the legislative, executive, and judicial branches.

The Republic evolved into an empire, and as the empire grew, political power became concentrated in the hands of the emperor.

The emperor played multiple roles, including commander-in-chief, high priest, head of government and bureaucracy, and even the source of all laws.[9] In the provinces, he was "God."[10] Yet, he was not the vicar of the gods, but a man on whom the Senate had conferred political power, and so his power flowed from men rather than from God, or gods – an important distinction.[11] Rulers who claimed that their authority flowed directly from God would also claim that they answered only to God for their decisions.

The emperor dominated political and administrative life in Rome. All major decisions, and even a number of minor ones, flowed to and from him. But there were some constraints. Roman emperors, for example, ignored the Senate at their peril. As Samuel Finer writes, "Experience ought to have shown this [i.e., confronting the Senate] to be unwise: the four emperors who openly terrorized the Senate – Caligula, Nero, Domitian, and Commodus – all came to bad ends; not so the Antonines, who made it their business to co-operate."[12] The point is that although the legislative branch may have been weak in relation to the emperor and his political power, it did exist, and emperors had to learn to deal with it or pay a steep price. The legislative branch would in time become the centrepiece of representative democracy throughout the Western world. It has, however, lost standing in recent years, and Canada is no exception.

There are two other relevant developments that need to be highlighted: Rome's code of laws and the role of the bureaucracy. Emperor Justinian drew on a long history of law-making in Rome to prepare his "Justinian Code." The code preserved for posterity a unique experience in Roman government, and it transmitted to Europe and beyond the basis for legal systems now found throughout the Western world, including Canada. The existence of a body of laws meant that all the power could not, or at least should not, rest in the hands of an absolute ruler. This was in sharp contrast to systems of government where power rested with an absolute monarch who enacted laws that applied to everyone except himself. Since he was the source of all laws, he was thus above them.

Unlike Ancient Greece, Rome developed a bureaucracy in order to manage its empire. Still, the imperial bureaucracy grew very slowly, reaching only 30,000 by the fourth century. It is important to stress that, although the civil service had an identity separate from the military, it adopted the military model. It, too, had a chain of command, hierarchy, and a graded salary scale. It divided responsibilities by function, with some looking after the emperor's household, others responsible for drafting legislation, and still others responsible for handling financial transactions. The civil service was made up of two grades – high posts and lower grades – much like the British civil service years later. The high posts were short-term appointments and were the preserve of the aristocracy. These positions were viewed as "distinctions to be won," the motive being neither to make money nor to gain political influence, since aristocrats already had both, but rather, to gain "honour." The lower posts were held by career officials whose salaries were quite modest; however, they could augment their salaries by charging fees for the services they provided.[13] Still, emperors recognized that they needed a bureaucracy to help them run government operations, and they embraced the military command and control model that has endured to this day, including in Canada.

LESSONS LEARNED FROM CICERO

Cicero was a keen observer and author as well as a practicing politician, which cost him his life. His observations of Roman political developments and his writings have had a profound influence on Western political thought. Thomas Jefferson, for example, pointed to Cicero as a major influence in drafting the Declaration of Independence and in gaining a better understanding of public rights.[14] French revolutionaries pointed to Cicero as a major influence with Camille Desmoulins, insisting that Cicero's work was an important force in the French Revolution.[15] Cicero's words are even inscribed on the north wall of the Canadian Senate: "It is the duty of the Nobles to oppose the fickleness of the Multitude." This speaks to Cicero's lasting influence and to the role John A. Macdonald decided to assign to the Senate – a place for sober second thought, a check on representative democracy.

Rome and Cicero's abiding contributions centre around a better understanding of public law and justice. Cicero wrote about a "moral higher law" that existed even before the written word. He stressed the importance of laws that transcend time and even settings, suggesting that laws should be the same in Athens and Rome. Cicero regarded government as a body with a moral obligation to serve the broader community. In essence, for Cicero, government exists to serve society, making the point that society is larger and more important than government. He saw a vital role for government in protecting private property and attached a great deal of importance to the rule of law and to written laws to give it life. While Plato would rely on philosopher kings to rule society, Cicero would rely on constitutions and written laws as expressions of natural laws that should guide and restrain tyrants, monarchs, and politics at large.[16]

BRITAIN AND FRANCE PAVED THE WAY

Kings and tyrants ruled throughout Europe until the French Revolution. Until 1701, English kings, like their European counterparts, enjoyed a divine right to rule and could make the case that they were accountable only to God.[17] Although parliaments were starting to make their presence felt after the seventeenth century, other European monarchs, at least those who remained in power, were able to cling to this notion much longer – until the early years of the twentieth century, in some cases.

Kings and queens had a unique authority, evidenced by the fact that they received their crowns from the pope or bishop. The message was clear: their mandates came from God, not the people. They were chosen by God in accordance with the doctrine of the "Divine Right of Kings."[18] There was no higher authority than God. Thus, no man could punish them if they broke the law, only God and only in the afterlife. Yet they were head of "their" people, and all political power flowed to and from their hands. The royal throne was not the throne of man but of God, and thus the royal power was absolute because it came from God, not from man.[19] The Crown had the authority to call upon its subjects for support in times of war or in raising revenues. King Charles I, though with no success, reminded his accusers that they should remember they were "born his subjects and born subjects to those laws which determined that the king can do no wrong."[20]

In the case of England, the Magna Carta, the Bill of Rights, and the Act of Settlement served to limit the power of the Crown and eventually hold it to account. As is well known, the barons revolted against tax increases and took London by force in 1215. Consequently, King John agreed to a document limiting his power, and in return they renewed their oaths of allegiance to him. Although King John reneged on the document, King Henry III later reissued a shorter version of the Magna Carta. The document contains a number of provisions, including freedom for the church, new feudal rights, judicial rights, and the establishment of a council consisting of the most powerful men of the country working for the benefit of the state and their own interest, not simply for the king. This council, though subservient to the monarch, would in time form the basis for Westminster-styled Parliamentary government. Thus began the long struggle that would establish Parliament – or rather the king in Parliament – to become a completely sovereign authority, at least in theory. The Magna Carta set in motion a number of reforms to strip away some of the power that had been concentrated in one individual. For this and other related reasons, it has been described as "one of the most important legal documents in the history of democracy."[21]

The council was actually transformed into Parliament during the reign of Henry III (circa 1216–72). Though monarchs would learn ways to circumvent it, the precedent was set then that no law could be made and no tax could be imposed without the consent of Parliament; however, it was hardly a representative body. Parliament was divided into two houses, one for the nobility and the higher clergy and the other for knights and landowners. But Parliament still functioned as a kind of temporary committee to be summoned or dismissed by the king to serve his interest. He would summon Parliament whenever he needed new tax revenues, and Parliament, apart from withholding financial resources, had no means to force its will on the monarch. Even here, monarchs had ways to raise money outside of Parliament if they had to, and they would exercise this option from time to time. As history has repeatedly shown, monarchs in England and elsewhere would not easily part with their levers of power.

About 400 years later, England was plunged into a civil war that would pit the Crown against Parliament. There were many grievances that led to civil war in England, but the one most relevant to our purpose was the king's desire to rule without Parliament. Charles I succeeded in deciding not to summon Parliament for a decade. Matters came to a head, however, when he needed new money to deal with a northern rebellion. Parliament responded by drawing up a list of grievances, which the king simply dismissed. He then dissolved Parliament. Without parliamentary consent, he had his forces attack Scotland and decided to raise funds by means outside Parliament's authority. His forces went down to defeat. The king then had no choice but to summon Parliament again, and once again Parliament presented a list of grievances. This time parliamentarians refused to be dismissed and were able to extract a number of concessions. The result was that Parliament became a permanent body, no longer a temporary or an intermittent feature of the country's constitution. Parliament was now able to block non-parliamentary means of taxation.

Parliament went further than it ever had in its dealings with the monarch when it refused a request from Charles I for new funding for the army and then transferred control of the army and navy to itself from the king. Charles I objected, and civil war broke out. Parliament, with this step, sent the message that the king's divine right to rule no longer held; it was taking over all key decisions of government. The king and his troops went to Parliament to arrest five of its members and directed the Speaker of the Commons to reveal where they were. The Speaker refused, stating that he was above all a servant of Parliament, not the king, thus establishing his loyalty to Parliament rather than to the monarch. This precedent has endured in Westminster-styled Parliamentary governments; Canada is no exception.

Oliver Cromwell was one of the signatories to Charles I's death warrant and later ruled as the Lord Protector of England, Scotland, and Ireland. Cromwell ruled much like a monarch. At one point, Parliament even offered Cromwell the "crown," which he rejected. Still, he was installed as Lord Protector for life, sitting on King Edward's chair, and he held the power to appoint his own successor, much like a monarch. He anointed his son Richard as Lord Protector. Lacking his father's strength and political support, Richard was forced to resign within a year. Charles II was invited from exile to restore the monarchy.[22]

A number of new constitutional experiments were tried and abandoned between 1648 and 1660. After Oliver Cromwell's death, proposals were again put forward to define a republican constitution. Nothing came of them. Instead, the monarchy was restored, and "with it the law-making authority of the king in Parliament." However, the Restoration left a distaste in Britain for constitutional innovations and a written constitution, and it instilled a strong bias for "pragmatic, incremental adaptation of customary institutions."[23] The bias for incremental change prompted Alfred, Lord Tennyson, to describe Britain as "A land of settled government, / A land of just and old renown."[24]

While it is true that when the monarchy was restored most of the legislation passed during the interregnum was declared null, the interregnum nonetheless had a lasting impact: the prerogative courts were never restored, and laws precluding the monarch from raising taxation and enacting legislation, except through Parliament, were left intact.[25] The more important legacy, which is still felt today in both Britain and Canada, is the inherent bias for incremental change in shaping our political and administrative institutions. Less than thirty years after the Restoration, however, the king and Parliament were again in conflict that this time would give rise to an important constitutional development.

THE GLORIOUS REVOLUTION

Britain had its own revolution, although not of the variety we later saw in the United States, France, and Russia. It was largely a bloodless revolution, at least in England. It held, however, an important message for democracy. James II made known his conversion to the Roman Catholic faith. This and the fact that France made military advances in Europe raised alarm among the general public and in political circles in England.

James II promoted Roman Catholics to key military posts and to senior government positions. He admitted them to the Privy Council and did not hesitate to dismiss members of the Anglican Church to make way for Roman Catholics. Some feared that the king was deliberately embracing Roman Catholicism to make it the exclusive religion of the state. In 1687, the king issued a Declaration of Indulgence, suspending all laws against Roman Catholics. Religious tensions had been brewing in England since the mid-1500s and many saw James II stoking the fire.[26]

Tension escalated with news that the queen, a Roman Catholic, was pregnant. The fear was that a Roman Catholic line of succession would be established. Leading English politicians of the day wrote to William of Orange, the husband of heiress Mary (daughter of James II) and the champion of Protestants in Europe against Louis XIV of France, to lead an English army to enable Parliament to hold a free vote on succession. William of Orange had little difficulty reaching London as Protestant officers in the king's army deserted to the enemy. James II fled to France. Parliament announced that he had abdicated and offered the Crown to William and Mary.[27]

But Parliament required something in return. William and Mary had to agree to conditions laid out in a Bill of Rights. The bill ensured that the transition from an absolute monarchy to a constitutional monarchy was complete, never to be reversed. The power had shifted from the Crown to Parliament, later to Cabinet, and later still to the prime minister. The Crown would now require parliamentary approval to make laws and spend public money. Parliament would decide who would succeed rather than having the decision rest in the hands of the king or queen. The Glorious Revolution thus brought to an end, at least in Britain, the doctrine of the divine right of kings.

Parliament passed the Bill of Rights, which was read to William and Mary during the ceremony when they were offered the Crown. The "rights" are those enjoyed by Parliament, and the central provisions of the bill remain in force to this day. The legislation essentially laid the foundations for affirming the ultimate sovereignty of Parliament.[28] It restricted many royal prerogatives, placed some power under the direct control of Parliament, and declared that raising money for the use of the Crown "by pretence of prerogative, without grant of Parliament" was illegal. It gave Parliament the ability to control the identity of the monarch by altering the line of succession (again, so much for the divine right to rule), and made Parliament master of its own affairs. One student of British politics sums up these developments succinctly: "Power started with the Crown, but it continues to vest in the Crown only because, and for only as long as, Parliament continues to wish it."[29] In brief, the Bill of Rights ensured that sovereignty and effective political power were vested in the king or queen in Parliament and not in the king or queen alone, a seminal moment in the development of the Westminster model.

By the end of the nineteenth century, Parliament had forced from the Crown virtually all the power it wanted. It would have been hard by then to find anyone claiming that Parliament did not in practice possess unlimited legislative authority. Walter Bagehot, the most celebrated student of government in Victorian Britain, maintained that Parliament, and more specifically the House of Commons, now firmly held the upper hand. He wrote that "no matter whether it concerns high matters of the essential constitution or small matters of daily detail ... a new House of Commons can despotically and finally resolve ... it is absolute, it can rule as it likes and decide as it likes." With respect to the role of Parliament and its relations with the monarch, Walter Bagehot wrote that the "Queen has no such veto. She must sign her own death-warrant if the two Houses unanimously send it up to her."[30] Bagehot very likely employed the word "rule" to signify laying down the rules, since Parliament does not rule in the sense of governing or managing the government. This is no less true in Canada than it is in Britain.

THE WORK OF POLITICAL PHILOSOPHERS

John Locke's work has been long associated with the Glorious Revolution and in strengthening the hand of Parliament in relation to the monarchy. Locke returned to England, a few weeks after William of Orange had arrived, and after five years in exile. Though there is a debate whether Locke's work had any influence in the Glorious Revolution, it has often been employed to justify it and to provide a defence for Parliament. To be sure, John Locke never accepted the old dictum "the King can do no wrong" and did not hesitate to point the finger at King James for his various "miscarriages."[31]

Locke saw a contract, a fiduciary responsibility, between the Crown and the people. He rejected the long-held notion that God had made "all people naturally subject to a monarch."[32] He explained, "Every man has a property in his own person: this, nobody has any right to but himself ... Despotical power is an absolute, arbitrary power one man has over another, to take away his life, whenever he pleases. This is a power, which neither nature gives, for it has made no such distinction between one man and another."[33] He insisted that no government can require obedience from a people who have not freely consented to it. If the Crown chose to play havoc with its fiduciary responsibility, then the people had the right to withdraw consent. In an era of the divine right of kings to rule, it was revolutionary to make the case that the people did were not duty-bound to obey a monarch who did not respect the citizen's right to life, liberty, and property.[34]

Locke provided the arguments for people to challenge the divine right of kings to rule and to launch the age of revolutions. The Glorious Revolution in England served notice that kings could be toppled, in some cases even beheaded. It was the age of revolution in Britain, the United States, and France that gave democracy "its positive modern meaning."[35] With kings and queens no longer invincible, the search was on to give life to the common good, and representative democracy showed the way ahead.

John Locke's influence extended to Canada. Janet Ajzenstat sees evidence of John Locke's work in the debates leading up to Confederation. She maintains that some Fathers of Confederation looked to Locke to make the case that Confederation offered more promise to protect individual rights than several smaller governments spread across half a continent.[36] In influencing or justifying the work of British political institutions in the eighteenth century and beyond, Locke also influenced the development of Canadian political institutions.

The Age of Reason provided answers, at least for the United States, France, and, to a lesser extent, Britain, on how to structure political institutions. Europe's intellectual ferment challenged monarchs and ecclesiastical tyranny. Intellectuals from Hobbes, Locke, Voltaire, and Montesquieu to Paine not only challenged one another but also how best to structure government. Charles Montesquieu, for one, argued that a constitutional monarchy offered the best promise for a system of government. He saw, in dividing power between several centres, a way to provide a necessary check against any one of them becoming despotic or too powerful.[37]

Two British political philosophers, John Locke and Thomas Paine, provided ideas and impetus in support of the American Revolution. Thomas Jefferson claimed that he turned to Locke's "life, liberty, and pursuit of happiness" for inspiration, while Paine authored the first pamphlet advocating the American Revolution. The impact was initially felt in the United States but it soon spread to other countries. No country in the Western world has been immune to their influence.

Paine was highly critical of government based on hereditary privileges. He put forward a revolutionary proposal that "men are born, and always continue, free and equal in respect of their rights."[38] He was widely applauded in the United States and, for a period, in France but much less so in Britain. He favoured republican government and became a strong proponent of equal rights among all citizens. The Crown and the aristocracy in Britain, he insisted, were "independent of the people" and "contribute nothing towards the freedom of the State." He wrote that "it is the pride of kings which throws mankind into confusion" and added, "To the evil of monarchy we have added that of hereditary succession; and as the first is a degradation and lessening of ourselves, so the second, claimed as a matter of right, is an insult and imposition on posterity."[39]

Paine left Britain in 1774 for the United States, where he wrote pamphlets advocating the independence of the Thirteen Colonies from Britain. He urged the Americans to embrace republicanism and representative democracy. Moreover, he warned Americans against concentrating too much power in the executive.[40] Writing in the pamphleteering style of his day, Paine published *Common Sense* anonymously in January 1776. It was widely read in the American colonies.

Paine later published *Rights of Man* to wide acclaim in 1791 and sought to reply to Edmund Burke's criticism of the French Revolution. However, he went further, notably in his second edition published in 1792, in which he produced a plan to reform England's institutions. The work challenged all aspects of society, including the Bible. Fearing that he would be arrested, Paine fled to France. There he became a fervent supporter of the French Revolution. He was tried *in absentia* in England and barely escaped with his life in France after Robespierre turned on his former ally.[41]

Paine and Locke provided the intellectual underpinning for representative democracy. They argued that "all" human beings were naturally free and, as a result, all rulers needed their consent to rule – a provocative idea in the eighteenth century. It was up to the people to decide what form of government and which representatives should rule over them.

Revolutions brought representative democracy to life. The Americans, the French, and the leading thinkers of the day showed that there was no need for "the people" to rely on the divine right of kings to rule without their consent. England's Glorious Revolution stripped the monarch of important powers. Paine and Locke, and revolutions, showed that there was another way to run the affairs of state, which relied on the people for guidance. But that was only half of the reform agenda. Institutions had to be created or refined to take over.

France, after Louis XVI, was hardly a model of political stability and provided few lessons for those wishing to pursue representative democracy. If anything, they constituted a warning that democracy itself required checks and balances. The National Assembly pledged in 1789 to pursue democracy by granting the male population the right to decide who should govern France. However, the objective was short-lived. The pledge was soon followed by the Reign of Terror, with Robespierre exercising absolute power. This, in turn, was followed by a succession of regimes, from constitutional monarchies and republics to dictatorships.[42]

Britain, by contrast, made the transition to a constitutional monarchy with limited political and social dislocation. However, the transition to a well-functioning representative democracy was slow

– from the Magna Carta in 1215 to the 1689 Bill of Rights that established the supremacy of Parliament, and to 1832, 1867, and 1929 in addressing the clamour for better representative government by extending the franchise to universal adult suffrage. Though gradual, Britain did make the transition without a sharp break from the past, unlike France and the United States.

In summary, regardless of how the nations initiated the transition to representative democracy, all could look to the ideas of political philosophers for guidance or, at least, justification. Locke insisted that a government can only secure legitimacy through the consent of the "people"; Montesquieu argued that it was possible to avoid abuse of power by a separation of power; and Paine asserted that a government can only be the creation of a constitution that establishes substantive limitations on the exercise of power.

Canada's Fathers of Confederation were pragmatic men dealing with practical issues: how best to break a crippling political deadlock between Canada West and East, how to resist the powerful economic pull of the United States, and how to remain loyal to Britain and to British institutions.[43] They concluded that the way forward was to look at how political institutions functioned in the mother country. They believed that these institutions provided ready-made solutions for their new country. Unlike their American counterparts, they felt that they did not need to invent new institutions or produce anything like the *Federalist Papers*. The work of political philosophers and the European Enlightenment had an important influence on Canadian institutions largely because they influenced the development of British institutions and the political debates of the day.

ESTABLISHING REPRESENTATIVE DEMOCRACY TO THE SOUTH

The Framers of the United States Constitution readily admitted that they looked to political philosophers from Cicero to Locke and Paine to shape their work. But they looked to their own seminal work as well. Alexander Hamilton and James Madison favoured a federal system of government and both made a substantial contribution to its literature. When they met in Philadelphia in May 1787 at the Constitutional Convention, they could draw on the experience from the Articles of Confederation that were put in place on 1 March 1781 to inspire their design of a new federal system.

The 1781 Articles of Confederation that united thirteen states had fallen far short of expectations. The Articles were designed to give full authority to the thirteen states and to keep the central government deliberately weak. The Articles failed to give the central government enough power to regulate foreign trade and interstate commerce, provided no executive branch to the national government or a court system to interpret laws, and all legislation required a 9/13 majority to pass in Congress.[44] The Articles, however, provided important lessons not only for those who met in Philadelphia in 1787 to define a new constitution, but also to the Fathers of the Canadian Confederation eighty years later.

The delegates to the Philadelphia Convention decided in 1787 to reject a unitary state and embrace federalism. Countries in Europe or elsewhere had little to offer on federalism. Some of the Framers of the Constitution – James Madison, Alexander Hamilton, and John Jay – decided to put pen to paper to define a federal system for the United States that reflected the country's socio-political and economic circumstances and its brief history. In short, they cut ties with the mother country and developed political institutions in accordance with the requirements of their new country and the pressures of society below. This required them to think about entirely new institutions and to bargain to accommodate regional interests. They had to think, too, about ways to incorporate checks and balances to ensure that, though the national government would have considerably more power than the 1781 Articles of Confederation provided, political power would not be concentrated in the hands of a few.

The authors of the American Constitution were confronting a daunting challenge – creating a new federal system and a central government that would work and would be seen, at least at home, to be superior to the political system found in Britain. It is important to stress that the authors "were men of penetrating sagacity." Eighty-one year old Benjamin Franklin brought wisdom to the exercise, having witnessed his share of crises. He teamed up with Alexander Hamilton and James Madison, two of the leading intellects of the era to build a true federal system.[45]

The *Federalist Papers* sought to strike a middle ground between a unitary state and a loose collection of regions. They rejected absolute sovereignty for each state and decided to grant them residual sovereignty in all areas that did not require national action. What is more, the *Federalist Papers* saw a bicameral legislature and the need to accommodate the requirements of the smaller states. The delegates at the Philadelphia Constitutional Convention came from both large and small states. Delegates from the small states insisted that representation in Congress be established on an equal basis, no matter the size, while the larger states insisted on a representation by population. The disagreement came close to preventing the union. But, by the end of the summer of 1787, the Constitutional Convention reached what Americans call the "Great Compromise." Small and large states got equal representation in the Senate and large states got a form of representation by population in the House of Representatives. Leaving aside Canada, other federations that followed have adopted essentially the same model.

This – and several other key features of the United States Constitution – points to the importance of "checks and balances," a theme that runs throughout the *Federalist Papers*. They warned against concentrating power in the hands of a monarch or in one branch of government and the tyranny of the majority.[46] They turned to the work of several leading philosophers of the day, from Montesquieu to Locke, to support their perspective.

The difference between American and Canadian federalism is stark. First, the United States has built-in checks and balances to guard against a concentration of power. Canada has concentrated power first in the hands of Cabinet and later in the prime minister's, a modern day monarch. Second, the United States has a built-in capacity in its national political institutions to give voice to the smaller states; Canada does not. More to the point, in Canada – unlike the United States – there has never been a Great Compromise between small and larger states. The Great Compromise that shaped Canada was between the two Canadas, or between Ontario and Quebec.

THE BAGEHOT INFLUENCE

Walter Bagehot had a deep influence on British policy-makers and on how a Westminster-style parliamentary government should work. K.C. Wheare even argued that Bagehot "invented" the English Constitution.[47] In 1867, the year Canada was born, Bagehot published *The English Constitution*, which outlines how British institutions relate to one another. His work has had a considerable impact on the development of both British and Canadian political and administrative institutions.

Bagehot summed up the shift from an absolute monarch to a constitutional monarchy by writing that "the Queen is only at the head of a dignified part of the constitution. The prime minister is at the head of the efficient part."[48] He surveyed all institutions and sought to define their proper role. The House of Lords had influence but he argued that it must yield to the opinion of the Commons, which embodies the opinion of the nation.[49] For Bagehot, the House of Commons was the centrepiece of Britain's representative democracy. It was the Commons and its ability to select, hold to account, and, if it so decides, to remove the prime minister and accompanying government that were the keys to make representative democracy work. He pointed to this ability to make the case that the model was superior to the American system.[50] He saw five functions for the House of Commons: "it must elect a ministry well, legislate well, teach the nation well, express the nation's will well, [and] bring matters to the nation's attention well."[51] This view applied no less to Canada than it did to Britain.

Bagehot saw Cabinet as a powerful body in its own right. He explained that it was a committee of the Legislative Assembly with "a power which no assembly would – unless for historical accidents and after happy experience – have been persuaded to intrust to any committee. It is a committee which can dissolve the assembly which appointed it; it is a committee with a suspensive veto ... Though appointed by one parliament, it can appeal if it chooses to the next."[52] Bagehot's emphasis was on the role of Cabinet, not the prime minister. One can only conclude that the English Constitution has been reinvented.

Bagehot had a number of warnings about government bureaucracy. He wrote that a "bureaucracy is sure to think that its duty is to augment official power, official business, or official members rather than to leave free the energies of mankind; it overdoes the quantity of government, as well as impairs its quality." He added, the "truth is, that a skilled bureaucracy ... is, though it boasts of an appearance of science, quite inconsistent with the true principles of the art of business." Bureaucracy, he argued 150 years ago, "will care more for routine than for results."[53] Although he was resigned to the inevitable defects of government bureaucracy, he saw it as an integral and necessary part of government.

It is important to underline once again that Britain saw its political institutions take shape over time and in the continuous struggle between monarchs and Parliament over who has, or should have, access to the levers of power. Vernon Bogdanor summed it up well when he pointed out that Britain's constitutional "progress has been evolutionary, unpunctuated by revolutionary upheaval or foreign occupation."[54] The Americans, meanwhile, invented their own political institutions. Some of the country's leading thinkers put pen to paper to design political institutions that reflected their society's socio-political reality as the country broke away from Britain. In both cases, they looked to the work of political philosophers to guide or justify their work. In both cases, national political institutions were shaped by political circumstances, by the work of political philosophers familiar with the country's socio-economic circumstances, and by practitioners.

What about Canada? The country was not able to draw on the work of its own political philosophers to shape its national political institutions. Our Fathers of Confederation were left to borrow ideas from away, largely from political philosophers who advanced ideas about how best to structure institutions to promote representative democracy, and from Britain. Those ideas did find their way in to our political institutions. The point is that none of our institutions are home-grown.

The concerns of these political philosophers who influenced the development of political institutions focused on who should have political power and how to control those who hold power. The Bill of Rights brought forward in the seventeenth century dealt with the rights of Parliament, not individuals. Neither that bill nor the politicians of the day were concerned about how best to accommodate regional circumstances in national political institutions or how to organize government bureaucracies. Although the Framers of the American Constitution offered ideas on how to accommodate regional interests when developing national political institutions, the leaders of the British colonies to the north were not about to borrow from the United States less than a century after it had broken away from the mother country in a revolution and in the midst of a brutal civil war. The next chapter explores how Canada's national political institutions took shape.

2

Understanding the Roots
of Canadian Democracy

Britain sent Lord Durham to solve problems in the British North American colonies. He came in the immediate aftermath of the 1837 rebellions in Lower and Upper Canada. Durham favoured a union of the British North American colonies, which New Brunswick and Nova Scotia wanted no part of. As is well known, Durham recommended a union of Lower and Upper Canada after he witnessed what he famously described as "two nations warring in the bosom of a single state." He urged the assimilation of French Canadians as quickly as possible, since they were a people with "no history, and no literature." Durham also urged the implementation of responsible government, which first saw the light of day not in the Canadas but in Nova Scotia. The British accepted the recommendation of a union of the two Canadas and pursued it in 1840 under the Act of Union.[1]

The colonies, however, were no model of political stability. Simply put, they did not work. The Act of Union provided for "equal" representation between English-speaking Canada West and mostly French-speaking Canada East, even though the population of the latter was 670,000 compared with only 480,000 for Canada West – hardly a way to ensure political stability. At the time, Canada West insisted on equal representation to protect its interests, fearing that a francophone and Roman Catholic–dominated Canada East would rule the roost. In addition, the capital moved between Kingston, Montreal, Toronto, Quebec City, and Ottawa – also not models of stability.

The government had two leaders – one from Canada West and one from Canada East. The Legislative Assembly had to produce a double majority on proposed legislation. By the 1850s, the population of Upper Canada had overtaken that of Lower Canada, and now Upper Canada no longer saw any merit in equal representation. George Brown, editor of the *Toronto Globe*, for one, began his long campaign for Canada to embrace representation by population to ensure fair, or better, representation for Upper Canada, or Canada West. Francophones in Canada East saw the development for what it was – changing the rules to square with Canada West's interest – and therefore Canada East consistently opposed the change. The union was continuously marred by political instability due, at least in part, to the inability of one political party to achieve a dominant position.[2] The colony saw four governments over a three-year period and two inconclusive elections in the early 1860s. As Richard Gwyn writes, "Canada's political system had degenerated into paralytic deadlock."[3]

Canada looked to the other British colonies to the east for several reasons, not least to solve its own internal political strife. As negotiations for uniting the British North American colonies evolved, Britain decided to aggressively support Canada's political leadership to bring its other colonies into the Canadian fold.

Thus, Canada was born to solve the political impasse between Canada West and East and also because Britain's Colonial Office wanted it, turning to undemocratic means to secure a union of its BNA colonies. John A. Macdonald, the principal architect of Canadian Confederation and frequently called Canada's Father of Confederation,[4] saw no need to tailor the country's political institutions to square with the local socio-economic setting or to accommodate regional circumstances. Macdonald, together with three other key architects of Confederation – George-Étienne Cartier, George Brown, and Alexander Galt – decided to import to Canada political-administrative institutions from a unitary state lock, stock, and barrel. To the extent that Canadian institutions were inspired by political philosophers, they were based on the British model whose aim was to sort out the relationship between monarch, Parliament, aristocracy, and citizens, and to make a unitary state function properly.

To understand Canadian democracy, we need to remember that there is little in Canada's political institutions that is home-grown. Indeed, Canada's Constitution begins: "Whereas the Provinces of Canada, Nova Scotia, and New Brunswick have expressed their Desire to be federally united into One Dominion under the Crown of the United Kingdom of Great Britain and Ireland, with a constitution similar in Principle to that of the United Kingdom."[5] British influence is evident in all of Canada's political, administrative, and judicial institutions.

Given that Britain had nothing to offer on federalism, the Fathers of Confederation had to look to the United States, however reluctantly, for guidance on how to structure a federal system of government. This posed a problem because they were loyal to the British Crown and had little interest in learned papers on the workings of federalism. Macdonald made it clear that he had no interest in wasting "the time of the Legislature, and the money of the people, in fruitless discussions of abstract and theoretical questions of government."[6] For Macdonald, British institutions would do just fine for Canada.

Only one of the thirty-three Fathers of Confederation present at the Quebec Conference had a university education, in contrast to the fifty-five leaders in Philadelphia at the 1787 Constitutional Convention, where more than half had a university education. Few of the Fathers of Confederation understood or even read about federalism. Richard Gwyn maintains that three or four of them, including Macdonald, Galt, and Oliver Mowat, all from Canada West, understood some of the finer points of federalism.[7] I would like to add that Albert Smith (from New Brunswick), Joseph Howe, and William Annand (from Nova Scotia) understood better than Macdonald that a federal system required a capacity to accommodate regional circumstances and that intrastate measures matter, or should matter, in a federation.[8]

It is not at all clear why Gwyn would make the case that Macdonald understood the finer points of federalism and why he – along with many historians from Central Canada – would ignore the points that Albert Smith made about federalism between 1864 and 1867. As is well known, Macdonald wanted a legislative union and a unitary state. He embraced federalism only because he had no choice. It was either federalism or Canada East (Quebec), New Brunswick, and Nova Scotia would have joined Newfoundland and Prince Edward Island and quickly walked away from the negotiations. Macdonald, however, came as close to a unitary state as one can get without a legislative union.[9] Some would argue that Macdonald got a unitary state in all but name or that, in the end, he was able to secure a legislative union in a federal disguise.[10]

Macdonald did consult James Madison's *Notes of Debates in the Federal Convention of 1787*, but it had little visible influence on his thinking, other than perhaps to reinforce his view that federalism was a deeply flawed concept. He saw merit only in British-inspired institutions which, again, had no experience with the workings of federalism. Thus, Macdonald could look to the United States for lessons learned on federalism only because it gave life to the concept. But those lessons, at least for Macdonald, were not positive when it came to managing regional tensions. He and his collaborators saw a civil war raging in the United States – fuelled by regional tensions – precisely at the time they were trying to craft a federal system for Canada. Macdonald and his colleagues knew that regionalism had brought the two Canadas to their knees, which forced them to look to the Maritime colonies to break their political impasse. Looking to the United States and to the 1840 Act of Union made the case, at least for Macdonald, that regionalism had to be downplayed and not given more life in national political institutions.

The result is that virtually all powers of the day went to the central government and precious little was done to make national institutions sensitive to regional circumstances. Peter Waite summed it up well in his observation, "Canada has become a federal state in spite of its constitution."[11] The provinces were viewed, particularly by Macdonald, as little more than a municipal government, as Macdonald argued, "The true principle of a confederation lies in giving to the general Government all the principles and powers of sovereignty, and in the provision that the subordinate or individual States should have no powers but those expressly bestowed upon them. We should thus have a powerful Central Government, a powerful Central Legislature, and a powerful decentralized system of minor Legislatures for local purposes."[12]

Macdonald had an agenda – uniting the British colonies north of the 49th parallel to break the political deadlock between Canada West and Canada East and to ensure that the colonies would remain loyal to the British Crown rather than fall into the American ambit. "Deadlock" was thus Confederation's real parent.[13] Ged Martin explains, "The old Canadian Union was condemned to death on 14 March 1864," when the political impasse between Canada West and East came to a head.[14]

Britain, meanwhile, wanted its colonies to unite, convinced that this would lessen their dependence on the British treasury and enhance their ability to finance their own defence requirements. Macdonald and other key political leaders from Canada West and East and the Colonial Office in London were on the same page with regard to the need to unite the colonies. The Maritime colonies, meanwhile, did not have a clear agenda to pursue and were pushed to the side as Macdonald and a handful of politicians from the Canadas drove the negotiations at the Charlottetown, Quebec, and London conferences. Indeed, the Canadians drove the negotiations to the point that the 72 Resolutions, which became Canada's Constitution, were already in draft form "before the Canadian delegates had ever disembarked at Charlottetown."[15] Ged Martin sums up the so-called negotiations: "The Maritimers were smacked into line by the British, acting on appeal from the Canadians."[16]

The key players among the Fathers of Confederation went about their work with single-minded purpose. Democratic concerns were not top of mind. Indeed, if today's democratic requirements applied between 1864 and 1867, Canada would not have been born or, more likely, would not look like it does today. The constitution that they came up with did not even meet the most basic requisites of a federal system, and the tactics employed fell far short of today's democratic requirements.

Richard Gwyn, in his sympathetic biography of Macdonald, describes him as a "scheming opportunist" and adds that he "hadn't so much created a nation as manipulated and seduced and connived and bullied it into existence against the wishes of most of its own citizens."[17] Macdonald put his considerable political skills to the task at hand and never wavered. He drove the negotiations, authoring fifty of the seventy-two Quebec Resolutions. According to Gwyn, Macdonald told a colleague, "Not one man of the Conference (except Galt on finance) had the slightest idea of Constitution making," and Gwyn adds that "Macdonald was the gathering's orchestra conductor, cheerleader, bookkeeper (of the law, not the finances), entertainer and diplomat."[18]

Macdonald, Galt, Brown, and Cartier staked their political careers on securing the Confederation deal. In doing so, they held an advantage that today's politicians do not enjoy: they were able to do much of their work away from media scrutiny. Moreover, they had the full support of the Colonial Office both in London and in all the colonies – no small political asset in 1867. They needed all the help they could get. Though Macdonald clearly overstated the point, he explained the challenge: "Every man in Lower Canada was against it, every man in New Brunswick, every man in Nova Scotia, every man in Newfoundland, and every man in Prince Edward Island."[19]

The observation makes the case that, as Macdonald saw it, Canada West, or Ontario, would be the main beneficiary of Confederation, and the other colonies would resist the deal.

The British Colonial Office in London, between 1864 and 1867, was small and inadequately staffed, a poor cousin to other portfolios. And yet, the colonial lieutenant-governor carried a big stick in the colonies with responsible government less than twenty years old around the time of Confederation. New Brunswick's senior colonial official, Arthur Gordon, was initially strongly and vocally opposed to Confederation and in favour of a union of the Maritime colonies. Gordon accused the Canadians at the Charlottetown Conference of being responsible for the "ruin" of the Maritime union project.[20]

Gordon, however, changed his mind after a visit to London and a reminder that his career depended on his ability to move New Brunswick towards Confederation. The colonial secretary wrote to Gordon in 1865 with a clear message: "You will impress the strong and deliberate opinion of her Majesty's Government that it is an object much to be desired that all the British North American colonies should agree to unite in one government."[21] The time had come for the Colonial Office to "turn the screw" on the Maritime colonies, and it did.[22] Gordon understood that without New Brunswick, Confederation would not be and he pledged to carry Confederation by every means in his power.[23]

Gordon happily took up the cause, and he did not let the requirements of responsible government get in his way. As Donald Creighton describes, Gordon pursued Confederation "with a nonchalant disregard for the constitutional niceties of responsible government."[24] He nevertheless faced stiff opposition. Albert Smith, a leading political figure in New Brunswick, urged New Brunswickers to reject the Confederation deal struck at the Quebec Conference. He fought against Confederation in the 1865 election and won handily. He astutely made the case that the Canadas were looking to the Maritime colonies to solve their own internal political problems and that, in time, Canadians would only increase their "dominance as their population and appetite grew."[25] Smith did not oppose a union of the British North American colonies but rather the deal negotiated at the Quebec Conference.

Gordon did not let an election deter him. He simply decided that Confederation was in the best interest of both the colony and his own career and set out to do something about it. He precipitated a crisis with the Smith government by accepting a strongly worded pro-Confederation reply to the Speech from the Throne from the Legislative Council, the colony's unelected Upper House. It flew in the face of responsible government, with Smith insisting that it was his right to be consulted and to recommend. Gordon had little time for the "rights of colonials" only a decade after responsible government came to New Brunswick. The Colonial Office was taken aback by Gordon's initiative because it was creating a constitutional precedent in having an appointed council address the Queen on a clearly political and controversial issue. Smith was forced to call an election.[26] If Smith lost the election, Gordon could then deliver New Brunswick to the pro-Confederation side.

Smith took to the hustings, denouncing both Gordon and the Quebec Resolutions once again. He told a packed hall in Saint John that Confederation would render the province "utterly powerless" and added that "the interests of Ontario were entirely distinct and at variance with all the other provinces."[27] Smith called for a referendum on any act of Confederation, equal and effective representation for provinces in the Upper House, a restricted number of MPs, an assurance of a Cabinet minister for each Maritime province, a court to deal with federal-provincial conflicts, and strict control over taxation.[28] Smith called for a Great Compromise between large and small colonies, much like the Americans had achieved in 1787 between large and small states. The Colonial Office saw no need for a referendum, and nothing came of his suggestion. Macdonald and his colleagues from the Canadas also saw no merit in Smith's other suggestions.

Smith lost the 1866 election to pro-Confederation candidate Sir S. Leonard Tilley. Tilley had the strong backing of the Colonial Office. He received funds from Macdonald to bribe voters and help persuade the undecided to support Confederation.[29] Luck, too, intervened on Tilley's side. The Fenians launched raids along the Maine and New Brunswick border precisely at the time Smith and Tilley, with Gordon's encouragement, were crossing swords over the merit of Confederation. Though the pro-Confederation forces overstated the Fenian threat, the raids considerably weakened anti-Confederation forces in the region in the weeks leading up to the election. Some even suggested that pro-Confederation forces brought the Fenians to the New Brunswick border "to frighten the people into Confederation."[30] For his part, Arthur Gordon was rewarded with an appointment as governor of Trinidad after he secured New Brunswick's assent to Confederation.

Charles Tupper had even greater challenges than Tilley in convincing Nova Scotians to accept Confederation. Few Nova Scotians shared Tupper's enthusiasm for Confederation as defined by the Quebec Resolutions.[31] Once the terms of the Quebec Resolutions were widely known, opposition to Confederation became rampant. Some of Tupper's key political allies, such as William Annand, broke ranks, insisting that the Quebec Resolutions were patently bad for Nova Scotia.

Annand saw problems on all fronts. He could not understand why Tupper would accept Confederation on the basis of representation by population, which would leave Nova Scotia with only 19 MPs out of 181, with the proportion declining as Canada expanded to the west and north. (Today Nova Scotia has 11 MPs out of 338.) With no capacity in the country's national political institutions to counterbalance rep by pop, he saw Central Canada dominating the federation at will. Joseph Howe led the anti-Confederation forces in Nova Scotia, insisting that the province would in time become a neglected member of Canada, given how national political institutions would be structured.

Tupper knew full well that he did not enjoy the support of Nova Scotians. He also knew that one of Confederation's main architects, George Brown from Canada West, would accept nothing less than rep by pop for the House of Commons and a non-elected Senate. In addition, Tupper had to deal with the colony's lieutenant-governor Richard MacDonnell, who made clear at every turn his strong opposition to Confederation. MacDonnell bluntly told Macdonald at the Quebec Conference, "You shall not make a mayor of me, I can tell you."[32] The Colonial Office, however, was quick to "promote" MacDonnell to Hong Kong and appointed in his stead William F. Williams, a high-ranking military officer who knew how to execute orders.

Tupper did not have to call a general election before 1867 and so could play for time. When thorny issues about the Quebec Resolutions were raised, Tupper said that he would fix them at the London Conference or in the next round of negotiations. To the surprise of many and to the annoyance of pro-Confederation forces in the Canadas, Tupper kept "a complete silence on the most important issue of the day" – Confederation – at key moments, including in the government's Speech from the Throne.[33] He was fully aware that he did not have the support either in the legislature or in the province for the Quebec Resolutions to carry the day.

Tupper did introduce a vaguely worded motion in 1866, calling for another look at Maritime union, hardly an endorsement for Confederation. An MLA – presumably in a side deal with Tupper – cleverly countered with another vaguely worded resolution, calling for the appointment of a delegation to explore "a scheme of union" with the Imperial Government and other governments. No mention was made of the Quebec Conference resolutions. Tupper secured the motion at half past two in the morning. This prompted Halifax newspapers to denounce the move as "a black crime, a deal of darkness, done like robbery and murder in the dead hours of the night."[34] Many who voted in favour of the motion believed that, at a minimum, they voted in favour of securing a better deal than the Quebec Resolutions offered.[35] The vote went 31 to 19.

Prince Edward Island rejected Confederation, with Island delegates insisting that a country built solely on representation by population would always work against the interest of the province. The proposed Confederation deal only allocated 5 MPs to Prince Edward Island, a number that would decline as the country expanded west. Island delegates argued essentially for a Triple-E Senate – elected, equal, and effective – to give a voice for the smaller provinces in Parliament. But Macdonald and other Canadian delegates rejected the notion out of hand.[36]

Maritime and Newfoundland delegates became convinced that "true political power" would always reside with the House of Commons. The Fathers of Confederation spent an inordinate amount of time debating the mandate and composition of the Senate – a full six of the fourteen days during the Quebec Conference. The proposed Senate mattered to Maritime delegates because they saw it as a way to bring regional balance in national political institutions. However, in the end, senators were to be appointed rather than elected, and representation would be based on regional, not provincial, equity. The Province of Canada would split in two for the purpose of negotiating Confederation and would later become Ontario and Quebec. This would ensure that the colony would get twice the number of senators than the Maritime colonies combined would receive.

Delegates from Ontario and Quebec rejected the call for an elected Senate. Ontario-elected delegates feared that the two Houses would be at loggerheads, and Quebec delegates feared the

Senate could not protect their cultural and linguistic position if it had the same number of elected senators as the smaller provinces.[37] Ontario, or Canada West, also argued that the new federation was too "oddly sized" for a United States–style Senate to work.[38] I note, however, that federations from the United States (California with a population of 38,802,500 and Wyoming with 584,153) to Australia (New South Wales with a population of 7,238,800 and Tasmania with 507,600) are no less oddly sized, and they have an equal and elected Upper House. Australia, like Canada, has a Westminster-style parliamentary government.

Macdonald quickly dismissed the call from A.J. Smith of New Brunswick to "give us [small provinces] at least, the guard which they have in the United States [i.e., an equal and effective Senate], although we ought to have more, because, here, the popular branch [i.e., the executive branch] is all-powerful."[39] Even Charles Tupper, a supporter of Confederation, argued in favour of a strong Senate to counterbalance the House of Commons' representation by population. He said, "In the Maritime Provinces we felt that the great preponderance of Canada [i.e., Canada West and East] could only be guarded against by equal representation" in the Upper House since Confederation "is not a Legislative Union, and we had sectional and local differences."[40] Macdonald, however, insisted that there was nothing to be gleaned from the Americans on their Senate, given that the country was plunged into a bloody civil war because of regional tensions. He saw more merit in looking to the mother country and its House of Lords as a model for the Canadian Parliament.

The Maritime colonies, however, disagreed: how could the Senate possibly speak on behalf of the regions and smaller provinces if senators were appointed by Ottawa? The argument did not carry much weight with the Canadian delegates.[41] Delegates from Canada at the Quebec Conference saw the Senate as a safeguard against the potential excesses of democracy rather than a voice for the regions. It was Macdonald who labelled the Senate a place of "sober second thought," thereby attenuating the importance of regionalism in Canada's politics, at least in the workings of national political institutions.[42] For Macdonald, a check on full-blown democracy was far more important than a check on power flowing from rep by pop. Macdonald and Brown saw Canada taking shape from the prism of the political and economic interests of Canada West, and Cartier, from the cultural, linguistic, and religious interests of Canada East.

The needs of the smaller regions were not on their political agenda nor on the agenda of the Colonial Office.

Margaret Conrad explains, "Any demand that the smaller provinces be accorded an equal voice, either in the Senate or in the House of Commons, was a deal breaker for delegates from the Province of Canada, who were determined to dominate the new federation. And this they did."[43] Philip Girard sums up the scenario best when he writes about an "'acquisition' of the Maritimes by the Canadas, as the United States had acquired Louisiana from France."[44]

Macdonald's "sober second thought" label for the Senate has stuck. It has taken away from the Senate's most crucial role according to the constitution – to "give the regions of Canada an equal voice in Parliament."[45] The national media, notably the *Globe and Mail*, the *National Post*, the *Ottawa Citizen*, and the CBC, very often refer to the Senate as the "chamber of sober second thought" rather than to its regional role.[46] Even the Library of Parliament ranks "regional representation" the second general role of the Senate behind its sober second thought role.[47] More recently, the *Globe and Mail* simply asked "what the Senate is for. It is hardly a necessity, yet a case can be made ... that the chamber can really provide sober second thought."[48] There is no reference to its role as a voice for the regions. This, combined with the tendency for prime ministers, until recently, to reward party faithfuls by appointing them to the Senate, has rendered the Upper House of little relevance when it comes to representing regional interests.

In a recent decision, the Supreme Court recognized three roles for the Senate. The first it identified was providing a sober second thought to the work of the Commons. The decision reads: "As in the United Kingdom, it was intended to provide 'sober second thought' on the legislation adopted by the popular representatives in the House of Commons." The court turned to the views of Macdonald to support its decision. The court then underlined the Senate's role in providing a voice for the regions and representing various groups that were under-represented in the House of Commons.[49]

Justin Trudeau has sought to overhaul the workings of the Senate by changing the appointment process. He established an independent committee mandated to come up with five names whenever a Senate vacancy occurs. I served on the advisory committee for New Brunswick in 2016–17. I note that the chair of the committee was from Ontario, the vice-chair from Quebec, and the third member overseeing the process for the ten provinces was from Alberta. The notion that a key role of the Senate is to speak for the smaller provinces and for the regional perspective was apparently lost on the prime minister and his senior advisers in establishing the committee. They know where political power is won in Canada – Ontario, Quebec, and in the two larger western provinces, Alberta and British Columbia.

The new appointment process is having an impact. Only time will tell if it will be a lasting one and if the Senate will embrace a regional role. The new senators have declined being identified with a political party, opting for the "Independent" label. Two former senators – a Liberal, Michael Kirby, and a Conservative, Hugh Segal – authored a report on the Trudeau reform. They warned that there is "nothing in the altered appointments process introduced in January 2016 that automatically assures a positive outcome for an independent Senate."[50] They remind Ottawa, "Make no mistake: without the Senate to provide a regionally based check and balance on the popularly elected House of Commons, the Confederation project would have failed."[51] They acknowledge that "mounting partisanship" undermines the Senate's effectiveness.[52] As a solution, they urge the Senate to return to its "regional roots" and that it should be reorganized "around the principle of regional caucuses"[53] that would include all senators from a given region regardless of any other affiliation. The government representative in the Senate, Peter Harder, declared his support for the Kirby-Segal recommendation that traditional party caucuses be replaced with regional caucuses.[54]

Voices were soon heard against a move to regional caucuses. Quebec senator Paul Massicotte argued that Canada in 1867 was "a dispersed and unconnected population, fearful and skeptical of a centralized government in far-away Ottawa" and that in "today's context," the shift would "lead to the resurgence of old conflicts, and supplant the national interest."[55] The implication is that an essentially unencumbered representation by population approach should be left to define Canada's "national interest" and that old regional conflicts have somehow been resolved. There are precious few voices in either Western or Atlantic Canada making this claim. Nothing has come out of the Kirby-Segal report.

Resistance to a more effective Senate, particularly an elected one, persists from Ontario and Quebec, the two regions that have benefitted from representation by population. Matthew Mendelsohn, the former head of Ontario's Mowat Centre and deputy secretary to the Cabinet in the Privy Council Office in the Justin Trudeau government, dismissed the prospect of a democratically elected Senate because, he insisted, the required provincial government consent is simply not in the cards. He made a revealing observation: "Today, the Senate does not really matter for decision-making ... So the fact that New Brunswick has ten seats in the Senate and British Columbia has only six is an oddity but not a big concern. It doesn't really matter because the Senate doesn't really matter."[56] That assertion, of course, serves the interest of the two most populous provinces, Ontario and Quebec.

Stéphane Dion argued, "So why not simply elect the future senators instead of letting the prime minister appoint them? There is a basic problem in that logic, one that derives from the unequal distribution of senators per province. To elect senators with the current distribution of seats would be unfair for the under-represented provinces, Alberta and British Columbia, who have only six senators each, whereas New Brunswick and Nova Scotia, with about one quarter of their population, have ten."[57] The whole point of having an effective Senate in a federation is to bring regional balance to national policy-making or, as a long-time supporter of Senate reform Roger Gibbins once argued, to bring "effective territorial representation within national political institutions."[58] The reason for having a federal system rather than a unitary one is that political structures need to be established to better accommodate regional interests. It should only take a moment's reflection to appreciate that to ensure this, smaller provinces or states need to be overrepresented in the Upper House. Dion is basically saying that the United States, Australia, Germany, and Russia have it all wrong with an equal number of senators for every state, no matter its population. I hear very few Americans, Australians, Germans, or Russians making the same point.

Dion, and others of like mind, offer no solution to counter rep by pop in a federation as large and as diverse as Canada, which suggests that they may not recognize the problem. One can only conclude that they believe smaller provinces and regions in a federation as large and as regionally diverse as Canada should simply rely on rep by pop if they want to be heard and have influence in a national setting. However, as Canadian history has so clearly demonstrated, this does not work for the smaller provinces. One thing is clear, either the status quo or the abolition of the Senate brings comfort to Ontario. Both play to its advantage.

Western Canada appears to be losing interest in a Triple-E Senate. The election of the Stephen Harper government and the shift of economic and political power to Western Canada changed its agenda. A Triple-E Senate was not a problem for Gibbins in the 1990s, but it became one when Harper held power. Roger Gibbins, former head of the Canada West Foundation, argued in 2012, "If we have a Senate that's elected and effective to some degree – but the seat distribution doesn't change – then we're into a situation where an elected Senate may be detrimental to the interests of the West."[59] He believed that "another reality is starting to sink in" and that "westerners must drop their demand for a Triple-E Senate." He explained, "To the extent that the Senate becomes a more influential body ... it would shift power into Atlantic Canada and away from the West."[60] Though it may come as a surprise to Gibbins, Ontario and Quebec would agree with him. Others in Western Canada, including former Saskatchewan premier Brad Wall, have echoed Gibbins's views on Senate reform, with Wall calling for abolition.[61]

Preston Manning has been more forthcoming. He once asked, how "will western interests be effectively represented in a one-house Parliament where Quebec and Ontario have an absolute majority of seats?" Today, things are different. He now writes: "With the rapid growth of population in the western provinces and the shift in the country's political centre of gravity from the old Laurentian region (Quebec and Ontario together) to the new alignment between Ontario and the West, Senate reform is not as high on the western agenda as it once was."[62]

One can only conclude that the West's push for Senate reform was motivated not by the "national interest" or by bringing balance to the Canadian federation, but rather solely by "the interests of the West." That is how Canada is governed, and where big dogs, or big provinces and regions, compete to eat first. Once Western Canada felt that it had the necessary political and economic clout to influence Ottawa, it lost interest in its old cry, "the West wants in." Ontario and Quebec, as noted, are hostile to Senate reform because it is in their economic interest to oppose reform, thus far at least. The 2015 election results have shifted some political power away from Western Canada back to Ontario and Quebec. Time will tell if Western Canada will have another change of heart on Senate reform.

ACCOMMODATING REGIONALISM
THROUGH OTHER MEANS

Rather than embrace an effective Upper House to deal with the demands of the Maritime delegates, the Canada West or Ontario representatives argued at the Charlottetown and Quebec conferences that the Maritime provinces could always count on Quebec if their province ever attempted to dominate Confederation. It would have been very difficult to assume in 1867 that Quebec would ever agree to support Ontario's economic interests, and vice versa, given the tension between the two provinces at the time. Delegates from Canada West argued that this should constitute enough assurance to the Maritime colonies that Ontario could never dominate the national political agenda. The Maritime colonies were thus being called upon to act as the "honest broker" between Ontario and Quebec, which would give them political influence whenever the need arose. History has demonstrated time and again that the Maritime provinces have not been able to play this role.[63]

In the pre-Confederation discussions, it was agreed that the Maritimes would have one-third of Cabinet posts to compensate somewhat for representation by population in the Commons. Maritime delegates pressed to have this enshrined in the constitution. This was firmly rejected by Canadian delegates, and it remained only an agreement of convenience designed for the moment. Macdonald and other representatives from the Canadas wanted no part of it in the constitution, convinced that it could never square with the Westminster-inspired parliamentary system and that it would fly in the face of the interest of their own region.[64]

SEALING THE DEAL

At the London Conference in December 1866, Macdonald, Brown, Galt, and Cartier knew that the Maritime colonies had no viable alternative but to join Canada.[65] The four had earlier made special trips to London to secure the support of the Colonial Secretary and his office. Maritime union was now off the table and joining the United States held only limited appeal for several reasons, even for the Maritime colonies. For one thing, the Colonial Office would not have entertained such an initiative. For another, it was less than one hundred years since Loyalists had left the United States to settle in

Nova Scotia, New Brunswick, and the Canadas to remain loyal to the Crown. The Loyalists were the political elite. Samuel Tilley of New Brunswick, for example, was a descendent of Loyalists on both sides of his family, as was Albert Smith. The same was true of Charles Tupper. And so loyalty to British institutions and to the Empire was as strong in the Maritimes as it was in Canada West.

The deliberations in London cannot be accurately described as negotiations. The London Conference simply reviewed the Quebec Resolutions and later essentially outlined them in a bill that would become law. There were no referenda anywhere in the colonies. The New Brunswick and Nova Scotia legislatures never approved the Quebec Resolutions, only a mandate to negotiate better terms. Tupper, for one, came with a specific list of demands and had told the anti-Confederation movement in Nova Scotia that he would push hard for amendments. However, the door to negotiations had been shut even before he arrived, and Tupper failed to secure a single amendment. The Canadian delegates, meanwhile, went to London with a mandate from their legislature not to negotiate but rather to proceed with the Quebec plan. Their Parliament had agreed to the Quebec Resolutions, and they won the day. Macdonald explained: "These resolutions were in the nature of a treaty, and if not adopted in their entirety, the proceedings would have to be commenced *de novo*."[66] The treaty was "negotiated" by and for Canada West and Canada East. That said, there were some modifications to the Quebec Resolutions, though nothing major and nothing that spoke to Tupper or Tilley's concerns.

Macdonald, Brown, Galt, and Cartier had negotiated a treaty between *deux nations*. I note, however, that *les Rouges* in Canada East vigorously opposed Confederation. The relationship between Canada West and Canada East had been stormy since the 1840 Act of Union, and they knew that the treaty could unravel if new concessions or revisions were made to it. Three colonies signed on to the Confederation deal: New Brunswick, Nova Scotia, and Canada. Ontario and Quebec were created since Canada West (Ontario) and Canada East (Quebec) did not have their own government or legislature. Confederation still fell short of what Macdonald wanted – a legislative union or a unitary state.

Although objections to the Quebec Resolutions from the Maritimes were politely heard in the end, little came of them. The Maritime delegates were up against a formidable force, as W.S. MacNutt observes: "The Canadians went to London as a disciplined team."[67] One New Brunswick delegate recalled no less than forty objections to the Quebec Resolutions debated in the New Brunswick legislature but, again, nothing came of those in London.[68] At one point, Tilley threatened to go home, but Macdonald knew that it was too late for Tilley to back away from the deal.[69] Tupper also failed to secure any meaningful improvements in London, notwithstanding his commitments to Nova Scotians. Phillip Buckner remarks that Canadian delegates "manipulated the Quebec Conference and outmanoeuvred the divided Maritimers."[70] In the end, Maritimers had a difficult choice: disregard their commitments to negotiate the Quebec Resolutions in London and sign on, or go home empty-handed. They signed on, realizing that Confederation was only possible through the Quebec Resolutions. They held out hope that, somehow, the construction of a national railway would mask the deficiencies the Quebec Resolutions had from a Maritime perspective. If anything, the London Conference weakened further the position of the two Maritime provinces, giving Ottawa full responsibility for the fishery rather than a shared responsibility like agriculture.[71]

Queen Victoria had considerable influence in the 1860s, and on the advice of her government and the Colonial Office, she sent a clear message to her Maritime colonies that "Her Majesty and her Canadian ministers were as one."[72] The Fathers of Confederation were colonials and they attached great importance to the monarchy, parliamentary government, and membership in the British Empire.[73] Britain was the mother country to English Canada. The mother country was able to preserve its monarchy and marry it to its parliamentary system. It had defeated its arch enemy France and was the world's economic powerhouse. Britain governed about a quarter of the world and had about a quarter of global trade flow through its ports.[74] When Queen Victoria spoke, British colonies in North America listened.

Macdonald's loyalty to the British Crown was well known. He had at one point actually opposed responsible government and extensions to the franchise "because such measures were un-British and could weaken the British connection or the authority of the governor and also the necessary propertied element within government and society."[75]

Though Britain was not prepared to abandon its North American colonies, many in Britain felt that the colonies imposed a cost on Britain greater than any benefits from them. Leading British politicians described the colonies as "a millstone around our necks," and they represented a "heavy expense" to Great Britain and "nothing else."[76] Donald Creighton explains: "Anti-colonial sentiment was running very strongly in England in the 1860s. Macdonald, Galt and Brown were all sadly aware of the fact that a great many British Tories, Whigs and Liberals would have preferred them to declare for separation and independence."[77] The next best solution from a British perspective was for the colonies to unite and begin the march to economic and financial independence.

In summary, the London Conference was a *fait accompli* even before it began. Macdonald insisted on few changes to the Quebec Resolutions and wanted to close the deal before Nova Scotia went to the polls. He knew that, failing this, it would kill Confederation. There were no minutes taken at the London Conference, and the media were deliberately kept in the dark. This, at Macdonald's request "to keep anti-Confederate critics in a state of sullen ignorance by making sure that everything done inside the room stayed there."[78]

Anti-Confederation sentiments did not die in the Maritime region. They became widespread in Nova Scotia after the London Conference. Many houses and businesses in Halifax and Yarmouth were draped in black in protest. Effigies of Tupper were burned in Halifax.[79] Nova Scotia elected 18 anti-Confederation MPs to Canada's first Parliament out of 19, and 5 out of 15 MPs from New Brunswick supported their position. Charles Tupper was the only pro-Confederation MP elected from Nova Scotia. The goal of the anti-Confederation MPs was to reverse the decision to join Confederation. Thomas Killam, an anti-Confederation MP elected in Yarmouth, Nova Scotia, declared that the election results in Nova Scotia "proved the hostility of the people to Confederation and the manner in which it was forced on them."[80] Thirty-six of the 38 provincial seats in the 1867 Nova Scotia election went to anti-Confederation candidates. On the two occasions that Nova Scotians were consulted on the merit of Confederation, they responded with a resounding no. Britain, however, was quick to serve notice that it would not allow Nova Scotia to secede from Canada. Responsible government, at the time, be damned, and Confederation was a done deal.

The anti-Confederation movement endured in the Maritimes for decades. William S. Fielding led his Liberal Party to victory in Nova Scotia in 1886 on a campaign to take Nova Scotia out of Confederation. He successfully secured a resolution from the

Legislative Assembly to ask Ottawa to help the province leave
Confederation. Federal politicians did not respond. Fielding went to
New Brunswick and Prince Edward Island to seek their support for
secession from Confederation and to promote Maritime union, but
they did not respond either. Fielding was prepared to proceed alone
to have Nova Scotia leave Confederation. However, once again,
Britain made clear that it would not agree to Nova Scotia's request
to secede and showed no interest in revisiting Maritime union if it
meant dismantling Confederation.

Prince Edward Island only decided to join Confederation in 1873.
The colony had rejected it in January 1866, when the Legislative
Assembly adopted a strongly worded resolution saying that it would
not send a delegation to the London Conference. The resolution
passed 21 to 7, despite strong pressure from the Colonial Office.
However, the Colonial Office and Macdonald did not accept the
rejection and continued to apply pressure at every turn, until the
Island became Canada's seventh province. By the early 1870s, the
Colonial Office had the helping hand of Canadian authorities – or
perhaps Canadian authorities had the helping hand of the Colonial
Office – to persuade Prince Edward Island to join after they heard
that the United States were making advances to the Island. Britain
made it clear that it was "the strong and deliberate opinion of Her
Majesty's government" that Prince Edward Island should unite with
Canada.[81] Macdonald sweetened considerably the earlier deal to the
Island, adding one member of Parliament and more generous financial incentives, among other things.

The gang of four from the Canadas – Macdonald, Brown, Galt, and
Cartier – controlled the agenda at the three conferences and drafted
the bulk of the Quebec Resolutions. They dismissed the regional factor, convinced that it had made Canada West and East dysfunctional
and that it had given rise to the American Civil War. The regional
voice, or the voice from the outer Canadas, was barely heard; both
Newfoundland and Prince Edward Island originally walked away
from the negotiations. The four western provinces were not yet born
but would have, in time, to work with national political institutions
as defined by the Quebec Conference.

Today's democratic standards did not apply in 1867. Consider
the following: The Quebec Resolutions were only approved by one
of the legislatures involved; they were at first rejected in a general
election in the case of New Brunswick and never submitted to the

Nova Scotia legislature; no delegates were elected to any especially convened constitutional convention; and the British Colonial Office intervened directly to secure the Confederation deal, paying lip service to responsible government.[82] Nova Scotians voted on two separate occasions to give a mandate to their provincial government to leave the Canadian federation but nothing came of it.

Macdonald, Brown, Galt, and Cartier were, above all, practical men, and they got what they wanted. Macdonald wanted Canada to retain strong ties to Britain, a strong central government with subordinate provincial governments, and a Senate appointed by the federal Cabinet that represents the well-to-do in Canadian society. Brown, meanwhile, insisted on representation by population to establish political power in Canada and made it a "fundamental part of confederation."[83] Canada West, or Ontario, politicians drafted the bulk of the BNA Act. The capital would be located in Ottawa, not Montreal, the country's largest city.

Cartier wanted the use of French in Parliament and in the courts and the continuation of the *Code Civil* in Quebec. Confederation meant that Quebec could now deal more effectively with threats from the Orangemen of Ontario. Galt, for his part, designed the new country's financial arrangements, which favoured Canada West and East. Tupper and Tilley fell far short of what was expected of them, but both could claim that they were able to secure commitments to build the Intercontinental Railway. When it came to the more fundamental questions – how best to design national political and administrative institutions to govern the new country – the Fathers of Confederation simply looked to ready-made solutions from Britain.

FEDERALISM IN NAME ONLY

The BNA Act, as a federal constitution, was deeply flawed. For one thing, it lacked a fundamental requirement: an amending formula. For another, it made no provision for counterbalancing representation by population with a voice for the regions within national political institutions. This is a fundamental requirement in a federal system, and even more so in the case of Canada, given its extensive and empty space and the vastly different political, cultural, and socio-economic circumstances among the regions.

It is unclear why the Fathers of Confederation decided not to define an amending formula for the BNA Act. There is little published discussion on the matter.[84] We are left to speculate. It could be that the Fathers of Confederation were not well versed about the requirements of federalism. It may be that they felt it was an act of the British Parliament and that the British Parliament would, if ever necessary, modify the act. It may be that the four leading architects of Confederation decided to focus their energies on the difficult task at hand – securing a union of the colonies – and leave the amending formula to a later time. Finally, it may well be that they could not come up with an amending formula that could satisfy one large colony – the Canadas – and two smaller ones. What we do know for certain is that Macdonald, the lead architect of Confederation, never argued for an amending formula at the Charlottetown, the Quebec, or the London conference.

Canadian democracy produced a Senate in 1867 that does not meet today's democratic standards because its original intention had little to do with giving a voice to Canada's regions to act as a counterpoint to the House of Commons' representation by population. Putting a safety valve on the House of Commons and the potential excesses of democracy was a sign of the times with the mob rule of the French Revolution still fresh in the collective memory of the new nation. In the United States, the Founding Fathers debated having a wealth requirement for entry into the Senate but rejected it.[85] Thus, unlike its Canadian counterpart, the United States Senate has no provision to exclude the poor from becoming a member.[86]

Macdonald wanted a highly centralized national government, as close to a unitary state as possible, and he got what he wanted. For example, shortly after Confederation, he went to Halifax to deal with calls from the region for "better terms." He completely ignored the provincial government and met with Joseph Howe, a member of Parliament in Ottawa, to deal with the matter. He refused to meet with any provincial politician, even the premier. He felt it best to ignore provincial governments even when dealing with purely regional or even provincial issues. For Macdonald, provincial governments were what he felt they should be – subordinate governments concerned only with local matters.

The Fathers of Confederation agreed to a provision in 1867 that did not square with the spirit of federalism. The BNA Act gave the provincial lieutenant-governors the power to stop provincial legislation from coming into force until the central government had approved it. Claude Bélanger explains: "Since the Statute of Westminster, in 1931, the British government does not disallow federal bills anymore but the provisions permitting the disallowance of provincial acts by the federal government are still in effect, although they have fallen into disuse. The right to disallow provincial acts by the federal government runs contrary to the true principles of federalism as it undermines the concept of the sovereignty of the provinces in their sphere of jurisdiction."[87]

The western provinces strongly opposed Ottawa's national policy (circa 1878) and passed legislation designed to attenuate its impact. Between 1867 and 1920, Ottawa disallowed ninety-six provincial laws with the bulk from Western Canada and dealing with the national policy.[88] In sharp contrast, Ottawa only disallowed a handful of acts from Ontario and Quebec between 1867 and 1943.[89] There is now a constitutional convention that the federal government will not use its disallowance and it has not, in fact, been used since 1943.[90] What made sense for Macdonald, for Parliament, and for representative democracy in 1867 no longer made sense in 1943, and makes even less sense today. The constitutional convention was quietly introduced over time with minimum fuss.

The difference between a federal and a unitary system is well known: a federal system provides for coordination between national and regional governments while a unitary one subordinates regional governments to the national one. Federations should require a capacity in their national institutions to give voice to the regions that extends beyond representation by population. Ronald Watts, a highly respected observer of federalism, writes that experience "would suggest that there is much to be said for bicameral institutions and that provision in some form or other for representation on a regional basis may be an important way to strengthen the commitment and loyalty of regional groups to the national institutions."[91] Macdonald and his colleagues, particularly those from Canada West, introduced strong unitary elements in Canada's Constitution and saw little need to strengthen the loyalty of regional groups. For them regionalism was not something to be encouraged or accommodated within national political institutions. Rather, it was something to be denied or, at least, downplayed. Politicians from Canada West and East had experienced regionalism and double majorities after the 1840 Act of Union and wished to avoid them in the new union.

Regionalism, in the second largest country in the world (9,984,670 sq km) and where regional political and economic interests are so varied, needs to be reflected in national political institutions. There are many forces that shape Canadian regionalism: size, race, class, historical events, language, and regional political and economic circumstances. Nelson Wiseman puts it succinctly when he writes: "To present Canadian political culture as an amalgam of its regional political cultures is akin to trying to tie a number of water-melons together with a piece of string. Canada's vast regions are not easily bound together."[92]

One keen observer of Canadian politics notes that "the political culture of Canada may be defined as a profound sense of regional grievance married to a discourse of entitlement ... Sixty-four per cent of Canadians feel their province gets back less in federal spending than the taxes sent to Ottawa. Nearly three quarters of Canadians feel that the federal government favours one region of Canada over the others, and very few feel that their region is the one favoured."[93] The fact that Queen Victoria decided to locate Canada's capital where the national government's political and bureaucratic power and influence are situated, smack in the middle of Canada East and West, has not helped matters.

For all the talk about special status for Quebec and difficulties associated with asymmetrical federalism, the Fathers of Confederation agreed to incorporate a special arrangement for Quebec for appointing senators. Unlike other provinces, Quebec senators have to be appointed to one of twenty-four constituencies and must own property in their designated areas. This, it was felt, would protect Quebec's English-speaking minorities.[94] The Fathers of Confederation chose not to do the same for the linguistic and religious minorities elsewhere.

THE BNA ACT

The bill to create the Canadian Confederation was introduced in the House of Lords rather than the Commons, and it passed the Lords without difficulty or even debate. The same can be said for the passing in the House of Commons, where the three readings were "swift, completed within two weeks with very little debate."[95] Few members of either the House of Lords or the Commons even bothered to show up to vote.

British politicians had far more important concerns at home. They were debating whether or not to extend the franchise. The 1832 reforms had left many issues unattended, and the question was now whether to extend the right to vote, which was then only held by a minority of the adult male population. There was also a need to establish constituencies on the basis of population. At the time, for example, Thetford had 11,000 inhabitants and only 200 voters, while Manchester had a population of over 300,000 and 14,000 voters. In addition, only 1 million out of 7 million male adults in Britain held the right to vote.

The issue was hotly debated and saw the Liberal Party split on the matter. There was still no question of giving women the right to vote, and the men's right to vote was still based on property qualification. The 1867 Reform Act "granted the vote to all householders in the boroughs as well as lodgers who paid rent of £10 a year or more; reduced the property threshold in the counties and gave the vote to agricultural landowners and tenants with very small amounts of land. Men in urban areas who met the property qualification were enfranchised and the Act roughly doubled the electorate in England and Wales from one to two million men."[96] Democracy was still something to be feared, or at least managed, in 1867. It is in this context that Canadian democracy was born and during this period that Canada decided to import its political institutions from Britain.

POLITICAL INSTITUTIONS IN 1867

Certainly, the Fathers of Confederation saw political institutions in a vastly different light in 1867 than we do today. Walter Bagehot provides important insights into how Westminster-inspired political institutions operated the day Canada became a federation. In his 1867 published classic *The English Constitution*, he sings their praises while openly criticizing the United States Constitution. The thinking among the Fathers of Confederation was that if the political institutions worked well in Britain, then they should work equally well in Canada – hence the preamble that makes it clear we have "a Constitution similar in Principle to that of the United Kingdom." The BNA Act even goes on to point out that members of the House of Commons and the Senate will have the same "privileges, immunities and powers" and should not exceed those enjoyed by members of Parliament in Britain.[97]

Bagehot described political institutions that reflected British society. These institutions were shaped in a country suited for a unitary state and home to a class-conscious society. In his second edition, and in response to enlarging the electorate, he wrote:

It must be remembered that a political combination of the lower classes, as such and for their own objects, is an evil of the first magnitude; that a permanent combination of them would make them (now that so many of them have the suffrage) supreme in the country; and that their supremacy, in the state they now are, means the supremacy of ignorance over instruction and of numbers over knowledge. So long as they are not taught to act together, there is a chance of this being averted, and it can only be averted by the greatest wisdom and the greatest foresight in the higher classes.[98]

He reported that the spirit of the House of Commons had become "plutocratic, not aristocratic."[99] Bagehot, better than anyone, understood the relationship between the Crown, the House of Commons, and the House of Lords. He explained how the monarchy, the aristocracy, and the democratic elements should work together, and added that the "Kings, lords and commons ... the principal characteristics of the English Constitution, are inapplicable in countries where the materials for a monarchy or an aristocracy do not exist."[100] Parliament in Bagehot's day was supreme, and the courts were there to interpret statutes *pur et simple*. Parliament then held "uncontrollable authority in the making, amending and repealing of laws. Nothing is beyond its capacity to legislate upon."[101] The same was to apply for the Canadian Parliament. That was then.

Bagehot attached considerable importance to the Crown and what he labelled "the dignified parts of the constitution." The Crown, he insisted, has no legislative power. However, Bagehot was quick to add that "the Crown does more than it seems."[102] The strength of the Crown stems from the fact that it is "of no party" and the monarch can draw on experience given the permanence of the place to warn or to encourage.[103] This remains an important part of the constitution, at least in Britain, but much less so in Canada. To date, thirteen British prime ministers have served under Elizabeth II, going back to 1952. Since 1952, Canada has had about the same number of governor generals (twelve) as prime ministers (twelve). In Canada, it is difficult to make the case that the Crown is "of no party" or that it is part of the "dignified part" of our constitution, given the bulk of past appointments.

Bagehot saw an important role for the House of Lords, pointing out that it could alter proposed legislation and even reject it by employing its "hypothetical veto." He explained how, "we reject your Bill for this once, or these twice or even these thrice; but if you keep on sending it up, at last we won't reject it."[104] In essence, for Bagehot, the House of Lords had the responsibility to keep the excesses of democracy in check – to play that sober second thought role on behalf of the aristocrats. He was deeply concerned about the "uneducated members"[105] of society and warned that if the "House of Peers ever goes, it will go in a storm, and the storm will not leave all else as it is."[106] Extending the suffrage should serve to strengthen the role of the House of Lords in Bagehot's eyes, as he explained: "the Reform Act of 1867 did not stop at skilled labour; it enfranchised the unskilled labour too. And no one will contend that the ordinary working-man who has no special skill … can judge much of intellectual matters."[107]

Regionalism did not figure in Bagehot's plans for the House of Lords. Indeed, the words *regionalism* or *regions* do not even appear much in his book, at least when it came to British politics. But the need to protect the interest of Britain's aristocracy did, as Bagehot asserted: "The aristocracy live in the fear of the middle classes – of the grocer and the merchant."[108] Macdonald certainly did not have an aristocracy on the scale found in Britain, but his goal was to import British institutions, as they were, to Canada. For this reason, he and his colleagues insisted that to qualify for appointment a senator must be at least thirty years old, have real property worth $4,000, and a net worth of $4,000, an amount unchanged from 1867. The goal was to protect the interests of the propertied class to the extent that it existed.

Canada's aristocracy was thin on the ground in 1867, as David E. Smith recounts, "In Canada, two-thirds of Bagehot's constitutional materials were unavailable – no aristocracy and a surrogate sovereign … In a vast transcontinental state where land was cheap, neither property nor class nor education provided a reliable or continuous basis for deference or, more to the point of the argument, for allegiance to government. Deference in Canada meant deference in electoral politics."[109] More to the point still, rep by pop would rule in the country's national political institutions and decide who should hold political power.

It is important to stress that the role of the House of Lords in 1867 was to ensure democracy would not be the ruin of Britain.[110] To be sure, deference in nineteenth-century Britain mattered. Students

of British politics at the close of the nineteenth century underlined
the importance of the House of Lords to British society. G. Lowes
Dickinson, for example, wrote, "An empire acquired and organised
by a strong and homogeneous aristocracy has to pass into the keeping of a nation increasingly engrossed by an economic feud, whose
tendency is at once to destroy the sense of corporate unity, and to
vitiate the sanity and strength that should be brought to bear on
imperial affairs. Under such conditions, I do not believe that the
democratic House will be a body competent to direct the destinies of
the Empire." He noted that for some colonists "the House of Lords
is more venerable than the House of Commons."[111]

The golden age for the British aristocracy extended from the
Glorious Revolution to the end of the nineteenth century.[112] As the
absolute monarchy came to an end, the British Empire was expanding
in all corners of the world, and the country's industrial power was
taking shape.[113] The aristocracy could claim to have led the charge in
Britain's political and economic successes. Accordingly, the political
institutions of the day were expected to speak to the interests of the
aristocracy, a role that the House of Lords would play by keeping
the work of the House of Commons in check. Looking back, one
can make the case that it made little sense for Canadian federalism
to establish a second House in Parliament patterned on the House
of Lords. Leaving aside loyalty to the mother country, Canada's and
Britain's political, social, and economic circumstances differed widely.
While Britain may have needed an unelected Upper House in its
Parliament to protect the interest of its aristocracy in 1867, Canada
had a different need, one to speak to the country's regional diversity.
James Allan summed it up best when he wrote, "Canada has bicameralism in name only ... in Canada ... bicameralism is a sham."[114]

Even Bagehot saw British political institutions suited to Britain
but less so for other jurisdictions and may well have had Canada in
mind when he explained, "The rude classes at the bottom felt that
they were equal to or better than the delicate classes at the top." He
added: "In theory, it is desirable that the highest class of wealth and
leisure should have an influence far out of proportion to its mere
number: a perfect constitution would find for it a delicate expedient
to make its fine thought tell upon the surrounding cruder thought."
He acknowledged that a young colony struggling to carve out an
economy based on agriculture does not have the maturity to establish a class of wealth and leisure or highly educated and cultivated

people needed to make political institutions based on a thousand years of history work.[115]

Bagehot had precious little advice for the British North American colonies. He did, however, identify the most important challenge – geography, not economic classes. He wrote that the greatest difficulty in North America was "geographical," adding that the "population is mostly scattered and where population is sparse, discussion is difficult."[116] However, he looked at the federal system in the United States and his verdict was not positive. He saw little merit in having sovereignty on important matters of state rest with what he labelled the "subordinate government."[117] Federalism was a foreign concept to Bagehot, to British policy-makers and, for that matter, to many of the Fathers of Confederation.

Reading Bagehot, one is struck by how he saw the ability of British political institutions to accommodate the country's socio-economic circumstances. Bagehot's England was elitist and, as he stressed time and again, accepted the importance of "deference." He argued that persons born in high positions should be given "generalized deference," and that if persons are born to a high place, they should retain it.[118]

Canadians, by contrast, had to deal with frontier conditions, not the need for "deference" to aristocracy. As David E. Smith writes, in Canada deference "was paid to electoral power and not social status."[119] Canada's political history was marked by conflicts between Britain and France as they played out in various colonies, efforts at building an economy resting on natural resources, and keeping a constant eye on American expansion. Historian Frank Underhill put it succinctly when he wrote that Canadians are the world's oldest anti-Americans. He made the case that Canadians have always been threatened by the United States, initially in a physical sense and, more recently, culturally and economically.[120]

Another important Bagehot contribution is important to feature for a better understanding of our political institutions. One of the most frequently quoted sentences in the public administration literature that explains the role of the Cabinet is Bagehot's: "A cabinet is a combining committee – a hyphen which joins, a buckle which fastens, the legislative part of the state to the executive part of the state. In its origin, it belongs to the one, in its functions it belongs to the other." He ascribes tremendous power to Cabinet even "the power of destroying its creators." In short, he saw Cabinet as the "efficient" element of the English Constitution.[121] That was then. Today, Cabinet government – particularly in Canada but also in Britain – has given way to a prime ministerial–centric government.[122]

LOOKING BACK

In conclusion, Canada was born to break the political deadlock between Canada West and Canada East. The British North American colonies had to deal with economic challenges as the American Civil War was coming to an end, and with the collapse of US-Canada reciprocity agreement there was a desire to keep American expansion in check, particularly in Western Canada, after the United States purchased Alaska in March 1867. The hope in Britain was that its colonies would become more economically self-sufficient in the midst of a deeply felt desire by many in Canada West and the Maritimes to remain loyal to the British Crown. The hope in Canada was that a national railway would open new economic opportunities everywhere. The architects of the Canadian Confederation decided that British cultural traditions and British-inspired political, administrative, and judicial institutions would shape how Canadians would govern themselves after 1867.

Macdonald, Cartier, Brown, and Galt got what they wanted – a treaty bringing together two colonies constantly at odds with one another. The treaty brought stability to Canada West and East. In sharp contrast to the 1841–67 period, Confederation would bring remarkable stability. For example, Macdonald would hold power for nineteen years after 1867.

Macdonald's strong favour for legislative union paired with his lack of appreciation for the benefits of federalism are worth emphasizing. As David E. Smith writes, "It is ironic that Macdonald, the feigned federalist of this interpretation, should a century and a half later be celebrated as the pre-eminent nation-builder of the world's most extensive federation."[123] The Senate, the one institution that speaks to the requirements of federalism, served one purpose – it made Confederation possible. Brown summed it up: "On no other condition could we have advanced a step." The Senate was compensation to Quebec for losing equal representation in the Parliament of United Canada and compensation to the Maritime colonies for a House of Commons based on representation by population.[124] Since 1867, the Senate has pursued several mandates with little success.

I can do no better on this point than, once again, quote David E. Smith: "There is and always has been talk, usually critical talk, about the upper chamber but nothing else."[125]

The United States struck a Great Compromise by giving small and large states equal representation in the Senate and large states a form of proportional representation in the House of Representatives. Canada never struck a Great Compromise between small and large provinces in defining its national political institutions. As we will see, to the extent that a compromise between large and small provinces in Canada has been achieved, it has been in the form of transfer payments.

The Senate speaks directly to Canada's national political institutions' inability to accommodate the country's regional diversity. Ontario and Quebec have consistently opposed attempts to rethink its role, to see it elected, effective, and equal. Western Canada was once highly supportive of a Triple-E Senate. Things began to change, however, when Stephen Harper, an Alberta MP, served as prime minister for ten years, and as the western population continues to grow and add more elected MPs.

Unlike their counterparts in the United States, the Fathers of Confederation did not see the need to bring fresh thinking on how best to organize political institutions to accommodate not only a distinct political culture but also the new country's linguistic, cultural, and regional diversities. They saw their task as bringing self-governing colonies together rather than creating a new political system.[126] Revolutions in the United States and France forced the political and intellectual elites in the United States to think of new approaches and define new institutions. That is what revolutions are good at. Wishing to import British political institutions in every detail spoke to the merit that the status quo held for the key architects of Confederation. Yet, Canadian society, its history and its people factor, looked quite different to that found in Britain in 1867. We explore the differences in the next chapter.

Canadian society has evolved since 1867, but the basic outline of our national political institutions has not. As was the case in 1867, these institutions still lack the capacity to accommodate regional circumstances and regional equality.

3

Canada: Setting, People, and Culture

We saw in the previous chapters that Canada adopted British-inspired political and administrative institutions. The contrast between British and Canadian society in 1867 was stark, and we need to gain insight into how our institutions have evolved to understand them. Unlike in Canada, British aristocracy dominated society in the nineteenth century, and it enjoyed the support of leading students of government from Walter Bagehot to Herbert Spencer.[1] One of Britain's most eminent political philosophers of that century, John Stuart Mill, argued three years before the Quebec Conference that "governments which have been remarkable in history for sustained mental ability and vigour in the conduct of affairs, have generally been aristocracies."[2]

Most of the senior Cabinet ministers in nineteenth-century Britain were drawn from aristocracies, and Parliament remained under the firm control of the landed interest until the twentieth century.[3] The *Oxford Companion to British History* sums up the eminent position of aristocrats in British society: "Their claims were still formidable – that they were superior in education, experienced in making decisions, enjoyed the leisure necessary to consider public affairs, and, above all, that their great possessions gave them a unique concern for the well-being of the country, since they had so much to lose. They also claimed a distinctive political role, as a balancing or stabilizing force, which prevented the country from sliding into royal despotism or democratic licence."[4] Royal despotism and democratic licence were both to be avoided and aristocracy provided the answer.

In 1867, many in Britain believed that they had achieved the proper balance between monarchy, aristocracy, and democracy that would ensure protection against a rush to a "simple" solution and provide for stable government.[5] The Americans had a different perspective. The American Constitution, Article 1, Section 9, Clause 8 expressly forbids titles: "No Title of Nobility shall be granted by the United States." Canada, in 1867, had no such prohibition. Indeed, several Fathers of Confederation were later knighted by Queen Victoria.

Britain highly valued its aristocracy in 1867. The argument was that aristocracy had led the way in making Britain the world's greatest colonial power, in promoting economic growth, and in providing wise and talented personnel to government. The sons of aristocrats went to Oxford or Cambridge where they established a network of like minds that would serve them and, they believed, their country well in the future. Family ties, until fairly recently, decided who was admitted to Oxford and Cambridge, and both universities became known as finishing schools for aristocrats.[6] It is revealing to note that of the fifty-four British prime ministers, from Robert Walpole (1721) to date, Oxford produced twenty-seven and Cambridge fourteen, or over 75 percent.[7] Privileges of birth, however, came with responsibility.

Canada has no university that compares to Oxford and Cambridge as a training ground for the country's political elites. McGill and University of Toronto do battle to be known as the "Harvard of the North," but neither can claim to have an Oxbridge influence on Canada's body politic.[8] Canada has had twenty-three prime ministers, and their education pedigree is diverse: five never attended university, three attended McGill for their first degree, one the University of Edinburgh, four the University of Toronto, one attended Dalhousie University, three l'Université Laval, one the University of Saskatchewan, one l'Université de Montréal, one the University of Alberta, three the University of British Columbia, one went to St Francis Xavier University, and one to the University of Calgary.

In Britain, the House of Lords, the epitome of aristocracy, played an important role in governing the country until the twentieth century. The consent of the House of Lords remained essential for all proposed legislation, except for money bills, until 1911. The Parliament Act of 1911 "freed most legislation of this undemocratic constraint"; nonetheless, the House of Lords still retains legislative influence.[9] Many believed that aristocracy provided stability and a sense of noblesse oblige to guide Britain, with the rationale that because most aristocrats are wealthy, they are not likely motivated by monetary gains and thus freer to pursue the broader public interest.

They have an interest in promoting gradual change, avoiding a complete break from the past, and fending off mob rule.[10]

The argument certainly resonated more in Britain, with its history, established families, and landed gentry, than it did in Canada in 1867. At that time Canada was, in many ways, alien to aristocracy. How could the country possibly produce a titled or landed class to act as legislative councillors and put the brakes on a rush to a "simple" democracy? There was no Oxford or Cambridge, no landed gentry, or families with a long tradition of distinguished military service.

Canada could take some comfort in the fact that aristocracy is not without its drawbacks and critics, which brought about its decline. Aristocracy did not square either with representative democracy or North American society in the nineteenth century. Alexis de Tocqueville made this very point when he wrote, "In America, where privileges of birth never existed and where wealth confers no particular rights on those who possess it, people who do not know one another easily frequent the same places and see neither advantage nor peril in communicating their thoughts freely. Should they meet by chance, they do not try to avoid one another."[11] That was not the British way. In Britain, the aristocracy hated and feared democracy, often pointing to the excesses of French and American revolutions to make their case. It was in Britain's interest to fear democracy and resist extending the suffrage. At the time of the Upper Canadian Rebellion, for instance, Britain looked to the "King, Lords and Commons" to define the national interest but was governed by class, more specifically the wealthy and aristocratic class.

The British North American colonies, by the mid-1850s, were more open to democracy than Britain. Canadian assemblies, were more democratic, perhaps because they had little power but also because there was no aristocracy to keep them in check. Members elected to these assemblies did not depend on class or wealth but rather on their popularity. Therein was the problem for the Colonial Office, which feared the rush to "simple" democracy as much for the colonies as it did at home. It explains why Britain was reluctant to grant the colonies responsible government, and accounts for the 1837 rebellions in Upper and Lower Canada.[12]

Even after responsible government finally arrived in the colonies, first to Nova Scotia in 1848, and then to the others, the elected legislative assemblies hardly represented the full repository of political power. We saw in the previous chapter that Arthur Hamilton Gordon,

New Brunswick's lieutenant-governor, completely sidestep the premier and elected members of the Legislative Assembly and sent a message to the Colonial Office in London calling for Confederation. In not rejecting Gordon's message, the Colonial Office violated its own directive sent by the British Secretary of State for the Colonies, Lord Grey, to the lieutenant-governor of Nova Scotia in November 1846. It read: "It is neither possible nor desirable, to govern any of the British provinces of North America in opposition to the opinion of its inhabitants."[13]

Exporting political and administrative institutions as is from one environment with deep historical roots, where aristocracy governed in a unitary state, to a young country that is home to two nations with disparate regional economies and a vast empty land posed substantial challenges. Durham's two nations were still warring in the bosom of a single state in 1867. Though the Canadian nation was larger with New Brunswick and Nova Scotia now a part of it, the prejudices did not die on 1 July 1867. Indeed, George Brown, one of the leading Fathers of Confederation from Canada West, saw the new country as a way to assimilate French Canadians. He certainly felt that the possibility of assimilation held more promise with the reliance on rep by pop to decide who should hold power rather than the equal representation formula provided under the 1840 Act of Union.[14]

The four key architects of Confederation – Macdonald, Brown, Galt, and Cartier – shared some objectives, if not beliefs. All four embraced the monarchy, with Cartier arguing that "in this country we must have a distinct form of government in which the monarchical spirit will be found."[15] Brown and Cartier agreed on the need for an unequal and appointed (rather than an elected) Senate, albeit for different reasons, as did Macdonald and Galt. Cartier strongly resisted an equal and effective Senate, maintaining that Quebec, given its distinct linguistic and cultural needs, could never agree to the same number of senators as a single small province. Brown opposed an elected Senate not because he "expected great things from an appointed federal Senate," but because, he insisted, "the principles of British cabinet government no less required that it should not be a competing elected body." He saw no advantage for Ontario in an equal and elected Senate. In addition, Brown, no less than Macdonald, Galt, and Cartier, "sought to maintain British institutions" in a Canadian setting.[16]

The Fathers of Confederation, including those from the Maritime colonies, saw political institutions through a British lens. This was even true for those who strongly opposed the Quebec Resolutions, including Joseph Howe. Loyalty to the British Crown was paramount. They saw only the British institutions to make their new country work. Howe, Smith, and delegates from Prince Edward Island and Newfoundland, however, wanted important adjustments for the new institutions, to give voice to regional considerations in Ottawa, but they would always remain loyal to the British Crown.

Canada is thus not the product of peoples wishing to live together. Rather, it is a product of two predominant peoples living in Canada West and Canada East who were unable to provide stable government, of a strong desire by Britain's Colonial Office to loosen ties with its colonies, of a strong willingness of the colonies to remain loyal to the British Crown, and of a strong desire of key leaders in the pro-Confederation movement to resist American expansion in what is now Western and Atlantic Canada.[17] These were the motivating forces that drove the agenda of Confederation's four primary architects.

For their part, Tupper in Nova Scotia and Tilley in New Brunswick saw advantages in the building of a national railway. It is important to stress that the many in Nova Scotia, New Brunswick, and Prince Edward Island who opposed Confederation were opposed to the Quebec Resolutions, not to a union of the British North American colonies. As students of Canadian history know, Macdonald and Brown did not see eye to eye on most issues, nor did Brown and Cartier. But they saw no alternative to Confederation as they defined it at the Quebec Conference, given their political agenda. They knew from experience that the status quo could only produce further political deadlock. What they sought and, in the end, secured, was a "pact" or a "treaty" between two nations: Canada West and Canada East. The Maritime colonies became, in many ways, convenient pawns in the negotiations between Macdonald, Brown, and Cartier to secure the treaty. The three and Galt had no interest in looking to the United States for solutions, but neither did Tupper or Tilley. They did not need to reflect long on the kind of democratic institutions required to give life to their agenda; all they had to do was import British institutions. How then did they square the circle and adapt political institutions without the experience, let alone the capacity, to deal with a vast geography and a large linguistic minority community?

TRANSPORTATION AND COMMUNICATIONS

In 1867, Canada had the most basic transportation means and communications capacities. Political leaders had to look to horse-drawn carriages, steamships, and – for some – trains to meet their constituents. It was a great deal easier then for a merchant from Halifax to make his way to London, Liverpool, Boston, New York, or the West Indies than to Toronto. In the 1872 election campaign, neither the leader of the Conservative nor the Liberal Party ventured outside of Ontario.[18] One argument for building a national railway was that it would bring "the most distant parts of the settled portion of the Dominion within the possibility of receiving a reply to a communication in less than a month."[19]

It was not easy for the Fathers of Confederation to get to the three Confederation conferences. Macdonald and Brown first had to make their way to Quebec City where they boarded the steamer *Queen Victoria* to Prince Edward Island. They left Quebec on 29 August 1864 and arrived at the Charlottetown harbour four days later.[20]

Canals were an important means of transportation for defence, goods, and people at the time of Confederation. The Lachine and Rideau Canals, for example, had already been operating for years.[21] But they had inherent limits due to geography, and thus the railway became a much more efficient mode of transportation.

Railways offered greater potential for opening up Canada's hinterland and for settling new areas. Indeed, the promise of a railway linking British Columbia to Nova Scotia became an important selling point for Confederation. It was only after the federal government committed to building the railway from the east to the west coast that British Columbia agreed to join Confederation. George Stanley, noted Canadian historian, maintained that "without railways there would be and could be no Canada."[22]

The first railway line in Canada was built in 1836, but it was only by the 1850s that major progress was achieved. The Grand Trunk Railway linking Sarnia, Toronto, Montreal, and Portland, Maine, was constructed in the early 1850s, and a few years later, the Great Western Railway line was completed, linking cities in Ontario with major urban US centres. The Sarnia to Montreal line was completed in 1860.

The railways, at the time of Confederation, held considerable promise for commerce and the military, and for linking regions to one another and enabling people to explore new markets and new communities. A leading promoter for the railways, Alexander Galt, was convinced that they would break down the economic isolation of the region he represented – Quebec's Eastern Townships. He took on the task of finding investors to build the railway from Montreal to Portland, Maine, to provide his constituency access to a year-round ocean port.[23]

The building of a "national" railway was slow. The Intercolonial, from the Maritime provinces to Central Canada, was completed in 1876. The Last Spike, as it was called, of the transcontinental railway to British Columbia was driven on 7 November 1885.[24] This was a commitment made in 1871 by the federal government to British Columbia, which had been an important factor in the province's decision to join Confederation.

Communications were no less rudimentary. It was only about twenty years before Confederation that the first telegram was successfully transmitted between Toronto and Hamilton.[25] Fifty years after Confederation, George M. Wrong wrote about the challenges confronting Canadian politicians in contrast to British politicians: "The very vastness of the Canadian union has created one of its chief difficulties. In Victoria, one can rarely secure a newspaper published in Toronto that is less than a week old. Distance is a great handicap in the building up of national life. In Britain, a political leader can make a speech in the south of England in the morning and repeat it in the capital of Scotland on the same day. In Canada, it takes about six days and nights to pass from one end of the country to the other."[26]

Politicians in 1867 had to be creative to reach out directly to citizens. The radio was still more than fifty years away. To reach the electorate, politicians had to turn to newspapers, political picnics, and public meetings. Political parties were just taking shape in 1867, and politicians did not have access to national party organizations with easy access to party members or voters.[27] The communication instrument of choice in 1867, and for many years after, was the newspaper. Newspapers of the day were openly partisan and closely identified with a political party. Khayyam Paltiel explains: "Thus at the very outset of the Dominion, Sir John A. Macdonald felt impelled in 1869 to stimulate the foundation of a friendly paper in Toronto (*The Mail*) and was periodically called upon to come to its assistance. A generation later, a group of Liberals put up the funds to purchase the *Toronto Evening Star*."[28]

CANADA'S PEOPLE FACTOR

Canada's population in 1867 totalled 3.4 million people thinly spread out over Ontario, Quebec, New Brunswick, and Nova Scotia. More than 80 percent of Canadians at the time were born in Canada, including about 100,000 Aboriginals and 1 million French Canadians, and the remaining were English, Welsh, Irish, Scottish, and other "foreign" origins.[29] Canada then was a rural country and its economy was based on agriculture (mostly small farms), lumber, and fish.

The delegates attending the Quebec Conference spoke to who had the upper hand in Canadian society. The thirty-three delegates at the conference were all males; there were no Aboriginal delegates and only four French Canadians. French-speaking minorities from Canada West and the Maritimes were not represented, but the English-speaking minorities from Canada East, led by Alexander Galt, were well represented. Three of the four key architects of Canada's Constitution (Macdonald, Galt, and Brown) were born in Britain. These three decided that a union of the British colonies was desirable for reasons outlined above, and as all politicians are wont to do, they set out to protect the interests of the region they represented.

The Indigenous communities were completely frozen out. It never even occurred to the Fathers of Confederation that the Aboriginal inhabitants should be involved in the negotiations. One can gain some appreciation of the position of the Aboriginal communities in Canadian society at the time of Confederation by reading the Indian Act. The act was passed in 1876, only nine years after Confederation. It is a highly paternalistic, even offensive document. The purpose of the act was to strip Aboriginal residents of their language and culture and assimilate them, as Sir John A. Macdonald put it, "with the other inhabitants of the Dominion as speedily as they are fit to change."[30] Indian agents were told, for example, to employ whatever means necessary to discourage dancing at traditional ceremonies. The act established a "reserve" system and only allowed Aboriginal residents to vote provided they renounced their Indian status.[31] The Fathers of Confederation did not see any need to hear the views of Aboriginal peoples in shaping new political institutions or draw from their experience in dealing with governance issues, as they were convinced these communities had precious little to offer to improve British-inspired institutions.

The idea of uniting the British North American colonies had been debated long before the Charlottetown Conference, with French Canadians essentially kept in the dark.[32] After the conquest, English Protestants in the colonies had the upper hand as the victors and some – notably George Brown – were openly hostile to French Canada.

George-Étienne Cartier was not bargaining from a position of strength with his counterparts from Canada West. But Canada West needed Cartier to secure the Confederation deal. Though there was resistance to Confederation in Canada East, there was hardly any in Canada West. Thus, Cartier was able to tell his constituents that French could now be used in Parliament and in the courts, that Confederation would break the political deadlock between the two Canadas, that Confederation would mean that Canada East would not be drowned in the American vortex, and that Quebec would have its own provincial government with jurisdiction over education. Jean-Charles Bonenfant sums up the crux of the matter: "Confederation was achieved because the English Canadians needed to have the French Canadians [here, read Quebec] in it." He adds, "French Canadians did not have a very advanced theoretical vision of it [federalism] and they would have been incapable of discussing most of the problems it poses today. They did not even suspect these problems."[33] Cartier, as the voice of Quebec and French-speaking minorities, had little knowledge of federalism. He explained why he joined forces with Macdonald, Brown, and Galt: "The question is reduced to this: we must either have a British North American federation or else be absorbed into the American federation."[34]

Cartier and much of Quebec's Roman Catholic clergy believed that Quebec's cultural and religious interests would be better served in joining Confederation than by becoming one of the American states. For Cartier and others of like mind in Quebec, that was the core of the issue and they got what they wanted – Quebec would have its own Legislative Assembly and the French language would have some degree of recognition, if not protection, in national political institutions. In any event, they understood that the die was cast: it was Confederation and British-inspired institutions or nothing. Even the status quo was in peril with everyone in the Canadas well aware that the end was at hand for the 1840 Act of Union. The political deadlock had become unsustainable for all parties.

FRENCH CANADA AT CONFEDERATION

It should come as no surprise that French Canadians (here read French Canadians in Canada East) were not negotiating from a position of strength and that Aboriginal communities were disregarded when Canada was born. We know that in French Canada, some of the richer and better educated colonists retreated the whole way back to France after the conquest, depriving the region of much of its economic and political elites and its innovative capacity. France itself showed little concern for the fate of its former colonists once the colony was lost. Far from helping it rebuild its economy after a damaging and costly war, France even renounced its debt to the colony. The impact of defeat was profound.

No longer in control of their own land and finding themselves, for one reason or another, at a disadvantage in competing with the British conquerors, the French withdrew, to a large extent, from economic competition. They looked to their traditions and cultivated a local nationalism, consoling themselves for their failure to participate fully in the economic life of their province by assuring themselves that they did not wish to do so anyway. They preferred the gentility and humanity of their own life, their own Roman Catholic faith, values, and culture to the vulgar materialism of the victors. As time went by, these attitudes became formalized and ritualized.

So persuasive was this ideal of a serene, agrarian society led by the Roman Catholic Church and a cultivated elite indifferent to wealth that many French Canadians began to think French Canada really was like that. Thus, in 1896, Sir John Bourinot, Clerk of the Canadian House of Commons and secretary of the Royal Society of Canada, wrote: "As a rule, the *habitant* lives contentedly on very little. Give him a pipe of native tobacco, a chance of discussing politics, a gossip with his fellows at the church door after service, a visit now and then to the county town, and he will be happy. It does not take much to amuse him, while he is quite satisfied that his spiritual safety is secured as long as he is within sound of the church bells, goes regularly to confession, and observes all the *fêtes d'obligation*. If he or one of his family can only get a little office in the municipality, or in the 'government,' then his happiness is nearly perfect."[35]

J.P. Beaulieu of the Quebec Department of Industry wrote in a similar vein, as recently as 1952, although showing more appreciation for industrialization, which was then taking place: "Quebec, barely half a century ago, a picturesque region in a vast country, over most of its extent farm lands alternated with forest, rivers, villages and freshly cleared colonization centres. This was Quebec little changed from pioneer days with the old ways kept alive from one generation to the other by the rural population."[36] I stress that both Bourinot and Beaulieu were French Canadians writing about their community.

This view permeated French Canada until fairly recently. Justin Trudeau writes that his father explained the "political and religious elites were concerned about protecting the province's French Catholic character within largely Protestant North America. Simply put, the emphasis was therefore on maintaining a society of farmers and lumberjacks, with a small cadre of lawyers, priests, doctors, and politicians to oversee it. Money and business were left to *les Anglais*."[37]

French Canadians had a strong interest in politics; it was a question of survival. But they had to play by the rules and institutions established by the British. No one was seriously suggesting – in Canada West, Canada East, or the Maritimes – that the new country could import institutions from France or the United States (leaving aside federalism). Designing new institutions from scratch was not possible. The talent was not there, in English or French Canada; neither was the self-confidence to define political institutions that would square with the forces from below and deal with the political and economic requirements of a new country.

In any event, Cartier and the powerful Roman Catholic clergy garnered as much as they could hope for from the Quebec Conference. They secured language and religious rights protection and their own political institutions in Quebec. Given the lack of transportation and communications infrastructures, they could continue to live in relative isolation from the "English." Cartier, like Macdonald, saw Confederation as a pact, a treaty that served the interest of his province. The treaty remains in place to this day.

INDIGENOUS COMMUNITIES AT CONFEDERATION

After Western Europeans arrived, European diseases wiped out a large percentage of the Indigenous populations. The highly ingrained egalitarianism in Indigenous cultures gave way when some members were able to acquire European goods. For those who did, the goods provided more prestige and more authority than they had in pre-contact bands of hunter-gatherers.[38]

The goal of policy-makers at the time of Confederation was to "civilize" Indigenous peoples,[39] who were given European names, and every effort was made to have them embrace Christianity. Policy-makers sought to have them abandon hunting and fishing, turn to agriculture, and adopt more sedentary ways of life. Government became the guardian of all Crown lands, including "Indian reserve land," sending a clear signal that the Crown assumed responsibility "to care for and protect interests of First Nations people."[40]

The Fathers of Confederation saw no value in the cultures or governance practices of Indigenous communities; therefore, it did not even occur to them that these populations should be consulted about joining Confederation or contributing fresh thinking in establishing political institutions for the societies they were designed to serve. Indeed, the Fathers of Confederation saw Indigenous populations as a problem that the new central government would have to address. The federal government did assume the "problem" in 1867 by simply taking over the responsibility that previously belonged to the British Crown. Section 91 (24) of the Constitution Act, 1867 gives the Parliament of Canada legislative authority to deal with "Indians, and Lands reserved for the Indians."[41]

Again, had the Fathers of Confederation applied today's standards of democracy and conflict of interest and ethics, as well as access to information requirements, to their work, they would have dealt with Indigenous communities in a very different manner. The new country simply embraced policies set before Confederation and then carried on with the status quo. The view had been long held that Indigenous peoples were "uncivilized, economically backward and morally inferior to Europeans."[42] Traditional forms of governance found in Indigenous communities were replaced by a system under the direct control of the central government and its "Indian agents." Chiefs and band councillors, elected by males only, would now serve at the pleasure of the government.

WOMEN AT CONFEDERATION

Looking at a painting by Robert Harris of the participants at the 1864 Quebec Conference, one is struck by the lack of diversity – no women, no Aboriginal peoples, and no representatives of visible minorities. The all-white, all-male participants saw no need to extend the membership or even to consult much beyond their immediate surroundings.[43]

The role of women at the Charlottetown and Quebec conferences was limited to entertaining the delegates and organizing "elaborate luncheons, dinners, and balls."[44] Edward Whelan's observations, quoted by Creighton, on how the Quebec Conference unfolded are nothing short of offensive: "Edward Whelan's first impression, at the Governor General's reception on Tuesday night, was that the Quebec women were a remarkably plain lot, usually quite short, and almost invariably much too stout. Mercy Coles recorded her opinion that the Maritime women, headed by the handsome Mrs. Tupper, were 'quite a credit to the Lower Provinces.' 'I have seen more pretty girls at a Government House ball in Charlottetown – more at the late banquet in the Province Building there – than I witnessed at the great Drawing Room,' Whelan wrote."[45]

One can only ascribe such impressions to the time. How else can one possibly explain Donald Creighton's added observations that

the French-Canadian women, who at first sight had looked rather stout and hearty, were now found to possess quite as much of that precious mid-Victorian quality "femininity" as the less robust and more languid beauties of Halifax and Saint John. The crinoline, then billowing out towards its greatest expanse, hardly flattered their stout figures; but the fashionable coiffures and the coquettishly elaborate ornamentation of the season's ball gowns could scarcely have suited them better. Little velvet ribbon caps festooned with tiny ostrich feathers, clusters of curls with a single dark ringlet falling forward coyly over a plump shoulder, tight-fitting bodices sparkling with crystal beads, blooming crino-lines lavishly adorned with braid, satin bows, and velvet inser-tions – all this elaborate prettiness became these short, dimpled, vivacious creatures extremely well.[46]

It was only in 1859, eight years before Confederation, that mar-ried women in Canada were allowed to own property. But, while they could own property, they could not sell it. They required the agreement of their husband to sell property. In 1867, the right to vote was restricted to males twenty-one and over, who were British subjects by birth or naturalization.[47] In response to a suffragette who asked why she did not have the right to vote, Macdonald said: "Madame, I cannot conceive."[48] Women finally won the right to vote in federal elections on 24 May 1918. Their work in the war effort, not concerns for representative democracy, paved the way. The Government of Canada explains: "Their service and sacrifice during the First World War helped influence the decision to grant federal voting rights to many Canadian women in 1917."[49]

Canada's representative democracy would be defined essentially by four white males (Macdonald, Brown, Galt, and Cartier) who saw little need to consult anyone outside their immediate circle. Minorities, women, Indigenous peoples, and small provinces were thus left on the outside looking in.

ELITES AT CONFEDERATION

The country's political and economic elites in the 1860s had a strong British connection. As already noted, Macdonald, Brown, and Galt were born in Britain, and so was John Langton, arguably the most powerful public servant in Canada's early years, serving as deputy minister of finance. As noted, Leonard Tilley, a Father of Confederation from New Brunswick, was of British Loyalist stock as was his New Brunswick counterpart, Albert Smith, and Nova Scotia's Joseph Howe.

The Loyalists had a profound impact on the British colonies and later on Canada. The sudden influx of Loyalists created two colonies from one, strengthened ties with the British Crown, and brought a new political culture to the colonies. The story of the Loyalists is well known. Those who were loyal to Britain during and after the American Revolution were subjected to severe hardships – they could not vote or sell land and were restricted from working in several professions. Some 70,000 Loyalists fled the American colonies and initially most made their way to Nova Scotia and New Brunswick and, to a lesser extent, Quebec and Ontario.

Loyalists were opposed to the revolution for several reasons. Many attached a great deal of importance to their ties with the mother country. For example, the Ontario coat of arms "Loyal she began, loyal she remains" speaks to the Loyalists' commitment to the British Crown. Some had a distrust of representative democracy. It is widely believed that Reverend Mather Byles, a community leader in his day, observed, "Which is better – to be ruled by one tyrant three thousand miles away, or by three thousand tyrants not a mile away?"[50]

The transition to the new colonies, however, was difficult for the Loyalists. They fled in a panic, leaving behind most of their possessions, to settle in a land where winters were harsh and economic opportunities modest. Some Loyalists had a great deal more difficulty than others in adapting to their new country. Black and Aboriginal Loyalists who had fought on the side of Britain did not fare nearly as well as the White Loyalists.[51] Another wave of Loyalists – labelled "Late Loyalists" – settled mostly in Upper Canada or Ontario.

Commitments made to Black and Aboriginal (i.e., mostly Iroquois) Loyalists were not honoured and the transition was particularly painful for them. A British company later decided to offer Black Loyalists relocation to Sierra Leone, in West Africa, and about half opted for the offer.[52] Barry Cahill writes that Black Loyalists in the region were more myth than reality: "Neither the Black Loyalist hypothesis nor the myth to which it gave rise allows for the fact that it was racism *tout court* which prevented the fugitive-slave refugees from being, or being seen to be, Loyalists."[53]

The White Loyalists – or the Chosen Loyalists – had the upper hand in their new colonies and were not about to loosen their ties to Britain or British institutions. They were handsomely rewarded for their loyalty. They were granted the best agricultural land with heads of families receiving 100 acres, which was later increased to 200 acres. They were given assistance – food, tools, and building materials to help settle the land. Military officers were awarded more land and resources. They arrived in the region with the attitude that they had sacrificed everything for their loyalty to the British Crown. Britain, they insisted, owed them land, financial support, and government jobs even if the incumbents had to be let go. Their deep sense of entitlement would "poison relations between them and the rest of the population for decades."[54]

Loyalists, at least in the early years, were anxious to show their loyalty to the British Crown and their resistance to American republicanism. They were conservatives, notably when it came to political institutions and to a unified British Empire. They pressed the colonies, particularly Quebec, to amend legislation to better correspond to British traditions and laws. They had a profound impact on Canadian geography and regionalism: their arrival led to the creation of a new colony, New Brunswick, and a division of Quebec into Lower and Upper Canada.[55]

LOOKING BACK

Canada in 1867 differed widely from the Canada of today in both important and unimportant ways. Certainly, Canadian democracy (circa 1867) had different requirements. The press was more easily controlled, as the London Conference deliberations revealed. Macdonald successfully kept the discussions inside the room, away from the media, fearing that leaks would only feed more opposition, notably in the Maritime colonies, to the Confederation deal struck at the Quebec Conference.

Public consultations, to the extent that they existed, were also easily controlled. Newspapers took a stand for or against Confederation; and they all wrote from a strongly held bias. They were on the receiving end of what politicians fed them. The negotiations were carried out by a closed club of white men with only a handful of them driving the negotiations.

Ties to Britain remained strong for a number of years – indeed, they are still strong in some parts of Canada. The country's coat of arms, updated in 1994, is revealing. It presents the flag of the United Kingdom, the royal flag of France, symbols of England and Ireland, symbols of the monarchy, maple leaves (a distinctive Canadian symbol), and Latin phrases that mean "They desire a better country" and "From sea to sea." Nothing is said about Indigenous populations. Nothing is said about Canada's regional diversity. The thinking was that the British Crown, the royal flag of France, and the maple leaf were the unifying symbols that could paper over regional diversity, at least regional diversity of the kind found in Ontario and Quebec. The 1867 Canadian setting reflected the way Europeans saw the world. They discovered the Americas, and they decided that everyone in the colonies would be subjected to their colonial power.[56]

French Canadians occupied a critical space in the new country and had to be involved in the negotiations to strike any Confederation deal. However, the impact of the British conquest was omnipresent in 1867 and, in some ways, it is felt to this day. Still, French Canadians in Quebec at the time felt that they got what they could out of the negotiations – their own provincial government, albeit with very limited power in the early years, and a commitment that either the English or French language may be used in Parliament and in the courts.[57] These were important concessions for Quebec. A leading Quebec newspaper in its day, *La Minerve*, applauded the Confederation deal, predicting that French Canada (here again, read Quebec) would be "*maître chez lui en tout ce qui regarde son économie sociale, civile et religieuse.*"[58] George Brown also got what he wanted – representation by population – that would henceforth decide who would hold power in the new Canada. The other key architects of Confederation, Macdonald and Galt, accomplished what they wanted too – breaking the political deadlock that had crippled Canada West and East and the ability to remain loyal to the British Crown while importing ready-made political institutions to Canada.

The Maritimes had a voice, which was politely heard but dismissed. Maritime political leaders did not have the strength to question a treaty negotiated a few thousand kilometers away by astute politicians wishing to break a crippling political impasse. No one – not even Albert Smith from New Brunswick or Joseph Howe from Nova Scotia – was a match to take on a combination of Macdonald, Brown, Galt, Cartier, and Britain's Colonial Office. The authors of the Quebec Resolutions gave the Maritimes a constitutional commitment to build a railway for the region and the region would have to be satisfied with that.

Again, space or regionalism did not figure to the extent that it should have in the negotiations leading to Confederation. Prince Edward Island and Newfoundland simply walked out of the negotiations, largely because of regionalism, convinced that their interests would not be heard in national political institutions. The vast expanse to the West had yet to be added, and so its voice was not heard. And, as already noted, the key players in the negotiations saw regionalism as something to be contained, or, if possible, ignored. They only needed to look to the Civil War raging to the south to see evidence of this. Political leaders from Canada West and East had a first-hand appreciation of how regionalism had crippled their political institutions. Therefore, they saw no problem in importing political institutions virtually as is, with little experience in dealing with regional issues. They had no better scheme to put forward, only a deep distrust of things regional. The decisions struck at the Quebec and London conferences were logical for the time, at least from the perspective of the Canadas. However, the choices made in 1867 have had a continuing and deterministic impact on Canadian politics, public policies, and public administration.[59]

The people factor had little influence in shaping the new country's political institutions. White middle-aged males, mostly Protestants with strong ties to Britain, brought their values and their preferences to the table and established how the new country would operate. French Canada was defined as Quebec, gender equality was a non-issue, and Indigenous communities were completely frozen out of the negotiations. The history of colonization continued on its track and Canada, to this day, deals with its consequences.

Confederation was a pact, a treaty between Canada West and Canada East or between two nations. Macdonald, Brown, Galt, and Cartier frequently employed the terms "pact," "treaty," or "compact" to describe the deal struck in Quebec in 1864. I can do no better than quote George Stanley on this issue: "The Canadian delegates to Quebec and London were thoroughly convinced that their bargain was a treaty or a pact; however, this conviction was always weaker among the Maritimers than among the Canadians, and especially the French Canadians, whose principal concern as a vital minority, has been and must be the survival of their culture and the pact which is the constitutional assurance of that survival." Stanley rightly observes: "If the population of Canada were one in race, language, and religion, our federation would be marked by flexibility; amendment would be a comparatively easy matter where there was agreement upon fundamental issues. Since history has given us a dual culture, with its diversities of race and language, we must maintain a precarious balance between the two groups; and our constitution is rigid and inflexible." He concludes: "It influenced both the political thinking and the political vocabulary," and it still does to this day.[60] What about the West and the Maritimes? The West did not have a voice at the table. Macdonald, with the help of the Colonial Office, drove the bargain that enabled Cartier to sign it.

British political institutions were designed to operate in a unitary state and to accommodate the interests of aristocrats. They had no experience in dealing with federalism, regionalism, and minority language rights. These institutions were designed for Britain's population, its history, and its socio-economic circumstances, and they would not have a capacity to give voice to the smaller regions in national policy-making.

In short, the Fathers of Confederation set the stage for several Canadas without designing national political institutions to accommodate them. One Canada had strong ties to Britain, another to the Roman Catholic Church and the French language and culture, another was for Indigenous communities, and yet another was housing different regional economies. The First Nations were stripped of political power or influence, divorced from the responsibilities of provincial and local governments, and relegated to live in communities "whose colonization was profound and immutable."[61] The Fathers of Confederation sowed the seeds for Indigenous peoples to turn to the courts rather than political and bureaucratic institutions to pursue their political agenda. The central government would keep full authority to manage what was deemed the "Indian problem" with band councils delegated meagre authority. The government's "Indian agents" held all the power to dictate the scope and pace of change in all key sectors.[62] The other Canadas have had to compete to promote their interests (with varying degrees of success) inside national political institutions. In their desire to bring British political institutions to Canada, Macdonald, Brown, Galt, and Cartier left K.C. Wheare – arguably the leading authority on federalism – to conclude that "the Canadian Constitution is quasi-federal in law."[63] Finally, Britain and Canada's population factors were markedly different in 1867. Economic and political class mattered a great deal more in political debates and conflicts in Britain than Canada.[64]

4

Canada Then

The next two chapters explore how Canadian society has evolved since 1867. They make the point that the country's national political and administrative institutions have not kept pace with changing socio-economic circumstances. The result is that policy-makers have made changes on the fly to meet the pressures of the day and to spot-weld the country's national political institutions to make Canada work.

If Macdonald, Brown, Cartier, and Galt could see Canada now, one can speculate that they would be pleased, but concerned. Macdonald would take a great deal of satisfaction in seeing that Canada extends from coast to coast to coast, that its ties to the British Crown remain intact, and that we have been able to resist the American pull to the south politically, if not economically or culturally. Macdonald would see, however, that the vision he had for Canada – a highly centralized national government as close to a unitary state as possible – has not lived up to expectations.

Macdonald would very likely think that regionalism has been running amok in Canada. Sitting in Ottawa or Kingston, he would be puzzled by the Maritime Rights Movement (circa 1920s), the sovereignty movement in Quebec, and the western alienation. Provincial governments are playing a much larger role in Canada than he ever envisaged, and he would likely be taken aback by the expanding role of government in several sectors. It is easy to speculate that Macdonald never imagined the role governments currently play in social services, health care, and education. Had he seen it, he would have called for the federal government to take the lead in these sectors. At the time of Confederation, the colonies spent 3.2 percent of their budgets on social services, health care, and education. Today, governments spend about 50 percent of their expenditure budgets in the same sectors. Macdonald would be at a loss to explain why the judiciary plays such a significant role in shaping public policy.

George Brown would likely be very pleased that political power in the national Parliament and government is still based on representation by population. He insisted on rep by pop throughout the negotiations leading to Confederation; it was his bottom line. Brown would not be surprised that the Senate has been largely ineffective – that is what he expected, if not hoped for. He may well be disappointed, however, that French Canada has not been assimilated.

Cartier would likely take great satisfaction in the vitality of French Canada in Quebec, in Canada's Official Languages Act, and in his province's ability to influence the nation's political direction. He would, however, be puzzled at the decline of the Roman Catholic Church and concerned that the two-nation concept is challenged by the growing political strength of Western Canada and discontent in Atlantic Canada. Macdonald, Brown, Galt, and Cartier would be left scratching their heads at the progress Aboriginal communities have been making in recent years, not through politics or political institutions, but through the courts. They would likely be surprised to see Parliament transformed from an all-white men's club into a multiracial and somewhat gender-balanced club.

Albert Smith could tell Maritimers, Macdonald, Brown, Galt, and Cartier, "I told you so."[1] As noted earlier, he asked the Fathers of Confederation – notably Macdonald, Brown, Galt, and Cartier – to give small provinces, "at least, the guard which they have in the United States [i.e., an equal and effective Senate], although we ought to have more, because, here, the popular branch [i.e., the executive branch] is all-powerful."[2] The call was rejected. Macdonald and Brown saw nothing in it for their respective provinces, and Cartier could not accept that French Canada, or in this case Quebec, would have the same number of senators as the smaller provinces.

Smith would point out that the ink had barely dried on the BNA Act when Canadian politicians made it clear that he was right. The notion that the Maritime provinces would be allocated one-third of the Cabinet never held. Cabinet ministers from the Maritimes quickly realized that they did not carry much weight. For example, one of New Brunswick's Fathers of Confederation, Leonard Tilley, did not get the finance portfolio he had hoped for in the first John

A. Macdonald government. He wrote to Macdonald as his minister of customs, pleading with him: "Do strengthen my hands ... I
want all the assistance I can get, to allay dissatisfaction that exists
... that I have no influence with the government."[3] Smith would
remind New Brunswickers that the province's media were making
the case that New Brunswick "had a right to be heard on these subjects – tariffs, postage, higher costs of foods – but the Government
by sheer force of numbers voted us down a course we shall resist
by every means in our power."[4] This was published in 1870, one
of many early signs that, though regionalism would dominate
Canadian politics, the regions would have a limited capacity to be
heard in national political institutions.

The idea that the Maritime region would gain power by being
the honest broker between the economic interests of Ontario and
Quebec never constituted a lasting arrangement, as history has so
often revealed. Ontario and Quebec have looked after each other's
economic interests when other Canadian regions have been involved.
This was true in building canals, managing the railways, and in planning the war effort during the Second World War.[5] Before Alberta
and Saskatchewan were created, some Prairie politicians called for
"one prairie province." The Laurier government rejected the proposal "for the simple reason that such an entity would threaten
the dominance of Ontario."[6] More recently, then Quebec premier
Philippe Couillard summed up the situation well in an address to
the Ontario legislature, making the point that Ontario and Quebec
are "natural allies" and that they are "a force to be reckoned with."[7]
The regional voice is always clearly heard in national political institutions, so long as it comes from Ontario or Quebec.

Albert Smith would be able to show that, time and again, the
unelected and unequal Senate was no match for the House of
Commons and its rep by pop. The executive – as it should be –
is drawn from the Commons. But there is no capacity in Canada's
national political institutions to bring regional circumstances to
light when shaping national policies. Denis Coderre, then Montreal's
mayor, bluntly put matters in perspective when he told former
Saskatchewan premier Brad Wall why he could oppose the Energy
East pipeline while Quebec received transfer payments from Ottawa,
generated in part by the energy sector: "Montreal's population: 4
million, Saskatchewan: 1.13 million."[8] That speaks to the tyranny
of rep by pop and the reality that Wall, or his province, and other

small provinces do not have access to an effective Upper House in Parliament to speak for Canada's regions. Coderre summed up in a five-word tweet why provincial governments can never be effective actors in influencing federal government policies or decisions.

Smith could make the case that the Macdonald-Cartier treaty saw the Maritimes as little more than a convenient and necessary appendage to the new Canada. How else, he may well ask, can one explain that the new federal public service consisted of nothing more than the old bureaucracy of the former United Province of Canada? Officials from the Maritimes were overlooked for government appointments in Ottawa. Shortly after Confederation, the civil service numbered 500 and only 10 came from the Maritimes.[9] Public servants from the Canadian colony occupied all the senior posts in post-Confederation Canada.

In the spirit of the two-nation treaty, Macdonald saw to it that three of the most important deputy ministers – agriculture, public works, and customs – came from Quebec. All deputy ministers, except one, came from Ontario and Quebec. There were thirteen deputy ministers at the time, and six of them had worked with Macdonald before Confederation. The deputy minister of justice was Macdonald's brother-in-law.[10]

Joseph Howe could echo Albert Smith's sentiment: "I told you so." Howe had warned Nova Scotians that, given the BNA Act, "the centre of power and influence will always be in Canada [i.e., Ontario and Quebec]. It can be nowhere else."[11] Howe would be deeply disappointed in the Senate's inability to represent regional interests in Ottawa. To the extent that the Senate has made a contribution, it has done so by embracing Macdonald's sober second thought vision. None of the Senate's standing committees (there are currently twenty-four) deal with regional issues. They – like their House of Commons counterparts – deal with economic sectors and Status of Women, Official Languages, and Justice and Human Rights. The Senate has sponsored a number of studies on mental health, aging, mass media, retirement age policies, and youth but none on regional economic circumstances, Canada's regions, or regionalism.[12] The Senate continues to blunt rather than sharpen regional perspectives.[13] Howe had the foresight to observe that political power could "be nowhere else" than in Ontario and Quebec.

All Fathers of Confederation would likely find it difficult to explain the fall of deference to the body politic in Canadian society. No one is suggesting that there is still a need to keep "simple" democracy in check through members of a propertied class sitting in an appointed second house in Parliament. Their political world was defined by Britain and the Westminster parliamentary system, where the Crown in Parliament ruled with nothing in its way. In their day, the courts were there to interpret statutes, nothing more. How could it be, they would ask, that a politically appointed court can tell Parliament not only what to do but also how quickly to do it, as it did in medically assisted dying legislation and on other issues?[14]

In the Macdonald days and for many years after 1867, Parliament was supreme, and no other institution had power to nullify its laws. Macdonald may ask whatever possessed politicians to make changes to enable Canada's former chief justice to observe that because politicians need to be re-elected, their work needs to "be supplemented by other non-elected bodies, like courts and ombudsmen."[15] She said nothing about the Senate and its sober second thought mandate because the Senate has not been up to the task even in pursuing this role. Macdonald would likely have asked why politicians ever agreed to implement such transparency requirements as access to information legislation, making it more difficult for them to govern.

POLITICAL PARTIES

The Fathers of Confederation would marvel at the state of political parties and how they have evolved over the years. The old Province of Canada – with one important exception – provided the political party infrastructure for the new Canada for more than seventy years. The two main parties, the Conservatives and the Liberals, had their origins in pre-Confederation Canada. The one exception was Joseph Howe's Anti-Confederation party. It captured 18 seats in the 181-seat House of Commons and won the popular vote in Nova Scotia in the 1867 election.

Macdonald led his Liberal-Conservative Party (commonly known as the Conservative Party) to victory, winning 101 seats, including his own Kingston constituency. Macdonald won handsomely in Ontario but lost badly in Nova Scotia where, as noted, anti-Confederate candidates won all but one seat. Macdonald dismissed election results in Nova Scotia as "a small cloud of opposition no bigger than a man's hand."[16] Macdonald understood better than anyone the power of representation by population: Ontario had 82 seats to Nova Scotia's 19.

The Liberal Party came second without a leader in the 1867 general election. George Brown was regarded as the party's elder statesman. He ran for both the House of Commons and Ontario's Legislative Assembly at the same time, but failed to win either constituency.

Political parties in 1867 were a loose collection of interests with little in the way of organizational capacity, and they were slow in organizing. The Conservative Party was the first off the mark, thanks to its access to patronage. Both the Conservative and Liberal parties had to strike new alliances as Canada took shape. The Ontario Conservatives struck an alliance with the Parti Bleu in Quebec, and the Liberal Party with the Clear Grits of Ontario and the Parti Rouge of Quebec. Both parties would mop up what they could in the two Maritime provinces.

Macdonald made every effort, initially at least, to have a non-partisan government, inviting as many Liberals as Conservatives in his Cabinet. He wanted a coalition government, arguing that party politics "is merely a struggle for office, the madness of many for the gain of a few."[17] He saw that Confederation was fragile and that the first few years were crucial to its success.

To that end, Macdonald appointed four other Cabinet ministers from Ontario, four from Quebec, and two each from Nova Scotia and New Brunswick. Macdonald's hope was that the federal Cabinet would give regions a voice at the centre of government. But the idea to house the voice from the regions in the Cabinet never lived up to expectations from the very beginning. Writing about Macdonald's first Cabinet, Richard Gwyn reports: "The intent was to give the regions a voice at the centre, as a substitute for the U.S. system of a powerful Senate with equal representation for all states. In fact, most ministers functioned principally the other way around – as voices speaking to their regions on behalf of the federal government."[18] Things have only deteriorated further in recent years as the federal Cabinet has been turned into a kind of "focus group" in a prime minister–centric government.[19]

I accept that prime ministers have always had the upper hand in Cabinet. Patrice Dutil makes the case in his excellent book *Prime Ministerial Power in Canada*. He explores how prime ministers Macdonald, Laurier, and Borden established levers of power in their own hands to shape policy and deal with the crises of the day. I maintain that recent prime ministers have, if anything, strengthened their hands on these levers, and I explain why and how below. In any event, prime ministers controlling the key levers of power, whether in 1870 or 2019, leaves unanswered how national political institutions can accommodate regional public policy. Prime ministers then and now are free to ignore regional circumstances or accommodate those that translate into more votes.

Some of the Fathers of Confederation would be puzzled by the "special place" regional protest parties have come to occupy in Canadian politics.[20] The Progressive Party, formed in 1920 and assisted by the United Farmers, was the first of several regional protest parties, followed by the Maritime Rights Movement, the Social Credit Party (mostly from Western Canada), the Ralliement créditiste (Quebec), the Bloc Québécois, and the Reform Party (Western Canada). Ontario is the only province that did not give rise to a regional protest party or movement. It is easy for Ontario to see its own regional interest mesh nicely with Canada's "national" interest. Ontario is where Parliament and the bulk of the senior echelons of the public service are located, and its MPs always have a strong presence in both the Commons and Cabinet. It is also the province that decides who holds power in Ottawa. More to the point, if political leaders cannot win a good number of seats in Ontario, they will never win power.

CANADA IS TEN TIMES DIFFERENT

Canada in 1867 consisted of four provinces, was largely rural, and had a population of 3.5 million. The bulk of Canada's population was of European descent (mostly from the United Kingdom and France) and Indigenous descent.

Today, Canada consists of ten provinces and three territories, is largely urban, and its population comes from diverse backgrounds. In 1871, Canada's population was 3,014,914 rural and 722,343 urban. In 2011, it was 6,329,414 rural and 27,147,274 urban.[21] In 1867, Canada was about two-thirds rural, one-third urban. In 2011, it was the opposite: Canada was well over two-thirds urban and less than one-third rural. The country has witnessed several periods of strong immigration since 1867: between 1895 and 1915, from 1955 to 1965, and from 1990 to 1995. The first wave of immigrants looked to rural Canada, particularly the Prairies, to start a new life. Saskatchewan saw its population grow by over 1,125 percent between 1891 and 1911.[22]

Clifford Sifton, a senior minister from Manitoba and minister of the interior in the Laurier government, pursued a deliberate policy to open up the West to new Canadians. He favoured Europeans because of their knowledge of agriculture and harsh climates. The Sifton immigrants were strongly encouraged to look to rural areas in the Prairies, which offered plenty of free fertile land. Sifton held a clear bias for immigrants. In descending order: British and Americans, French, Belgians, Dutch, Scandinavians, Swiss, Finns, Russians, Austro-Hungarians, Germans, Ukrainians, and Poles. He described the ideal immigrant in one of the most often quoted sentences in immigration policy: "a stalwart peasant in a sheep-skin coat, born on the soil, whose forefathers have been farmers for ten generations, with a stout wife and a half-dozen children is good quality."[23] He left it unsaid but he could well have added "white" to the sentence. Sifton, a Winnipeg MP, spoke to the eco-nomic interest of his region and he wanted farmers to develop the region he represented, not what he labelled "A Trades Union arti-san who will not work more than eight hours a day."[24] Sifton – like all politicians – held a clear regional bias in defining the country's immigration policy, a bias that squared with the interest of the region he represented.

Canada welcomed another wave of immigrants in the aftermath of the Second World War. Many Europeans looked to Canada to start anew after the war years had destroyed many communities and livelihoods. This wave of new Canadians looked to major urban areas rather than rural Canada – thus began the country's rapid urbanization.[25]

The next wave of newcomers came from Vietnam, India, and Pakistan, and they, too, would look to major cities, more specifically to ethnic neighbourhoods in Toronto, Vancouver, and Montreal, to start anew. The trend continues to this day – the great majority of new Canadians continue to go where new Canadians are. In recent years, for example, 95 percent of new Canadians have chosen to locate in the major urban centres of four provinces: Ontario, British Columbia, Quebec, and Alberta.[26]

New Canadians have changed Canada in a fundamental way. They now almost invariably look to urban areas, and thus urban Canada dominates the political landscape today in the same fashion that rural Canada dominated it when Canada was formed. Canada's people factor is no longer tied to Britain to the extent that it was in 1867. Today, one out of five people in Canada are foreign-born, the highest proportion among G8 countries. New Canadians report close to 200 countries as a place of birth, and Asia and the Middle East now account for about 60 percent of immigrants. This is in sharp contrast to Canada before 1970, when nearly 80 percent of new Canadians came from Europe. In addition, about 20 percent of Canadians identify themselves today as visible minorities.[27] Asian countries now account for seven out of the top ten source countries for new Canadians. Today, new Canadians represent 46 percent of Toronto's population and 40 percent of Vancouver's.[28]

THE ECONOMY THEN AND NOW

Population composition is not all that has changed. Today's economy is unlike Canada's economy in 1867. Canada had a relatively closed economy at Confederation and for many years after. The United States pushed Canada towards a closed economy when it killed the United States-Canada reciprocity treaty on 16 March 1866.

Canada tried to re-establish free trade arrangements with the United States after 1867, with limited success. At times, Americans resisted, at other times, Canadians did. Pro-British and pro-protectionist sentiments surfaced in Ottawa at critical moments to hinder the removal of trade barriers between the two countries. Protectionist sentiments were always stronger in some regions (i.e., Ontario). It has long been recognized that Ontario benefitted the most from a closed economy and east-west trade.

Trade broke open in the late 1980s, when Canada and the United States negotiated a Free Trade Agreement (FTA) and again in 1994 when Canada signed a Free Trade Agreement with the United States and Mexico (NAFTA). We have since seen a veritable plethora of free trade agreements and proposed trade agreements. Though it is a moving target, by my count, Canada entered into nine free trade agreements over the past twenty years, and it is negotiating another nine agreements. Even if Donald Trump has seemingly tried to apply the brakes to its growth, the global economy has arrived to stay, and Canada is an active participant.

Economic development in 1867 was relatively straightforward. Canadians in the western part of the new Confederation worked almost exclusively in agriculture. In the eastern part, they worked predominantly in the fishery, forestry, and shipbuilding, while in the central part, lumbering and mining, and manufacturing was in the early stages. Exports were spotty and limited. Today, exports account for more than 30 percent of Canada's GDP.[29]

There were 837,718 labourers at the time of Confederation, with 41 percent of them employed on farms. Nova Scotia, New Brunswick, and Prince Edward Island had a very healthy shipbuilding industry. They produced 572 ships in 1865, and in 1867, the *Year-Book and Almanac of British North America* reported that "owing principally to the abundance and excellence of timber, but partially to other causes, ships can be built here much more cheaply than in Europe, and 40 per cent cheaper than even in the United States."[30]

For the most part, Canada's exports went to Great Britain and the United States. However, Nova Scotia and New Brunswick were able to secure new markets in the Caribbean for their foodstuffs. The railway linking the provinces was still on the drawing board in 1867.

Canada's economy today is much more complex and more diversified. It accounts for 16,272,568 jobs, many in sectors that had yet to see the light of day in 1867. The knowledge economy dominates Canada's economic landscape to the same extent traditional sectors like farming, forestry, and fishery did in 1867. The retail trade industry leads the way with nearly 2 million jobs, followed by health care and social assistance with 1,916,241, manufacturing 1,508,942, and education 1,278,405.[31]

Canada now looks first to the United States for its exports, followed by China, the United Kingdom, Japan, and Mexico. Exports to the United States account for 76 percent of total exports.[32] Canada's exports reflect the mix of traditional and new economy sectors that make up the nation's economy. Mineral fuels exports lead the way with 20.1 percent of total exports, while electrical equipment takes the sixth spot with 3.1 percent.[33]

The Canadian economy is far more open, complex, and diversified than it was in 1867. This is no different in other economies of the Western world. But Canada's efforts to diversify its economy, to pursue new markets and lessen its dependence on the US markets, and to have two orders of government involved in promoting economic development continue to have an important impact in Canada's political and administrative institutions and, by ricochet, on Canadian democracy.

GOVERNMENTS THEN AND NOW

The federal government had very limited responsibilities in 1867 when compared to today because the role of government in society was very limited. As it was, Macdonald and the other leading Fathers of Confederation gave all important responsibilities of the day to the central government – national defence, trade and commerce, currency, banking and finance, and the ability to ensure "peace, order and good government," as the Constitution Act, 1867 reads.

Macdonald's first Cabinet had thirteen ministers, Justin Trudeau's has thirty-one. The size of Macdonald's first government was no bigger than a regional office in one of Ottawa's current line departments – and a small one at that. It would have been easy for Macdonald to understand all facets of government activities and to control all levers of power and influence. Similarly, it would have been easy for members of Parliament to probe, to ask questions down to the last-minute detail of administration – and they did.

The government's first full-year budget totalled $7.9 million.[34] Three line items – railways, militia and gunboats, and canals – accounted for over $3 million. The expenditure budget was simple to follow; everything was boiled down to specific items: first to specific activities such as the cost of running Rideau Hall, penitentiaries, harbours and lighthouses, and then further broken down for such items as salaries.[35] All one needed to know about the budget was outlined in a seven-page budget speech tabled in the House of Commons.

Government departments were few and small. They included: agriculture, marine and fisheries, immigration and statistics, justice, public works, post office, finance, customs, inland revenue, militia, privy council, Secretary of State for Canada, Secretary of State for the Provinces, and Receiver General. Departments were mostly concerned with administration and had little policy capacity. The Department of Finance, for example, had a total staff of twenty-eight, mostly clerks.[36]

The machinery of government in Ottawa in 1867 was essentially a continuation of the machinery that had served the Canadian colony before Confederation. Thus, the Privy Council Office (PCO) simply assumed the responsibilities that were carried out by the Executive Council under colonial government. PCO in 1867 "was only responsible for preparing and registering Orders-in-Council."[37]

At Confederation, and for many years after, the government made
every effort to live by the theory, principles, and practices established
by the Westminster-inspired parliamentary system. Its simplicity and
limited number of government activities encouraged government
officials and Parliament to live by well-known rules of Parliament
and Cabinet government. We saw in earlier chapters that the rules
flowed from struggles between king and Parliament. Underpinning
the relationship were three overriding principles: "i) The executive
should have no income which is not granted to it, or otherwise sanc-
tioned, by Parliament; ii) the executive should make no expenditures except those approved by Parliament, in ways approved by
Parliament ... Parliament has the right to debate and criticize the
budget fully, both as it affects past or current executive activities,
and the executive's proposals for future spending."[38] It was easy then
(and for many years after) to respect both the theory and spirit of
Westminster-inspired parliamentary government.

When the budget and spending estimates arrived before the House
of Commons, they were remarkably straightforward. A newly
elected member of Parliament with no experience in government
could easily grasp the contents. Reading government documents
from the immediate post-Confederation period reveals the extent to
which MPs were able to drill down not only into government policy
but also into government operations.

It was not uncommon for an MP to inquire about the position
and salary of individual public servants. One MP, for example, asked
the government to give "the names of all inland places at which the
customs duty is collected, the name of the officer, his salary and
expenses connected with the office, and the amount of duty collected
at each office from the first day of July, 1867, until January 1st,
1869."[39] Answers to such questions were provided.

It was easy then to make the doctrine of ministerial responsibility
work. There was no need to invent terms such as "answerability," to
distinguish it from "responsibility" and "accountability." The minister had no difficulty accessing information to answer questions in
a timely fashion. The Department of Justice, for example, only had
two lawyers and "a few clerks who had worked in the office of the
Attorney General of Upper Canada before Confederation."[40]

It is likely difficult for the reader to appreciate how small government was when Canada was constituted, and for about seventy-five years after, and what this meant for representative democracy

and accountability. Prime Minister Alexander Mackenzie was able to answer all correspondence himself.[41] In 1909, the newly created Department of External Affairs was entirely housed above a barbershop in Ottawa. During the Second World War, the East Block housed the prime minister and his office, PCO, the under-secretary of External Affairs, and the Department of External Affairs.[42] Britain looked after a number of responsibilities, which now belong to Ottawa. It was only in 1946, for example, that the Canadian Parliament adopted the Canadian Citizenship Act, which created a Canadian citizenship distinct from British citizenship. Canada did not enjoy full control over its external relations until 1931, with the Statute of Westminster.[43]

Early politicians and a handful of senior public servants laid the groundwork for how Parliament and government would operate. As in other things, they looked to Britain for guidance. In any event, the constitution required it. The broad contours of the relationship between government and Parliament in Britain and Canada are similar. The same is true for the allocation and spending of public funds. Responsible government requires that government enjoys the support of Parliament; it also requires a process to estimate in advance the government's financial needs for the ensuing year or years, that departments be organized so that ministers can exercise control for which they can be held responsible in Parliament, and that the expenditure budget permits a full audit.[44]

There are, however, some differences between Britain and Canada's machinery of government. Britain turned over responsibility for raising, collecting, and distributing public funds to a department. This made it easy for Parliament to keep an eye on government spending. In 1867, the government of Canada had four departments that shared responsibility for raising, collecting, and spending public money – customs, inland revenue, finance, and Receiver General. The result was that officials in the Department of Customs, for example, were spending money from sums which they had collected rather than turn over the money to a consolidated revenue fund. The auditor, which did not enjoy an independent status from government until 1878, explained the problem: "unless the rule is strongly enforced that all receipts are to be paid in to the Receiver General intact, it will be impossible for the Auditor to prevent an expenditure in excess of the Parliamentary authority."[45] This, even though the BNA Act established a Consolidated Revenue Fund under section 102.

Norman Ward, author of the classic *The Public Purse*, argues that Canadian regionalism explains why Canada did not fully embrace the British machinery of government when it came to public spending. To explain the difference, he points to Macdonald's decision to look to Cabinet to accommodate the interests of the four regions – Ontario, Quebec, New Brunswick, and Nova Scotia. Ward writes, "The need for several cabinet posts had a secondary and lasting effect on parliamentary control of finance" since it inhibited turning over responsibility to "a single department of finance discharging all the functions of raising, collecting, and distributing public money."[46]

Government departments were relatively autonomous, operating with a minimum of intervention from central agencies. The prime minister was the boss, and he had little help from central agencies. The modern PCO was still about seventy-five years away, and the PMO had no policy advisory capacity. Departments had their own accounting system operating in relative isolation from one another, which made it difficult for central agencies to exert control.

Few politicians were complaining about faceless bureaucrats wielding too much influence. Public servants were, for the most part, clerks and front-line workers. They owed their jobs to patronage. John A. Macdonald argued that political patronage was an important component of responsible government: "I think that in the distribution of governmental patronage we carry out the true constitutional principle. Whenever an office is vacant it belongs to the party supporting the Government, if within that party there is to be found a person competent to perform the duties. Responsible Government cannot be carried on on any other principle."[47]

The prime minister and ministers did not hesitate to attend to the details of the day. They had a direct hand in exhaustively reviewing the management of departments down "to the last low-grade clerk."[48] Prime ministers and ministers took to heart the doctrine of ministerial responsibility, insisting that they should have a hand in all facets of government activities, even in unimportant and purely administrative matters, if they were to be held responsible for the decisions. Sir George Murray, the British expert brought in to review the work of the Canadian public service, observed that "ministers ... both have too much to do and do too much."[49]

From day one, Canadian ministers were able to dig deeper into departmental operations than their British or American counterparts. As noted, Macdonald and indeed the Confederation deal itself, looked to Cabinet to give voice to the regional perspective which, in turn, would give rise to a larger Cabinet. Abraham Lincoln had seven Cabinet secretaries, British prime minister Benjamin Disraeli had twelve ministers, and Sir John A. Macdonald, as mentioned, had thirteen ministers (including himself), even though Canada's population was much smaller than either the United States' or Britain's, and at the time, Britain held some government responsibilities on behalf of Canada (e.g., Foreign Affairs). In addition, the government of Britain operated in a unitary state, which meant that it held some responsibilities that belonged to provincial governments in Canada.

Geography cuts both ways. It generated a bigger Cabinet and encouraged ministers to dig deeper in departmental operations. And yet it was the one factor that inhibited the ability of ministers to get personally and directly involved in some administrative issues. Departments had to open up the West, build canals, deal with the railways that linked communities over a continent, manage customs and ports, and look after the fishery. The means of communication and transportation between Ottawa and field offices were rudimentary so that ministers had to rely on reports from the field to see if their directives had been followed. I note that only about 25 percent of federal public servants worked out of Ottawa for much of the first 120 years of Confederation.[50]

ACCOUNTABILITY: SOMETHING DIFFERENT

Statutes in Britain mostly conferred power on individual ministers to act, while statutes in Canada conferred it on the "Governor General in Council" or Cabinet.[51] This, too, has given a mandate to both Cabinet and individual ministers to deal with management or administrative issues.

Canada's decision to rely on the Governor General in Council or Cabinet in delegating power rather than on individual ministers, as Britain continues to do, has had important implications for accountability. Britain embraced the "accounting officer" concept in the nineteenth century to strengthen accountability but Canada did not. After a few false starts, the government of Canada only embraced a highly watered-down version of the concept in 2006. Norman Ward writes: "The British practice of leaving the accounting officers on the staffs of their departments was hardly feasible in Canada, for reasons which are not entirely palatable."[52] Ward adds that the government's accounting and auditing systems were not up to the task.[53] More is said about this further on.

THERE WAS LITTLE BLEEDING

Luther Gulick, a leading student of government of his day, had advice for those designing the machinery of government: ensure that there is "little bleeding."[54] Government departments, he argued, should have a clear mandate. To the extent possible, they should be self-contained and watertight and go about their work with limited concerns for the work of other departments. Two years after Canadian Confederation, John Stuart Mill argued in his *Representative Government* that responsibility in government is best provided and the work best done if all functions of a similar subject are allocated to single departments.[55]

J.E. Hodgetts maintains that the most important legacy of the pre-Confederation bureaucracy was the departmental framework. It was widely believed in the 1850s that, without a clear departmental structure, responsible government would be, at best fraught with danger, and at worse, impossible to achieve. Departments with clear mandates, he pointed out, encourage unity of command and a hierarchy of responsibilities.[56] This, in turn, would give life to Earl Grey's point that "the first principle of our system of government" is "the control of all branches of administration by Parliament."[57]

The early years of public administration were about establishing boundaries, sorting out departmental mandates, and linking the departmental structures to responsible government. Clear mandates and hierarchy allowed ministers to turn to their departments when they needed to secure answers for themselves, MPs, the media, and citizens.

It was easy in 1867 to establish clear mandates, departmental hierarchy, and ensure that there was little bleeding so that ministers and their departments could go about their work with limited concern for the work of other departments. It remained easy for a number of years after Confederation for ministers and their officials to work within clear mandates and organizational boundaries. Departments even had their own accounting system, which complicated the work of auditors and the Parliament's Public Accounts Committee.[58] Ministers and a handful of public servants were able to run their departments as closed shops, keeping important information to themselves. The Department of Agriculture, for example, was established in 1867 and employed only twenty-seven people. It had a clear mandate for the sector, and it housed all responsibilities for agriculture. The Department of Agriculture was not an isolated case.

Managing federal-provincial relations was also fairly straightforward. The federal and provincial governments operated in relative isolation from one another. The one issue that linked the federal government to provincial governments was subsidies to provinces because the BNA Act limited the ability of provincial governments to raise revenues (they essentially only had access to direct taxation, a highly unpopular tax field in 1867). Section 118 of the BNA Act gave federal government the authority to transfer payments to the provinces: a fixed amount paid annually and an annual grant of eighty cents per head based on the 1861 population. From day one to this day, provincial governments would push the federal government to increase the transfers.

There were, however, precious few other contacts between federal and provincial public servants. Macdonald saw provincial governments as small local governments with limited power – that is how he and the other key architects of Confederation had designed it. Macdonald preferred to deal with federal MPs when he had to address provincial or regional issues. He could, and often did, turn to lieutenant-governors to look after provincial issues. J.R. Mallory sums up the relationship: "The office [of lieutenant-governor] was conceived by the federal government as an important element in preserving the dominant role of Ottawa over the provinces. Canadian federalism in the beginning was ... 'quasi-federal.' It was clearly based on the old colonial model, with the government in Ottawa playing the role previously played by the British government."[59]

Macdonald went further than the Colonial Office. He argued in 1868 that "under the present constitution of Canada, the general government will be called upon to consider the propriety of allowance or disallowance of provincial Acts much more frequently than Her Majesty's Government has been with respect to colonial enactments."[60] The Macdonald government followed suit shortly after coming to power, with the justice department issuing a Cabinet-approved directive to "emphasize a new and exacting use of disallowance, so that even the strongest of provincial rights was to be subject to central surveillance."[61] Ottawa could rely on federal government–appointed lieutenant-governors to keep an eye on the provinces and deal with provincial government matters whenever there was a need. Ottawa exercised its power of disallowance ninety-six times between 1867 and 1920.[62]

Macdonald believed that, in time, Canada would abandon Confederation in favour of a unitary state. He envisaged one government for Canada, much like Britain had one government for Great Britain, because provincial governments would be born fatally weak. He said in 1864, "if the Confederation goes on you ... will see both Local Parliaments & Governments absorbed in the General Power. This is as plain to me as if I saw it accomplished but of course it does not do to adopt that point of view in discussing the subject in Lower Canada."[63] He could have added, when discussing the subject in the Maritime colonies, but his focus was on Canada East because the problem he was trying to fix was the difficult relationship between Canada West and East.

LOOKING BACK

The role of government in 1867 was limited. The federal government dominated the country's policy agenda, the machinery of government was small, and clear boundaries existed not only between levels of government but also between government departments. Whenever the federal government decided that a provincial government had stepped beyond its narrowly defined boundary, the former would exercise its power of disallowance on a number of occasions for over seventy years. There was no need to distinguish "accountability" from words like "responsibility" and "answerability" to make the process work. Ministers had an intimate knowledge of the work and activities of their departments and did not hesitate to get directly involved in purely administrative matters to give direction or to get answers.

Macdonald had little interest in dealing with provincial governments. He had lieutenant-governors to look after provincial governments and to ensure they stayed in line. He had an ambitious agenda, albeit with limited resources, in pursuing his vision of Canada from sea to sea, the building of a national railway, and establishing the political and administrative capacity to govern the new country.

Canada in 1867 was ten times different from Canada today, while the machinery of government was different in every way. The basic outline of Canada's democratic institutions remains intact, but most everything has changed. Before we review how the country's political and administrative institutions are dealing with current democratic requirements, we need to review today's political and public policy environment.

5

Canadian Federalism Now

Canada had a Westminster parliamentary system in 1867 and, in the Westminster tradition, Parliament was supreme. The courts operated on the periphery of public policy issues. Provincial governments were viewed as junior partners, and their work was subject to federal government review. The prime minister and ministers could be held accountable for all facets of government activities. Government bureaucracy was small, and partisan political patronage was the sure route to an appointment, at virtually all levels.

Today, things are different, up to a point. Parliament is no longer supreme. We have a federal system in more than name. The courts are now very important public policy actors. The prime minister and his office have transformed today's Cabinet into little more than a focus group.[1] Accountability has taken on different forms, depending on who is asking and who is answering the questions. Bureaucracy is larger and deeper, and appointments are made on merit – at least, that is the argument – and political parties are more defined than they were in 1867.

There are important attributes, however, that have remained constant. Politicians pursue political power in Canada much like politicians did in the nineteenth century, and they still focus on the regions that can best secure power. Parliament has not changed its rules of engagement in any fundamental fashion, though everything around it has.

In several significant ways, political institutions have largely adjusted to changing circumstances by standing still. The wide scope and fast pace of government activities are now evident in every sector, even though the allocation of power and jurisdiction between the two senior orders of government have remained essentially intact since 1867. The Supreme Court has, since the mid-1980s, played a key role in shaping public policy and has expanded its role to have a say not only on policy but even on program implementation. Though consultation processes have been introduced in recent years, Supreme Court members are appointed in basically the same fashion they were a hundred years ago; the key to an appointment is still the prime minister.

Bureaucracy, however, no longer resembles how it was 150 years ago in size, purpose, organization, complexity, staffing, and management. Relations between politicians and public servants have come full circle a few times, and relations between the two senior orders of government have taken a 180 degree turn from what the Fathers of Confederation envisaged. All have important implications for the state of Canadian democracy.

FEDERAL-PROVINCIAL RELATIONS

Provincial governments in 1867 were small and viewed as "amateurish." In 1869, the Quebec government, for instance, only had ninety-two public servants, with virtually all of them providing routine clerical services.[2] As noted, even as prime minister, Macdonald saw little need to deal with provincial governments. To make matters worse, the political talent left provincial capitals for Ottawa. This outmigration even included leading anti-Confederation voices, notably Joseph Howe from Nova Scotia and Albert Smith from New Brunswick, as well as pro-Confederation voices, including Leonard Tilley from New Brunswick and Charles Tupper from Nova Scotia. Politicians, at the time, were allowed to hold dual seats: George Brown tried to get elected in both the Ontario legislature and Parliament but failed in both cases, while Alexander Mackenzie, Edward Blake, and George-Étienne Cartier, as well as the premiers of Ontario and Quebec, sat in both Parliament and their provincial legislatures. This and other forces reduced provincial legislatures and provincial governments "to the political equivalent of railway sidings."[3]

When Macdonald and his ministers needed to deal with regional or provincial issues, they looked to their own parliamentary caucus or across the aisle in Parliament. There was only one undisputed voice that spoke for Canada and for Canadian regions – Parliament – more specifically, Cabinet. Federal-provincial relations hardly existed during much of Macdonald's terms in office. As noted, when Nova Scotia argued for better terms, Macdonald dealt with Joseph Howe and Charles Tupper, ignoring the provincial government.[4]

If provincial governments embarked on a wrong course (from an Ottawa perspective), Macdonald and future prime ministers could – and many times did – turn to Ottawa's power of disallowance. Macdonald summed up his view of provincial governments when he observed that they warranted no more attention than the City of Montreal and maintained that provincial governments should be subordinate to the federal government in all things.[5]

Macdonald's view of federalism made it clear which order of government held power over a given jurisdiction and who should be held to account – Ottawa – the disallowance confirmed as much. K.C. Wheare's classic definition of federalism could never square with Macdonald's view of federalism. Wheare writes: "By the federal principle I mean the method of dividing powers so that the general and regional governments are each, within a sphere, co-ordinate and independent."[6] The disallowance clause compromised less formal and less rigid definitions of federalism. American political scientist W.H. Riker, for example, maintains that a constitution is federal if "each level has at least one area of action in which it is autonomous, and there is some guarantee (even though merely a statement in the constitution) of the autonomy of each government in its own sphere."[7] Ronald Watts, for his part, maintains that in a federation there must be "an explicit constitutional demarcation of powers and functions between the general and regional governments. Governments at both levels must each be limited to their own sphere of action and must each be independent within their own sphere."[8] Macdonald did not see federalism this way. Today, Wheare's, Riker's, and Watts's views of federalism have been discarded. Canadian federalism is now as far removed from classical federalism as the BNA Act crafted in 1867 was.

Three forces have fundamentally reshaped Canadian federalism to the point that Macdonald would not recognize it today: Britain's Judicial Committee of the Privy Council, a rigid constitution that lacked an amending formula, and the development of the modern state. Parliament – the institution the BNA Act viewed as supreme – has stood on the sidelines, acting more as an observer than a participant. In short, it was forces largely outside of our political institutions that reshaped Canadian federalism, Canada's political and bureaucratic institutions, as well as Canadian representative democracy.

Canada was only able to establish its Supreme Court in 1875, eight years after Confederation. In its early years, at least, the court was not busy, hearing only four cases in year one.[9] It was the Judicial Committee of the Privy Council that served as Canada's Court of Appeal until 1949. The committee essentially turned Macdonald's view of federalism on its head in striking 173 judgments interpreting the BNA Act.[10] The decisions strongly favoured the provincial governments, while cutting short some federal government powers, notably in the area of trade and commerce.

The Judicial Committee interpreted the BNA Act for what it was: an ordinary statute passed by the British Parliament. Because the Fathers of Confederation never struck a process to amend the constitution, the committee's work played a pivotal role in revising it. Members of the committee, though highly respected at home, operated more than 3,000 miles away and knew very little about Canada, about Macdonald's views on federalism, or for that matter, the finer points of federalism. As established, federalism was not a system of government that was well understood in Britain.[11]

The work of the committee has, over the years, come under heavy criticism in Canada. Alan Cairns identified two groups critical of the committee's work and its impact on Canada's constitution. One he labelled the constitutionalists, who advocated a "flexible, pragmatic approach" so that judges could keep the BNA Act up to date. The second, the fundamentalists, were highly critical of the committee for "not providing a technically correct, logical interpretation of a clearly worded document," the BNA Act.[12] Either way, the argument goes, Canada was not well served by the Judicial Committee. A persistent criticism was that the committee played havoc with the wishes of the Fathers of Confederation when they set out to create a highly centralized federation, if not a unitary state. In brief, critics insisted that the committee did not give sufficient weight to the "peace, order, and good government" clause designed to favour the federal government, that it misinterpreted the division of powers in sections 91 and 92, and that it mishandled Ottawa's responsibilities for trade and commerce.[13]

I note, however, that five prominent women asked Canada's Supreme Court to answer the question, does the word "person" in section 24 of the BNA Act include female persons? The Supreme

Court said no. But an appeal to the Judicial Committee of the Privy Council of Great Britain overruled the Supreme Court's decision by saying, "why should it not."[14]

Amending Canada's constitution, as history has often shown, has not been for the faint of heart. As is well known, it has only been since 1982 that Canada has a made-in-Canada amending formula.[15] Before then, amendments to the BNA Act could only be passed by Britain, given that it was a British statute. Ironically, however, we saw more amendments to the BNA Act before 1982 than we have seen, *toutes proportions gardées*, since to the Constitution Act of 1982.

Prior to 1982, the practice was for Canada to request amendments to the BNA Act through a joint address of the Commons and the Senate, asking the UK government to lay before its Parliament a bill proposing the amendment. The procedure, established in 1895, remained in force until 1982. What was not clear was the role provincial governments had in the amending process. The federal government did not have a consistent practice, though it obtained unanimous provincial consent when the proposed amendment affected provincial powers.[16] Therein lay the rigidity of the constitution, leaving it to the Judicial Committee to interpret it.

A rigid constitution, a division of powers that made sense to the Fathers of Confederation but became untenable as the welfare state started to take shape, and the work of the Judicial Committee forced the hand of Canadian policy-makers to look for solutions outside the constitution and even outside national political institutions. Bora Laskin, who later became Canada's chief justice, reflecting on the work of the Judicial Committee, summed up the problem: "But has provincial autonomy been secured? In terms of positive ability to meet economic and social problems of interprovincial scope, the answer is no. A destructive negative autonomy exists, however, which has as a corollary that the citizens of a province are citizens of the Dominion for certain limited purposes only."[17] It was left to policy-makers to design new processes to deal with emerging economic challenges.

SOMETHING HAD TO GIVE

The Great Depression, more than anything else, rendered John A. Macdonald's view of Canadian federalism obsolete. Although the work of the Judicial Committee of the Privy Council essentially denied a role for the federal government to implement measures to address the economic crisis, the Depression called for government intervention to deal with unemployment relief, regional economic disparities, and serious financial difficulties among several provincial governments. For example, the government of Alberta defaulted on loans in 1936.

The four Western and three Maritime provinces were the hardest hit.[18] The Prairie farmers were particularly hard hit by falling wheat prices and drought. Ottawa had the financial resources but not the jurisdiction to address some of the economic issues, while the provinces had the jurisdiction but not the financial resources. Macdonald's 1867 Canada, which saw vastly different challenges – building railways and canals, opening up the West, and attracting immigrants – had met most of these challenges by the 1920s, and the federal government was running surpluses. In 1935, the R.B. Bennett government tried to follow the lead set by Franklin Roosevelt and his New Deal efforts.[19] However, the courts declared Bennett's initiative *ultra vires*, or violating provincial jurisdictions. This did not alter the fact that some provincial governments had only limited or no financial resources to support new measures.

Prime Minister William Lyon Mackenzie King decided to establish a Royal Commission on Dominion-Provincial Relations (better known as the Rowell-Sirois Commission) to come up with solutions to the federal-provincial jurisdiction conundrum. He selected N.W. Rowell, a well-known Ontario politician and lawyer, to chair the commission. When Rowell was forced to step down for health reasons, Mackenzie King turned to Joseph Sirois, a prominent Quebec lawyer, to take over as chair.

The commission was given an ambitious and timely agenda. It was asked "to consider and report upon the facts disclosed by their investigations; and to express what in their opinion, subject to the retention of the distribution of legislative powers essential to a proper carrying out of the federal system in harmony with national needs and the promotion of national unity, will best effect a balanced relationship between the financial powers and the obligations and functions of each governing body, and conduce to a more efficient, independent and economical discharge of government responsibilities in Canada."[20] In short, it was asked to fix Canadian federalism. The commission hired leading economists and political scientists of the day from Canada, Britain, and the United States to carry out the necessary research. This, however, was not without challenges. John W. Dafoe, a member of the commission, explains that as he reviewed the work of leading British constitutional experts, he realized they were not suited to undertake an examination of Canadian federalism because of "the difficulty which a person, brought up under English conditions, has in adjusting himself to the atmosphere of a federal combination."[21] Dafoe urged the commission to "examine the connection between past national policies and the current crisis. These fundamental historical problems could not be solved by a return to the centrist goals and tactics that lay behind Macdonald's National Policy."[22]

Thomas Crerar, a one-time federal Cabinet minister and leader of the newly formed Progressive Party insisted that the central issue before the commission and confronting Canada was the struggle against the domination of central Canada in national politics. He pointed to Macdonald's National Policy to explain Canada's uneven development and to the inability of national political institutions to recognize the country's different regional circumstances; many others from Western Canada and the Maritimes have continued to make this point.[23]

The commission took three years to consult Canadians and carry out its research. It concluded that Canadian federalism had "buckled under the strain of the Depression."[24] The constitution, the commission insisted, was making it impossible for governments, notably the federal government, to intervene at a time when Canadians were crying out for help and when the country required government intervention. The commission recommended that the federal government should assume responsibility in social services – a field that constitutionally belonged to the provinces. It favoured a constitutional reallocation of powers between the two senior orders of government to have responsibilities correspond with fiscal capacities and deal with pressures to equalize standards of services across Canada.

Mackenzie King embraced the findings of the Rowell-Sirois Commission, notably its call to reassign responsibilities through constitutional amendments. He insisted that "it is not wise for one government to raise revenue for others to spend,"[25] a point that has been lost on Canadian policy-makers since they formed the welfare state. Rowell-Sirois rejected turning to shared-cost programs "on the grounds of administrative complexity, provincial autonomy and the need for legislative accountability."[26] The commission argued that such programs would seriously inhibit accountability requirements because determination of which government was responsible for what would be extremely difficult.

Mackenzie King called a federal-provincial conference in January 1941 to pursue the Rowell-Sirois recommendations. Though he had reasons to be optimistic, given that he was able to secure a constitutional amendment a year earlier to transfer jurisdiction over unemployment insurance from the provinces to the federal government, he met with little success.[27] The war years and vocal opposition to the commission findings, particularly from premiers Hepburn and Duplessis of Ontario and Quebec respectively, killed any hope of implementing Rowell-Sirois. Ontario had made clear its opposition by joining forces earlier with Quebec in refusing to participate in the Rowell-Sirois Commission's public consultation exercises.[28]

Still, the Rowell-Sirois Commission was able to break new ground. It sponsored studies from leading scholars from Canada and other countries. It raised fundamental questions that went to the heart of Canadian federalism. W.A. Mackintosh, a highly regarded professor of economics at Queen's University and a senior official in Ottawa's Department of Finance during the war years, wrote about the challenges of promoting unity in a highly regionalized country, making the point that Canada hardly constituted an economic unit.[29] John W. Dafoe believed that the root of Canada's problems was as "much regional as constitutional" and that Macdonald sought to create an "Empire within the greater empire." Dafoe argued that Macdonald was both a "centrist and an enemy of federalism," who saw the provinces as "colonies with self-governing rights, but if they didn't use them in the way he thought right he would crack down on them with disallowance – which he did on a number of occasions."[30]

Though the written constitution was left pretty well intact, the Rowell-Sirois Commission did have a lasting impact that essentially reshaped Canadian federalism. Keith Banting has documented the rise of the welfare state through the Rowell-Sirois Report. He makes the point that the federal government could only secure three amendments in 1940, 1951, and 1964, which gave Ottawa jurisdiction over employment insurance, contributory pensions, and supplementary benefits, with the rest done through federal-provincial agreements and Ottawa's spending power.[31]

What is of interest here is why and how Canada's welfare state has reshaped not only Canadian federalism but also Canadian representative democracy. It is important to underline the point that two federal-provincial conferences aiming to give life to Rowell-Sirois and the welfare state – one in 1941 and the other in 1945 – failed to secure permanent arrangements through the constitution. But, as Donald Smiley writes, "Almost from the day the Conference [of 1945] was finished federal officials began to seek limited and piece-meal agreements with the provinces on particular matters" designed to change how Canadian federalism operates.[32] They set out to address through other means the "inflexibility of the system in effecting periodic redistributions of the powers and responsibilities of government between the two levels by constitutional amendment, judicial review or the delegation of legislative powers by one level on the other."[33]

Thus, the federal spending power was born, a development unique to Canadian federalism.[34] Ottawa's spending power led to Old Age Security and assistance for those with visual impairments and disabilities in 1951, hospital insurance in 1958, the Canada Pension Plan in 1965, medicare in 1968, and countless federal-provincial agreements in virtually every economic sector beginning in 1972.[35] Peter Hogg, one of Canada's leading constitutionalists, points out that it is now a constitutional convention for the Canadian Parliament to "spend or lend its funds to any government or institution or individual it chooses, for any purpose it chooses; and that it may attach to any grant or loan any conditions it chooses, including conditions it could not directly legislate."[36] The federal government's spending power, when boiled down to its core, is about territory or space, or about which level of government has the authority to act in a policy field in a given space, whether in a province, an area within a province or a region, or a group of provinces. In brief, Ottawa's spending power gives the federal government licence to roam in all policy fields and in all regions with cash, enticing provincial governments to do things that they may not otherwise do or be able to afford.

The United States struck the Great Compromise between large and small states by building in its constitution the ability for national political institutions to give a strong voice to small states to shape policy. Canada, instead, turned to Ottawa's spending power to flow money to the provinces with a bias towards the smaller have-less provinces.

Ottawa's spending power, however, has a lot to answer for. It has thrown overboard classical federalism and spawned new forms of federalism, including executive federalism, co-operative federalism, collaborative federalism, shared-cost federalism, joint-decision federalism, and fiscal federalism.[37] It has shifted some of Canada's political power outside of public view, made accountability more difficult, and punched holes in Canada's democratic requirements. The locus of decision-making in government has, as a result, become a moving target, difficult to follow with wide implications for accountability. And yet, hyphenated federalism has been widely applauded in Canada because it has delivered important government programs that the constitution would not otherwise allow.[38]

MAKING HYPHENATED FEDERALISM WORK

Hyphenated federalism became the way to work with a deeply flawed constitution designed to give the appearance of a federal state when its main authors set out to establish democratic institutions for a unitary state. Parliament, legislative assemblies, and even Cabinet have been pushed to the sidelines to make hyphenated federalism work. Prime ministers, premiers, their close advisers, some key Cabinet ministers, and senior public servants – many of them operating in central agencies – are at the centre of the federal-provincial policy and decision-making apparatus. This is a distinctly Canadian development, with Anthony Sayers and Andrew Banfield making the case that Canada "invented" hyphenated federalism.[39]

Richard Simeon in his 1972 seminal book, *Federal-Provincial Diplomacy: The Making of Recent Policy in Canada*, looked to international diplomacy and treaty negotiations to shed light on relations between the federal and provincial governments. Simeon decided to revisit the book's findings in 2005 and concluded that "intergovernmental players from the 1960s would be on familiar ground were they to join the fray today. Indeed, many of the elements of the process that we observe today were first coming into focus in the tumultuous decade of the 1960s."[40]

Hyphenated federalism has had remarkable staying power because, in Canada, governments have nowhere else to go. It is the key to getting things done. The constitution continues to force the hand of policy-makers to look for solutions through federal-provincial diplomacy or negotiations. They saw it as the only avenue available to give life to the Rowell-Sirois Report, to the welfare state, and to develop a modern economy, with only limited concerns for the workings of democratic institutions.

The Rowell-Sirois Commission had issued a clear warning to policy-makers against relying too heavily on federal-provincial agreements as the way ahead to pursue new measures. It argued that "if the
cooperative projects are to be continued the governments involved
must be their own arbitrators. Arbitration conducted solely by the
interested parties leads to delay and sometimes to deadlock which
is ruinous to administrative efficiency. It always leads in the end to
compromise. While compromise is inherent in the political process,
it is rarely conducive to good administration ... Where legislative
power over a particular subject matter is divided, it is ordinarily
desirable that these powers should be pooled under the control of
a single government in order to secure a unified effort in administration."[41] Before he became prime minister, Pierre E. Trudeau
saw problems with hyphenated federalism and its impact on representative democracy: "A fundamental condition of representative
democracy is a clear allocation of responsibilities: a citizen who dis-
approves of a policy, a law, a municipal by-law, or an educational
system must know precisely whose work it is so that he can hold
someone responsible for it at the next election."[42] Canada no longer
meets this fundamental condition of representative democracy.

W.L. Mackenzie King, Louis St Laurent, and John Diefenbaker
ignored Rowell-Sirois's warning. Pierre E. Trudeau did not follow
his own advice once in office; within a year of becoming prime minister, Trudeau described Ottawa's spending power as "the power of
Parliament to make payments to people or institutions or governments for purposes on which it [Parliament] does not necessarily have
the power to legislate."[43] We have seen a plethora of federal-provincial
agreements in every sector since the end of the Second World War.
Indeed, one would be hard-pressed to identify a single sector that has
not been covered by a federal-provincial agreement or a policy field
that belongs exclusively to one level of government or the other.[44]

Canadian federalism has become a potpourri of federal-provincial
agreements, federal-provincial policies, federal-provincial measures,
federal-provincial initiatives, and federal-provincial regulations. It
has given rise to a multitude of federal-provincial committees managing a myriad of shared-cost programs. All federations have different
forms of collaborative arrangements between levels of government,
but no other federation has taken the matter as far as Canada.

There are things peculiar to Canadian federalism. Ronald Watts
points out that the ability of the federal government to spend in

areas of sub-national jurisdictions is unique among federations.[45] Not only did Canada invent hyphenated federalism, there is now very little that is beyond the reach of the federal government's spending power. As noted above, hyphenated federalism is free to roam wherever it wishes to go and to do whatever it wishes to do. The result is that politicians and public servants from eleven governments have become the constitutional decision-makers for Canada.[46] They operate behind closed doors, and when agreements are struck, it is difficult to discern who proposed what, who opposed what, and how the consensus was struck.

A defining characteristic of international diplomacy is that participants keep their objectives and strategies close to their chest until the deal is done. The same applies in federal-provincial negotiations.[47] To be sure, hyphenated federalism can get things done, as the past seventy years have shown in both the social and economic development fields. However, it comes at a cost for representative democracy. Hyphenated federalism is the preserve of political and bureaucratic elites. Andrew Petter explains that Ottawa's spending power under hyphenated federalism allows "political responsibility to be shifted from one order of government to the other but, by causing responsibility to become interspersed, made it virtually impossible for citizens to determine which order of government to hold accountable for policies that fail or, for that matter, for ones that succeed. The result was to reduce the influence of ordinary citizens over the policy-making process and to increase the influence of governmental elites."[48] The same can be said for the House of Commons and even ministers.

Hyphenated federalism comes at a cost to both our country's political and bureaucratic institutions. It requires public servants in Ottawa, in regional offices, and in provincial capitals to negotiate, manage, and implement federal-provincial agreements. In many ways, they report to one another rather than to their political masters. Hyphenated federalism has created another level of government, one that can operate outside of accountability requirements. Public servants are the key players in making it work, and most everything takes place on their turf. At one point, Ottawa even co-financed the salaries of provincial public servants to ensure that there was a capacity at the other end to negotiate and implement the agreements.[49]

Federal-provincial negotiations can generate federal-provincial conflicts among status-seeking politicians and public servants. The negotiations can lead to conflicts that hold very little importance to those not actually involved in the negotiations, as Donald Smiley once pointed out.[50] The conflicts, which can be both costly and counterproductive, are often known only to those sitting at the negotiation table and in central agencies and line departments in Ottawa and provincial capitals.

Hyphenated federalism is an important factor in making it exceedingly difficult for Parliament to play its role of holding the government to account. How is a member of Parliament to know who negotiated what and to determine what order of government gave in when reaching an agreement? Even responsible ministers, let alone backbench MPs, often have a trying time to understand the give and take required to strike an agreement.[51] All eleven governments in Canada now have well-staffed federal-provincial or intergovernmental units working with line departments to manage a very complex federal-provincial government machinery and numerous policy and decision-making processes. Hierarchy matters less in this environment, and in government, if hierarchy matters less, then so does accountability.

Hyphenated federalism provides federal and provincial public servants many opportunities to pursue their self-interest. They have an interest in enlarging the number and scope of federal-provincial agreements. Many federal and provincial public servants may well regard their role as complementary rather than competitive. If one government walks away from an agreement or a federal-provincial program, then some public servants would either be assigned new tasks or lose their jobs. Donald Smiley makes the case that "provincial program officials, along with their federal counterparts, usually believe that more financial resources are expended on their functions when shared-cost arrangements prevail than would be the case if the provinces had equivalent funds at their disposal with no strings attached."[52]

Hyphenated federalism adds layers of bureaucracy in both levels of government. It strengthens the hands of central agencies that are tasked with, among other things, keeping an eye on line departments. It also adds to oversight bodies in both levels of government. The auditor general in Ottawa and its provincial counterparts will audit the same programs. The different access to information requirements have to be coordinated, and this, too, necessitates financial and human resources.

THE SCOPE OF HYPHENATED FEDERALISM

At one point, there was not one department in the government of New Brunswick that did not have a federal-provincial agreement to manage. The same can be said for several other provinces. For have-less provinces, the promise of federal government money was enough to reorient priorities and reshape, in a fundamental fashion, the electoral platform of the party in power during the election campaign.[53] When it came to economic development in certain provinces, it did not matter which political party was in power. Federal-provincial agreements kept on rolling from one generation to the next with few changes.[54] For provincial governments, particularly in have-less regions, the risk of losing federal dollars was too high to challenge the status quo or to pursue major initiatives without federal government funding.

There have been instances when line ministers directed officials to pursue an initiative but were told that the federal-provincial committee would not approve and best to drop the request for fear of losing federal government funding. Ministers were not about to admit this before their legislative assemblies for fear of being perceived as weak. In any event, said ministers had nowhere to appeal a decision struck by a committee made up of federal and provincial public servants. Their federal government counterpart not only had nine other provinces to deal with, but they also had to turn to federal-provincial committees of officials.[55] This is an important factor that has shifted the locus of power from the political arena to permanent officials. It explains why politicians – starting in the early 1980s – decided to push back on public servants, convinced that they had too much influence.

Hyphenated federalism has taken various shapes over the years, making it difficult for Members of Parliament, let alone Canadians, to understand who should be held accountable for what. No matter the phase, hyphenated federalism has made provincial governments more assertive, to be sure, far more assertive than John A. Macdonald ever imagined. At times, federal-provincial conflicts broke out in the open, as they did in the early 1980s when the Trudeau government sought to patriate the constitution. At other times, Ottawa bought peace with provincial governments by signing a generous federal-provincial agreement in health care, as the Paul

Martin government did. At still other times, the Federal-Provincial Conference of First Ministers enjoyed a high profile (e.g., the Pierre Trudeau years), while at other times, not at all (e.g., the Harper years). Deciding who would get visibility for federal-provincial programs has always dogged hyphenated federalism. This is a particularly sore point whenever a different political party holds power in Ottawa and in a provincial capital.

The above makes the point that hyphenated federalism is a continuously moving target. It has no set form that can be easily grasped by members of Parliament, let alone average Canadians. It also leaves unresolved fundamental issues confronting Canada. National unity remains the preoccupation of many Canadians, despite a long-standing dissatisfaction with federalism in Quebec, Western Canada, Atlantic Canada, and in Indigenous communities.[56]

Hyphenated federalism has not always been smooth sailing. It has given rise to numerous federal-provincial and interprovincial conflicts. Mackenzie King showed great foresight when he argued that "it is not wise for one government to raise revenue for others to spend." Not only does it muddy the accountability waters, it fuels the battle of the balance sheets. Provincial governments insist that there is a growing imbalance between the capacities of both orders of government to finance their responsibilities. The BNA Act was largely silent on federal-provincial fiscal matters, except sections 114–18 that outline the liabilities of Nova Scotia and New Brunswick and the grants in aid to these provinces. The BNA Act gave the federal government the power to raise revenues "by any mode or system of taxation" while restricting provincial governments to "direct taxation."

The Canadian Constitution Act, 1982 goes further on fiscal federalism and commits Canada to the principle of equalization payments to have-less provinces to ensure that they are able to provide reasonably comparable levels of public services at reasonably comparable levels of taxation.[57] This, however, has created a new set of problems and conflicts – have provinces are often critical of needs-based programs and will pressure Ottawa to revert to per capita funding, while have-less provinces insist that Ottawa and National Policy explain in no small measure their have-less status. This, they argue, should require Ottawa to have an equalization principle built into every federal government program.

THE BATTLE OVER FEDERAL TRANSFERS

At its core, the battle over how to calculate federal transfers is about space, about which regions benefit the most from federal government transfers. It is a very important debate given that federal transfers to the provinces represent 22 percent of total federal spending.[58] Have provinces argue that a per capita calculation for federal transfers is straightforward and speaks to fairness in federal government spending. The have provinces are vote-rich (i.e., Ontario and Alberta). Readers will recall that former prime minister Harper, from Alberta, was supportive of a per capita approach to federal transfers and did overhaul federal transfers along this line while in power. More is said about this later.

Have-less provinces have a different perspective, insisting on a needs-based approach. Prime ministers from Quebec, from Trudeau *père*, Mulroney, and Chrétien to Trudeau *fils*, have been reluctant to embrace a per capita approach. The argument is that when Ottawa transfers tax points as part of its transfer payments, it should rely, at least in part, on a needs basis because the value of tax points transferred to a have province is greater than to a have-less province. Janine Brodie explains that federal transfers "help to underwrite some of the social costs of uneven development" in certain political jurisdictions so that "the economic relationships that promoted uneven development remained unchallenged."[59]

Leaving aside Ottawa's equalization program – albeit a very important aside – the have provinces recently won the day. The Stephen Harper government, with strong representation from Ontario, overhauled federal transfers to provinces in the 2007 budget, deciding that equalization payments can no longer exceed growth in nominal GDP, and other transfer payments will, in future, be calculated on a per capita cash basis. The big winner under the new arrangement – Alberta – is Harper's home province. The province saw a 37.8 percent increase in federal transfers from 2013/14 to 2014/15, while Nova Scotia, for example, saw a 2 percent increase.[60]

Provincial governments have long argued that there is a serious fiscal imbalance in Canada. The provinces insist that Ottawa, because of the BNA Act and other developments, has more revenues than necessary, given the federal government's limited responsibilities in the modern economy and welfare state. The opposite is true in the case of provincial governments because of their constitutional responsibilities

in education, health care, and social services. While provincial governments have no choice but to deliver programs in these sectors, Ottawa
can move in and out, depending on its priorities.

Though Saskatchewan pioneered medicare, the program went
national when the Canadian Parliament passed the Medical Care
Act in 1966. Ottawa would pay about half of medicare costs for
eligible items in any province, provided that the provincial plan met
several criteria – the program had to be universal, portable, and publicly managed.[61] Ottawa has, over the years, lessened its financial
contribution to the program. Today, the federal government contributes no more than 25 percent to the cost of medicare, leaving
provincial governments juggling priorities to pay a greater share of
the cost. One can assume that if the federal government had declared
it would gradually lower its share of the cost to 25 percent (less in
some provinces) in 1966, then we would have had fewer provinces
signing on to medicare, and we would not have a national program
that, today – at least for some – helps define Canada and its values.[62]

Many federal public servants posit that the fiscal imbalance argument is flawed because they do not accept that it calls for an unduly
rigid interpretation of the division of responsibilities between the
federal and provincial governments.[63] They essentially assert that the
Fathers of Confederation had it wrong when they drafted the BNA
Act, and they maintain that our inability to amend the constitution
forced the federal government's hand to get involved by whatever
means were available.

THE IMMIGRATION FACTOR

Michael Wilson, a former finance minister in the Mulroney government, told me of an eye-opening experience he had when he first ran
for Parliament in 1979. He spoke before a gathering in his constituency, Etobicoke, a suburb of Toronto, where he employed the word
"freedom" on three occasions. The reaction was markedly different between "old stock" Canadians and new Canadians. Old stock
Canadians, he reports, had a somewhat "blasé" reaction to the word,
while new Canadians reacted very positively. He added that Toronto
alone now welcomes about 100,000 new Canadians every year, and
this is having an important impact on Canada's body politic.[64]

Ontario, notably Toronto, leads the way in attracting new
Canadians. The province has welcomed between 90,000 and

133,000 new Canadians every year over the past ten years; Quebec, Alberta, and British Columbia have each attracted between 20,000 and 55,000 a year during the same period. The smaller provinces trail badly, attracting between 352, in the case of Prince Edward Island, and 2,000, in the case of New Brunswick during that period.[65] This only tells part of the story. Once in Canada, new Canadians have a much greater tendency to move to Toronto, Montreal, and Vancouver than to the smaller provinces, affirming the case that new Canadians want to be where new Canadians are.[66]

Immigration is the driver of population growth in Canada, and it is having a profound political and economic impact. Today, 22 percent of Canadians are immigrants, the highest number in eighty-five years.[67] The political participation of new Canadians is not much different than that of the broader Canadian population. But there are important differences on other levels. There is evidence to suggest that new Canadians are more socially conservative than old stock Canadians, and they are more satisfied with the state of Canadian democracy than the broader Canadian population.[68] A study explains why. "Many new citizens in the focus groups related their feelings towards Canadian democracy in reference to their lives before coming to Canada. Those who came from countries such as Mexico, Colombia, Ukraine, or Russia commented that while Canadian democracy has its problems, it is much better than in the countries they left."[69] New Canadians also believe that Canada's political institutions represent well the wishes of the Canadian population (64 percent agree or strongly agree).[70] They see Canada not as a treaty between two nations but a country that gives them a new beginning. They are not well-versed with regional grievances and unlikely to be concerned with the issue that Donald Smiley and Ronald Watts, two of Canada's leading students of federalism, debated – the inability of federal institutions to "accommodate and reconcile the variety of regional interests."[71]

Though they may not realize it, they, too, have a regional bias. There is evidence that new Canadians are having a profound impact on politics in the Greater Toronto Area (GTA). EKOS Research reports that they played a "critical" role in the "restoration of Liberal Party dominance in the 905 and other areas surrounding the GTA."[72] It will also be recalled that Jason Kenney, the immigration minister in the Harper government, met with some success in attracting new Canadians to the Conservative Party, which led to breakthroughs in the GTA in the 2011 general election for the Conservative Party.[73]

New Canadians may have different values than old stock Canadians when they arrive, as Michael Wilson and other politicians have discovered. For one thing, new Canadians tend to be much more supportive of immigration policy than old stock Canadians.[74] They attached a great deal of importance to freedom and equality. Public opinion surveys reveal that Canadian-born citizens have a greater attachment to their local community and to their province than new Canadians; 42 percent of Canadian-born citizens see themselves as citizens of their province (strongly agree). This is in contrast to only 26 percent of recent immigrants who strongly agree that they see themselves as citizens of their province.[75]

In time, however, they will identify with the regional interests of the communities where they settle, thus reinforcing the representation by population factor in deciding who holds political power in Canada. Public opinion surveys reveal that, over time, new Canadians adopt similar values as native-born Canadians, just as they develop attachment to community and province.[76]

The country's reliance on representation by population to decide who holds power maintains a bias for regions that are better able to attract new Canadians. They arrive with limited knowledge of the BNA Act 1867, Canadian regionalism, and the reasons that led Ottawa to enshrine the principle of equalization in the Canada Constitution Act, 1982.

LOOKING BACK

What to do when a country has a federal system in name only? What to do when the Fathers of Confederation never foresaw the growth of government and the requirements of the welfare state when designing the constitution with no amending formula? What to do in a country when the federal government and several national commissions of inquiry concluded that some regions benefitted more from Confederation than others?[77] Successive Canadian governments from W.L. Mackenzie King to Justin Trudeau have come up with the following answers: embrace a form of hyphenated federalism, push the constitution aside, turn to the federal spending power to enable Ottawa to move in with plans in every policy field, and worry not about implications for the country's democratic institutions. Alain Noël went to the heart of the issue when he reviewed possible measures to limit Ottawa's spending power: how, he asked, "do you limit a power that does not exist."[78] The federal government's spending power is a power placed in the hands of politicians and public servants with a limited capacity to hold them to account.

The Fathers of Confederation put a straightjacket on policy-makers, and the consequences still account for much of Canada's political conflicts. Unlike their American counterparts, they were in no mood to embrace a great compromise by ensuring that national political institutions reflected the country's regional composition as does the Senate in the United States. The main architects of Canada's constitution were from Ontario, and the only great compromise they were willing to accept was with Canada East (Quebec) by recognizing the French language in Parliament and the courts. At the risk of sounding repetitive, British-inspired institutions designed for a unitary state made no provision for the regional factor. The Fathers of Confederation would leave unattended arguably the most important facet of Canadian federalism – how to give life to the regional factor in national political and administrative institutions. Transfer payments of one type or another became Canada's version of the Great Compromise. But the compromise has been a moving target since it was first introduced. The federal government can move in and out of policy fields at will, depending on its own priorities and fiscal capacity.

Canada's compromise laid the groundwork for hyphenated federalism and how policy and program changes are introduced. Hyphenated federalism, however, has been much better at managing issues and conflicts than resolving them.

Yet, hyphenated federalism can claim success on a number of policy fronts – it was either hyphenated federalism or many policy issues would have been left unattended. Canadians appear comfortable with hyphenated federalism. A leading Canadian pollster reports that "the fight between 'a strong central government,' on one side, and 'a community of communities,' on the other side, is over, and both sides won."[79] Hyphenated federalism made it possible for both sides to win, at least temporarily. It is, however, at a cost to our political and administrative institutions and cracks are now appearing in the Canadian version of the Great Compromise.

Hyphenated federalism is not without problems for representative democracy. It has made federal and provincial governments thicker, added new layers of bureaucracy, muddied accountability, and made it more difficult for politicians to direct the work of their public servants. It has pushed our elected representatives, notably our members of Parliament and, to some extent, Cabinet ministers to the sidelines. MPs, and even Cabinet ministers, have become convinced that they have been shunted to the sidelines to make hyphenated federalism work. They are correct.

Everything Canadian Is Regional, Except National Political Institutions

One is hard-pressed to identify an issue, large or small, in Canadian politics that does not arouse regional tensions. This chapter contends that, while virtually all issues in Canada have an important regional dimension, the country's national political and administrative institutions are not designed to accommodate regional perspectives other than those from heavily populated regions. Furthermore, the inability of these institutions to accommodate regional circumstances have made it more difficult for Canada to manage regional tensions. For instance, the initiative to have a woman on a Canadian bank note presented a regional twist as soon as the names of the five finalists were announced. Nellie McClung, the Prairies activist who led the charge to grant women the right to vote, did not make the short list, while Idola Saint-Jean, the Quebec activist who led the same campaign in her province, did. The Winnipeg-based McClung Foundation asked why there was not "a single woman from any of the prairie provinces, the part of the country where the women's rights movement first took off in Canada."[1]

The Canadian Broadcasting Corporation (CBC) assumed that it would help Canada celebrate its 150th anniversary when it decided to tell Canada's story. Prime Minister Justin Trudeau launched the series, declaring that it was designed to celebrate Canada. However, the series was met with immediate criticism from Nova Scotians, Acadians, Indigenous communities, and Quebecers. Stephen McNeil, premier of Nova Scotia, and Bill MacDonald, mayor of Annapolis Royal, called on the CBC to add an episode to the series to "set the record straight." Nova Scotia, Mr MacDonald explained, is the "cradle of our nation ... an omission that substantial is pretty profound."[2] A history professor from Quebec dismissed the series out of hand, insisting that CBC was "presenting alternative history based on alternative facts."[3] It seems that Canada was not wholly represented on its sesquicentennial anniversary.

Prime Minister Trudeau laid out a well-planned summit to bring provinces and territories to address climate change. The December 2016 federal-provincial summit was well timed with the Liberal Party holding power in Ottawa and in seven of the ten provinces, and the NDP in just one – in fossil-fuel-rich Alberta. Trudeau made it clear that he supported measures to deal with climate change. The summit did not work out as planned for Trudeau. The premiers insisted on special clauses to deal with their regional concerns. Christy Clark, then premier of British Columbia, went before the television cameras at the summit meeting to say that the deal before the First Ministers was "unfair to BC," insisting that her province would pay twice as much as Ontario and Quebec under the proposed plan. In the end, she got a side deal.[4] Other premiers secured addendums to the deal as concessions for their province.[5] The point is that Canadian federalism has become a collection of side deals to accommodate regional grievances. The side deals, which address matters mostly under provincial jurisdiction, are technocratic rather than structural and can therefore be adjusted or terminated whenever Ottawa decides.

Attempts to negotiate a federal-provincial health care agreement in late 2016 broke down along regional lines as well. Initially, all ten provincial governments demanded more federal funding, insisting that Ottawa's "take it or leave it" approach was not acceptable. The media reported that some provincial governments were prepared to walk out of the meeting if the federal government did not put more funds on the table.[6] In the end, the federal government shut down the talks and began negotiating one-on-one with the provinces. First, New Brunswick, then Nova Scotia and Newfoundland and Labrador, and later, the other provinces one by one agreed to side deals with Ottawa.[7] We later learned that Ottawa signed a side deal with New Brunswick in the form of a $75 million pilot project to help the province manage its aging population and health care.[8]

Canada is a "country of regions."[9] Michael Ornstein sheds further light on the notion: "The people of different regions exhibit regional loyalties, in the sense of preferring the quality of life of their province and/or supporting their province's claims against the federal government."[10] Americans define themselves as Americans while Canadians identify themselves as Maritimers, *Québécois*, or "from Western Canada."[11] Canada is home to regionally distinct patterns of political behaviour, vastly different geographical features encompassing the world's second largest territory – which includes the Canadian Shield, the Interior Plains, the Great Lakes, the Rockies, the Artic, and territories that touch three oceans – diverse regional economic structures, two official languages, all amounting to strong regional identities.

A leading Canadian journalist writes that Canada has a "malignant sense of regional envy."[12] He points to "Quebec's restlessness" and Western Canada's "angst and anger about the raw deal the region asserted that it had always received within Canada."[13] He made no reference to Atlantic Canada's "angst" but it is there, even though the region does not have the political or economic clout of Western Canada to get the attention of the Ontario media. The journalist said nothing about Ontario, though the province has been critical of Ottawa's transfer payments to have-less provinces in recent years.

The Mowat Centre, which labelled itself Ontario's voice on public policy, published a report making the case that Ontario is receiving a lower share of federal government spending than it contributes to federal government coffers.[14] We have now reached the point in Canadian federalism where, if a province gives a dime to Ottawa in taxes, it expects a dime back in government spending. The Mowat Centre ignored all the benefits that flow to Ontario from the federal government, ranging from large investments in economic development to the location of head offices of federal government departments, agencies, and Crown corporations.

The two main cleavages in Canadian politics remain language and regionalism, and in many ways, the language issue has become tied to regionalism. The French-Canadian population is largely concentrated in the province of Quebec and in some communities of Nova Scotia and Western Canada (e.g., St Boniface), adjoining regions of New Brunswick, and eastern and northern Ontario. Notwithstanding the concentration of French Canadians in several provinces, the language issue has become regionalized within French Canada to the point that French Canada itself no longer exists as a community.

The Royal Commission on Bilingualism and Biculturalism, combined with the election of the Trudeau government in 1968, constituted a turning point, a defining moment in English-French relations in

Canada and within the French-Canadian community. Pierre Trudeau himself summed up the task at hand and the resulting benefits if fully implemented when he declared that once francophone-language rights across Canada are constitutionally entrenched, the French-Canadian nation will stretch from coast to coast. "Nobody will be able to say ... [in Quebec], 'I need more power because I speak for the French-Canadian nation.'"[15] For Trudeau, the challenge was to secure a strong future for the French-Canadian community, which extended beyond the Quebec borders. In brief, *la survivance* was the challenge. But no sooner had Trudeau secured francophone-language rights than the challenge took on different forms. While francophones outside Quebec still saw the challenge, at least in part, as *la survivance*, for many French-speaking Quebecers, *l'épanouissement national* now better reflect their purpose, that is, the wish to develop their society to its full potential and, in doing so, to have a free hand in shaping their political, economic, and cultural institutions.

The result is that French Canada is now regionalized. The language issue has rediscovered the borders that Macdonald and Cartier first defined in 1867 when they negotiated the Confederation pact between two nations. The cleavage and the political tensions between Québecois and Acadiens today are nearly as pronounced as they may be between English Canada and Quebec. Indeed, there is a growing tension among French-speaking communities in Canada, and it is increasingly difficult to find a commonality of interests. When, for example, the New Brunswick Acadian community wanted to play host to the 8th Sommet de la Francophonie, it soon discovered that it could not count on support from their Quebec cousins. Those who would have been its most natural ally, say, forty years ago, now wished to downplay the French-speaking presence outside Quebec in order to further their own objectives. Thus, French Canada no longer speaks with one voice, even on the language issue, and it is in this sense that there are now two, three, or four regional French Canadas pursuing different objectives.[16]

Public opinion surveys reveal that English Canada, too, has distinct regional identities. Leaving aside stark differences in the economy of Canadian regions, there are regional differences on questions of morality and dialects. When it comes to determining what is morally acceptable or morally wrong, for example, Albertans have more in common with Quebecers than with some other English-speaking provinces.[17] Kevin O'Leary, a leading candidate for the leadership of the Conservative Party in 2017, decided to drop out of the race because he realized further into the campaign that he "didn't grasp the complexity of the country's regional dynamics."[18] Pollster David Herle explains: "Residents of the major western cities share most values and attitudes with residents of major central Canadian cities." Yet they see, for example, the gun registry program very differently "because their perceptions were shaped by their region, rather than by their status as urbanites."[19]

Political parties in Canada are also highly regionalized. The Liberal Party has been a Quebec-Ontario– and, at times, Atlantic Canada–dominated party. The Reform, Alliance, and Conservative parties have been Western-based, with the Conservative Party occasionally making inroads into vote-rich Ontario to win power. The NDP has enjoyed only modest support in Atlantic Canada. On very rare occasions can a political party win power in Canada while enjoying support in all regions. A leading *Globe and Mail* journalist had a warning for the Conservative Party in 2017: "Conservatives can't win without support from Quebec."[20] He had no such warning with respect to Atlantic or Western Canada. I note, however, that Stephen Harper won power with a strong majority of seats in Western Canada and Ontario. No matter the combination, Ontario is always the key to power in Ottawa.

There is no other national institution to counterbalance this political reality in Parliament, making it difficult for the national government to speak for all of Canada, to secure support for its policies in all regions, and to have the political legitimacy to act on behalf of all regions. This has led Western and Atlantic Canada to argue that "national policy" is in reality only a "regional policy" designed for Ontario and Quebec.[21] As noted in the Introduction, a public opinion survey asked Canadians whether their province has its fair share of influence in making important national decisions and whether it was treated with respect. Only in Ontario and Quebec did a majority of respondents say yes.[22]

Some equate regions with the ten provinces and the North, others see Canada as five regions – Atlantic Canada, Quebec, Ontario, the Prairies, and British Columbia, and still others see Newfoundland and Labrador as a distinct region, and the list goes on.[23] Richard Simeon has a different take: "Regions are simply containers, whose contents may or may not differ. And how we draw the boundaries around them depends entirely on what our purposes are: it is an

a priori question, determined by theoretical needs or political purposes. We can have regions within provinces, or regions made up
of groups of provinces, or regions cutting across provincial lines."[24]

Three students of Canadian politics from Ontario and Quebec
make the case that Canadians are divided more by values than
regions and that disagreements on policy issues exist because of
"differing values not because of territorial fracture lines." They are
quick to add, however, that in promoting national policies, there
is a "need to adopt regionally sensitive communications strategies,
notably to appeal to values that have been overlooked in the past in
given regions by policy makers." They explain: "Compared with the
national average, egalitarianism is more prominent in the Atlantic
region, Quebec and Ontario. Legal rigorism is relatively more prominent on the Prairies and in Atlantic Canada, and above the national
average in Quebec. It is under the national average in Ontario and
British Columbia. Traditionalism is relatively more pronounced on
the Prairies and in British Columbia."[25]

Provincial political institutions and their politicians give life to
regionalism; they speak on behalf of their "containers." Provincial
boundaries establish where voters elect politicians to represent them
and their interests. Territorial politics, or the containers, can be
amplified by politicians coming together to speak to the interests
of regions that extend beyond provincial boundaries. I am thinking of the Council of Atlantic Premiers and the Western Premiers'
Conference. However, the Council of Atlantic Premiers does not
decide who becomes premier of Nova Scotia. Nova Scotians make
that decision, which explains why the council has met with little
success. The main territorial divides remain provincial boundaries.

Quebec, Ontario, and Manitoba substantially expanded their
territories over time. Manitoba and Ontario clashed over borders
between 1881 and 1889, when the issue was finally "settled in
Ontario's favour."[26] The three Maritime provinces, meanwhile, have
clung to their defined territories, or their containers, despite urg-
ings from a tri-province study.[27] *The Economist* magazine summed it
up well when a contributor observed: "By any administrative logic,
the three provinces should be bundled into one. But nobody will be
crazy enough to try."[28] Once containers are defined, it is extremely
difficult for those operating in them, either at the political or bureaucratic level, to see merit in forging a broader union with neighbours,
even if it makes economic sense to do so.

Rather than go over the same material from early chapters, suffice to note that federalism calls, or should call, for a capacity in national political institutions to reconcile the political power that flows out of representation by population with the need to represent territorial or regional diversities. As noted, Canada's national institutions fall far short of this requirement, and provincial premiers continue to try to fill the void. To be sure, they are the voice of regionalism in Canada, but they have no capacity to be heard or to shape policy in national political institutions. The voices are largely for the benefit of those who reside in the containers, and in the end, they have had limited impact within national institutions.

In summary, when it comes to shaping national policies and measures, premiers have a voice but little else. They do not have the power to "exit," given both Ottawa's spending power in areas of provincial jurisdiction and its ability to shape economic policy and economic development. Their loyalty is to the defined political boundaries they represent. Their voice can be loud – particularly when it comes to economic policy, economic development, and federal transfers. National political actors are free to listen to or ignore these voices. If the voices come from heavily populated provinces, however, they stand a better chance of being heard.

TRYING TO MAKE IT WORK

The *Canadian Encyclopedia* reports that the existence of regional tensions is "hardly surprising, considering that a national state was imposed, [over] 150 years ago, over a vast territory and over scattered different peoples."[29] Trying to make a Parliament and a machinery of government designed for a unitary state work in a federation, all the while coping with a rigid constitution, has made it exceedingly difficult for Canadian society to manage regional diversity. This is in contrast to other countries. Alexander Hamilton, for example, warned in the *Federalist Papers*, number 1, that "among the most formidable of the obstacles which the new Constitution will have to encounter may readily be distinguished the obvious interest of a certain class of men in every State to resist all changes which may hazard a diminution of the power, emolument, and consequence of the offices they hold under the State establishments."[30] The same warning applies to Canada, except that we need to substitute "class of men" with "regions."

Ganesh Sitaraman, in his widely acclaimed book, makes the case that the United States is confronting the crisis of the middle-class constitution, arguing that "'the system is rigged' to work for wealthy and corporate interests."[31] He looks to political institutions and maintains that economic elites "manipulate and deform the structures of government" to pursue their economic interests.[32]

Canada is confronting a similar crisis that is regional in nature. The political language of Canadian federalism has encouraged provincial governments to speak to regional particularism and to remain federal funds claimants.[33] Ottawa has tried to manage regional tensions by throwing money at the problem through its spending power. In more recent years, it has tried to refocus more of its efforts on Canadians' individual rights by stressing the importance of the Charter of Rights and Freedoms and providing resources to groups to pursue the government under the charter.

Though parts of Canada's national political institutions were originally designed to address class (e.g., the Senate), given their British influence, tensions in Canadian federalism have never been about class. They have always been about regions and language.[34] It is no exaggeration to write that every crisis in Canadian federalism that has surfaced since 1867 has been regionally based, and Ottawa has looked to federal-provincial agreements for solutions. The result is that, leaving aside waste collection, the postal service, and perhaps National Defence, governments in Canada do not act alone.[35]

Canada has three sets of political and bureaucratic institutions operating at the two senior orders of government: institutions associated with the federal government, institutions associated with provincial governments, and institutions associated with federal-provincial relations. Vote-rich regions control the levers of institutions associated with the federal government. All provincial governments control the levers tied to their legislature, Cabinet, and public service but many of their decisions are tied to federal-provincial agreements. As noted, provincial governments direct criticism at the federal government for policies and decisions that hold, or are perceived to hold, a negative impact for their province. The voices of the Ontario and Quebec premiers, however, carry far more weight in both political and bureaucratic circles in Ottawa than those of Prince Edward Island, New Brunswick, Nova Scotia, British Columbia, Alberta, Manitoba, Saskatchewan, and Newfoundland and Labrador combined.

From time to time, a bombastic and high-profile premier from a small province, such as Premier Danny Williams from Newfoundland and Labrador, will enjoy a high profile in the national media. It is not at all clear that the profile translates into action for the province. The votes for winning power in Ottawa are in Ontario and Quebec, the senior bureaucracy straddles the Ontario-Quebec border, and the national media speak from these two provinces.

OTTAWA IS THE PROBLEM

Canada's three sets of political institutions provide ready-made arguments for regions to explain their economic woes or their unfair treatment from Ottawa. Provincial premiers rarely hesitate to say Ottawa is to blame for a lack of funds in virtually all sectors, from health care and education to economic development. All ten provincial premiers can point at Ottawa as the culprit, as the federal government moves in and out of sectors or adjusts its funding to the provinces to suit its policy agenda or manage its own fiscal challenges.

In this sense, all provinces should be on the same page, but they are not. Some provinces receive more federal transfers than others, notably the have-less provinces. The Equalization Program, by definition, is designed to flow funds to have-less regions.[36] But other transfer payments have been adjusted to flow less money to have-less provinces. We saw earlier, for example, that the Harper government adjusted transfer payments for health care, social services, and education to equal per capita payments, making them less redistributive. The winners of this move: the have provinces.

The decision to tie the Canada Health Transfer (CHT) to an equal per capita basis came into force in 2014–15. The Parliamentary Budget Office reports that, as a result, Alberta and the Northwest Territories experience substantial growth in their CHT entitlements (37.8 per cent and 45.2 per cent respectively), while most other provinces and territories experience increases of less than 4 per cent.[37] Prior to 2014–15, federal transfers for health care combined cash and tax points, which saw larger transfers for equalization-receiving provinces.[38] Former prime minister Harper responded to pressures from the more populated provinces, including his home province, fast-growing Alberta, to move to a per capita basis to calculate transfer payments. Ontario applauded the move but then was quick to note the need for a further increase to retain more of the funding it sends to Ottawa.[39] Harper spoke to the interest of his region much like W.L. Mackenzie King, Louis St Laurent, John Diefenbaker, the Trudeaus, Mulroney, and Chrétien spoke to the interest of theirs, with Ontario always in the equation given its political clout.

Focusing on federal transfers and what the government spends in a given province only tells part of the story – and not the most important part at that. Government spending can take many forms. Some spending can create an economic dependency while other spending can have a positive structural impact on a region's economy. A federal dollar spent under the Employment Insurance program, for example, will have a far different impact than a dollar spent on a consulting contract, to create jobs in the automobile sector or help launch a new IT business, such as BlackBerry. A federal dollar spent on a federal public servant's salary will have a different impact than a dollar spent on Old Age Security. As has been well documented, have-less and older provinces rely a great deal more on transfer payments to individuals and provincial governments than the have provinces.[40]

A simple accounting of the redistributive impact of the federal government's tax and spend activities invariably reveals that provinces like Ontario and Alberta contribute more to federal coffers than they receive in federal spending.[41] A review of federal government spending that has a structural impact has not been documented but would likely reveal a different story.

I reported in another publication that in the early 1980s, the Department of Regional Economic Expansion (DREE) decided to launch an in-depth study to break down the federal government's expenditure budget by location (i.e., by region), expense type (i.e., economic development measures versus transfer payments), cost of operations, and so on. The report divided government spending further into different categories: spending by point of outlay in terms of wages and salaries, economic development, social programs, investments in infrastructures, the purchase of goods, money spent for consultants and services, and here too, the list goes on.[42] Before the study could be properly launched, word came from the Privy Council Office, which reports to the prime minister, that the department "had to" discontinue the project – PCO officials feared that the study would have a negative impact on national unity and fuel further regional tensions. The department did as it was told and dropped the project.[43] DREE was disbanded in 1982 on the advice of PCO officials.[44] The study, if completed, would have provided a more thorough look at federal government spending by region. As it is now, there is a tendency to simply add up total spending in four or five regions, without differentiating investments in research and development from transfer payments provided by Ottawa's Employment Insurance program.

I hold the view that an effective Upper House, responsible for bringing a regional perspective to bear on National Policy, would have likely seen merit in a thorough analysis of federal government spending vis-à-vis where funds are spent and for what purpose. It could have challenged such directives as seen above, from the prime minister or the PCO to a line department. The Rowell-Sirois Commission had this to say: "Any fair system of accounting would have to include gains and losses from all federal policies not only at any given time, but also for the whole period since federation."[45] Atlantic and Western Canada have long argued that the country's National Policy introduced in 1878, which lasted until the 1940s and 1950s, strongly favoured Ontario and Quebec at their expense and had a long-term impact, which is felt to this day.[46] A fair accounting system, as called for by the Rowell-Sirois Commission, has never been implemented.

WHAT DOES "NATIONAL" MEAN?

It is much easier for Britain, the United States, and Australia to speak about the "national" interest than it is for Canada. Former prime minister Paul Martin, among many other politicians, spoke about the problem. Martin lamented the fact that "when a regional issue arises in central Canada, it very quickly becomes a national issue," but this is not the case for other regions. He remarked, "We cannot allow national issues in British Columbia to be relegated to the sidelines as regional issues,"[47] and clarified, "What I am talking about is the absolute necessity of reducing the distance between the nation's capital and the regions of the country, a distance which is not measured in kilometres, but a distance which is often measured in attitude."[48] Stephen Harper, for his part, stressed the need for "a greater voice for regions outside Quebec and Ontario."[49] Little actually changed under either prime minister, although during Harper's stay in power, he tilted some federal government programs to favour Western Canada. The changes were technocratic, not structural.

Liberal member of Parliament David McGuinty spoke directly to the problem in his remarks that Alberta politicians in Ottawa were being too "provincial" when they focused on the energy sector. He said, "They are national legislators with a national responsibility, but they come across as very, very small-p provincial individuals who are jealously guarding one industrial sector, picking the fossil-fuel business and the oil-sands business specifically, as one that they're going to fight to the death for."[50]

The "one industrial sector," fossil fuel, matters greatly to British Columbia, Alberta, Saskatchewan, Nova Scotia, New Brunswick, and Newfoundland and Labrador (six out of ten provinces). No matter, in the eyes of McGuinty, it is a regional sector and politicians who focus on it are parochial, unable to pursue a national perspective. McGuinty, other MPs from Ontario, and the national media, however, view the automobile sector as a "national sector." Yet, for nine of Canada's ten provinces, the automobile industry is a regional sector – far more than fossil fuel – and, for half of the Canadian provinces the fossil-fuel sector is a critical element to their economic growth.

The Automotive Products Trade Agreement (also known as the Auto Pact) is not a product of the market or Adam Smith's hidden hand. This Canada-US agreement stems from the federal government. Ontario's automobile sector is tied to a historical event initiated by the Canadian government. The Auto Pact allowed firms to bring parts and automobiles into Canada without any tariff, provided that these firms created jobs and generated investments in Canada. The Auto Pact was signed in January 1965 by Prime Minister Lester B. Pearson and President Lyndon B. Johnson after months of Ottawa-Washington negotiations.

The agreement benefited large American automakers and Southern Ontario. In exchange for tariff-free access to the Canadian market, the Big Three US automakers agreed that automobile production in Canada would not fall below 1964 levels and that for every five new cars sold in Canada, three new ones would be built there. The Auto Pact had an immediate effect. In 1964, only 7 percent of the automobiles built in Canada were sold in the United States; the proportion jumped to 60 percent by 1968.[51] By 1999, Canada had become the fourth largest automaker in the world. This sector was the largest component of Canada-US trade: it went from just $715 million in 1964 to about $92.7 billion in 2000, but dropped to $65.3 billion in 2012.[52] Ontario was home to 130,000 of these jobs – that is, about

90 percent of all jobs in the industry in Canada.[53] The 2008 reces-
sion hit Canada's auto industry hard, losing 43,500 jobs between
2007 and 2009. The sector has since witnessed modest job growth.
It remains largely concentrated in Ontario where it still employs
over 90,000 people.[54]

The industry has been able to secure federal funding in recent years
to modernize its operations.[55] When the auto sector confronted serious financial difficulties in 2008–09, the federal government rushed
in to save GM and Chrysler from bankruptcy with financial support amounting to $9.1 billion. I note, however, that other countries,
including the United States, bailed out their auto sector at the same
time. The minister of industry claimed that the move "saved more
than 50,000 jobs." However, the auditor general would later report
that the government came to the rescue with "limited analysis showing how the restructuring actions would improve the financial situations of GM and Chrysler's Canadian subsidiaries, what concessions
had been made by stakeholders and how the companies would repay
their loans."[56] Ottawa sold all its GM shares in April 2015 at a loss
of $3.5 billion.[57] It takes the Atlantic Canada Opportunities Agency
about ten years to spend that amount of money with a good chunk
of it in repayable loans. In other words, a dollar spent in the automotive sector or the Auto Pact will have a greater impact on restructuring the local economy than a dollar spent on transfer payments,
and the automotive sector, viewed from Ottawa and Ontario, is
regarded as "national," but, viewed from the other nine provinces, it
is regarded as regional.

Quebec-based business Davie Shipbuilder has been living on a
federal government lifeline for about forty years. In a competitive
bidding process in the early 1980s, Davie lost in its bid to build
frigates for the Canadian navy to the Irving Saint John shipyard.
The Quebec caucus led by Marc Lalonde, the province's regional
minister in the federal Cabinet, successfully pressured the federal
government to allocate part of the contract to the Davie shipyard
outside of Quebec City. Davie, again, lost the $25 billion contract
to build navy ships in 2011. Davie was later awarded a sole-source
contract to provide a supply vessel to the navy only weeks before
the 2015 general election. Shortly after the Trudeau government was
elected, the Cabinet asked to review this contract. A senior Davie
executive wrote to company executives and lobbyists in Ottawa
and threatened to purchase a full-page plea in the *Globe and Mail,*

asking that Scott Brison, the Nova Scotia minister in Cabinet, "put his regional bias aside for matters of national security."[58] Regional biases, it seems, are not tolerated outside Ontario and Quebec. It remains that the shipyards based in Saint John (New Brunswick), Vancouver, and Halifax won bids to build ships for the navy through the open competition bidding process. The same is not true for the Quebec-based shipyard.

In October 2017, TransCanada Corp decided to drop plans for the Energy East pipeline. It pointed to changed conditions for its decision, but many looked to Ottawa and politics for an explanation. Jeffrey Jones explained: "The National Energy Board review process was a tragedy of errors with proceedings having to be rebooted with a new panel after members of the first one were discovered to have attended ill-advised meetings with Trans Canada lobbyists."[59] New conditions were later introduced to guide the review process, including adding upstream and downstream emissions. Thus, greenhouse gas emission created by extracting oil before it flows in the pipeline and those created by refining and burning after it leaves the pipeline would need to be evaluated. That killed the project.

The Trudeau government had political problems with the Energy East pipeline project because Quebec had problems with the project. It did not square with the province's economic interest. The main beneficiaries were Alberta and New Brunswick. Saskatchewan Premier Brad Wall urged Montreal mayor Denis Coderre to support the Energy East project, making the case that it was in the interest of the national economy. Coderre dismissed Wall's position out of hand when – as already noted – he "tweeted the respective populations of metropolitan Montreal versus Saskatchewan: four million compared to 1.13 million."[60] Coderre was making the case that premiers from the smaller provinces have little standing in Ottawa. No mayor or elected politician from a large city or state in a federation having an effective Upper House would make this argument in hope of making it stick.

Alberta and New Brunswick politicians reacted strongly to the decision not to pursue the Energy East pipeline. Prime Minister Trudeau was quick to evoke national unity concerns and accused proponents of Energy East of "stoking national divisions."[61] Trudeau said nothing to Mayor Denis Coderre about his response to Premier Brad Wall's plea to support the pipeline. Trudeau and his close political advisers can count: Quebec has 78 seats up for grabs while

Alberta and New Brunswick combined only have 48. Three leading Quebec pollsters warned the Trudeau government that a yes to the Energy East project could create a perfect storm in the province, arguing that it would not only make winning 2018 provincial election difficult for the provincial Liberal Party, and that it could "lead to a resurgence for sovereignty in Quebec."[62]

Many in Western Canada insist that the Justin Trudeau government does not give pipeline issues the attention they warrant. According to Gary Mason, "in the West, the pipeline is the biggest issue, one now enveloped in generations-old complaints. If the aggrieved party was Quebec, instead of Alberta, this matter likely would have been solved by now. (Mostly by ensuring Quebec got whatever it wanted.) At least, that is the sentiment this clash has sown west of Ontario."[63]

The perception is that Quebec, in the name of national unity, has held the Damocles sword over the rest of Canada. Mathieu Bouchard, senior policy adviser to Justin Trudeau, explains: "If Quebeckers don't feel represented by the government for a period of time, unlike in other provinces, it becomes a question of national unity. We always have to be conscious of the fact."[64] According to Bouchard, that logic only applies to Quebec.

DEUX POIDS, DEUX MESURES
DEPENDING ON THE REGION

In the 1980s, Germany's Thyssen Industrie AG called on the federal government asking to establish a manufacturing plant in Bear Head, Cape Breton. Thyssen wanted to set up a heavy industrial manufacturing plant in eastern Nova Scotia to produce military vehicles and a range of environmental protection products.

What Thyssen asked of the government was a sole-sourced start-up order from the Department of National Defence (DND) to design and build 250 Light Armoured Vehicles (LAVs) from the department's 1,600 LAV requirements. The Atlantic Canada Opportunities Agency (ACOA) gave the proposal a strong endorsement.[65]

The project went nowhere beyond an understanding in principle between ACOA and the firm. The proposal soon ran into stiff opposition from Ontario ministers in the federal Cabinet, senior public servants in Ottawa, and the Ontario-based defence manufacturing industries. The Toronto Star reported that the proposal "sparked a split within Mulroney's Cabinet, between ministers from Atlantic

Canada – the proposed site of the Bear Head plant – and the manufacturing heartland of Ontario."[66] Whenever that happens, the Atlantic region is no match against Ontario's political weight in the House of Commons or in Cabinet. The Senate, meanwhile, was relegated to the sidelines and it had nothing to say or contribute on the issue.

Senior public servants in the PCO, the Industry Department, and Foreign Affairs teamed up to oppose the project. Industry officials feared that it would "undermine existing domestic manufacturer General Motors, located in southern Ontario." PCO and Foreign Affairs officials argued that the proposal "could jeopardize Canadian foreign policy by selling military vehicles to volatile areas such as the Middle East." Robert Fowler, who was then a senior PCO official, explained, "at bottom this is a moral choice, a point of principle, a decision not to build a stall in the Middle East arms bazaar."[67] The project never advanced beyond the discussion stage in Ottawa.

Now, fast-forward to 2015. Somehow, moral choices and points of principle are thrown out the window. The Government of Canada agreed to a multibillion-dollar deal to sell "made-in-Canada light-armoured vehicles" to Saudi Arabia. The deal was approved by the federal government's Canadian Commercial Corporation in support of General Dynamics Land Systems Canada, based in London, Ontario. The government has refused to make public the requirements of the deal, insisting that it needs to protect the "commercial confidentiality" of the firm.[68] The federal government refused "to divulge how it was justifying this massive sale to Saudi Arabia under Ottawa's strict export control regime" given that "rules oblige Ottawa to examine whether arms shipments would further endanger the civilian population in countries with poor human-rights records."[69] Departmental emails revealed that the Department of Foreign Affairs issued no red flags over the proposed deal and that "General Dynamics has little to fear concerning official approval of its export permits." Steven Chase for the *Globe and Mail* explained: "Selling General Dynamics light armoured vehicles to the Saudi government will help sustain more than 3,000 jobs in Canada, including many in London, Ont., where the factory is located. There are 10 federal ridings in the London region, many of them held by Conservatives, and the Tories are eager to retain this foothold in the October election."[70]

The newly elected Justin Trudeau government had an opportunity to cancel the contract shortly after coming to power. Global Affairs Canada has a responsibility to audit requests to export military goods to countries "whose governments have a persistent record of serious violations of the human rights of their citizens."[71] Stéphane Dion, the responsible minister, declared that "the contract is not something that we will revisit."[72] Political and business leaders in London, Ontario, jumped to the defence of the contract to Saudi Arabia, insisting that it was "a pivotal component of the region's effort to become a major hub for defence-industry manufacturing."[73] No federal minister and no senior federal public servant spoke about "a moral choice" or building a "stall in the Middle East arms bazaar." That argument, it seems, does not apply to all regions.

Controversy over the Saudi arms deal negotiated previously by the Harper government continued to dog the Justin Trudeau government for months. The United Nations released a report documenting human rights violations by Saudi Arabia.[74] The Foreign Affairs minister, Stéphane Dion, described Saudi Arabia's human rights record as "terrible."[75] No matter, the government announced that the contract "will be exempt from the global arms deal" – a standard practice for countries that sign the treaty – and stood firm behind the Saudi contract and the arms deal.[76] As noted above, Steven Chase explained why: "The $15 billion deal will keep 3,000 Canadians employed for 14 years – many of them in Southwestern Ontario."[77] The Globe and Mail later argued in an editorial that cancelling the contract "would be a futile gesture because another country would simply supply the combat vehicles."[78]

Trudeau changed his mind after the murder of journalist Jamal Khashoggi at the hands of Saudi Arabia officials. Trudeau reported that he was exploring ways to stop arms exports to Saudi Arabia. He added, however, that the government would pursue other buyers for the Light Armoured Vehicles or "purchase them outright for the Canadian military."[79]

A former senior ACOA official explains what amounts to regional bias: "The lack of support for the Bear Head plant has everything to do with regional stereotyping and the Ottawa mindset. When the Ottawa system looks to Atlantic Canada, it looks to the fishery, tourism and the region's reliance on transfer payments. The more sexy stuff from the IT sector and manufacturing belongs to Central Canada. We see the bias but they don't."[80] His point is that regions outside of Ontario-Quebec have to cope not only with market forces, like all regions, but also powerful political and bureaucratic forces that favour the heavily populated regions. Atlantic and

Western Canada have to pull against gravity when promoting their economic interests.

This speaks to *deux poids, deux mesures* and, once again, to the inability of our national political institutions to manage regional circumstances. If anyone needed another example where provincial premiers can never play the role that the Senate ought to be playing, one need look no further than Ottawa's decision to award the CF-18 maintenance contract to a Montreal-based firm, even if Winnipeg-based Bristol won the bid. The head of Bristol told then Manitoba premier Howard Pawley, "If this is the way Canada wishes to do business, we will avoid smaller provinces; they have too little political clout. It's better for us to choose provinces like Quebec or Ontario, they can pull the political strings."[81] Western and Atlantic Canadians understand both the issue and history but less so, it seems, central Canadians.

Negotiations leading up to trade agreements demonstrate that Canada is home to different regional economies. Western, central Canadian, and Atlantic premiers produced "duelling letters" to press federal delegates negotiating a Trans-Pacific Partnership agreement to promote their regions' interest.[82] Canadian negotiators had to contend with sharp regional tensions between Western and central Canadians, and Maritimers in their attempt to negotiate a softwood trade deal with the United States in 2016–17.[83]

Canadian economic history is littered with federal government decisions that favoured Ontario and Quebec. The building and rebuilding of canals was one of two major infrastructure investments made in the years that followed Confederation. A deal was struck to work on canals in Canada West, Canada East, and the Maritimes. An 1870 Royal Commission on canals established three lists of canals to be built – first, second, third, and fourth classes. All the canals in Ontario and Quebec that made the first list were built. The canals in the Canadas that were built or rebuilt include, among others, a third Welland Canal, the Carillon Canal, and a costly upgrade of the Ottawa River canal system. The one canal from the Maritimes that made the first list was never built – the Chignecto Canal.[84]

Canada's National Policy (introduced in 1878) favoured Ontario and Quebec at the expense of Western and Atlantic Canada, while Canada's National Energy Program (early 1980s) favoured Ontario and Quebec at the expense of Western Canada. Canada's War Efforts in the Second World War brought economic prosperity to Ontario and Quebec, while it had modest impact on the other regions. Even navy ships were built in Central Canada against the advice of British and American military personnel.[85] The state-sponsored building of the St Lawrence Seaway had a negative impact on the port of Halifax. The decision to award the CF-18 maintenance contract to a Montreal firm, although a Winnipeg firm had the lowest bid; and decisions to award sole-source contracts to the Davie shipyard in Quebec City while Maritime and British Columbia shipyards always won contracts in a competitive process; the decision to support contracts to build Light Armoured Vehicles in London (Ontario) after saying no to Thyssen wishing to build similar vehicles in Nova Scotia; and the list goes on. I have, over the years, raised the issue with senior government officials in Ottawa and leading "national" journalists and columnists. The answers are equally dismissive: "it is what it is," "well, what is done is done," "there is no merit in dwelling on the past," and one that speaks to a misunderstanding of what federalism is about, "most Canadians live in Ontario and Quebec."

Deux poids, deux mesures extends even to the construction of bridges. When Prince Edward Island joined Confederation in 1873, the Government of Canada accepted responsibility for assuming the costs of "continuous communication" for mail and passengers between the Island and Canada. Ottawa insisted that Prince Edward Island agree to a constitutional amendment prior to the construction of a fixed link to allow a toll to help pay for the $1.3 billion construction of the Confederation Bridge. However, the federal government decided not to impose a toll to help pay for the construction of a new $5 billion Champlain Bridge in Montreal. Justin Trudeau explained: "The Champlain Bridge is a replacement bridge. There's an existing bridge that doesn't have a toll on it." Trudeau neglected to mention that the Champlain Bridge had a toll until 1990.[86]

REVISITING THE *STORY OF US*

CBC felt the need to issue an apology soon after it aired its *Story of Us*, the ten-part series to celebrate Canada's 150th anniversary. Konrad Yakabuski explains why: "The story of Canada is that there is no us in this country, but many of them. Most Canadians outside of Ottawa and Toronto see nothing wrong with that. It is what it is."[87] Regional identities are strong and regional economic circumstances widely different, making "regionalism an inescapable part of society, economy and politics in Canada."[88]

In the closing days of 2017, journalists began asking why Canada's 150 anniversary was a "bust." Charlotte Gray provides an answer: "Canada 150 commemorated an event – the passage of the BNA Act, which established Confederation in 1867 – that for vast numbers of Canadians was either irrelevant or, more seriously, damaging. The attempt to have a coast-to-coast carnival was doomed from the start."[89]

Regionalism exists in all things Canadian, except in national political institutions. Preston Manning pinpointed the problem when he asked, "How will western interests be effectively represented in a one-house Parliament where Quebec and Ontario have an absolute majority of seats?"[90] At the time of Confederation, Macdonald, Brown, and Cartier only saw the need to offset Ontario's rep by pop dominance by offering equality between Ontario and Quebec in the Senate. It reiterates the point that Confederation was a treaty between *deux nations,* or between Ontario and Quebec.

One of Canada's leading historians, J.M.S. Careless, wrote prophetically fifty years ago that "the experience of regionalism remains prominent and distinctive in Canadian history, time has tended less to erode it than to develop it."[91] More recently, David Herle maintains that "regional identity continues to be one of the most important prisms through which people see government policy and political behaviour." He adds that "it is important to understand how people in different regions view the same things differently." More revealing, he explains,

> In the 2004 and 2006 election campaigns, the Liberal Party was competing in at least five different campaigns across the country, with different primary opponents and different issues in each. We ran specially tailored advertising in almost every province. It is still the case that outside Ontario, the federal government is often seen as an outside force that does not have that region's best interests at heart. It means that everything the government does has to pass through a barrier of cynicism. This puts a special onus on the government to find ways to communicate what it is doing, and to do so in a way and a language that makes sense to people in that region.[92]

It is one thing to run five different regional campaigns but quite another to tailor federal government policies to accommodate five regional socioeconomic circumstances. In politics, it is important to work from five different regional perspectives. The same does not apply, however, when it come to the federal government's policy and decision-making processes.

Premiers from the four Western and the four Atlantic provinces and from different political parties have, time and again, charged that Ottawa demonstrates "favouritism toward central Canada."[93] Quebec premiers insist that their province holds a special status in the federation and can point to the pact struck in 1867 to protect its distinct identity. Given its minority situation in North America, it has little interest in promoting or even accommodating other regional considerations. It employs its political clout in Ottawa and its geographical location to promote Quebec's political and economic interest.

The point is worth underlining that Canada's national political institutions were designed for another country lacking the integrative capacity to accommodate marked regional diversity.[94] The Westminster parliamentary model, built around strict party discipline, "greatly weakens the federal Parliament as an arena of accommodation for regional differences" and thus unable to "integrate the country."[95] One political scientist took stock and concluded Canada is facing not a "crisis of language, culture, or even economy, but a political crisis – a crisis of political communities and their institutions."[96]

LOOKING BACK

Regional interests and regional stereotypes define Canada. All things Canadian are regional, except the working of our national political institutions. Consider the following: political power in Canada is still decided by rep by pop much like it was in 1867, no structural change here. The Supreme Court has been playing a much larger role since the Charter of Rights and Freedoms – the province of Quebec is guaranteed three of the nine seats. The four Atlantic provinces have been home to one seat, though Prime Minister Justin Trudeau mused about taking it away a few years ago. The four Western provinces have two seats. Ontario has three. The National Capital Commission is located smack in the middle of Ontario and Quebec. It is home to the federal government's political power, bureaucratic power and influence, and to Canada's mainstream media.

Canada has been immunized against structural change because the *deux nations* treaty struck in 1867 has not allowed it. Senior politicians and senior public servants operate in institutions designed for a unitary state. They do not see – and they have no interest in seeing – that everything Canadian is regional. It is telling that John Diefenbaker, Robert Stanfield, Joe Clark, Preston Manning, and Stephen Harper were viewed in Central Canada as regional politicians, while Pearson, Trudeau, *père et fils*, Brian Mulroney, and Jean Chrétien were not. Regional politicians, the argument goes, are not very skilful at building "coalitions" and at "nation building."[97]

Politicians on the hustings recognize Canada's regional diversity, as Paul Martin did when he observed, as mentioned earlier in the chapter, that "we cannot allow national issues in British Columbia to be relegated to the sidelines as regional issues." Royal commissions from the Rowell-Sirois to national task forces do, too. The 1977 Task Force on Canadian Unity, the Pépin-Robarts Task Force, made the case that Canada was defined by regional variations in political behaviour, uneven economic development, and geographical barriers that separate regions, which have led to tenuous connections between regions.[98]

Strong regional narratives exist on campaign trails and in Royal Commissions, but much less so in Ottawa's political and bureaucratic circles where policies are shaped and decisions struck. There, the *deux nations* treaty still rules. Ontario's regionalism, meanwhile, is largely invisible, passing itself as Canadian nationalism.[99] All political voices in Quebec have been strongly opposed to a structural reform of the Senate – elected rather than appointed – because such a development would violate the *deux nations* treaty.

Western and Atlantic Canadians have, in the past, expressed their regionalism through political movements – for example, the Reform Party and the Maritime Rights Movement. These had more to do with space or territory than a political ideology. They speak to the belief that these regions are separated from the country's political process. They identify with the plight of colonies of old in the "sense that power over them resides and is wielded elsewhere."[100]

Canadian federalism has been turned into a series of side deals because its national institutions have not been able to address the reality that everything Canadian is regional. Structural deficiencies have given rise to buying peace, at least temporarily, by adjusting federal transfers to the provinces to address political pressures of the moment. Donald V. Smiley sums up the issue well when he writes: "The institutions of the central government have ceased to be an adequate outlet for interests that are territorially demarcated. This then confers upon the provinces the almost exclusive franchise to be vehicles for the representation of such interests."[101] Provincial premiers have voice but little else. They are non-players in Ottawa's internal policy and decision-making processes.

All things Canadian are regional. Different regional economic circumstances cry out for policies to acknowledge these differences rather than national policies that apply to all regions, whether they fit or not. Some regions, notably Southern Ontario, British Columbia's lower mainland, and southern Quebec, required important investments in public infrastructure. The federal government unveiled a national $180 billion plus infrastructure program in 2016.[102] It is a "national" effort, even though it is not at all clear that the Maritime provinces required new investment in infrastructure. They are struggling to maintain existing infrastructure while their population growth remains stagnant and aging. The region's economic circumstances require different investments better suited to their economic circumstances. As noted, the region needs more people not more infrastructure. However, Canada's national political institutions, including the executive, are not able to view matters from a regional perspective or see that Toronto and other major urban centres require infrastructure investments, but communities in the smaller provinces require different policy prescriptions.

Regional tensions are only getting worse. Prime Minister Justin Trudeau, recently abolished regional ministers. In addition, Trudeau has all the regional economic development agencies (i.e., ACOA, WD, DEDNOR, CED, CanNor, FedDev Ontario) reporting to one minister from the Greater Toronto Area (GTA) responsible for Innovation, Science and Economic Development, formerly known as Industry Canada. One member of Parliament identified the problem succinctly: "Instead of being able to develop programs that would be customized for the needs of the regions, more and more of those agencies are being asked to implement centralized decisions made by the department."[103] Many, even non-Canadians, can see that Canada needs to shape policies to fit regional economic circumstances. Christine Lagarde, the head of the International Monetary Fund (IMF), in a recent visit to Ottawa told Prime Minister Trudeau that Canada should tackle Canada's housing market from a regional perspective because "Canada's housing market has strong regional differences."[104]

A leading Canadian journalist remarked: "It seems to be impossible to conduct national politics in Canada without pitting one region of the country against the other."[105] This has been true virtually from the first day Canada was constituted. It makes the case that Canada's democratic deficit, at least from a comparative perspective, is tied to the inability of the country's national institutions to promote regional equality. Evidence of this deficit can be found in the constitution, in the executive, and in the bureaucracy.

The inability of our institutions to cope with regional circumstances is not the whole story. Our national political and administrative institutions are facing powerful new forces that are at play in other Anglo-American democracies. The next sections explore these issues and their implications for Canada.

PART TWO

The Changing Face
of Canadian Democracy

Getting Elected:
The Deinstitutionalization of Political Parties

Politicians aspiring to be elected to Parliament must carefully navigate a number of steps. They must enjoy a solid profile in the community, should be a member in good standing of a major political party, and should be prepared to make sacrifices emotionally and financially. A candidate needs to commit considerable time and effort to the task and be subject to developments over which they have little control. The moment they become candidates for Parliament, they are subjected to intense public scrutiny, including a review of bad deeds, even those that may be long past. The Internet and Google mean that yesterday's news is never old news. In short, running for Parliament is now only for the brave.

There are disincentives for those contemplating running for Parliament. Leaving aside former prime ministers and former ministers of finance or industry, politicians are finding it increasingly difficult to carve out a post-political career. Raymond Garneau, a former senior provincial and federal politician, reports that many young professionals are avoiding politics, reluctant to even join a political party, for fear of losing contracts or employment opportunities.[1] Former senior politicians have told me that they did not apply for a Senate appointment, knowing that ex-politicians, no matter their party affiliation, stood little chance of securing an appointment. Politicians and public servants now have to contend with a demanding policy on conflict of interest and post-employment guidelines.[2]

Rem C. Westland provides a detailed account of his attempt to win the Ottawa-Vanier constituency for the Conservative Party in the 2011 federal election. His account gives important insights for those wishing to serve as a member of Parliament. Though he urges his readers to run for Parliament, his experience hardly encourages them to do so.[3] Westland draws a sharp distinction between a "novice" and a career politician, and between a safe seat and a competitive one. Novice politicians typically "run for the people," and career politicians "run for the party."[4] If you are a novice politician not running in a safe seat, "you are almost certain to be returning to the world from which you came."

Westland may have been somewhat of a novice to partisan politics but not to government or to the public policy process. He had been a sessional lecturer in political theory at Carleton University, an executive assistant to a federal Cabinet minister, a federal public servant for twenty-two years reaching the rank of assistant deputy minister in a line department, and then a senior executive in a mid-sized Ottawa-based consulting firm.

He writes that an unsuccessful politician soon comes face to face with the "collective interest, which immediately follows the reporting of election results but also the inspiration to get back to work. There is a whole lot of money for a novice to recover."[5] When he told family and friends that he was thinking about running for Parliament, he met a chorus of "why the heck are you doing it." From family members he heard, "Please don't do this to us," and from work colleagues, "Take a leave of absence and good luck." Westland points out that once you are a candidate, your partisanship becomes forever stamped on your forehead. You become a "Conservative," a "Liberal," or a "New Democratic Party" for the rest of your life, at least in the eyes of the public. Once back in the private sector, and if your firm loses a contract, you may well hear, "We lost because of your political stripes."[6]

Westland's experience on the campaign trail is revealing. He did the required door to door campaigning, worked with local party members, and did his part in raising money. But when it came to substantive issues, he notes that "party leaders and their staffs" ran the show. He had no say. They did not even like to see him participate in public debates, and he reports that "party officials expect that candidates will do exactly what the party directs."[7]

Notwithstanding the challenges and expense in running for Parliament, Westland was only one of 1,587 candidates running for 308 seats in the 2011 general election, representing 18 political parties. The lure of sitting in Parliament has remained strong. There were 1,792 candidates for 338 seats representing 23 political parties in the 2015 general election.[8]

There are important differences for aspiring politicians running in a safe seat, in a swing seat, or in a constituency where the party candidate has little chance of winning. As Westland points out, paths are quite different for career and novice politicians seeking a party's nomination. For example, career politicians already enjoy a strong media profile, the support of influential individuals in the party and community, and local party members as well as party headquarters.[9]

Alison Loat and Michael MacMillan heard a great deal of criticism over the nomination processes from the eighty exit interviews they conducted with former MPs. They report that the criticism came from those who won, and that we can only imagine what those who lost have to say. They conclude: "The nomination process is a manifestation of the negative perceptions that people tend to have of politics – an opaque, manipulative and even cruel game that turns both citizens and candidates away from the democratic process. The process can be confusing, mysterious and inconsistent. As many Canadians suspect, the inner workings are subject to manipulation by riding associates and the national leadership of a party."[10]

Brent Rathgeber, a former member of Parliament, confirms this view and adds that the ability to win a nomination often rests on a candidate's ability to "sell $10 party memberships," at least when party leaders and their senior advisers have no interest in intervening. Rathgeber echoes Westland when he writes that the "party brass" is not interested in recruiting "critical thinkers," who are able to produce "informed discussion." Rather, it looks for "women, especially telegenic ones, and visible minorities" and especially for candidates who know how to toe the party line.[11] He insists that the latter attribute is highly valued by the party brass.

A CANDIDATE IS WORTH 5 PERCENT

There is a theme that runs through the views of many former MPs and defeated candidates who go on to write about their experience: they are not the key to winning. Westland writes: "'Remember,' I would be told, 'your chance of being elected in this riding has very little to do with who you are.' By now, I was reading in the literature on electoral politics and already knew that the results obtained by a candidate in a federal or provincial election these days are explained over 95% by central party messaging and under 5% by the candidate. The influence from the centre can even be as much as 100%."[12] Rathgeber comes to the same conclusion. Students of politics have also come to the same conclusion.[13] Yet, anyone wishing to become a member of Parliament needs to join a political party and seek the party's nomination. Independent MPs have been rare in Canada's Parliament.

We now have personality and leader-centric election campaigns. For instance, Stephen Harper defined the Conservative Party much more than the party defined him. The same can be said for Justin Trudeau and the 2015 election campaign. Elisabeth Gidengil and André Blais point to several reasons why party leaders have become "the superstars of Canadian politics."[14] Among these reasons are the weakening of partisan ties among Canadians; televised debates between party leaders; the absence of well-defined political ideologies, leaving it to party leaders and their advisers to define a campaign strategy to hold a loyal core of supporters; and the need to attract as many floating voters as possible.[15]

Canadian political parties do not have as clear and as distinctive ideologies as their counterparts in Britain, Australia, or New Zealand.[16] Social or economic class have historically held little impact on Canadian politics or voting behaviour. And party leaders in Canada have difficulty capturing the voters' attention by appealing to a political ideology.[17]

Canadian political scientists have long debated the merit of the ideological and brokerage models to explain the behaviour of political parties. A number of political scientists have found, at best, modest evidence of political ideology in shaping the views of political parties.[18] Janine Brodie and Jane Jenson argue that political parties adopt principled positions only occasionally and that "these fragile constructions are easily reversed when conditions change."[19] I leave the last word to Richard Johnston, arguably the leading authority in Canada on the matter: "The brokerage image of Canadian parties does seem to be the dominant one. Indeed, it has been characterized as the textbook theory of the party system."[20] Brokerage politics is unique to Canada, as it refers to the ability of a political party to broker regional divides.[21] It speaks to Canada's democratic deficit as well.

Johnston opens his highly acclaimed book, *The Canadian Party System*, with two telling sentences: "The Canadian party system is unruly yet inscrutable ... [I]t defies the most powerful generalization in empirical political theory."[22] He looks to history, among other factors, to make sense of Canada's party system. He ties the Liberal Party's success to its links to Quebec, and the rise of new or "insurgent" political parties to geography. He writes that new parties have, at different points in Canada's history, entered the political system but old ones do not die.

David Herle, a leading Canadian pollster and political adviser, explained that the Liberals ran at least five different campaigns in the 2004 and 2006 general elections, so that the campaigns made sense in the regions. Political ideology has to take a back seat in this political environment.[23] William Cross maintains that the rise of regional parties, notably the Reform/Canadian Alliance and the Bloc Québécois had little to do with ideology. They were able to find their roots in defining and articulating "regional interest."[24]

Linguistic and regional cleavages, not ideology or economic class, continue to dominate Canadian politics. Much like Macdonald and Cartier sought to do over 150 years ago, political leaders continue to try as best they can to define and manage an approach to gain political support in Quebec without losing support elsewhere, particularly in Ontario where federal elections are won or lost. This is a delicate undertaking fraught with pitfalls and best left to the party leader and close associates.[25]

Herle has advice for aspiring MPs: "Parties don't run on what their members think and can't if they want to be successful. They run on what will get them the most votes. It is a strategic marketing exercise rather than a genuine contest of ideas."[26] Political ideology and the clash of ideas are no match for strategic marketing, political branding, and managing the election campaigns at the region, notably in regions with the most voters.

Managing regional cleavages is much more difficult today than when Macdonald was prime minister. Leaving aside Quebec, Macdonald essentially denied regionalism as a political force. He and Cartier struck a deal to accommodate Quebec's interest in national institutions, from a guaranteed number of seats in Parliament to an appointed Senate, based on regional rather than provincial representations and later on a guaranteed number of judges in the Supreme Court. As noted, the West was not present at the Charlottetown and Quebec conferences, and as we have seen, the smaller Maritime colonies were regarded by Macdonald and Cartier as members of the new country that were conveniently brought in to break the impasse between Canada West and East. It is not an exaggeration to write that Macdonald, Cartier, the Colonial Office decided to annex New Brunswick and Nova Scotia to make their Canada work.[27]

The regional factor is still more difficult to manage today than in the era of limited government. Premiers and provincial governments play a much larger role and Western Canada now has a voice that gains in importance every time the electoral map changes. However, the regional factor serves to strengthen the hand of party leaders and their advisers because political parties lack the capacity to "reconcile inside themselves regional interests from across the whole country."[28] Party leaders and their advisers consider regional issues to be so politically explosive that they are best left in their capable hands to sort out. They know how to reconcile issues by placing a premium on not annoying voting-rich regions.

One misstep by a candidate in one region can have a highly negative impact in another region that dominates the news cycle for several days. Andrew Perez writes that national political campaigns in Canada can "more aptly be described as a set of regional elections; in each region, vastly different dynamics – that are bound to influence the parties' electoral strategies and communication approaches – are at play."[29] Once elections are over, however, the regional factor often takes a back seat to matters "national."

And yet, Canada's regional factor has dogged political parties since 1867. It is a rare occurrence when a party is able to win a strong majority and at least one seat in all provinces. Trudeau *père* did it in 1968 and Trudeau *fils* in 2015. Trudeau *père*, however, only won three seats in the three Prairie provinces in the 1972 election. Harper won a majority mandate in 2011 but did not get much traction in Quebec or any of the four Atlantic provinces. It was under Mulroney's watch that the Western-based Reform Party and the Bloc Québécois were born. The regional factor can be contained in Ottawa's political and bureaucratic world but much less on the political hustings.

Pollsters have become both key players in campaigns and close advisers to party leaders. They are there, according to Bob Rae, able to "slice, dice, dissect and divide the electorate to strengthen the hand of the party leader to win the election."[30] Kenneth Carty, William Cross, and Lisa Young make the case that it is not possible to overstate the importance of party pollsters: "Party pollsters are assuming an increasingly important position among the parties' wartime personnel. As the parties attempt to target specific groups of voters with tailored measures, the pollsters play a key role in identifying the regions of the country [and groups] where the party should concentrate its resources."[31] Party pollsters, party leaders and their close advisers are better at managing regional issues in mapping out political strategies than local candidates who may wish to respond to the pressure of their electors.

Where does this leave the MP or aspiring MP? David Herle, veteran pollster for the Liberal Party, has an answer: "One criticism of the use of polling in government comes from those who say it has diminished the role of the member of Parliament. I think that it is a fair comment ... [N]o person could possibly replicate through personal consultations the reliable information polling provides ... [M]y experience has been that many MPs either have no idea what people in their riding think or want, or they know but have no interest in reflecting it, which makes taking their advice on public opinion a dubious proposition."[32] It leads to the question, Why have MPs at all, if they have no idea what people in their constituencies believe or have no interest in reflecting it?

Pollsters will invariably point to Ontario, Quebec, and increasingly Western Canada to win power. There is an old saying, you win the election in Ontario and a majority in Quebec. David Herle maintains that "regional identity continues to be one of the most important prisms through which people see government policy and political behaviour. This may seem like an obvious thing to say because it has been the case for so long."[33] The prism has to be managed to win power in Canada, and its importance to winning is such that it is best left to party leaders and their immediate advisers. National political institutions, however, have little capacity to manage the prism once a government is elected. It is one of the legacies that the Fathers of Confederation left to Canada, a prism that focuses on Ontario and Quebec and that neither province will let go.

IT'S ONLY ABOUT WINNING

One of the most important roles of political parties in a healthy democracy is to educate citizens.[34] They are there or should be there to outline the socio-economic challenges confronting the nation and prescribe policy solutions for citizens to ponder. In theory, political parties win elections based on their electoral platforms. They make Parliament work by imposing discipline and making responsible government work by shedding light on who decided what, how, and when. Parties are the link between people and power and, as Paul

Pross argues, they make Parliament "the pre-eminent legitimating institution."[35]

I would not suggest that political parties had a golden age when they and their rank and file members were particularly adroit at shaping policies that later became government policies. They continue to be largely empty vessels on policy. There was a time, however, when party leaders and their close advisers did not dominate politics and policy-making to the extent they do today. At a minimum, they had to give a hearing to powerful regional party stalwarts from C.D. Howe, James Gardner, and Marc Lalonde, to Allan J. MacEachen, among many others.[36]

Powerful regional ministers, however, are personalities of the past in Canadian politics. They have been replaced by pollsters and a new class of courtiers working with the party leaders. Party leaders have their favourite pollsters in court, and they no longer have to rely on local candidates to know where voters stand on any given issue. In addition, prime ministers no longer have to rely on regional ministers to know how a region views a proposed government measure. It is a great deal easier to deal with a favourite pollster and a courtier than with a regional minister. Public opinion surveys are more reliable, more objective, more to the point, less demanding, and a much easier to address than ministers and party candidates. Prime Minister Trudeau decided, when he came to power, simply to do away with regional ministers.[37] He did away with the concept because he could not make it work in Ontario and Quebec. Both provinces are home to several senior ministers, and it is difficult to pick one over another.[38] For example, how can the minister of finance be junior to the regional minister when Ontario is the traditional home for ministers of finance?

Today political parties have become little more than election-day organizations, fundraising machines, and a convenient venue to select candidates to help them win elections. William Cross sums it up well when he observes: "Canada's political parties are not effective vehicles for policy study and development. They neither offer voters meaningful opportunity for involvement in the policy-making process nor do they regularly generate policy alternatives for consideration and examination by those in elected office of in the senior bureaucracy."[39] Cross adds that the inability of party members to shape policies may well explain the sharp drop in party memberships and the growing attractiveness of interest groups for those

Canadians interested in influencing public policy.[40] Party members on the ground are to concern themselves only with local personnel matters and managing the local ground wars of election campaigns.[41]

IT'S ABOUT BRANDING

Party leaders, their close advisers, and their favourite pollsters are quite happy to "play the politics of image and strategic vagueness, [and to] take office with little sense of direction."[42] It is all about winning elections, and branding has come to matter greatly, both in election campaigns and in governing. The goal is to ensure that Canadians perceive the party leader in a positive light. The approach has everything to do with impressions, images, reputations, and less to do with tangible policy issues or substance.[43]

Political scientists are showing a growing interest in branding and marketing in Canadian politics. Their verdict for democracy is not positive. Alex Marland remarks that "branding threatens idealized notions of democratic government and party politics. It harmonizes and dumbs down. It requires strict message control and image management. Above all, public sector branding contributes to the centralization of decision making within the prime minister's inner circle."[44] Leaders of political parties become the brand to promote rather than the party itself. We have the Trudeau and the Harper brands in Canada and the Bush, Clinton, and Trump brands in the United States.

Once in power, the brand continues to be associated with the party leader so that it becomes the Chrétien, Harper, or Trudeau governments. And, when in power, prime ministers do not hesitate to leverage public resources, communications specialists who are career public servants, and information subsidies to promote their brand.[45] For branding purposes, the prime minister, the party, and the government now come as one.

Branding and marketing are tied to the rise of permanent election campaigns. Permanent election campaigns speak to all political parties and to an unrelenting approach to politics and governing. They "describe a mindset that efforts to win the next election begin immediately after election day. [Permanent election campaigns are] fuelled by a desire to achieve positive media coverage that treats all manner of political issues as mini-contests with winners and losers. Public opinion polls, by-elections, legislative votes, policy announcements

– they all must be won as though the outcome of the next election is at stake."[46]

The process of branding, de-branding, or attempts to brand opposition parties and their leaders is ongoing. Branding involves all means of communications tied to an underlying message. If the party is in power, then branding will access communication tools available to government, notably logos, colour schemes, and visual backdrops. Party branding is tied at the hip to party leaders. De-branding involves political parties employing communication tools to discredit other parties by taking aim at their leaders often through negative advertisements.[47] The Harper Conservatives successfully employed this strategy to brand Stéphane Dion as weak and Michael Ignatieff as "just visiting" Canada.

Governments now govern with an eye constantly on the politics of every issue and every development. In some instances, the government has even put in place "shadow MPs" in some "winnable" constituencies, ready to fight the next election. The government employs former candidates on contract to keep an eye on the constituency and to act as a "liaison between Ottawa and their communities."[48] This tactic gives the individual a leg up in winning the party's nomination and in winning the next election.

The twenty-four-hour news cycle and social media have given impetus to permanent election campaigns, and more is said about this later. Sitting MPs or aspiring MPs ignore these and other developments tied to permanent elections at their peril. Because of the insatiable appetite for political news to feed the twenty-four-hour news cycle, they have to be on a constant election footing. In short, the government will always try to brand its activities in a positive light while other parties will try to cast the government in a negative light. It is a never-ending process. Aspiring MPs in election campaigns know – or should know – their leaders' brand, and if they wish to have the support of the party's key strategists they need to campaign respecting the brand.

Party leaders and their courtiers will carefully select surrogates to speak on their behalf before television audiences to feed cable news programs. One is hard-pressed to find just one instance when a surrogate is even mildly critical of their party leader. The sole purpose is to spin every issue, every development, to cast the party leader in a positive light and the opposition parties in a negative one. Facts and evidence-based arguments do not feature much in their work. If facts do not work in your leader's favour, you can always try "alternate facts," as Donald Trump's adviser Kellyanne Conway did in his inaugural days.[49]

David McLaughlin, a former Conservative chief of staff and campaign strategist, explains: "Faithful to the partisan glue binding them to their parties, our political class is doing everything possible to diminish, demean, and destroy the precious commodity they actually hold in common: their own political integrity. In their relentless attacks on everything and everyone on the opposite political divide, they continue to devalue the basic political currency – trust – essential between electors and elected in a democracy. We, the voters, are the losers."[50] Party leaders and their courtiers are there to ensure that partisan politics now run on their tracks. Again, local party candidates are there to defend their party leader's brand, not to create a separate one. The role of party leaders and their closest advisers, permanent election campaigning and, branding are key to understanding those seeking election or re-election. Those in government will employ every available tool to brand the prime minister in a positive light. Those in opposition will offer "new ideas" for a "new day" without outlining in any detail what these new ideas are. The goal to win or retain power dominates all.

WHY JOIN A PARTY?

Political parties in Canada face a daunting challenge in pursuing their primary role in a representative democracy to reflect and articulate society's basic divisions whether social, economic, ethnic, or geographic, given that Canada has been defined time and again as a "country of regions imperfectly balanced, unequally resourced and unevenly committed."[51] William Cross points to the challenge and the need to bridge "regional and linguistic cleavages."[52] Alan Cairns asserts that political parties have not been adroit at managing regional tensions; they do not generate "compromises between representation of competing territorial interests. The capacity to bargain and block is based vastly on the size of the electorates behind the region, making it difficult, if not impossible, for the smaller regions to be heard."[53]

Representative democracy is not possible without political parties.[54] John Meisel observes that political parties "are among the relatively few genuinely national forces in Canada."[55] They perform five critical roles: they offer candidates for elected office; engage citizens in politics; facilitate communications between Parliament, government, and citizens; educate citizens on policy; and make Parliamentary government work.

So, how well are Canadian political parties performing in pursuing their five critical roles? Practitioners like Rem Westland, Brent Rathgeber, and those interviewed for the Samara research projects insist that there are different candidate-nominating processes. The Canadian Association of Former Parliamentarians reviewed the processes and concluded that "current practices are badly flawed and in need of substantive amendments in order to bring them into line with accepted democratic principles."[56]

Students of politics have come to the same conclusion. William Cross observes that a party's "central campaign's involvement is typically uneven, leaving the electorally poor boroughs on their own while closely scrutinizing, sometimes orchestrating, the nomination process in constituencies that are electorally important to the party."[57] Cross goes on to identify several characteristics of Canada's approach to candidate nomination. He writes about the high degree of regionalization of political parties that often reduce them to secondary importance – the choice of an MP is made during the nomination contest – the near-monopoly of candidates nominated by major parties elected to Parliament, and the limited ability of voters to select their preferred local representative in general elections.

Party leaders hold the power to decide who can run under their party's banner. The Liberal Party has a number of leader-centric rules on the selection of its candidates. Rule 1.2 gives the leaders "authority to designate a person to be a candidate in any election, without the need for the conduct of a meeting." Rule 9.3 gives the leader the authority "not to endorse any candidate."[58] The Conservative Party has similar rules. Rule 4.d gives authority to its National Candidate Selection Committee to "disallow a candidacy on such grounds as it sees fit."[59] Such rules are among the many signs that party leaders and their courtiers own the party, not the other way around.

Political parties fall short in their capacity or willingness to engage citizens in politics. A Public Policy Forum study sponsored by Elections Canada interviewed twenty-six leading practitioners. It concluded that political parties equate "democratic engagement for the act of casting a ballot." The study goes on to report that the vast majority of participants believe that political parties fall short – they are not the vehicles for bold new ideas, do not have strong roots in the community, do not empower members, have little identity beyond their leader, and do not lead on issues of the day.[60]

R. Kenneth Carty writes that the major Canadian political parties "were designed to obfuscate rather than articulate interests, blur rather than sharpen divisions." [61] The thinking is that Canadian society is so fragile, so fragmented that political parties have to be careful not to provoke one segment of society against another or, more importantly, one region against another. The same applies when asked to facilitate communications between Parliament, government, and citizens. Political parties have to tread carefully for fear of alienating important segments of Canadian society. A political misstep or a loosely worded policy position can kick-start the blame game in Parliament or the media. Again, best to leave this in the hands of the party leaders and their courtiers and pollsters.

Do political parties make Parliamentary government work? MPs – nearly all of them and nearly all the time – are elected as a member of a political party. A government can only stay in power if it enjoys the confidence of the House of Commons. In this sense, political parties serve an important role – making parliamentary government work.

Political parties in Canada have a special challenge in addressing Kenneth Carty's opening sentence in his book *Big Tent Politics*, "Canada's national politics is neither natural nor easy."[62] One political party – the Liberal Party – has emerged as "Canada's Natural Governing Party." It has been able to become Canada's dominant party by being "shapeless" and by offering "continual and shifting compromise."[63] The party has stood for everything and nothing but always focusing on managing forces that can tear the country apart. At times, it was the party of protectionism, at times it favoured free trade, at times it favoured bigger government (e.g., the Trudeau years 1968–83), while at still other times, it favoured smaller government and balanced budget (e.g., the Chrétien years 1993–97). Through it all, it has been able to somewhat assuage regional tensions while never losing sight of its home base (Ontario and Quebec). All Liberal Party leaders have had either Ontario or Quebec as their base and all but two were born in the two provinces – the other two, Alexander Mackenzie and John Turner, were born in Britain. I note that the Liberal Party is the only major party that has not been led by a woman.

In contrast, the Conservative – the Progressive Conservative – Party has had twenty leaders since Confederation. Two were born in Britain, eight in Ontario or Quebec, and ten either in Western or Atlantic Canada. Only the Liberals and Conservatives – Progressive Conservatives – have held power in Ottawa – the Liberal Party for 81 years and the Conservative Party 69 over the past 150 years, and some 43 years for the past 67 years (1950–2017). The Liberal Party has won 19 of the last 29 elections.[64]

How does one explain the success of the Liberal Party? As we saw earlier, Richard Johnston ties it to its standing in Quebec. Other Canadian political scientists have broken the evolution of partisan politics into distinct periods: a clientelistic period that lasted from 1867 to the end of the First World War, where voters traded their support for goods or services; a second period of brokerage politics from the 1920s to the 1950s; a third, the pan-Canadian system, starting in the early 1960s; and a fourth period that saw Canadian politics transformed from pan-Canadian to a regionally balkanized system.[65]

The pan-Canadian period squares with the growth of the welfare state, the post Rowell-Sirois period. Janine Brodie sums up the period well when she writes that the transfer payments "would simply help to underwrite some of the social costs of uneven development within certain political jurisdictions (for example, New Brunswick) while the economic relationships that promoted uneven development remained unchallenged."[66] Free trade agreements and a more competitive and integrated global economy are changing this dynamic.[67]

I recall attending a roundtable discussion in the months leading up to the Canada-US Free Trade Agreement. Tom Courchene supported the agreement but warned there was risk of a "maritimization" of the Ontario economy. His point: economically stronger United States regions would, in time, come to dominate the North American economy much like Ontario came to dominate the Canadian economy. Somehow, it does not hurt the national interest, however defined, to see the "maritimization" of the Maritimes, but it becomes a different story when Ontario may suffer the same fate. Space, it seems, matters when it is cast at the national level (here, read Ontario and Quebec), but less so at the regional level.

Regionalism explains, at least in part, why Maurice Duverger's theory on political parties has not taken root in Canada. Duverger maintained that countries like Canada with a first-past-the-post voting system are doomed to have two-party partisan politics.[68] The theory explains politics in the United States but not in Canada. Duverger argued that voters are unwilling to waste their votes on a third party, but willing to vote for a party that does not square completely with their views because it has a better chance of winning. In Canada, many have prepared "to waste their votes" to speak to their region's interest.

The Liberal Party has dominated Canadian politics with the Progressive Conservative – now Conservative – Party acting as a spare tire.[69] Canadians have looked to the spare tire whenever the Liberal government became either plagued with scandals or became "depoliticized" and "transformed into the electoral arm of the government of Canada ... and preoccupied with administrative issues."[70]

Liberal Party leaders from Laurier, Mackenzie King, St. Laurent, Pearson, and Chrétien to Trudeau *père* and *fils*, who governed Canada for over 80 years in the last 121 years, are products of the Macdonald-Cartier *deux nations* treaty. Laurier refused to promote minority rights of Catholics in Manitoba through legislation.[71] Laurier's focus was on Ontario-Quebec and how issues played out in these two provinces. Recall, too, that Laurier pressed Alberta and Saskatchewan to create two provinces rather than one, in part because of the fear that one large Western province bringing together Alberta, Saskatchewan, and the Northwest Territories would, in time, challenge Ontario's position in Confederation.

We know that Mackenzie King impressed "the business communities in Montreal and Toronto" with his "responsiveness to their concerns" and his "tariff protection for manufacturers in central Canada."[72] As is well known, Mackenzie King and C.D. Howe decided to concentrate Canada's war efforts for World War II in Ontario and Quebec. Thirty-two Crown corporations were established for the war effort, all in Ontario and Quebec. The Crown corporations represented a significant new source of investments, with the potential to generate a great deal of new economic activity. Indeed, they would provide the basis for future development in the manufacturing sector in the postwar years.[73] For example, wartime Crown corporations gave rise to aircraft manufacturers, synthetic rubber producers, and an advanced technology company called Research Enterprises Limited.

As noted, Ottawa situated the bulk of the war effort in Central Canada, even when military considerations suggested otherwise. After a visit to Canada in 1940, the British Admiralty Technical Mission concluded, "Political issues weigh heavily" in military decisions. They underlined the problems with building ships in yards cut off from the Atlantic Ocean for five months and questioned the need for vessels to make the long trip down the St Lawrence. American military advisers made the same point.[74] The first ten ships built for Britain barely escaped getting trapped in the St Lawrence in the winter freeze-up and "required substantial work in the Maritimes before they could risk an Atlantic crossing."[75] The British tried as best they could to convince Ottawa to make Halifax the logical naval headquarters for their Canadian convoys and as the repair centre for the larger vessels. They were not successful.[76] Mackenzie King and C.D. Howe, senior public servants located in Ottawa, understood the political importance of locating the bulk of activities in vote-rich Ontario and Quebec. They were free to do as they wished, and there was no Upper House in Parliament with the legitimacy to speak to the interest of the smaller provinces.

Pierre Trudeau looked to Ontario's and Quebec's interest when he launched his National Energy Program (NEP). He decided to overhaul his regional development efforts to focus more and more on Quebec in his fight against Quebec's secessionist movement. Jean Chrétien, meanwhile, focused the bulk of his economic development efforts in Ontario and Quebec. Chrétien, a career politician, understood better than anyone that the key to his success was Ontario and that there was nothing in national political institutions to inhibit him from focusing on vote-rich Ontario and Quebec. The Chrétien government suffered heavy losses in the 1997 general election in Western Canada (as expected) and in Atlantic Canada (not as expected). Chrétien won 101 out of 103 seats in Ontario, but only 9 out of 54 seats in the three Prairie provinces.

His government suffered heavy losses in Atlantic Canada, including two senior Cabinet ministers, Doug Young and David Dingwall. He even saw hand-picked candidate Dominic LeBlanc lose in his former temporary New Brunswick riding of Beauséjour. Chrétien's Liberal Party lost all eleven seats in Nova Scotia. Chrétien knew that Ontario, not Atlantic and Western Canada, would remain the key to a majority in the next election. As Atlantic provinces had turned away from his government, the best the region could expect from this seasoned politician was benign neglect, and that is precisely what it received. Chrétien would turn his back on the region, much like the region had turned its back on him.

In the post-program budgetary exercises of the late 1990s, budget speeches provided for new spending and new economic development measures. The focus was on the Ontario economy. The 1999 budget, for example, added $200 million to the Canada Foundation for Innovation; $75 million to the Natural Sciences and Engineering Research Council of Canada; $6 million for National Research Council Canada; $55 million for biotechnology R&D; $50 million for Networks of Centres of Excellence; $150 million for Technology Partnerships Canada; and $430 million for the Canadian Space Agency. There was very little here that would benefit Western or Atlantic Canada. The Technology Partnerships Canada program was viewed for what it was, a program designed for the economic circumstances of Ontario and Quebec, which always secured the bulk of the programs budget, while the Canadian Space Agency was seen as mostly benefitting Ottawa and Montreal.[77]

The 2000 federal budget held no greater promise for the Atlantic provinces. It established a $60 million Canadian Foundation for Climate and Atmospheric Sciences but located its head office in Ottawa; provided $46 million for national pollution enforcement and the Great Lakes Action Plan; and added $900 million to the Canadian Foundation for Innovation. It also gave the Montreal-based Business Development Bank of Canada an $80 million injection of new money to support its financing activities.[78] There was nothing in the country's national political institutions to shape policies and programs to favour regions that supported Chrétien politically and to penalize regions that did not.

Stephen Harper rode to power with strong support from his Western region and Ontario. Western Canada had long made the case that the "West wants in." As long ago as 1980, Roger Gibbins explained the essence of Western alienation. He wrote that it is "a political ideology of regional discontent rooted in the dissatisfaction of western Canadians with their relationship to and representation within the federal government."[79]

Stephen Harper's Conservative Party won 124 out of 308 seats in the 2006 general election. He won 48 out of 56 seats in the three Prairie provinces, and 40 out of 106 Ontario seats in the general election. Harper sought to address Western alienation and met with some success. He overhauled federal transfer payments, pegging them to a per capital basis which, as shown earlier, favoured his home province of Alberta. Among other things, he directed more federal infrastructure funds to Western Canada, strongly supported the energy sector, and did away with the Canadian Wheat Board monopoly.[80] John Ibbitson, a *Globe and Mail* columnist, wrote that Harper "brought the West into the heart of the federal government," suggesting that it had never been there before.[81]

Shortly after the Justin Trudeau government was elected to power in October 2015, a senior public servant with Global Affairs Canada observed that "Ontario and Quebec are back in."[82] Justin Trudeau sent out an important message when he appointed his Cabinet: all key portfolios went either to Ontario or Quebec ministers from finance, global affairs, transportation, and to the Environment and Climate Change Canada. In addition to doing away with regional ministers, Trudeau decided, for the first time, to have all regional development agencies report to an Ontario minister.

WHAT DIVIDES CANADIANS?

Canada's political landscape is deeply fractured along geographical lines. Elections are won or lost in two to three provinces and they turn on campaign missteps, the work of political war rooms, how well leaders do in the debates, and the ballot question or questions. Political parties contribute precious little to the issues that divides Canadians. Their main purpose is to provide candidates at election time but always under the watchful eye of party leaders and their courtiers.

Both Canadian politics and governing are now managed by the centre. Prime ministers govern from the centre and political leaders manage political issues from their offices. Political parties in Canada are non-actors as institutionalized mediators defining solutions to the challenges and conflicts found in Canadian civil society. On all important issues that confront Canadians, political parties are empty vessels.

Political parties have abdicated their responsibility for the most important issue that divides Canadians – regionalism – to party leaders and their trusted courtiers. The issue is considered to be too important and too difficult to grasp fully to be left to anyone else, even party candidates at election time, precisely when the issue should be fully aired in all regions.

LOOKING BACK

The deinstitutionalization of political parties has accelerated in recent years. As many observers now agree, political parties are little more than election-day organizations. Political parties have been deinstitutionalized in that they have lost both status in society and their institutional character. Political parties in Canada have lost their brand to their leaders. The Trudeau, Harper, and Scheer brands are now what count at election time.

Sophisticated political expertise, notably pollsters and political strategists, are required to develop and manage political brands. Candidates for Parliament are now worth "5 percent," while members of political parties are on the outside looking in as party policies and strategies are defined. Too many Canadians regard politics as too complex to engage, opting instead to ignore it or get angry with it. We now have data to make the case that Canadian politics has become the preserve of those who engage with it and those who have the resources to retain lobbyists or professional politicians to do their bidding.[83]

The Commons: The Institution that Fails

Kelly Blidook has a stern warning for those elected to Parliament: "It would be an enormous and probably fruitless task to argue in the next 120 pages that Parliament matters."[1] No one is happy with Parliament, including many members of Parliament. They have been labelled "trained seals" by Gordon Aiken and opposition MPs as "nobodies" by former prime minister Pierre E. Trudeau.[2] Ned Franks, one of Canada's leading students of Parliament, maintains that the role of an MP is "confused and obscure."[3] John Ibbitson, a widely read columnist, writes that "our Parliament has become the most dysfunctional in the English-speaking world, weaker and more irrelevant than the U.S. Congress or the parliaments of Britain, Australia or New Zealand." He adds: "If Britain is the mother of Parliaments, her Canadian daughter [has] ... fallen. Government MPs are cowed; parliamentary committees are too often irrelevant."[4]

This chapter explores why Canada's Parliament has fallen. Walter Bagehot ascribes a number of functions to the House of Commons. He argues that the Commons has the power to decide who holds executive offices and holds them to account and to dismiss executive office holders, at the political level, if the need arises. Bagehot ascribes a number of deliberative functions for the Commons. He saw the Commons as the one body able to give voice to the "sentiments, the interests, the opinions, the prejudices, the wants of all classes of the nation."[5] He also saw the Commons teaching the nation what it does not know, expressing the nation's will, and bringing matters to the attention of the nation.[6]

Today, the Commons falls short in pursuing these functions. No one, it seems, believes that the House of Commons is performing at an acceptable level under any of Bagehot's functions. Students of government are making the case that the role of Parliament, and more specifically the House of Commons, has been relegated to little more than providing democratic legitimacy for decisions made elsewhere.[7] Michael Atkinson and Paul Thomas write, "Parliament's role in lawmaking is restricted to refining, ratifying and legitimating decisions."[8] Well-known journalist Andrew Coyne concludes that "nothing in our present system works as it is supposed to. The dominance of the executive over Parliament, and of party leaders over caucus, pervades everything, from how we nominate candidates to how we elect party leaders, from how elections are conducted to how Parliament works, or fails to."[9] A survey revealed only 27 percent of Canadians believe that the House of Commons deals with issues important to them.[10]

Many practitioners, or those who have served in the House of Commons, have been no less critical. For example, Brent Rathgeber maintains that the government runs Parliament rather than being accountable to it and insists that the House of Commons falls short on several fronts.[11] Still, the Commons has a critical constitutional role – notwithstanding Canada's vast geography, widely different regional economic circumstances, and its federal system, only the House of Commons decides who forms the Government of Canada, and it is the one legitimate institution in which all communities can be heard through their MPs.

ARRIVING IN OTTAWA

Canadian MPs come from diverse backgrounds. You do not need to have attended a select few universities to become an MP, pursued specialized courses, or even an internship program. They come to Parliament as lawyers, teachers, university professors, community workers, small business owners, physicians, and former public servants. Many are newcomers – turnover in Canada's House of Commons is high when compared with other jurisdictions. They join career politicians who survive elections usually because they run in safe constituencies.[12]

MPs represent a geographical space – a constituency – and become the spokesperson for its economic and political interest. For most MPs, that is as close as the work gets to a job description. There is evidence to suggest that politicians who run for Parliament to promote the interest of their constituencies are more likely to be successful than those who run to contribute to policy-making, to hold the government to account, or to find flaws in the spending estimates.[13] There are far more opportunities for MPs in the Canadian Parliament to be seen back home as acting as a spokesperson for their constituencies than trying to hold the government to account. Bagehot's functions for the House of Commons resonate more in a unitary state like Britain in the nineteenth century than they do in Canada, where space and territory dominate Canadian politics.

NO TRAINING

A typical member of Parliament arrives in Ottawa with limited knowledge of the ways of Parliament and government, and with limited capacity to learn from others. A non-partisan report, prepared by the Library of Parliament under the direction of three MPs, sums up the challenge: "It takes eight years to train a doctor but only 36 days to elect an MP."[14]

MPs soon learn that Wednesday mornings are the busy mornings in Ottawa: they meet in regional caucuses between 7:00 and 8:45, and in their national caucus between 9:00 and 11:00. All three major parties have regional and national caucuses so that there are Atlantic, Quebec, Ontario, and Western caucuses. In the case of the Conservative Party, the Western regional caucus can also meet as provincial caucuses. The daily business of the House of Commons, meanwhile, begins at 2:00 p.m. on Wednesday.

Caucus sessions can, in the words of an MP, turn into "bitching sessions."[15] The "bitching" can be directed at the leader (only by brave souls if the leader is the prime minister) or at a Cabinet minister for a political misstep, at senior public servants, at a government or party miscue, and at perceived or real slights to their regions. Former prime ministers and premiers report that it was more difficult for them to manage caucuses than Cabinet. Frank McKenna told me this on several occasions.[16] Brian Mulroney said it many times in interviews, and Jean Chrétien's difficult days were caused by caucus, not Cabinet.[17] Ministers can be dropped from Cabinet – they have something to lose, less so in the case of backbench MPs, particularly when they come to terms with the reality that they will not make it to Cabinet with the current prime minister. Caucuses are closed meetings where rules of secrecy apply.[18]

MPs view their work and the work of government from a spatial or territorial perspective, that is, the territory they represent. They identify with their constituencies, the province, and the region they represent – that is their job and many believe that keeping their job depends on how well they represent these interests. I recall a conversation with Maurice Dionne, MP for Northumberland-Miramichi, in the early 1980s. He looked out his office window at the building cranes dotting the downtown Ottawa skyline and said, "I only want one of those for my constituency – only one – that is what I want from my government." That was his measure of success. He understood that his constituencies would appreciate anything that he could bring back home. He understood that they would have little appreciation for the work he might do in committees to hold the government to account.

MPs on the government side are free to voice the concerns of their constituencies and to compare what the government is doing in their constituencies and regions with what it is doing in others, something they often do. They are free to criticize how a national policy applies and how a proposed initiative will be accepted in their regions. These concerns, however strongly felt by MPs on the government side, remain in caucus. It is a rare occurrence for MPs on the government side to publicly voice criticism at the inability of national policies to perform in their region. That is best said in private in regional or national caucuses or in one-on-one meetings with a minister or a Prime Minister's Office (PMO) official. It is left to the prime minister or the party leader, however, to establish the consensus in caucus on the way ahead on any given issue. At that point, party discipline kicks in.

MPs on the government side soon learn they have to be on good terms with the prime minister and his key advisers to get things done for their constituencies. Best not to offend them. It was widely reported that Prime Minister Justin Trudeau "verbally attacked" a first-term MP who raised issues over proposed gun control legislation. T.J. Harvey argued that there was a lack of meaningful consultation with caucus. Several MPs reported that the prime minister "went after" Harvey with an "unusually angry tone," which MPs insisted had an "intimidating effect" on future discussions in caucus. MPs are questioning why Trudeau's principal secretary and his chief of staff regularly attend national caucus meetings, which they maintain should only be attended by elected MPs. I note that other than

Stephen Harper, previous prime ministers limited caucus meetings to elected MPs.[19]

When several or more MPs on the government side voice criticism publicly of government policy or decisions, one can assume that the prime minister has given them a green light to do so. Several government MPs were openly critical of the government's 2017 proposal to reform its income tax for small business that had implications for doctors and other professionals who decided to opt for incorporation to retain income. The chair of the Commons Finance Committee, a government MP, said that the proposed changes "triggered an unprecedented backlash from his constituents."[20] The minister of finance heard a barrage of criticism from government MPs at a caucus session held in British Columbia in early September 2017.[21] The prime minister and his advisers decided to back away from some of the proposed changes and let government backbenchers voice some of their criticism in public and claim credit in their constituencies for having influenced the government. I recognize that, faced with this "backlash," the prime minister and his courtiers decided best to give government MPs the green light to criticize proposed changes to the income tax on small businesses rather than stick with the proposal.

Atlantic Canada government MPs – at the time all MPs from the region – privately took aim, and some opposition MPs from other regions publicly took aim at Prime Minister Justin Trudeau's musing that Atlantic Canada could lose its one seat on the Supreme Court. Justice Thomas Cromwell announced his retirement for 1 September 2016, and Trudeau declared that he could not "guarantee the country's top court will continue to have a judge from Atlantic Canada."[22] Many Atlantic Canadians soon took Trudeau to task, making the case that his position was counter to a constitutional convention and that he would never consider taking away a Supreme Court appointment from the other more populous regions. The Atlantic Provinces Trial Lawyers Association decided to turn to the courts to make the case that the government would need to amend the constitution if it wanted to drop regional representation as an unwritten constitutional convention.[23]

Initially, Atlantic MPs remained quiet, at least publicly. It was left to trial lawyers and academics to speak up for Atlantic Canada's Supreme Court seat.[24] In time, pressure mounted. Atlantic Canada MPs made it clear in their regional caucus that the issue was causing serious problems in their constituencies. Opposition justice critic

Rob Nicholson tabled a motion calling on the government to "respect the custom of regional representation ... in particular, when replacing the retiring Justice Thomas Cromwell, who is Atlantic Canada's representation on the Supreme Court."[25] Trudeau signalled to his Atlantic MPs that he had shifted his position and would support the motion, which was unanimously approved.[26]

However, when the prime minister tells caucus to support the government on any issue, government MPs listen. I know several government MPs from Atlantic Canada who told me in private conversations that they were unhappy when the prime minister appointed an Ontario MP, Navdeep Bains, to head the Atlantic Canada Opportunities Agency (ACOA). It was a very different story, however, when speaking with the media. They either were supportive or said nothing. One told the local media that "a central Canadian" as head of ACOA "gives the east more profile at the cabinet table."[27] Party discipline carries the day.

The current level of party discipline was largely unknown in the early post-Confederation period. For one thing, political parties were just starting to take shape in 1867, and as Jean-François Godbout and Bjørn Høyland point out, partisan behaviour and strong party discipline only became evident around the turn of the twentieth century.[28] It was during the early Parliaments that a number of MPs became known as "loose fish" who did not always walk in step with their parties.[29] They would trade their support in exchange for something for their constituencies.

It is worth quoting Jonathan Lemco on party discipline in Canada's early years: "Members were not particularly concerned about acting cohesively to achieve party goals. Their primary aim was to be on the winning side so that they would secure as many benefits as they could for their constituents. Their independence gave the Commons its collective character and its most important check on the executive."[30] MPs did not hesitate to vote against their party – for example, 72 percent of MPs voted against their party in 1867.[31] In addition, the John A. Macdonald government was defeated six times on government bills and twice on supply votes. It is worth underlining the point that Macdonald did not see the need to recommend to the Governor General to dissolve Parliament and call a general election.[32]

For a number of years after Confederation, political parties were not clearly defined. Macdonald, for example, led the Liberal-Conservative

Party until 1873. A number of Nova Scotia and New Brunswick MPs sat in Parliament opposed to Confederation and had their own partisan considerations. They did not wish to align themselves with political parties at the expense of the regions they represented. Godbout and Høyland, in their review of the development of Canadian political parties between 1867 and 1908, make the case that "the regional ties between members of Parliament (MPs) gradually weakened at the expense of partisanship."[33]

Partisanship and party discipline are tied at the hip, and partisanship now rules the roost in Parliament. It has become even more evident with the arrival of permanent election campaigns and the new media. Michael Ignatieff calls partisanship the "essence of politics" and explains, "You join a team, choose your leader, issue a platform and then march forth to do battle with the other side. Partisanship means putting party line first and personal judgment second. Loyalty is the moral core of partisanship, the value that trumps all others. Once you become a partisan, you enter an information bubble of political positioning. You abjure the other side, do not keep company with them, and define them as everything you oppose. Partisanship defines the world you take as normal."[34] Party politics is a team sport. If you go against your team, you are disloyal to your team and team leader.

The first lesson learned for a new elected MP arriving in Ottawa is that loyalty, partisanship, and party discipline trump everything; you are a team player or you are a nobody shunned by your caucus. Students of Canadian politics insist that party discipline in the Canadian Parliament is the strictest in the world. Richard Simeon points out that "we are worse than the Australians and much worse than the British in terms of giving MPs the ability to act and to somehow make a difference." Leslie Seidle adds: "There may be some exceptions in those African dictatorships that are part of the Commonwealth but in the advanced parliamentary democracies, there is nowhere that has heavier, tighter party discipline than the Canadian House of Commons. People are kicked out of their party temporarily for what are really very minor matters."[35] MPs in Britain are much more willing to challenge their party's leaders than is the case in Canada, and party discipline there or in Australia is not nearly as tight.

Ambitious MPs know that toeing the party line is a prerequisite for success in Ottawa – it comes with the territory. The overriding goal of MPs is to get "re-elected," and this is where loyalty kicks in.[36] Loyalty is the lifeblood of politics and nothing is more valued by party leaders. More to the point, loyalty is rewarded and disloyalty is severely punished. Party leaders have several levers to ensure loyalty and party discipline: the power of appointment to Cabinet, parliamentary secretaries and shadow Cabinet, even the ability to decide who runs for Parliament for the party and the widely held belief that Canadians vote for party leaders and their brand, not local candidates. They control memberships to committees and even those who ask questions in question period.

Party discipline is regarded as a crucial ingredient for winning elections – the need to present a united front and avoid creating political grief for one's party leader. A member of Parliament breaking rank with the leader is certain to be widely reported in the media, always with a negative spin for the party leader. However, an MP who is always vocally supportive of the party leader and toes the party line stands to gain on a personal level. Former MP David Kilgour explains: "A 'loyal' MP who votes the party line will be a candidate for promotion – if in the government party, perhaps Cabinet – or other benefits from the party such as interesting trips or appointment to an interesting House committee ... In light of this, 'caucus solidarity and my constituents be damned' might be the real oath of office for most honourable members in all political parties."[37]

In Canada, MPs openly challenging their leaders are often shown the door. For example, Stephen Harper kicked Bill Casey out of caucus when he voted against the budget, arguing that it would cost Nova Scotia as much as a billion dollars.[38] In another example, Jean Chrétien tossed John Nunziata out of caucus after he decided to vote against the budget in protest against the government for reneging on its election campaign commitment to do away with the Goods and Services Tax (GST).[39] David Kilgour, who, together with two colleagues, was expelled from the government caucus for voting against the GST, explains that "an expelled MP is forced to sit as an independent and is virtually excommunicated from the political process."[40]

Government MPs know, or should know, of the long-standing convention that voting against the budget is tantamount to being removed from caucus. There are, however, other less obvious reasons. For instance, Garth Turner was kicked out of caucus for running a blog, Hunter Tootoo for having an affair with a staff member, and Carolyn Parrish for stomping on a doll of George W. Bush.[41]

Free votes in the Commons can loosen party discipline. However, in Canada free votes are rare. Not only are they rare, they tend to cross party lines, and very often deal with questions of morality and conscience such as capital punishment, abortion, and same-sex marriage. Canada did try to introduce, albeit in the end with limited success, the "three-line" whip, a practice employed in Britain. The concept works in this fashion: 1) On one-line votes all MPs on the government side, including ministers, are free to vote as they wish; 2) On two-line votes the government recommends a preferred position and ministers and parliamentary secretaries are expected to vote with the government; 3) Three-line votes are questions of confidence and all MPs on the government side are expected to vote with the government.[42]

In Britain, on occasions, government MPs even defy three-line whips. For example, eighty-one government MPs voted for a motion for the Brexit referendum in opposition to their party leader.[43] In Britain, Margaret Thatcher lost four votes in the Commons, John Major six, Tony Blair four, David Cameron six – all were a three-line whip vote. In Canada, Stephen Harper did not lose a single whipped vote, nor Justin Trudeau.[44] The concept has had little traction in Canada since the Paul Martin government introduced it in 2004.[45]

Few Canadian MPs are prepared to break rank with their party, at least publicly. As Jonathan Malloy maintains, Canada's House of Commons has highly disciplined political parties "even by Westminster standards."[46] But how does one explain that party discipline is stronger in Canada than Britain, Australia, or New Zealand, given that they all operate under the Westminster parliamentary model? Why do party leaders in Canada show less tolerance for dissent than their British counterparts?

WHY DISCIPLINE QUELLS DISSENSION IN CANADA'S POLITICAL PARTIES

I contend that Canadian party leaders often feel compelled to keep a tight rope on their MPs to keep the regional factor under control, and keeping the regional factor under control speaks to the interest of vote-rich Ontario and Quebec.[47] Leaving aside the Senate, with its equal number of senators for every state, large or small, the United States has other ways to give voice to the regional factor. On numerous occasions, for example, it has witnessed regional or territorial block voting. Representatives of the Republican and Democratic parties can and do vote "in block," and often work hand in hand in committees to promote regional interests.[48] Regional blocks include "New England," the "Sun Belt," the "Mountain States," among others. It is well known the Southern block played a key role in securing military and space expenditures that contributed to the economic revival of the Sun Belt – the coalition of Southern Democrats and Republicans was successful in 85 percent of the cases it tried to influence.[49] Regional or block voting is unknown in Canada – party discipline and permanent election campaigns simply do not allow it.

As noted, Britain's MPs are more willing to vote against the party line. For one thing, votes of non-confidence are made much more explicit than in Canada. In addition, Britain's political parties are more ideologically polarized than their Canadian counterparts. Jonathan Lemco argues that Canadians' two main parties only have a "small number of real differences in their public policy initiatives and ideological beliefs ... As a result, the line between the two parties is often a narrow one and strict party discipline is required to avoid cross-party voting."[50]

Robert Jackman insists that strict party discipline in Canada has inhibited the ability of political parties to become effective national integrating bodies which, he believes, explains why Canada lags behind other jurisdictions in promoting national integration.[51] Canadian MPs do not have the freedom to respond to regional pressures before Parliament or in public for fear that it would be regarded as a criticism of the party leader. Given the potential of throwing fuel on the fire, party leaders and advisers will keep a close watch on the activities of MPs to ensure that regional tensions do not flare up or create a problem for the party in another region. Managing regional tensions from the leader's office so that they remain under control has, in turn, promoted the growth of third parties in Canada which are often region-based.[52]

There is a wide consensus that the Canadian Parliament and government MPs have little ability to constrain prime ministerial power.[53] Neither are political parties much of a factor in checking the power of the prime minister. Brian Tobin, a long-serving MP and high-profile Cabinet minister, laments the decision to give party leaders the power to accept or reject a candidate. He argues that the rules now in place point to a "massive shift of power from riding associations and provincial organizations to the national leader and the national campaign committee."[54] Recall that Justin Trudeau did an about-face on his commitment to end the practice of protecting incumbents from nomination challenges. The Liberal Party decided in 2018 that incumbent MPs who meet certain conditions would be acclaimed as candidates for the 2019 election.[55]

The many reports tabled to deal with the decline of Parliament have often focused on the need to turn MPs into something more than "trained seals."[56] This has wide implications not only for national integration but also for holding the government to account. This is particularly evident in the management of government spending. Robert Marleau, a highly respected former clerk of the House of Commons, maintains that the Commons has "almost abandoned its constitutional responsibility of supply."[57]

Parliament under the Westminster model holds the power – at least, it should – over both taxation and government spending. The prime minister, notwithstanding his access to a multitude of levers of power, Cabinet, and the public service cannot raise taxes or spend a single dollar without first obtaining Parliament's explicit approval.[58] Parliament, as earlier chapters point out, carved out its constitutional role through struggles with the Crown over who should have the power to tax and spend.

THE BUSINESS OF SUPPLY:
FINDING A NEEDLE IN A HAYSTACK

MPs should readily understand the budget's importance. The Canadian House of Commons has the ability to dismiss a government by withholding supply. The budget states, in the clearest terms, who wins, who loses, and in – dollars and cents – who gets what from government. Two students of government have observed that "budgeting is the most important annual ritual of government – the World Series of Government or perhaps the Grey Cup of Government within the Canadian context."[59]

For MPs, the budget is where the rubber meets the road. They understand the political impact of raising or lowering taxes and – better than anyone – the impact of raising or lowering spending in their constituencies. Ministers, too, have a keen interest in the budget process – they know that they will be evaluated on their ability to bring home the bacon, so to speak. They rank their ability to secure funding for initiatives in their constituencies and for their departments as the most objective way to assess their performance both in government and in their region.

LOOKING FOR SOMETHING TO DO

The decline of Parliament and the role of MPs, particularly over the past forty years, has been well documented. There are precious few publications or reports making the case that all is well with Parliament. We have, however, a catalogue of reports with recommendations for strengthening the role of Members of Parliament. The McGrath report, the Bennett-Gray report, various Samara reports, and speeches and articles produced by many MPs all call for parliamentary reform to give MPs a stronger role.[60] Party leaders invariably pledge to give MPs a greater say while in opposition but little comes of it when they become prime minister. They very often do "the opposite."[61]

Canadians should look to MPs to provide assurance that the government is properly managing public resources. The Canadian government points out that "Parliament has a broad range of means to hold the government to account. The oldest and still among the most powerful is control of the public purse."[62] The Library of Parliament argues that the "study of departmental estimates gives MPs the chance to criticize and possibly alter appropriation projections. Committee rules empower Members to accede, to revise downward, or even deny the government's appropriation demands outright."[63] The Library's report continues, "The scrutiny of government spending is an important element of the MP's surveillance role."[64] Things, however, are not working out as the government or the Library of Parliament envisage.

The government has tried on several occasions to overhaul its budget process with little success. I outlined the various attempts, from line item budgeting, Planning, Programming and Budgeting System (PPBS), to Policy and Expenditure Management System (PEMS) in my book *The Politics of Public Spending in Canada*, and there is no need to go over the same territory. Suffice to note that all the reforms failed badly and both PPBS and PEMS were jettisoned only a few years after their introduction.

I sought to explain in the book why the reforms failed: "Ten people meet for the first time over lunch. They must decide whether they will share one check or ask for ten separate ones. In theory, if they decide on one shared check they will all choose the most expensive items. But if each were paying individually they would probably have chosen differently: nobody would want to miss the best food while paying for someone else to have it."[65] This sums up the politics of public spending in Canada – regionalism, the politics of regional envy, and departmental pressure to spend fuel new spending demands, and no budget process wisely constituted can cope with the pressure. The result is that the prime minister and the minister of finance – with an emphasis on prime ministers and their courtiers – decide who gets what, end of debate.

Prime ministers from Trudeau *père*, Mulroney, Chrétien, and Harper to Trudeau *fils* have all given up on the ability of Cabinet to manage the government's budget process. When Cabinet ministers sit down for lunch to review budget requirements, they tend to order the most expensive items in the hope that the regions they represent or their departments will get a share of the spending. Prime ministers have pushed aside ministers and decided to sit down solely with the minister of finance to make all the key budgetary decisions.

Ministers looking for new spending now make the case before the prime minister, not Cabinet or even the minister of finance. It is the prime minister with the minister of finance who decide on the luncheon menu, and together with senior advisers in the PMO, the PCO, and the Department of Finance, they decide who gets what. Prime ministers and their courtiers know better than anyone where the votes required to form government are located. Though the Senate is recently trying to show that it is becoming a more credible and no-partisan independent actor, it has not had much of a say in the budget process over the years.

WHAT ABOUT PARLIAMENT?

Imagine that you are a newly elected member of Parliament. Some MPs have experience in government, most do not. Some have experience in management, many do not. Some have experience in budget-making, most do not. MPs enter Parliament with a demanding "to-do list." They need to hire staff for both their Ottawa and constituency offices and some MPs have never hired or managed staff before being elected to Parliament. They need to establish office procedures with staff to deal with mail, phone calls, procurement, and the media.

Newly elected MPs need to understand how Ottawa works, and many look to veteran MPs as role models. Veteran MPs will underline the importance of following party discipline, raising contentious issues only in private, and avoiding creating problems for the party leader. Ambitious MPs soon learn to abide by these golden rules to promote their own career advancement and help their party win the next election.

What about one of Bagehot's most important roles for MPs – holding the government to account for its spending? MPs sit at the end of the assembly line in the budget process. All competing demands and all decisions have been struck by the time the budget and the estimates are tabled in Parliament. Thousands and thousands of pages are tabled every year in Parliament for MPs to review. However, little ever comes out of this process.

I know of no one who is prepared to make the case that Parliament is able to hold the government to account on budget matters or that MPs play a meaningful role in reviewing the government's spending plans. However, I know many credible voices who argue the contrary. Sheila Fraser, who served as Canada's auditor general, argued before she stepped down that MPs are "failing Canadians" in one of their most fundamental roles: the scrutiny of yearly spending estimates.[66]

Herb Gray, a veteran MP who knew his way around Parliament, explains: "The examination of the Main Estimates has become rather cursory and there has been no focus for parliamentary debate on government spending before its spending priorities are actually set."[67] Shawn Murphy, the former chair of Parliament's Public Accounts Committee, exposed the problem when he met senior public servants. He told them to insert some blank pages in the budget documents they send to Parliament to see if any MP would notice; he told them that none would. He reminded the committee that the Department of Justice simply "forgot" to include financial statements for the firearms registry, a controversial initiative widely reported in the media. No one noticed, let alone raised questions about it.[68] Lowell Murray, a highly respected Cabinet minister in the Mulroney government, observed: "Parliament – specifically the House of Commons – over a period of more than forty years, has allowed its most vital power, the power of the purse, to become a dead letter, their Supply and Estimates process an empty ritual."[69]

Government MPs, on the government side, are expected to support the budget and the estimates – no question asked. Opposition MPs, meanwhile, are expected to find fault. Few, however, will invest the time to go through the mountain of documents tabled in Parliament. They and their staff will keep an eye on media reports, of which they are many, that can generate questions or give rise to a fifteen-second clip on the evening news. Such reports include, among many others, "Over $350-Million Spent to Clean Up Abandoned Mine in Yukon and Not an Inch Has Been Remediated."[70] Departments, meanwhile, will counter with well-controlled information difficult to challenge.

The Department of Finance, for example, maintains that it plays "a vital role in helping the Government of Canada develop the social and economic policies that will further improve the standard of living and quality of life of Canadians, their families and their communities in the years to come." And adds it does all of this "with fewer than 1,000 people."[71] How can an MP, or for that matter anyone else, possibly know that a 1,000-strong finance department is good value for Canadians? Consider the following: The Department of Finance is a central agency and does not deliver programs directly to Canadians, and there are several other central agencies in the federal government – the PMO, the PCO, and the Treasury Board Secretariat (with a total staff of 1,800) – that can argue they, too, play a vital role in helping the government develop social and economic policies. Ten provincial governments and three territorial governments each have a finance department that carry out similar tasks. Could the Department of Finance Canada perform as well or even better with only 700 or 500 staff members? No one knows, other than perhaps finance officials, and they will never tell – why should they?

MPs can look to a myriad of documents produced by the Treasury Board Secretariat and Department of Finance for answers. I wish them well. I can do no better than quote a senior Treasury Board Secretariat official from a paper he gave to "CPA Canada's 2016 Public Sector Conference," when he remarked, "We did a lot of reporting that was not widely read (and produced) a large quantity of low-quality performance information."[72] A consultant hired to assist the secretariat in revising its approach had this to say: "Reducing the level of detail in performance reports is unlikely to result in a significant loss of meaningful information for Parliamentarians and the public." No one, it seems, asked why one produced the information in the first place.

Ottawa's Management, Resources and Results Structure Policy (MRRS) was the latest of a long line of approaches to manage public spending and report on it to Parliament. It has fared no better than previous approaches and was dismissed by the Justin Trudeau government, shortly after it came to office. We are told that the MRRS had the following shortcomings: it was viewed as "inefficient" because it "imposed 'an unnecessary burden' on departments by asking for too much detailed program data and 'ineffective' because the resulting reports were of 'little use to Parliamentarians, public managers and the public.'"[73]

The Justin Trudeau government tried its hand at yet another new approach, *Policy on Results*, introduced on 1 July 2016. Like previous efforts, the approach was designed to improve achievement of results, enhance the understanding of results to be achieved, and make clear the resources employed to pursue them. It was designed to ensure that "Parliamentarians and the public receive transparent, clear and useful information."[74] The government added that the new approach would ensure "resources are allocated based on performance using the resulting information to optimize results."[75] This is precisely what Ottawa said, almost word for word, when it introduced its Planning, Programming and Budgeting System (PPBS) in 1968.[76] The federal government never explained why the new approach would work where PPBS failed. It never even mentioned PPBS in introducing its new approach, though the similarities between the two were obvious. One can only conclude that institutional memory inside the federal government is non-existent.

There is a disconnect between Parliament and government on many fronts, but nowhere is it more evident than in the management of public spending. The main casualty is accountability – one of Parliament's most important functions, if not the most important one. The deck is stacked against accountability, starting with all key policy actors having an interest in taking the edge off accountability requirements. MPs have slight interest – to say nothing of competence – in struggling through performance and evaluation reports while senior public servants have little reason to produce revealing and easily accessible evaluation reports about their programs or operations.

MPs have two overriding interests: making their political parties and, in particular, their party leader, appealing to voters and to promote, as best they can, the interest of their constituencies. Government MPs are not about to raise difficult questions about government spending, for fear of making the prime minister or the government look bad. Opposition MPs have an interest in pushing accountability requirements but not the means. Public servants have every interest in operating below the radar screen. Visibility, in either Parliament or the media, is a sure-fire way to inhibit career advancement.[77]

If the goal is to encourage Parliament or MPs to take an interest in spending plans, then the government should make every effort to present its spending plans in a highly accessible and transparent format. It does not. If the government wants to capture the attention of MPs when tabling its spending plans, it needs to give life to them by presenting the estimates from a regional perspective or in manner and format that will grab their attention. This is a timely opportunity to emphasize that MPs always think in regional or spatial terms. However, leaving aside a few exceptions, the spending plans are presented from a sectoral perspective (e.g., health, agriculture, and natural resources). They are then packaged in what a senior Treasury Board Secretariat official describes as a "large quantity of low-quality performance information," which gives "Canadians and Parliamentarians a hard time understanding what departments do and how well they are doing it."[78] This is far from a "user friendly" approach for MPs.

Senior government officials, meanwhile, have little incentive to produce clear, well-documented, and revealing evaluation and performance reports or to produce budget papers from a regional perspective. For one thing, prime ministers and their courtiers are not asking for it, preferring to have the estimates operate under the radar of MPs and the media, unless and until they announce spending commitments. For another, Ottawa-based senior public servants know that such an approach would be fraught with political problems in so far as it would generate material to fuel the blame game.

A journalist attending budget briefings prepared by the Department of Finance officials for budget day wrote about the challenges confronting MPs in their efforts to understand what they were being asked to approve. He indicated that he and his colleagues were left "scratching their head. And not just because, in a 419-page document, the critical headline numbers – total revenue, total spending and the deficit – didn't appear until page 268. A key table breaking revenue and spending ... was missing."[79] Opposition MPs, central agencies, the Office of the Auditor General, and the media are not in the business of looking to the estimate or evaluation and performance reports to applaud the work of senior public servants, who know this better than anyone. Doug Hartle remarks, "It is a strange dog that willingly carries the stick with which it is to be beaten."[80] Senior public servants are not about to walk around Ottawa with such a stick in the form of well-documented evaluation or performance reports painting for their departmental or program failures.

Recall that private sector-inspired New Public Management measures, about which more is said below, were designed to do away with many centrally prescribed rules and regulations in order to let managers manage like their private sector counterparts. Many centrally prescribed rules and regulations were tossed aside in favour of performance and evaluation reports, ostensibly designed to determine how well senior officials managed operations and programs. Senior public servants soon learned that it is much easier to fudge evaluation reports than centrally prescribed rules. Accountability both to Parliament and in government continues to pay a heavy price.[81] Public servants know how to fudge reports. They are, however, less adroit at sidestepping clearly articulated rules.

A former assistant to Prime Minister Chrétien summed up how most political problems surface through "small issues, not big dollars."[82] He gave examples: "sixteen-dollar orange juice, Gucci loafers, gold-plated faucets on a plane, $6,000 a minister spends on a photographer or $3,700 for two days of private car service or claiming per diems for a house you don't actually live in."[83] Opposition MPs are always on the lookout for the "gotcha" headlines aimed at the prime minister or ministers, while Cabinet ministers, government MPs, and senior public servants are on the lookout to protect the government from providing such "gotcha" moments. The less the opposition parties and the media know, the better. That is now what drives the budget process in Parliament.

HERE, YOU DRIVE

Members of Parliament have, to a large extent, turned over some of their responsibilities to the "audit society," notably officers of Parliament. David Smith writes about officers of Parliament making the transition from servants of Parliament to become Parliament's masters.[84] The following can claim some status as officers of Parliament: Office of the Auditor General; Office of the Commissioner of Official Languages; Office of the Information Commissioner; Office of the Privacy Commissioner; Office of the Public Sector Integrity Commissioner; Public Service Commission of Canada (one can, however, debate whether the commission is an agency of government); the Conflict of Interest and Ethics Commissioner; the Office of the Procurement Ombudsman; the Parliamentary Budget Officer (albeit part of the Library of Parliament); the commissioner of lobbying; the director of public prosecutions; and the chief electoral officer.

Canada has more officers or agents of Parliament than the other Westminster-inspired parliamentary systems of government, and they have increased their staff considerably and expanded their mandates in recent years. The dozen offices employ more than 2,000 persons and spend over $250 million. Many of those employees in Offices of Parliament go to work every morning looking for administrative miscues; they seek to put in place processes to prevent such miscues and to monitor and evaluate the performance of individual public servants, departments, and programs. Several years ago, one department had 286 of its 700 employees working on various accountability reports.[85] This explains why officers of Parliament are very often viewed – in the words of a senior line department official – as "the enemy in the room."[86]

Their measure of success centres on what miscues they identified or what processes they can claim to have championed and implemented. Officers of Parliament, such as the auditor general, have sought to break out of the traditional boundaries to establish new turf for themselves, but not necessarily at the urging of Parliament. Indeed, in some ways, they now appear to function as free agents, accountable to no one but themselves. Of course, they cannot be subordinate or accountable to the government of the day, because that in itself would compromise their *raison d'être*. But once established, agents of Parliament, like members of other bureaucratic organizations, will seek to expand their sphere of influence, and Parliament has not been very effective in its dealings with them. Predictably, opposition parties and the media support an expanded role for officers of Parliament, while those on the government side of the House do not. Political parties that supported agents of Parliament while in opposition can very quickly turn sour on them once they themselves are in power.[87] They often do, as they discover that things look very different, depending on which side of Parliament one sits.

The Liberal Party pledged, in its 1993 Red Book election platforms, to restore integrity in government by appointing an officer of Parliament to ensure proper ethical conduct in government.[88] Prime Minister Jean Chrétien, by then a veteran politician who knew how the blame game operated, had a change of heart once in power. He appointed an officer who reported to him, arguing that he was ultimately responsible for the ethical conduct of his government.[89] Opposition parties immediately cried foul and pledged to rectify the situation once in office. Prime Minister Stephen Harper put in place the Conflict of Interest Act as part of his government's 2006 Federal Accountability Act, which made the ethics commissioner an officer of Parliament. One can easily speculate that Harper probably had regrets about the decision once in power, though he stayed the course with his commitment.[90]

The Office of the Auditor General, for example, once had clear boundaries defining its roles and responsibilities. Its purpose was to assist the Public Accounts Committee of the House of Commons and report to the committee the results of its investigations of financial probity and compliance with appropriation authority. Today, 50 percent of its budget goes to "qualitative" or "soft reviews" that "bear little apparent relationship to efficiency or economy in the use of funds, human resources, or material."[91] A good number of reports published by the office now have little to do with financial probity. They are essentially political document, in that they stake out policy positions or explore issues that have nothing to do with financial audits. Yet the office continues to insist on its non-political nature, even though it regularly engages in policy debates. Neither it nor the media bothers to explain that qualitative or soft reviews can never be as certain or conclusive as financial audits. Yet, the office has become particularly adroit at attracting media attention, and it now reports its findings to the media as much as to Parliament.

The Canadian auditor general became a media star during the sponsorship scandal. There was talk on a number of open-line shows of "Sheila Fraser for prime minister," and she was described as a "folk hero with the electorate."[92] The office has successfully created its own distinct voice and essentially views Parliament as just another consumer of its reports. Its activities are no longer based on the exact work of accountants but increasingly on comprehensive policy work. The voice may not be partisan, but it is political. It is sufficiently influential that the prime minister, ministers, and senior public servants must invest time and effort to deal with it. In fact, it has become an important policy actor in its own right, a far cry from its original mandate.

The officers of Parliament all speak from a narrow viewpoint, according to their particular mandates or interests, and no one is charged with bringing a broad overarching perspective. Consequently, those in government have several independent officers looking over their shoulders from different, and at times conflicting, perspectives (for example, privacy versus access to information). Opposition parties view officers of Parliament as their natural allies and do not want to challenge them, let alone hold them to account, preferring to let them wander wherever they want in the hope that they will uncover a situation embarrassing to the government.

An excellent case in point is the parliamentary budget officer, a position established by the Harper government as part of its Federal Accountability Act. The government's insistence that the office was created to "ensure truth in budgeting" could not have been lost on the minister of finance and his officials or parliamentary committees, who apparently are not as credible as a budget officer and cannot ensure truth in budgeting. It was not long after Harper came to power that the budget officer became embroiled in a political controversy. He began to challenge the government's spending estimates, its economic forecasts, and its projected revenues. He questioned whether the government's 2009 economic stimulus package would actually create the 189,000 jobs it projected,[93] and he said it would "push the country to the brink of a persistent deficit."[94] Somehow, he was able to arrive at this and other conclusions with a handful of employees, while the Department of Finance and the PCO could not.

The media gave the budget officer wide coverage, and overnight he made the transition from an obscure bureaucrat to someone in high demand by journalists. In some ways, he was playing the role that the leader of the opposition once played; he enabled the media to challenge the government without having to do the legwork. Veteran MP Carolyn Bennett, who at the time sat in opposition, went to the bottom of the matter when she observed that the parliamentary budget officer should "work for parliamentarians, not the public." She took exception to his "habit of releasing reports to the public at the same time as he gave them to the MPs requesting the information, or tabled them in the Commons and Senate."[95]

The Harper government, in establishing the position of a parliamentary budget officer, borrowed a page from the United States and the Congressional Budget Office. The goal was to help MPs understand the government's budget process. But the first incumbent saw his role as less about helping MPs understand it and more about providing a second set of numbers to the Department of Finance's short- and mid-term budget forecast.[96] He has made it clear on several occasions that his mandate was to tell the "truth in budgeting" and that his $2.8 million annual budget was not sufficient to allow him to do so. He asked for more people and more resources for his office. Like other officers of Parliament, his reporting relationship has been geared more to the media than to parliamentarians.

The first incumbent revisited his mandate and his relations with the Harper government, the government that established the office. He recalled, "To the Conservatives, what looked like a great idea in opposition became less so in government." He reported sustained attempts by the Harper government and senior public servants to undermine the office. He applauded, however, the Liberal Party's pledge while in opposition to strengthen the role of the Parliamentary Budget Office (PBO) by making it an independent officer of Parliament. He signalled out the media's support for the office in his call to strengthen the PBO.[97]

Officers of Parliament have become autonomous bodies with uncertain ties to Parliament. They decide on their priorities, the agenda to pursue, and it is not clear to whom they are accountable. The government is often critical of them while opposition MPs will urge them to press on since they have little to lose, at least as long as they sit in opposition. More by stealth, officers of Parliament – as David Smith argues – have made the transition from servants to Parliament to Parliament's masters. Though they have, in their own way, strengthened accountability in government, they have done little to strengthen the role of the House of Commons. Officers of Parliament have gained in recent years at the expense of the institution they are ostensibly asked to serve – Parliament. While they have strengthened transparency in government, they have contributed to making government operations thicker, slower, costlier, and more risk-averse.

LOOKING BACK

Canada's House of Commons now falls short on the roles Walter Bagehot gave to Parliament under the Westminster model. The Commons still decides who holds executive power but no longer delivers on the other responsibilities Bagehot outlined. It falls short in giving voice to the sentiments, interests, and opinions of Canadians.

The House of Commons does not teach the nation what it does not know, becoming political theatre *pur et simple*. It is revealing that few have been more critical of the House of Commons than the MPs who have served in it.

The failure of the House of Commons to hold the government to account, notably in its spending, has been particularly glaring. The prime minister, ministers, and MPs on the government side have no interest in pursuing accountability issues. The same can be said for senior public servants as they associate accountability with the blame game. Opposition MPs will turn to the media for clues on what accountability issues to pursue, and in turn, the media will look to officers of Parliament for their clues.

To MPs, the $300-plus billion federal government budget consists of thousands of pages that make little sense. Government MPs will applaud it because that is what is expected of them – opposition will look to the media and latch on to something, anything, to find fault with it because that is what is expected of them. Canadians, meanwhile, perceive the budget process as a document produced by a handful of political and bureaucratic elites for their own benefit and the benefit of economic elites. The budget is viewed for what it is – a closed process, closed because our political institutions encourage it and because all actors involved in preparing it and spending it have an interest in keeping it that way.

The 2017–18 federal budget speaks to this point: finance officials spent $212,000 to produce a cover for the report and related material to promote the budget. Andrew Coyne remarks that "other countries do not allow their budgets to be covered in advertising in this way. Neither did we once." To Coyne and others, the $212,000 speaks to a contempt for the public purse, for Canadians trying to make ends meet and that only those in power are entitled to spend such an amount of public money for such misguided purpose. Coyne labels it the "last shred of institutional dignity."[98] It speaks to Parliament failing in one of its most important constitutional duties: its constitutional responsibility of supply and holding the government to account for its spending.

The Senate: The Institution That Never Was

Responding to criticism that the Senate did nothing to support the proposed Energy East pipeline, Senator Percy Mockler wrote that two Senate committees debated how to "modernize and depoliticize the pipeline approval process," and made a series of recommendations, but the "recommendations were ignored."[1] In the eyes of most Canadians, that has been the history of the Canadian Senate.

Some Fathers of Confederation, particularly in the early years, believed that Parliament through the Senate would speak for the regions, notably the smaller ones. The Supreme Court of Canada pointed out that "the smaller provinces only consented to Confederation, on the understanding that there would be a regional Upper House."[2] This did not prevent the court from stating in its *Reference re Senate Reform* that the "Senate's fundamental nature and role [is] as a complementary legislative body of sober second thought."[3]

The Upper House has consistently failed in its ability to speak to regional interests. Alan Cairns points out that the Senate should be "an important body designed to allow regional-provincial interests an effective influence in the central government. This was particularly the case with the first batch of senators nominated." He adds, however, that "democratic practice and values increasingly put an appointed chamber which lacked on an aristocratic base ... on the defensive." The result, according to Cairns, is that the House of Commons and the government are left on their own "to allow regional-provincial interests an effective influence in the central government."[4] That, too, has failed, at least from a Western and Atlantic Canada perspective, going back virtually to the day Canada was born.

I can produce a catalogue of criticisms directed at the Senate, going back 150 years. The New Democratic Party has repeatedly called for its abolition.⁵ A Royal Commission on Economic Union and Development Prospects for Canada, known as the Macdonald Commission, labelled the Senate an "institutional failure."⁶ *Maclean's* magazine has called for its abolition, arguing that "from a practical perspective, Canada already has a unicameral legislature. Why not make it official? ... The Senate's lack of democratic legitimacy prevents it from pushing back against government initiatives in the name of regional fairness."⁷ Political scientists have also been, for the most part, highly critical. David Docherty remarks that "the Canadian Senate ranks as one of the last unreformed chambers in Westminster-based parliamentary democracies ... It represents and embodies some of the most anti-democratic features of representative assemblies." That the Senate "looks remarkably similar to the 1867 Senate in terms of its democratic qualities is worth discussion,"⁸ he adds.

Some regions have paid a higher price than others for the Senate's institutional failure. The Senate, David E. Smith points out, "was designed to secure the voice of Maritime interests ... in a Parliament whose lower house, based on rep-by-pop overwhelmingly advanced the concerns of central Canada."⁹ In time, Western Canada would look to the same body to advance its interests, as its campaign for a Triple E (Equal, Elected, and Effective) Senate became the rallying cry for the "West Wants In" that was heard throughout the 1980s and 1990s. Alberta held a province-wide election in 1989 to elect senators, and former prime minister Brian Mulroney appointed Stan Waters on this basis. As noted, the West's push for a Triple E Senate lost momentum when Stephen Harper came to power. With Harper as prime minister, the West was in where it truly matters – in the prime minister's chair.

The national media or the Ontario and Quebec-based media have not been supportive of the Senate or Senate reform. The *Globe and Mail*, the *National Post*, *La Presse*, and *Maclean's* magazine have either called for its abolition or for the status quo. The Quebec-based media have largely favoured the status quo, while the Ontario-based media, notably the *Globe and Mail*, continue to underline the Senate's "sober second thought" role, more often than not ignoring its responsibility to speak on behalf of the smaller regions.¹⁰ The Ontario and Quebec media have not, however, answered the question, Who should speak for the interest of Western or Atlantic Canada in national institutions if the Senate cannot do so or if it were abolished?[11]

Robert MacGregor Dawson, the dean of Canadian political scientists, reminds us that the hopes of the Fathers of Confederation "were not excessively high" when it came to the Senate.[12] Janet Ajzenstat notes a similar expectation: "The founders could have not believed representation of regions in the Upper Chamber would be enough to satisfy local feeling."[13] But many did. They saw the Senate and Cabinet becoming the institutions that would look after regional interests. The Senate never performed to expectations while Cabinet did, but only up to a point and only until recently.

THE MUCH-MALIGNED INSTITUTION

Most who have looked at the Senate have labelled it "a much-maligned institution" and "a tarnished" appointed body.[14] In numerous discussions over the years with several senators, I have expressed my reservations on the Senate's work. I have pointed to its apparent inability or unwillingness to promote the regions' interests. Few deny this point, but they invariably point to important studies the Senate has produced over the years. For example, they often refer to a 2006 study on mental health.[15] The study made an important contribution, as many observers have pointed out.[16] I remind senators, however, that the Senate's annual budget is now over $100 million, and if the goal is to produce important studies, then there are more effective and less costly ways to produce them.

The Senate has confronted a crisis of legitimacy for much of its existence. The legitimacy issue is tied directly to how senators have been appointed. David E. Smith concludes his widely consulted book, *The Canadian Senate in Bicameral Perspective*, with this observation: "If a theme were sought for the story of Canada's second chamber, the motif of legitimacy would warrant attention. To be more precise, the claim has long been that, because the Senate of Canada is not elected, it is illegitimate."[17] Indeed, count me as one who has questioned the Senate's legitimacy.

Calls for reforming the Senate go back to its very beginning. Canada's Supreme Court made the point that "from its first sittings, voices have called for reform of the Senate and even, on occasion, for its outright abolition."[18] The Senate itself debated its own abolition in 1906 and the Co-operative Commonwealth Federation (CCF) and its successor the NDP, a political party which has held power at in several provinces and was at one time the leading opposition party in the House of Commons, has favoured Senate abolition. This has been the party's position since it was established in 1935.[19]

GROUNDS OF SENATE FORMATION

One has to look far and wide to find anyone, or any group, at any time in Canada's history pleased with the Senate. I cannot identify another issue that has generated as much interest or as many reports as the Senate and its future. The issue generates ongoing interest from individuals, associations, and politicians from British Columbia to Newfoundland and Labrador. Public opinion surveys consistently report that a majority of Canadians would like to see the Senate reformed or abolished.[20] Various reports' recommendations have sought to deal with Senate issues extending back to the debates that led to Confederation and the Constitution Act, 1867. Two issues have dominated such debates about the Senate: its roles and responsibilities and the appointment process.

Three colonies – the Canadas, Nova Scotia, and New Brunswick – came together to define the country's political institutions. The Canadas population in 1867 was 3,090,936 compared with 295,084 for New Brunswick and 368,781 for Nova Scotia.[21] The Canadian colony was led by an influential trio: George Brown, who insisted on a form of representation by population for the House of Commons; George-Étienne Cartier, who sought to accommodate the interest of Canada East; and John A. Macdonald, who sought to strike a compromise between the Canada East and West in part by looking to the Maritime colonies to break the impasse. They decided to create two provinces from the Canadian colony. Canada East, which sought to counterbalance the power of Canada West because of its larger population through the Senate, would not accept the same number of senators as the two smaller colonies. Thus, the Senate's composition would be along regional rather than provincial lines in contrast to other federations, notably, the United States, Australia, and Russia upper houses that have all provinces or states, not regions, represented by an equal number of members.

ROLES AND RESPONSIBILITIES

David E. Smith observes that a good part of the Senate's criticism over the years has been levelled at its role.[22] The Senate's role has never been made clear. Macdonald's "sober second thought" has met the test of time, at least for some, particularly in Ontario. Moreover, the Supreme Court, the media, Royal Commissions, and independent associations have bought into this role. Fathers of Confederation from New Brunswick and Nova Scotia saw the appointed Senate's role as focused on its ability to speak to regional interests. And they were optimistic this would bear out. But this would be hindered by Quebec representatives' insistence on an equal number of senators as Ontario and the Maritime colonies combined for continuing to negotiate the terms of Confederation.[23]

The Supreme Court maintains that the Senate has, over the years, taken on a third responsibility: "The Senate also came to represent various groups that were under-represented in the House of Commons. It served as a forum for ethnic, gender, religious, linguistic, and Aboriginal groups that did not always have a meaningful opportunity to present their views through the popular democratic process."[24]

We have seen widespread criticism directed at the Senate under all three roles. It has even been accused of falling short in pursuing its "sober second thought" role. The argument goes that the Senate has, until recently, reflected the same partisan spirit as the House of Commons.[25] Leaving aside recent developments, the Senate has been divided along partisan lines with Liberals on one side, Conservatives on the other with a sprinkling of independents, and the debates have been all too often politically partisan-fuelled by politically partisan considerations.

Many, particularly in Western and Atlantic Canada, and a number of reports, too, have made the case that the Senate has not been able to promote regional interests and that it has failed as an instrument of intrastate federalism. Because the Fathers of Confederation gave Ottawa all the primary powers in key sectors with the provincial governments to be junior partners, and because our parliamentary system concentrates power in the executive, the Senate was expected to speak up on behalf of the regions. The national government was even granted the power to disallow provincial government legislation if it was deemed not to serve national interest, or whatever other reason that suited Ottawa.

However, the Senate, the argument goes, has lacked the democratic legitimacy to perform this role.[26] The appointment process, at least until a few years ago, was "regularly cited to disparage the second chamber."[27] The test for the Senate was then, and it remains, straightforward: if appointments are suspect and if the Senate lacks democratic legitimacy, then the work it does is also suspect and lacks legitimacy. This argument applies to all three roles ascribed to the Senate by the Supreme Court and by others.[28]

Arguably other than senators themselves, few have been willing to defend the Senate. The actions of some senators have further tarnished the institution.[29] Students of Canadian politics and the media have, for the most part, been critical of the Senate's inability to pursue its roles.[30] I note, however, that one prominent student of government has pointed to several benefits. David E. Smith reminds us that the Senate is not a confidence chamber with the ability to make and unmake governments. He notes that the Senate holds some advantages over the House of Commons: the small number of senators means fewer speeches, procedures are more informal, and the Senate has the ability to produce highly regarded studies.[31]

ATTEMPTS AT REFORM

Particularly since the 1970s, we have seen numerous reports on Senate reforms. There is no need to review them in detail. Suffice to note that the reports came from a variety of sources, that all have pointed to important shortcomings, and all called for reforming the institution. Canada was only seven years old when the House of Commons debated a proposal to amend the constitution to allow provinces to select senators. In 1909, the Senate considered limiting terms to seven years and having two-thirds of senators elected.[32] Both proposals were rejected. In more recent years, the government of Canada tabled a report and Bill-60 in 1978 on reforming the Senate. The government, however, rejected an elected Senate, arguing it would compromise the supremacy of the House of Commons. A year later, the Pépin-Robarts Task Force rejected an elected Senate, on the argument that it would only promote further party politics and partisanship rather than regional concerns.[33]

The Canada West Foundation launched a debate on the merits of an elected Senate – the Triple E variety. It called for an equal number of senators per province, the election of all senators, and the power to challenge the House of Commons.[34] Later, the Canada West Foundation insisted that a reformed Senate "would serve as a valuable balance to the House of Commons and the power of the Prime Minister."[35]

The Macdonald Commission applauded parliamentary government but went on to recommend an elected Senate. The argument was a need to "sensitize the federal government more fully to the aspirations of Canada's diverse regions," making the case that national political institutions lacked this capacity.[36] The Macdonald Commission recommended that Senate elections be held at the same time as the House of Commons, to lessen the risk of having a sharp contrast between party representation in both houses in order to avoid paralysis in Parliament.[37]

The failed 1987 Meech Lake Accord envisaged a reformed Senate, where provincial governments would have had a say in the selection of senators. However, many in Western Canada insisted that the accord did not go far enough in proposing Senate reforms.[38] The failed 1992 Charlottetown Accord sought to go further and proposed an elected Senate, albeit without recommending a system to elect members. It would set aside Senate seats for Indigenous members, while expanding the Senate's power by delegating to it the ability to ratify senior appointments and the authority of a suspensive veto over revenue and expenditure bills.[39]

The above is an all too brief description of past efforts to reform the Senate. I could have added to the list by reporting on the Molgat-Cosgrove Committee (1984) and the Beaudoin-Dobbie Committee (1992).[40] I could also have commented on the reports produced by associations like the Canadian Bar Association, the Public Policy Forum, the Fédération des communautés francophones et acadienne du Canada, and the list goes on.[41]

Leaving aside senators (and not all of them), few are happy with the status quo. Various efforts to reform the Senate, combined with public opinion surveys, reveal a strong willingness to reform or abolish the Senate. Scandals over expense accounts and controversies over place of residence on the part of some senators have not helped matters. I know of no other Upper House, including Britain's House of Lords, that has been so openly and so often challenged.

AN UPPER HOUSE CRITICIZED,
YET CONDEMNED TO SURVIVE UNCHANGED[42]

Roger Gibbins, the former head of the Canada West Foundation, had in his office a carved wooden pig with wings, which he called "my Senate reform pig, as in 'the Canadian Senate will be reformed when pigs can fly.'"[43] The Senate still operates much like it did in its first sitting in 1867. When it comes to the Senate, Canada is like a deer caught in the headlights; Canadians know that they need to reform the Senate, but they simply cannot get it done.

One has to refer back to the Fathers of Confederation in 1867 to understand why. As noted earlier and for reasons that are not clear, they decided not to attach an amending formula to the constitution. The best explanation is that they saw the BNA Act for what it was – an act of the British Parliament that it could amend, if it so decided. In any event, given Macdonald's lack of appreciation for the workings of a federal system, he may well have concluded that the provinces should have no say in amending the constitution.

Starting in 1927, the federal government sought on several occasions – albeit with no success – to patriate the constitution with an amending formula. Ottawa finally secured enough support to patriate the constitution through the Constitution Act, 1982. We saw the 1927 Conference, the 1935 Conference, the 1950 Conference, the Fulton-Favreau formula, the Victoria Charter, and the 1980 Federal Government Initiative all end in failure.[44] In the case of the Fulton-Favreau formula and the Victoria Charter, Quebec balked. I remind readers that Quebec has yet to sign on to the Constitution Act, 1982. Quebec has long argued that it is not a province like the others and points to the Constitution Act, 1867 to make the case that it holds a special status. That Act gives Quebec, among other things, its French civil law system, enshrines the use of French and English in its National Assembly and courts, and gives the province special status when calculating representation by population to determine the number of seats in the House of Commons.[45]

The Constitution Act, 1982 provides an amending formula. However, we have not seen any major amendment since 1982. One of the first attempts to amend the constitution under the formula dealt with the powers of the Senate. The Mulroney government sought in 1984 to give the Senate a suspensive veto of thirty days on many bills and forty-five days on other bills. The amendment fell by the wayside when Quebec and Manitoba, followed later by Ontario, decided to oppose it.[46]

The constitution's amending formula is now clear enough. Stephen Harper turned to the Supreme Court when he sought to reform the Senate in 2013. He asked the Supreme Court to determine if it was within Parliament's authority to reform the Senate in several areas, and if it could abolish the institution.

THE PIG STILL DOES NOT FLY

The Harper government did what Canadian governments do when confronting a high-profile political issue that requires constitutional clarification – refer the matter to the Supreme Court. The Pierre Trudeau government turned to the same when it decided to patriate the constitution, as did the Chrétien government on the issue of Quebec secession, and the Harper government on same-sex marriage.[47]

Harper, a long-time strong proponent of Senate reform, would finally have his day in court. Harper asked the Supreme Court to rule whether Parliament could amend the constitution to establish new term limits for senators, to enable consultations with Canadians to identify nominees for appointment to the Senate, to revise property qualification for senators, and whether the Senate could be abolished without securing unanimous consent of the federal and provincial governments.[48] The reference generated a great deal of interest and all ten provincial governments and territorial governments sought public interest standing on the case.

Harper had promoted Senate reform from the day he first entered politics as a member of the Reform Party. He represented the West, a fast-growing region that "wanted in" in Ottawa, and he and others in the Reform Party saw a reformed Senate as the way ahead. I note that Harper's first Speech from the Throne made Senate reform a priority, making the case that the Senate should better reflect "the needs of Canada's regions."[49]

Nik Nanos, a leading Canadian pollster, suggests that Harper spent considerable time in government creating the circumstances for Senate reform. However, he met with stiff resistance. The Liberal-dominated Senate resisted, as did Conservative senators, even when they gained the majority. Harper met with resistance in caucus particularly from some of his House of Commons members from Ontario and Quebec.[50]

Conservative members of the Commons and the Senate from Ontario and Quebec were one thing, but the constitution and the courts were quite another. Quebec had already taken Harper's proposed legislation on Senate reform to its Court of Appeal. The Quebec court ruled in 2013 that Harper's Bill C-7 designed to create Senate elections and set term limits without consulting the provinces was unconstitutional.[51]

Canada's Supreme Court fast tracked both the hearings and its decision. The court delivered a unanimous verdict, which was "largely expected."[52] The court decided that "Parliament cannot unilaterally achieve most of the proposed changes to the Senate which require the consent of at least seven provinces representing, in the aggregate, at least half of the population of all the provinces."[53] The court added: "The abolition of the Senate requires the consent of all of the provinces." The Canadian Parliament, however, could repeal the requirement ($4,000) to own land in the province for which they are appointed. The decision, however, did not apply in Quebec, where the provincial government would need to agree to do away with special arrangements made in 1867 for the province.[54]

The Supreme Court made it clear that it was only answering questions put before it, that it did not take a position on "possible changes to the Senate," insisting that "the desirability of these changes is not a question for the Court, it is an issue for Canadians and their legislatures."[55] The court, in its rulings, however, referred to the Senate's "sober second thought" thirteen times, underlying its importance. In addition, when the Supreme Court ruled on Canada's efforts to patriate the constitution in 1981, it forced the hand of the federal government to go back to the negotiating table with the provinces. The Supreme Court did not offer the same direction when it ruled on Senate reform.

. In the immediate aftermath of the court's decision, the media and observers were quick to conclude that Senate reform was dead, that it was now off the table, or that the court "just kill[ed] Senate reform."[56] Emmett Macfarlane wrote that the court's ruling "may help to cement Canada's troubling constitutional stasis" and added that it "may not be an absurdity of the Court's making, but of the Constitution's."[57]

Those who wish to see the Senate abolished, including members of the NDP party, now have a very high bar to overcome: the federal government and all ten provincial governments would have to agree.

It is highly unlikely that Quebec would agree to open the constitution on abolishing the Senate without tabling demands that may be difficult for the other provinces to accept. Quebec would not be the only stumbling block. I put the question to Wade MacLauchlan, former premier of Prince Edward Island, whether he would ever accept abolishing the Senate. He answered, "You have my word, never."

INDEPENDENT SENATORS

Justin Trudeau decided in January 2014, with little forewarning, that he would ask all Liberal senators to sit as "independent" senators, meaning they would no longer sit with the Liberal caucus, and henceforth, they would be free to vote as they saw fit. The Liberal Party, in its 2015 election platform, declared that "the Senate needs to change. The status quo is not an option." Trudeau pledged to "create a new non-partisan, merit-based process to advise the Prime Minister on Senate appointments."[58] To that end, shortly after coming to power, Trudeau established an Independent Advisory Board for Senate Appointments with a mandate to "provide non-binding, merit-based recommendations to the Prime Minister on Senate appointments." The board consists of "three permanent federal members and two members from each of the provinces or territories where a vacancy is to be filled."[59]

I accepted to serve on the board as a member for New Brunswick. I note that my experience as a board member was positive. The process worked as it was intended. I did not see or feel any interference from the political level. All Canadians were free to apply, and our deliberations were held in a non-partisan and professional way. If there were a bias, it was against former politicians, including Liberal ones. Word circulated that former politicians need not apply and, if they did, they stood little chance. We were asked to submit five names for every vacancy and in all cases the prime minister selected from the five names. It was made clear that the prime minister would decide, and that he may or may not consult ministers.

The Trudeau reform is making a difference. One senior government official told me, "The best thing to happen to the Senate is that Senators are now independent. The worse thing to happen to the Senate is that Senators are now independent."[60] The point is that the government, particularly the senior public servants, likes the idea of independent senators, but it is uncertain about the impact they will have on government policy and operations.

To be sure, Trudeau sent the Senate into uncharted territory. He explained why: "I'm giving the Senate a chance to save itself."[61] He could do little else, given the country's regional diversity and interests, the rigidity of our constitution, and the Supreme Court's ruling.

What has actually changed? The appointment process, little else. Still, it is important not to underestimate the impact of the independent appointment process. In October 2017, independent senators first held a plurality of seats. This, however, could be short-lived. Andrew Scheer, the opposition leader, pledged to abandon the pursuit of an independent Senate. He has declared that his Senate appointees "would be Conservative senators who would help implement a Conservative vision for Canada."[62]

The change has generated a great deal of interest in and out of government. Many in the media maintain that the Senate remains an "undemocratic" institution. The *Globe and Mail* reminded its readers that the Senate remains unchanged and underlined the point that we have yet "to redistribute its seats to better represent Canada's provincial populations."[63] Here read that the smaller provinces have too many senators and the more populated provinces not enough, seemingly unaware of the role of an Upper House in a federation; look to the United States and Australia, among other nations. It is interesting to read, however, that the *Globe and Mail* sees things differently in the United States where, as pointed out earlier, the executive is less powerful than it is in Canada, and where California (population nearly 40,000,000) and Wyoming (population 590,000) have two senators respectively, or in Australia, with a Westminster-inspired parliamentary system, where New South Wales (population 7,272,800) and Tasmania (population 516,000) have twelve senators respectively.

Another *Globe and Mail* editorial offered, "The Senate, that unelected house of sober second thought ... is currently blocking two bills passed by the elected MPs of the House of Commons. If it persists in doing so, it will face justified criticism that it is acting in an anti-democratic fashion ... There are moments when the credibility of our unelected senators hangs by a thread, and this is one of them."[64] It appears the newspaper has problems with all three roles of the Senate because it remains unelected.

Le Devoir has had little to say about Trudeau's changes to the Senate appointment process. It did, however, make it clear that Quebec was correct in not supporting the Harper reform proposals.[65]

La Presse reported on the Trudeau reform to say that the prime minister was essentially shutting the door on constitutional negotiations to reform the Senate.[66]

The *National Post*'s Andrew Coyne remarked:

> Among the many questions the government has yet to address is: who asked for this? The vast majority of the public, when asked, say the Senate should either be elected or abolished. Almost no one merely wants a better quality of appointee ... There are three kinds of possible reform to the Senate. There is what is desirable – namely, a democratically elected upper house, though this is famously difficult to do. There is what's necessary – namely, to prevent the Senate from thwarting the democratic will of the people. This could be done by a mere change to the Senate's own rules of order. And there is what's beside the point. Strange that the Liberals should be so focused upon the last.[67]

Earlier, an editorial in the *National Post* called for Senate reform – the Triple E variety.[68]

The media have also expressed concern about the work of "an august body" with no political ties to either the government or the opposition. Few journalists or non-partisan observers dispute that the Justin Trudeau appointed senators are non-partisan, thoughtful, with a solid track record of achievements. Many observers acknowledge that independent senators accepted the appointment to make Canada a better place. The Trudeau appointed senators, however, are not representative of the average Canadian. They are the elite in that they are leaders in the arts, literature, business, government, academe, and community associations. Many make the point, however, that in pursuing a better Canada as they see it, they are accountable to no one and owe no allegiance to a political party. This, according to the *Globe and Mail*, "is precisely why they are dangerous."[69]

IN SEARCH OF A JOB DESCRIPTION

Justin Trudeau went as far as he could in reforming the Senate without opening up the constitution. The Justin Trudeau senators are free to define their work as they see fit. They do not answer to a partisan caucus, a political party, or a party leader.

The government's website on Senate appointments outlines the constitutional eligibility requirements (i.e., thirty years of age, a Canadian citizen, residency requirements, and a net worth of $4,000) for those seeking a Senate appointment. It calls for "an outstanding record of achievement in the individual's profession or chosen field of expertise" and stresses the importance of having professional experience to review legislation. It informs applicants that the appointment process will give preference to individuals that will re-balance the Senate in terms of "gender, indigenous, and minority representation."[70]

The government's website has nothing to say about what is expected of independent senators. There is no job description. However, by underlining the importance of "gender indigenous, and minority representation," the government appears to be giving a nod to one of the roles the Supreme Court identified for the Senate when it wrote that it serves "as a forum for ethnic, gender, religious, linguistic, and Aboriginal groups that did not always have a meaningful opportunity to present their views through the popular democratic process."[71]

The government sent an important message to the regions when it announced the Independent Advisory Board. As noted earlier, the chair is from Ontario, Canada's largest province, one member from Quebec, the second largest province, and the other from Alberta, the fourth largest province by population. This suggests that the federal government favours the sober second thought role for the Senate.[72] The Trudeau government would have sent an important message to the smaller provinces, let alone the more heavily populated provinces, had it appointed the chair from Manitoba, the vice-chair from Nova Scotia, and the third federal member from Ontario or Quebec.

The Trudeau Senate reforms did, however, stimulate discussions about the Senate's role and job description for senators. One newly appointed senator wrote that "the only thing asked of us by the PM was that we should bring an independent perspective to our work."[73] He said nothing about the Senate's role in promoting a regional perspective. Another pointed to his contributions in the promotion of LGBTQ rights in his work in the Senate.[74] It would seem that independent senators are free to define their job descriptions as they see fit. Gloria Galloway described the post–Justin Trudeau Senate as "unpredictable. It is a chamber populated with members who do not agree amongst themselves on the basic nature of their job description."[75]

I noted earlier that two high-profile former senators, Michael Kirby and Hugh Segal, penned a 2016 paper with suggestions on how to strengthen the Senate in light of Trudeau's new appointment process. They labelled Justin Trudeau's changes as "perhaps the greatest actual reform of the institution – as opposed to the many mooted ones since Confederation" but then added that "the Prime Minister has provided little guidance as to how their independent Senate should function." They sought to fill the void and offer guidance to the new Senate, while acknowledging its merit: "Make no mistake, without the Senate to provide a regionally-based check and balance on the popularly elected House of Commons, the Confederation project would have failed." They reminded their readers that "such was the sensitivity of this issue that Prince Edward Island remained outside of Canada for six years because the demand for equal provincial rather than equal regional representation was not met."[76]

Among their recommendations included a structure based on regional representation: "As the Senate was originally organized on the basis of regional representation, we recommend this as a sound way to proceed in replacing the prerogatives of partisanship." They acknowledged that some senators will want to come together to pursue objectives such as LGBTQ rights and anti-poverty measures, but "it is not a sustainable base upon which the Senate should organize itself." They urged independent senators to "hang together" or else "no meaningful change will occur." To achieve this unity, they urged that the Senate be organized around regional caucuses that would bring together all senators, regardless of any other affiliation. These caucuses would meet weekly while the Senate was in session. They see the four regional caucuses "contemplated" by the founders of Confederation – Atlantic, Ontario, Quebec, and the West – and the three senators from Northern Canada be given "a one-time election as to which caucus to join." Other recommendations mostly addressed the rules of the Senate and proposed five changes of a statutory nature dealing, among other things, the removal of the net worth requirement.[77]

The Kirby-Segal report went nowhere. Michael Kirby told me, "It was dead on arrival." Senators had little interest in its findings, and few – outside of Western Canada and Atlantic Canada – saw merit in organizing the Senate into regional caucuses. Kirby said that "it was like no one wanted to hear about regional caucuses."[78] Hugh Segal appears to have given up on the report's recommendations and now writes about the Senate's sober second thought role. His views are worthy of mention:

> The Senate, in which I served from 2005 to 2014, was largely driven by partisan directives from the parliamentary wings of the two old-line parties. The appointments by them when in office reflected those partisan priorities. Creating a mirror Upper Chamber with the same divisions and tensions as the lower and elected House was not what the negotiators of Confederation had in mind. Their intent was for a revising chamber that improved legislation, asked more detailed questions and was a thoughtful source of unhurried judgement, all the while respecting the democratic will of Canadians as mandated by an election and expressed by the duly elected government.[79]

Indeed, senators are reverting to what they know best, reviewing legislation. Independent senators, many with limited political experiences given the reluctance to appoint former politicians, are looking to others to guide their contributions. In their report on modernizing the Senate in light of Justin Trudeau's changes, a non-partisan group of senators focused efforts on rules of the Senate, how best to review legislation in committees, and how committee members should be selected. It made only a passing reference to regional caucuses.[80] As noted, a Quebec senator warned publicly against reorganizing the Senate in regional caucuses for fear of fuelling regional tensions. He was not the only Quebec senator to oppose such reorganization, as we will see later.

Senator Peter Harder, the government representative in the Senate, produced a thoughtful discussion paper on the role of the Senate in light of the new appointment process. He outlined a series of principles to guide senators' work. He called for a balanced approach to amending government legislation, including a "sober review of the interplay of legislation with the Constitution ... treaties and international agreements ... the detrimental impact of legislation on minorities and economically disadvantaged groups ... the text of the legislation for drafting errors, serious unintended consequences or other potential oversights." With regard to regions, Harder downplayed the issue and wrote about the need to review legislation for the impact on "regions, provinces and territories, but with a view to the national interest of the federation as a whole."[81] The whole of the Ottawa system from representation by population to determine who holds power, the Cabinet always with strong representation from Ontario, and the senior federal public service concentrated as it is in Ottawa are designed to ensure "a view to the national interest."

THINGS ARE DIFFERENT

The Senate, with a rising coterie of independent senators, is less predictable and more demanding for the government of the day. The ties between the government and the Senate are not as strong as they were. Formerly the government leader in the Senate sat in Cabinet and helped move legislation through Parliament. In the Justin Trudeau government, the government representative in the Senate is not a Cabinet member but does attend Cabinet when there is a need to discuss the government's legislative agenda.[82]

Lobbyists have taken note and they are often a reliable source of where power and influence lie. We have seen a six-fold increase in Senate lobbying since Justin Trudeau came to power. Independent senators, rather than partisan ones, are taking most of the meetings. Members of the House of Commons still hold a strong lead in meetings or communications accepted (about 8,000 versus 1,250 for senators on a monthly basis); however, the Senate is slowly catching up. The twenty-eight Trudeau-appointed senators account for more than a third of the meetings. Senator Terry Mercer explains that "senators are being lobbied more because we've been more active. We're been very proactive." A lobbyist reports that it is now a "new normal, a reflection of the reality that independent senators are changing how decisions get made."[83]

Though it is too early to assess the impact of the new appointment, and though a number of journalists have expressed concerns over the appointment process, some informed observers are applauding the "new" Senate. Paul Thomas, for instance, writes that "it is probably time to revise our negative stereotype of the Senate as a complete failure." Though he acknowledges that the future of the Senate "remains uncertain," he acknowledges "there is tangible evidence that the emerging Senate is becoming less deferential to the prime minister and the government and more willing to amend legislation already passed by the House of Commons."[84] This is a positive development, particularly in pursuing the Senate's "sober second thought" role.

Though I maintain that Justin Trudeau's reforms have done little to clarify the Senate's role, the Trudeau appointees are having an impact. Trudeau appointed Peter Harder, a widely respected government representative in the Senate, who knows well the corridors of power in Ottawa and the legislative process. He has been successful in working with both independent and many partisan senators, and they have made the Senate more relevant inside government and with Canadians – no small achievement in itself. Time will tell if the change can be sustained. Given the reactions to the Kirby-Segal report, it is unlikely the Senate will develop a strong capacity to be the voice of the regions in Ottawa.

LOOKING BACK

It does not much matter what Canadians think of it, the Senate is here to stay and, chances are, stay as is. The shift to appointing independent senators may well be short-lived if Andrew Scheer becomes prime minister. He has made it clear that he is a "believer in an elected Senate," but failing that, his appointments "would be Conservative senators who would help implement a conservative vision for Canada."[85]

One still has to search far and wide to find someone applauding the senators' contributions. In introducing his new appointment process, Prime Minister Justin Trudeau described the Senate as "a powerful, negative force."[86] The national media, for the most part, see little use for the Senate. The *Globe and Mail*, for example, argues that "Canada may not need a Senate, but it's stuck with one."[87] Some senators, meanwhile, see merit in their institution, with one labelling the Senate "one of Canada's most important democratic institutions."[88] He did not explain why he labelled it thus.

Leaving aside the new appointment process, every attempt at Senate reform in recent years has failed. Harper's efforts produced a Supreme Court decision that effectively killed future major reform efforts. Trudeau's new appointment process remains a work in progress.

Senate reform did not rank as priority for Pierre Trudeau when he decided to patriate the constitution, opting instead for a Charter of Rights and Freedoms. After patriation, we saw a number of reports – from the Macdonald Commission to the Beaudoin-Dobbie report – calling for Senate reform. Nothing came of them. The result is that the Senate remains "the whipping post of democratic institutions."

Defending it, as David Docherty points out, "is a thankless task that few outside the Senate feel inclined to take on." Docherty points to the senators' most critical failure in concluding that the Senate "does a poor job of representing regional interests in Ottawa."[89]

Senators, independent or partisan, are juggling several job descriptions. And yet, expectations should be more precise for senators than for members of the House of Commons. Voters decide expectations and performance every four years for elected MPs. Senators have no such requirement. As one journalist observes, the Senate "is elected by no one, accountable to no one."[90] The Kirby-Segal report recommending the Senate rediscover its roots by calling for "a regionally organized Senate" also went nowhere. Rather, independent senators have sought to refine their "sober second thought" role with various reports essentially calling for a "Sober Second Thought Checklist."[91] The fear, as always in Ottawa, is to fuel further regional tensions. Viewed from Ontario, Quebec, and the Prime Minister's Office, it is much safer to pursue a sober second thought role than give more potency to regional voices.

Consequently, we are appointing senators struggling with three different roles, two defined by the Fathers of Confederation when representative democracy was still taking shape – providing sober second thought to an elected House of Commons and providing a regional perspective in Ottawa. We have, over time, added or promoted a third role: speaking on behalf of minorities. Senators are free to pick and choose from any of these roles. The Senate remains an institution that lacks a clear role and norms that its members can easily grasp. The institution was born of a compromise struck by the Fathers of Confederation that avoided dealing with basic requirements of federalism. Virtually from day one, Canadians saw that the institution would not serve their country well.

The new appointment process sees senators with different backgrounds, skills, and notably less partisans than those of past years. However, the institution continues to prescribe expected patterns of behaviour, as the rejection of the Kirby-Segal report reveals. The Senate, starting with the Fathers of Confederation who allowed confusion to set in over its role, continues to mould the behaviour of senators and to generate self-perpetuating characteristics. Delegates from Ontario (then Canada West) did not want power flowing from representation by population compromised by an Upper House, and Quebec (then Canada East) did not want equal representation on a provincial basis. The fact that the Senate remains unelected further delegitimizes its work in the eyes of many Canadians. Given Canada's constitution and recent court decisions, Canada's Upper House will continue to be both criticized and condemned to survive unchanged. Institutions – and the Senate is no different – consist of individuals "bound together by some common purpose to achieve certain objectives."[92]

The Senate continues to be an institution that never was for at least eight of Canada's ten provinces and three territories. The Canadian Senate fails to confer greater democratic legitimacy when it comes to important decisions by providing a double majority – one based on representation by population in the Lower House, and the other by constitutionally recognized communities in the federation in the Upper House. That is what is expected in a federal system. Canada is the exception.

At the risk of stating the obvious, provincial premiers cannot perform that task because they do not have the constitutional power to participate in Ottawa's decisions about national policies or interests.[93] Macdonald and other Fathers of Confederation made sure of that when they decided that provincial governments are responsible for "all matters of a merely local or private Nature in the Province." A former senior provincial government official responsible for intergovernmental relations wrote: "Premiers today are, in Ottawa, about as influential as the MP nobodies Pierre Trudeau dismissed. There is no national forum for Premiers to represent their interests and interact with the federal government."[94]

The Cabinet: The Institution That Once Was

Canada has Cabinet government, so we are told. Cabinet government means government by Cabinet, not government directed by an individual. Under Cabinet government, ministers are involved in setting the government's policy agenda, in striking important government decisions, and in the government's political and administrative life. In a Westminster-inspired parliament government, Cabinet government means that ministers are individually and collectively responsible to Parliament and must retain its confidence.[1] It is their government – at least in theory.

Walter Bagehot wrote that "Cabinet, in a word, is a board of control chosen by the legislature out of persons whom it trusts and knows, to rule the nation."[2] Bagehot had full confidence in Cabinet government and insisted that it was far superior to presidential government. He remarked: "Cabinet government educates the nation; the presidential does not educate it, and may corrupt it."[3]

I wrote in *Governing from the Centre* in 1999 that we had *primus*, and that there is no longer any *inter* or *pares*. Twenty years later, only a few former practitioners dispute this claim.[4] We now have *primus* in all things: in establishing the broad policy agenda; in defining the government's brand; in striking decisions, both large and small, according to the prime minister's wishes; in making all order-in-council appointments, including deputy ministers, senators, and judges; and in shaping the budget, notably in deciding new spending commitments.

In the 2015 general election, Justin Trudeau pledged to return Ottawa to Cabinet government. He told CBC's Peter Mansbridge that though his father launched governing from the centre, he would be the one to return Canada to Cabinet government. He boldly declared on the day that his government was sworn to office that "government by Cabinet is back," in effect acknowledging that Canada no longer had Cabinet government in 2015.[5] However, government by Cabinet is not back. If anything, we have moved further away from it.

Trudeau *fils* has not only abolished regional ministers, he has also made it obvious that he is *primus* and sees no *pares*. At a press conference, for example, Trudeau told journalists to direct questions to him rather than his minister of finance, who was present and traditionally the government's most powerful minister. This, he told the assembled journalists, because he was the prime minister. A *Globe and Mail* journalist persisted and made a second attempt to question the minister of finance, who was standing next to the prime minister. Trudeau replied, "You have to ask a question of me first because you get a chance to talk to the prime minister."[6] I cannot imagine Prime Minister Lester Pearson making a similar claim or, for that matter, his ministers of finance, either Walter Gordon or Mitchell Sharp, putting up with it.

WHERE HAVE ALL MY CHARACTERS GONE?

Ottawa has had powerful ministers through the ages. They had their own brands and could point to major accomplishments that they had successfully promoted and that became part of their brand. I am thinking, among others, of Clifford Sifton and immigration policy, C.D. Howe and economic development, Allan J. MacEachen and social policy, Lionel Chevrier and transportation policy, and Judy LaMarsh and the Canada Pension Plan (CPP). I could go on.

In my book *Politics of Public Spending in Canada*, published in 1990, I grouped ministers under four categories: status, mission, policy, and process participants. Briefly restated, status participants took public visibility to the extreme. They usually worked very well with their departments, I explained, and are always on the prowl in their departments, or elsewhere in government, for initiatives or announcements that enabled them to gain public visibility. The challenges for their departments were to ensure that their ministers were always cast in a positive light in public. If they could do this, these ministers and their departments made for a happy and productive partnership. Status ministers did not want to jeopardize any opportunities to be cast in a favourable light by challenging policy positions of their departments. So long as these ministers did not create problems for the prime minister or the government, they were free to pursue opportunities to be more visible in the media.

Mission participants brought strongly held views to the government and did not avoid confrontations with colleagues or their departments. They were tenacious in pushing their views and were, if needed, prepared to challenge their senior departmental officials. Mission participants had a strong standing in government, in caucus with like-minded colleagues, and in their parties. They, more often than not, pushed far more government spending rather than less. Because mission participants had their own brand and power base within the party, the prime minister had to tread carefully in dealing with them (see, for example, Louis St-Laurent, C.D. Howe, John Diefenbaker, and Alvin Hamilton).

Policy participants went into politics to shape public policies, and they welcomed long debates with their departmental officials and Cabinet colleagues. They came to government with a specific area of expertise and arrived at the Cabinet table with more than the generalities of their own party election platforms. They were not career politicians having gained an expertise in a sector or policy area before coming to Parliament.

Process participants, meanwhile, did not usually question policy or the policy process, nor did they have strongly held views. They went to government to strike deals with colleagues, their departments, or with senior public servants to secure a project for their departments, the sectors for which they were responsible, or their constituencies. They went into politics to deliver projects, to make things happen, and to strike deals.[7] In short, they were deal-makers. They made it a point of understanding how Parliament and government operated to enable them to make things happen. Prime ministers and their advisers worked closely with process participants to ensure that they kept track of the deals being struck.

When I wrote about these four different categories of ministers in the late 1980s, I could still slot ministers as status, mission, policy, or process participants. I saw, among others, Ed Lumley and Jean-Jacques Blais as status participants in the Trudeau *père* Cabinet. I saw Jake Epp and John Wise in the Mulroney Cabinet, and Roméo LeBlanc and Monique Bégin in the Trudeau *père* Cabinet as mission participants. I saw Donald Johnston in the Trudeau *père* Cabinet as a policy participant, given his expertise in tax policy. I saw, among others, André Ouellet in the Trudeau *père* Cabinet as a process participant.

I am hard-pressed in the Trudeau *fils* Cabinet to slot any of his ministers into the four different categories. I can make the same observation for the former Harper government. We no longer have ministers with their own brand that compare to those listed above or, even more recently, with Paul Martin, Brian Tobin, and Sheila Copps in the Chrétien government. We now have the Stephen Harper or Justin Trudeau brand, end of story. Ministers simply blend into these brands and ride the waves wherever the waves take them. As Alex Marland explains, "Ministers and MPs cannot have their own brands. Party leaders own the brand."[8]

There is now only one brand for ministers – the prime minister as Trudeau *fils*. Competing brands from ministers only dilute the prime minister's brand, and it is not tolerated. Prime ministers now have in their hands all the levers of power to dominate every issue they wish to dominate and to have their ministers and MPs blend into their brand. The media now understand that the government belongs to the prime minister, not ministers. Doug Saunders pointed to Stephen Harper, not ministers or even the minister of foreign affairs, in striking program decisions when he wrote, "The $3.4-million Zimbabwe Civil Society Fund II, dried up in 2013 after Prime Minister Stephen Harper shut down its major democracy-promotion agencies, and withdrew resources from countries such as Zimbabwe."[9] Nothing was said about the minister or Cabinet because the decision that involved modest funding belonged to Prime Minister Harper and his senior advisers, no one else, not even the minister.

The Liberal Party won the 2015 general election because Justin Trudeau ran a solid campaign, because of his brand and the work of his pollsters in his court, as well as his political advisers. They understood that the call for "change narrative" would resonate with Canadians.[10] The Trudeau brand dominated the campaign; there were no regional power brokers helping the party win local constituencies.

Politics in Canada is now leader-centric, much like the government is prime minister–centric. Everything revolves around the party leader. MPs, aspiring MPs, and political advisers know that if a leader's weaknesses are exposed, the opposition and the media will pounce. The media's focus is also on party leaders – they are television personalities – and the leaders' debates during the campaign can have a profound impact.[11] Party candidates and party members, meanwhile, are left to show loyalty to their leaders and applaud their performance.

Once the party leader wins election with a majority mandate, his power in government is near absolute. The prime minister's many levers of power are extensive: chair Cabinet; appoint ministers and deputy ministers, senators and judges; establish all Cabinet committees; and decide all machinery of government issues without consulting Cabinet. All orders-in-council initiating machinery of government changes make it clear that the action belongs to the prime minister, not Cabinet. The prime minister articulates the government's strategic direction through the Speech from the Throne, has the final say in establishing the government's fiscal framework and on all major budget items, and is the final arbiter in all interdepartmental conflicts, leads the federal government side in federal-provincial relations, represents Canada abroad, and is the only politician with a "national" constituency. There is no constitutional requirement for the prime minister to consult Cabinet – there are only conventions. The prime minister heads the PMO, the largest partisan political office in government, by a wide margin. Winning a majority of seats sees party discipline kick in, leaving Parliament essentially on the sidelines until the next election. British monarchs of yesteryear would be comfortable with these levers.

Ministers continue to lose influence to the centre of government, that is, to prime ministers and their courtiers. To be sure, prime ministers from John A. Macdonald to Justin Trudeau have always had the upper hand in shaping their government's policy agenda. Patrice Dutil's *Prime Ministerial Power in Canada* documents prime ministerial power under Macdonald, Laurier, and Borden.[12] The story went around Ottawa that R.B. Bennett held Cabinet meetings by walking alone and talking to himself.[13] In brief, prime ministers in Canada, as in Britain and other Westminster-inspired parliament systems, have always been powerful. They gradually replaced all-powerful monarchs to lead the executive, and they have kept for themselves many of their levers of power.[14]

However, today's prime ministers have more tools to govern from the centre, tools that were not available fifty years ago. Cabinets of old had powerful ministers (think of John A. Macdonald's first Cabinet and George-Étienne Cartier; Wilfrid Laurier, Clifford Sifton, and John Cartwright; Mackenzie King, Ernest Lapointe, and

Charles "Chubby" Power; Louis St-Laurent, C.D. Howe, and Jack Pickersgill; John Diefenbaker, Alvin Hamilton, and Donald Fleming; Lester B. Pearson, Donald Gordon, Paul Martin, and Mitchell Sharp; Pierre E. Trudeau, Lloyd Axworthy, and Marc Lalonde; Brian Mulroney, John Crosbie, and Don Mazankowski). The above prime ministers, as noted, had to deal with powerful regional ministers. Alan C. Cairns sums up well the balance of power: "Early Cabinets were collections of regional notables with power bases of their own who powerfully asserted the needs of their provinces at the highest level in the land ... [N]ow, however, regional spokesmen of such power and authenticity are only memories, although the regional basis of Cabinet appointment continues."[15] That argument, as well as the concept of regional ministers, now belong to the history books.

Canada no longer has "big beasts" of Cabinet, like it once did.[16] They enjoyed strong support within the party, their region, caucus, and Cabinet. As noted, Trudeau *fils* has done away with regional ministers because he and his advisers concluded they could not make the concept work in Ontario and Quebec. Before Trudeau *fils*, prime ministers would consult their regional ministers in many areas: from infrastructure projects in their regions to order-in-council appointments.[17] Today, the prime minister turns to independent advisory groups for advice on Senate and judicial appointments and to central agencies for advice on infrastructure projects.

This may well explain why the Trudeau *fils* government set a new record for the number of unfilled government appointments within two years of coming to office. In November 2017, there were 594 positions vacant or occupied by someone whose appointment was past expired. There were another 54 judicial appointments waiting to be made, and a third of federal government agencies had more than half of their positions waiting to be filled.[18] The government came under heavy criticism for the slow pace of striking decisions in implementing its electoral platform to make the largest infrastructure investment in Canadian history.[19] It appears that governing from the centre and bureaucratic processes are not able to produce decisions as quickly as regional ministers once could.

In any event, prime ministers no longer have to turn to ministers, including regional ministers – even if they were still in place – to gain an appreciation of political developments, a proposed initiative, or how a government program is viewed in selected regions. Prime ministers and their courtiers can turn to a variety of public opinion surveys to challenge their ministers' views. There are now timely surveys documenting Canadians' views on virtually every public policy issue. After all, how can the most senior minister dispute what polls say? Public opinion surveys are more reliable, more objective, less regionally biased, more focused, and easier to deal with than ministers.

Governing from the centre, however, is not without problems. Government and bureaucracy are far too complex for one individual and a handful of courtiers to manage and control the whole show. When all important decisions, and even some minor ones, are struck by the prime minister and his courtiers, too much of the system has to be put on hold. Ministers and senior public servants now have to look to the prime minister and PMO for the green light to proceed with major initiatives or even to strike many decisions. This, in turn, overloads the system and the logjams only break when the prime minister and PMO decide what proposed initiative can go forward. This, combined with the growing number of oversight bodies, is stifling the system, making it even more risk-averse than it was in years past. The centre can only focus on carefully selected issues. It has to allow time to manage unforeseen political controversies, which are rarely in shortage.

The rarest commodity in Ottawa is time with the prime minister. Canadian prime ministers lead incredibly harassed lives, with scarcely an open spot on their agenda.[20] Consider the following: prime ministers have some thirty ministers reporting to them; they oversee the work of over one hundred deputy ministers, heads of agencies, and Crown corporations; they have an office with about one hundred staffers; they must pay attention to caucus and, on occasions, be accessible to a caucus member. They must pay attention to their political party, deal with the party president, attend fundraising events and party policy conferences. There are always telephone calls to return, correspondence to attend to, documents to read, and appointments to make. Prime ministers meet the clerk of the Privy Council most mornings when in Ottawa to attend to issues of the day.

There is more. Prime ministers have to be accessible to the ten provincial premiers. They need to be accessible to senior business leaders, the media, and heads of high-profile associations. They have to be available when heads of government call or come to visit. They attend international meetings, notably those of G8, G20, Commonwealth Heads of Government Meeting, and Organisation Internationale de La Francophonie. They have to make time to attend question period and a select number of parliamentary events, from the Budget Speech to special votes. They, and their staff, always have to keep an eye on current or emerging political controversies. Prime ministers, like all MPs, have their own constituencies to attend to. Contrast this with Canada's early years, when Prime Minister Alexander Mackenzie had no secretary and answered all correspondence himself.[21]

Leading students of management insist that a manager's proper span of control should have no more than ten to fifteen people.[22] Elliott Jaques maintains that ten to fifteen subordinates is about right and that one can increase the number of subordinates reporting to a manager "where the manager has no scheduling or technical problems, does not have to go to any meetings, and can spend his/her time overseeing subordinates."[23] This hardly describes the prime minister's workload.

The result is a crushing overload problem, creating a bottleneck at the centre of government where important decisions are made and where green lights are granted for new initiatives. Ministers, departments, agencies, and senior public servants that do not get a green light are expected to run on their tracks, leave well enough alone, and avoid providing fuel for the blame game. This, in turn, makes for a constipated bureaucratic system and decision-making process.

David Mulroney, a former senior PCO official and Canada's former ambassador to China, explains how Ottawa's decision-making process now works:

> Trade negotiating, once an elite art in Ottawa, is now a more mundane bureaucratic function. Back when the Canada-U.S. free-trade agreement and NAFTA were negotiated, we fielded a team of deeply experienced negotiators, giants in a discipline in which Canada then wielded global influence. They worked closely, often directly, with ministers and with the prime minister. There were few – if any – surprises.
>
> Today, the distance between the people who negotiate the deal and the person who signs it – the prime minister – is far greater, and many other people, among them congenitally cautious mandarins from Ottawa's 'central agencies' and legions of hyperpartisan political staffers, stand between negotiators and the PM. That makes us more susceptible to second-guessing and last-minute surprises.[24]

IF THE HEAD GOES ...

Gordon Robertson, clerk of the Privy Council and secretary at a time when Cabinet government was much more evident, observed: "Ministers are responsible. It is their government."[25] The PCO asserts in one of its publications, "We operate under the theory of a confederal nature of decision making where powers flow from ministers."[26] I argue, to the contrary, that power no longer flows from ministers but from the prime minister. In commenting on my book *Governing from the Centre*, Robertson wrote that I "was the first to perceive a change in the governing of Canada that has already had injurious consequences for our country."[27]

Robertson served the Mackenzie King, St-Laurent, and Diefenbaker governments and was clerk of the Privy Council to both the Pearson and Trudeau *père* governments. Prime ministers from Trudeau *père* to today have all sought to strengthen their hands within the federal government. Central agencies have grown in size and influence, starting with the PMO. Trudeau *père* is the architect of the modern PMO. He felt that the Pearson years lacked a proper planning capacity at the centre, and as a result were marked by confusion and chaos. He resolved that things would be different in his government: "One of the reasons why I wanted this job, when I was told that it might be there, is because I felt it very important to have a strong central government, build up the executive, build up the Prime Minister's Office."[28] As a result, Trudeau *père* considerably expanded the size of the PMO and identified its specific functions and tasks. Tom Kent, principal secretary to Prime Minister Pearson, described the PMO before Trudeau: "The PMO was then utterly different from what it became in the Trudeau era and has since remained. There was no bevy of deputies and assistants and principal this-and-that, with crowds of support staff."[29]

No prime minister since Pierre Trudeau has sought to turn back the clock by reducing the size of the office or limiting its functions to what they were before his time in office. Mulroney, in fact, did the opposite. He increased the staff at the PMO by one-third, increased the office's budget by 50 percent, and added eight professional staff concerned with policy.[30] When Chrétien came to office, one of his first decisions was to abolish the chief of staff position in all ministerial offices, a position that Mulroney had established. However, Chrétien decided to retain a chief of staff for his own office who enjoys a deputy minister rank.

Stephen Harper's PMO dominated government. Both Justice John Gomery and Justice Charles Vaillancourt went as far as suggesting that Harper's PMO was a threat to democracy. Gomery urged that "power be taken out of the hands of the scores of unelected and unaccountable people working in the PMO." He emphasized: "I suggest this trend is a danger to Canadian democracy and leaves the door wide open to the kind of political interference in the day-to-day administration of government."[31] Justice Vaillancourt, in his ruling on the Mike Duffy Senate scandal, said that Harper's PMO actions were "shocking and unacceptable in a democratic society."[32] Political observers such as Jeffrey Simpson, Lawrence Martin, Jonathan Rose, and Nik Nanos have all commented on Harper running a tight government controlled from the PMO.[33]

Trudeau *fils*, as noted, pointed to his father for putting in place measures to concentrate power and starting the shift to governing from the centre. He said: "One of the things we've seen throughout the past decades in government is the trend toward more control in the Prime Minister's Office. Actually, it can be traced as far back as my father, who kicked it off in the first place. And I think we've reached the end point on that."[34] We do not know when we will reach the end point but it has not been reached under Justin Trudeau's watch.

Trudeau *fils* has strengthened the centre of government rather than rolled it back. Shortly after being sworn in to power, he established a "deliverology" unit in the PCO. He invited Michael Barber, a British political consultant, to his Cabinet's first three retreat meetings to sing the praises of deliverology. Barber stressed the importance of "results-oriented management" in the public sector, far from the first consultant to make that pitch.[35] As noted, Trudeau asked Matthew Mendelsohn, with close ties to the Ontario government and the Liberal Party, to head the unit. He also decided to chair the Cabinet Committee on Agenda, Results and Communication.[36]

The unit's role is to ensure that the government delivers on its election commitments and key priorities. Mendelsohn was part of Trudeau's transition team and helped draft mandate letters to ministers. The letters, which Trudeau has made public, outline the priorities that ministers and their departments are asked to pursue. How ministers perform in pursuing their mandates became an important criteria for the unit and Cabinet committee. The unit attaches a great deal of importance to established targets and generating the needed data to assess performance. This, ironically, is precisely what Trudeau *père* sought to do when his government adopted a Planning Programming Budget System (PPBS), a scientific process designed to assess whether programs delivered what they had promised.[37] The PPBS failed to deliver because the objectives were too broadly stated, it could never generate the needed data, and budgeting in government is basically a political document not a scientific exercise.[38]

It appears that Trudeau *fils*'s efforts are not faring any better. Deliverology is facing the same challenges that PPBS did – we still do not have the knowledge required to evaluate many programs. With some exceptions, program goals are too abstract or too subjective to measure their impact. The challenge in defining clear objectives, establishing evaluating criteria, and securing the needed information to assess 364 different priorities has yet to be met. In addition, having 364 priorities identified in the mandate letters may well mean having no priorities at all. We know that many things government do are simply not measurable. How, for example, can one possibly evaluate programs to improve the socio-economic circumstances of Indigenous communities or selected regions or communities; how – when assessing economic development measures – do you, isolate the impact of interest rates or volatility with the Canadian currency?

Ottawa-based journalists were reporting, only a few years after its introduction, that deliverology is falling far short of expectations. Adam Radwanski notes that "even some of those more enthusiastic about deliverology in principle have grown skeptical." He asks how one can possibly measure Trudeau's goal of "helping the middle class" and labels the deliverology approach as "the Liberals' attempt to write their own report card."[39] One can ask how one can possibly assess, in any meaningful fashion, Justin Trudeau's efforts to promote "international engagement that makes a difference in the world."[40]

Deliverology itself has not even answered how one could tell if it is successful. Some dismiss it as simply a public relations exercise.[41] The deliverology unit has kept track of commitments made in the 2015 election, something that other units in the PCO and the Treasury Board Secretariat did for years. These older units, however, were not disbanded when the deliverology unit was established, thus making government thicker. This is how government operates: it is excellent at launching new bureaucratic units but largely incapable of doing away with them, even though they have outlived their purpose. In any event, the ability of the Justin Trudeau government to pursue successfully commitments made during the 2015 election is on par with, or no better than, what previous governments accomplished between 1945 and 2014. Other governments did it without a deliverology unit.[42]

The deliverology unit's mandate closely resembles that of the Treasury Board Secretariat. The latter is responsible for assessing the impact of programs, how they perform, and how departments manage operations.[43] When the deliverology unit was established, the mandate of the Treasury Board Secretariat was not adjusted, nor was its staff reduced. As is the way of government, both simply continue to operate with overlapping mandates generating still more demands on line departments and agencies to provide data to the centre. These developments also strengthen the hand of the centre in its ability to ensure that line departments run on their tracks. It is unlikely, however, that it will have any lasting impact on government decision-making. Richard French sums up deliverology's potential nicely: "Deliverology is simply the latest in a continuing flow of fads and fashions that invade ... the public sector with metronomic regularity ... [T]hey never revolutionize government ... because the enduring challenges ... are deeply rooted in a human nature highly resistant to fundamental change, in institutional inertia and – in a democracy – in the additional constraint of democratic constitutions rightly focussed upon legitimacy rather than efficiency."[44]

The key to understanding Ottawa's decision-making process is to focus on prime ministers and their courtiers, on new measures unveiled from time to time (particularly after the budget is tabled), and on the ability of ministers and public servants to ensure that their departments and agencies run on the track. The prime minister is always in the thick of things and is invariably consulted on all issues that matter. The same cannot be said for Cabinet. Prime ministers and their courtiers can remind ministers that they are expendable and the government can carry on. Not so for the prime minister – if he goes, the government goes.

ALL THE PRIME MINISTER'S MEN AND WOMEN

The government of Canada is top-heavy in central agencies, more so than other Westminster parliamentary systems. There is the PMO (100 full-time equivalents), PCO (1,022 full-time equivalents), Treasury Board Secretariat (1,849 full-time equivalents), and Department of Finance (735 full-time equivalents).[45] There are approximately 4,000 full-time equivalents working in central agencies that do not deliver programs or services to Canadians – line departments and agencies do that. They provide political (PMO) and policy (PCO) advice to the government, or rather to the prime minister, and they take direction from prime ministers and their courtiers.[46]

Central agency officials are the bureaucratic and policy elites of the government. If one aspires to be a deputy minister, there is no better route to the top than through central agencies. There was a time when deputy ministers could make it to the top of their department by climbing the ranks within their department. No more. There is not a single deputy minister at the time of writing this book that made it to the top in this manner. Those who make it as deputy ministers will look to the centre for guidance as much, if not more, than to their minister. Deputy ministers know not to shortcut the system: not only do their future promotions depend on the clerk of the Privy Council and the prime minister, but also attempts at making end runs around central agencies to get things done for the department tend to backfire.[47]

The PMO has more power now than ever before in staffing ministerial offices. There was a time when ministers were free to pick their own political staff. The PMO, more often than not, now decides who works in ministerial offices. We were told that Prime Minister Harper trained people in his office and then sent them out to run ministerial offices "in the image of the PMO." The same appears to apply in the case of the Justin Trudeau government. Six chiefs of staff in ministerial offices in the Trudeau *fils* government worked at one time in his PMO.[48] A former federal Liberal member of Parliament suggests that when it comes to governing from the centre, the Justin Trudeau government is "identical, in fact it might be even worse" than the Harper government.[49]

WHAT HAPPENED TO CABINET GOVERNMENT?

In a Westminster-inspired parliament system, constitutional conventions and tradition require that the executive shall be directed by a collective body.[50] I argue that we have moved away from Cabinet government to a form of court government. At the risk of sounding repetitive, the government is directed not by Cabinet but rather by an individual – the prime minister – and carefully selected courtiers.

Though it has gone further than other Westminster-inspired parliamentary governments, Canada is not alone in moving away from Cabinet government. Mark Bevir and R.A.W. Rhodes reviewed a series of media articles that document the rise of "Blair Presidency" in Britain between 1997 and 2005. They consulted a number of practitioners who offered observations suggesting that "more and more decisions were being taken at No. 10 without consultation with the relevant Minister or Secretary of State"; there was a "lack of inclusiveness of the Cabinet"; and the "Cabinet Office now serves the prime minister rather than the Cabinet collectively."[51] Practitioners reported a series of important decisions that were "never even reported to Cabinet," including "independence for the Bank of England, postponement of joining the Euro, cuts in lone-parent benefit and the future of hereditary peers."[52] A long-serving senior public servant in Australia wrote as far back as 2003 that the "power of the Prime Minister and the Prime Minister's Office continues to rise."[53]

Canada has taken governing from the centre to new heights.[54] The clerk of the Privy Council and secretary to the Cabinet saw the job mandate take a new form in the 1990s. No secretary to the Cabinet since Gordon Robertson has sought to describe their main job as secretary to the Cabinet. The PCO now serves the prime minister rather than the Cabinet collectively. In 1997, the PCO produced a document on its role and structure whose opening page makes it clear that the secretary's first responsibility is to the prime minister. It states that the

> Clerk of the Privy Council and Secretary to the Cabinet has three primary responsibilities:
> 1) As the Prime Minister's Deputy Minister, provides advice and support to the Prime Minister on a full range of responsibilities as head of government, including management of the federation.
> 2) As the Secretary to the Cabinet, provides support and advice to the Ministry as a whole and oversees the provision of policy and secretariat support to Cabinet and Cabinet committee.
> 3) As Head of the Public Service, is responsible for the quality of expert, professional and non-partisan advice and service provided by the Public Service to the Prime Minister, the Ministry and to all Canadians.[55]

The direct link between the prime minister and the secretary to the Cabinet and the PCO is made clearer still in the office's *mission* and *values* statement. Its mission is "to serve Canada and Canadians by providing the best non-partisan advice and support to the Prime Minister and Cabinet." Its values statement makes absolutely no mention of Cabinet: "We recognize the special need of the Prime Minister for timely advice and support. We dedicate ourselves to our work and to the effective functioning of government. We believe that integrity, judgment and discretion are essential to achieving our mission."[56] The prime minister, not Cabinet, appoints and dismisses the clerk of the Privy Council. Since 1997 federal government officials see the clerk of the Privy Council far more as the deputy minister to the prime minister than as secretary to the Cabinet. The prime minister, on the advice of the clerk of the Privy Council, not Cabinet, appoints all deputy ministers, heads of agencies, and heads of Crown corporations. The ambitious public servants are well aware of this.

Clerks of the Privy Council in recent years attach considerable importance to their number one role in the list of three: the "Prime Minister's Deputy Minister," which gives them all the influence they need. In her report to the Gomery Commission, Sharon Sutherland remarked: "There is a lack of restraint in brandishing the title. It seems to imply an unlimited power acquired through access to the Prime Minister. As one interviewee said, Gordon Robertson, as a kind of gold standard as Clerk, would have been offended to be called 'DM to the PM.' The Clerk is, before anything else, 'the guardian of the system of responsible government, which includes Cabinet government.'"[57]

I invite those who believe that Canada still has Cabinet government to ponder the point made earlier: "Two key decisions regarding Canada's deployment in Afghanistan – one by a Liberal government, one by a Conservative government – were made in the Prime Minister's Office with the help of a handful of political advisers and civilian and military officials. The relevant ministers – of National Defence and Foreign Affairs – were not even in the room." Cabinet was later told of the decision. Former cabinet minister Lowell Murray adds that this is "far from atypical illustration."[58]

Former prime minister Jean Chrétien summed up the role of Cabinet ministers when he wrote that the minister "may have great authority within his department, but within the cabinet he is merely part of a collectivity, just another adviser to the prime minister. He can be told what to do, and on important matters his only choice is to do it or resign."[59] Ministers, for Chrétien, were no more than other political advisers – offering counsel on a variety of issues, assessing political conditions, and providing support to the prime minister. Prime ministers have many political advisers, including senior members of their office, and Cabinet ministers are no match to the prime minister's chief of staff. Today, Cabinet's role, in its essence, is to be a symbolic representation of government unity before Parliament, the media, and Canadians.

The *Hill Times*, an Ottawa-based publication that closely follows the federal government's political and bureaucratic developments, provides a list of the most powerful and influential people. In 2018, it ranked Justin Trudeau, followed by his principal secretary, and then his chief of staff as the three most powerful individuals in Ottawa. The clerk of the Privy Council and secretary to Cabinet ranked fourth on the list. There were only six Cabinet ministers on the top twenty-five list, while PMO-PCO had nine.[60] Other Ottawa watchers came to the same conclusion. For instance, John Ibbitson writes that "in reality, power rests in only a few hands," including "the small team of powerful ministers that a prime minister trusts to manage the crucial files, with all the others kept on a short leash."[61]

DOES IT MATTER?

Collective ministerial responsibility is, at least in theory, fundamental to the Westminster-inspired system. At the risk of stating the obvious, it requires that ministers collectively decide and collectively take responsibility for their decisions. Robert Marleau and Camille Montpetit's widely consulted book *House of Commons Procedure and Practice* makes it clear that, as in Britain, "Ministers are expected to take responsibility for, and defend, all Cabinet decisions. The principle provides stability within the framework of ministerial government by uniting the responsibilities of individual Ministers under the collective responsibility of the Crown."[62] In Canada, as it is in other Westminster-inspired parliamentary government, this principle should remain "one of the cornerstones of Westminster government."[63]

Canada's government maintains that it has stood firm on the principle. It continues to make the case that it remains "a vibrant part of the Canadian – indeed the Westminster – constitution."[64] The government continues to cling to the requirements of Cabinet government. Former Cabinet secretary Bob Bryce struck a seminal decision in 1957, when he asked Prime Ministers Louis St-Laurent and John Diefenbaker to accept to protect Cabinet confidences that reveal "differences of view between Ministers or opinions of Ministers which would not be put on paper if it were felt they would ultimately fall into the hands of members of another political party."[65] The principle of Cabinet confidences is still brought home with the prime minister, occasionally reminding ministers of the strict rule against taking notes in Cabinet, other than by official note-takers from the Cabinet secretariat.[66]

Nicholas D'Ombrain, a former senior official with the PCO in Ottawa, explains in his award-winning article that the constitutional convention of secrecy of Cabinet proceedings "was established to protect the process of decision-making, which is quintessentially political in a system of government built on the collective responsibility of ministers to the House of Commons." D'Ombrain attaches more importance to protecting the process and "the views and opinions of ministers than the substance of the policy decision struck in Cabinet."[67] He writes that for the Cabinet decision-making process to work properly, "ministers must be able to speak frankly without fear that divergent views or disagreements may become known and exploited through the political process, and thus potentially undermine parliamentary confidence in the ministry."[68] Cabinet government prevents the government from pitting one minister against another in public, a key element of the Westminster parliamentary model. This requirement is key because, in theory at least, the government belongs to ministers – it is their government.

Ministers have a choice: respect the Cabinet process and accept – at least, in the Commons and publicly – the decisions that flow from it, or resign. When Cabinet resolves an issue, any ministers who previously opposed the resolution must now make it their choice and support it as if they had authored it. Again, if ministers cannot live by this rule, they must resign. For example, James Richardson resigned as minister of Defence from the Trudeau government in 1976 because he disagreed with the government's policy on official languages. Michael Chong resigned from the Harper Cabinet to express his opposition to the government's decision to recognize Quebec "as a nation within a united Canada."[69] Both resignations dealt with language policy or Quebec's place in Canada. Both instances make the case that ministers in Canada are not prone to resign on matters of principle.

Some observers of Canadian politics have pointed to my own work to ask some fundamental questions about the role of Cabinet.

For example, David E. Smith writes, "Donald Savoie has argued that to the extent power is concentrated, it is lodged in central agencies answerable to the Prime Minister," suggesting that Cabinet is losing some of its policy-making role and that ministers may no longer be collectively responsible.[70] Nicholas D'Ombrain pointed to my book *Governing from the Centre: The Concentration of Power in Canadian Politics* and went further. He observes that as "Donald Savoie has argued, there is doubt that the cabinet continues to fulfil its central role of uniting ministers in order that they may be collectively responsible for government."[71] If ministers are no longer collectively responsible for the government, then a number of constitutional conventions need to be revisited.

If much of the requirements for Cabinet secrecy no longer apply, it raises fundamental questions about the continued relevance of what underpins the Westminster model. If Cabinet is little more than a focus group for the prime minister or a "pep talk session" for the most senior members of caucus, one needs to ask if Cabinet still requires "immunity from the disclosure of its proceedings, still less factual material laid before it."[72] I can do no better than quote D'Ombrain once more to sum up what this means for Cabinet government: "Canada's version of Westminster democracy is being eroded by lack of appreciation – and, hence, respect – for the conventions of responsible government and the important principles of constitutional government they underpin. The political and informal character of the cabinet lies at the heart of the conventions of the constitution. The cabinet secrecy convention is the foundation for the maintenance of collective cabinet responsibility, but if cabinet secrecy is to remain part of our constitutional arrangements, it is essential that the cabinet remain the mainspring of government."[73] The point is that if Cabinet is no longer the mainspring of government, then one can legitimately ask what underpins the conventions of responsible government, and if Cabinet secrecy should remain an important part of our constitution.

I argue that prime ministers and their courtiers – not Cabinet – are now the mainspring of government. The Cabinet minister is all too often left on the outside looking in, as it was, for example, regarding Canada's military deployment in Afghanistan. Several years ago, I was invited to meet with some senior staff members of Stephen Harper's PMO. Two asked if I would autograph their copies of my book *Governing from the Centre*. One had clearly read the book with parts of it underlined. As I signed it, I said: "I hope that you learned something from reading it." One of them responded: "Oh yes, we use it as a manual." I assure the reader that my purpose in writing the book was not to empower PMO staff members or other senior central agency officials to strengthen their hands and the governing from the centre process.

One former deputy minister told me that governing from the centre became more obvious after the book was published. He argued that many university graduates came to government after reading the book, thinking that it was how government operated and best to adjust their thinking accordingly. His point was that the book served to reinforce the shift toward the governing from the centre approach rather than help to keep it in check.[74]

LOOKING BACK

Cabinet government is failing. It is no longer the key policy and decision-making body. More and more decisions are struck at bilateral meetings, which are preferred by the prime minister. No other Cabinet minister hears what was discussed at these bilateral meetings where decisions struck are final – who in the system can question a decision struck by the prime minister? The new norm as described is that ministers are required to subscribe to the prime minister's views and decisions or resign, and history shows that few ministers are prepared to resign, no matter the issue or the policy-making process.

It is more than ironic that ministers developed Cabinet confidences in Britain as protection against the monarch. The idea that ministers should speak with one voice became a way to prevent the British monarch from adopting a divide-and-conquer strategy against them. The monarch, in the eighteenth century, performed a role that now belongs to the prime minister. George III (circa 1760–1820) met his ministers not as a group but rather one by one. Ministers decided that the best way to deal with the king's desire to confine them to address a particular issue was to speak with one voice. When it came to general political issues, ministers would agree beforehand what to say and then meet the king and repeat the identical story. This allowed ministers to be able to debate issues and strike decisions through frank discussions without fear that their deliberations – who spoke in favour and who spoke against – would make their way to the king. Hence the birth of Cabinet confidences.[75] The reason for Cabinet confidences has come full circle.

Cabinet is failing in recent years to bring the regional perspective in the federal government as some Fathers of Confederation insisted it would. We know that Macdonald pointed to the role of Cabinet in promoting regional interests as the way to entice Nova Scotia and New Brunswick to sign on to Confederation. In addition, powerful regional ministers and powerful personalities in Cabinet are no more. Prime ministers since Trudeau *père* have interpreted the wide degree of discretion under the Westminster model to make decisions that once belonged to Cabinet and individual ministers.[76] Prime ministers now increasingly turn to a governing body of senior officials in PMO and PCO who have seen their influence grow in recent years at the expense of Cabinet.[77]

The Cabinet's failings have wide implications for representative democracy, for accountability, and for our constitution. If it no longer underpins our Westminster-inspired parliamentary model, then what does? What happens to the requirements of Cabinet confidences? What does it mean for bureaucracy? Who, if anyone, now speaks for the regions inside the federal government?

11

The Media: The Lost Institution

Post-truth politics is here. Donald Trump demonstrated that he was a master at it during the 2016 presidential election. Brexit supporters, too, were successful in promoting misinformation claiming, for example, that EU membership was costing Britain nearly $500 million a week, money which, they argued, would be better spent on the country's National Health Service.[1] Canada is not immune to post-truth politics. The publication *iPolitics* documented the top fifteen untruths voiced by leading Canadian politicians during the 2015 federal election.[2] The FactsCan website was also kept busy throughout the 2015 general election.[3]

The *Oxford Dictionary* declared "post-truth" as its international word of the year for 2016, defining it as "relating to or denoting circumstances in which objective facts are less influential in shaping public opinion than appeals to emotion and personal belief."[4] According to the same source, post-truth has "gone from a peripheral term to being a mainstay in political commentary."[5]

The digital world has made it possible for the post-truth world to flourish. The traditional media are under attack as both readership and revenues continue to plummet. As revenues shrink, so do newsrooms. Politicians, as recently as the early 1980s, would not recognize today's political landscape. They would see their profession debased by the new media, as well as other forces, and many may well conclude that they could not function in the current political environment. They would wonder why the class of politicians that came after them would ever support developments that made the post-truth world possible and their job much more difficult by accepting what was once unacceptable.

Until the mid-1980s, politicians did not have to deal with access to information legislation, a twenty-four-hour news cycle continually looking for something new to report, mostly negative, and social media were not even on the drawing board. The traditional print media were healthy, widely read, and had editorial oversight. Both the print and electronic media were the important source of non-partisan political information, at least they were widely perceived as such. They had considerable influence on the country's political discourse as they played their traditional referee role between competing political parties or points of view. Newspapers and the evening news on television and radio enabled a small number of journalists to speak to millions of Canadians about politics. Canadians, however, could not speak back to them.

Politicians in the 1980s were still years away from what Lawrence Martin, a widely read *Globe and Mail* columnist, describes as "a crisis in the journalism industry unprecedented in scope." He observes that we are witnessing a "media implosion. Newspapers being reduced to digital editions, large numbers losing their jobs, circulation falling, ad revenues plunging ... the old business model in a state of collapse."[6] One can only imagine how difficult it must be for journalists working under the old business model.

THE MEDIA: DEMOCRACY'S BACKBONE

Representative democracy requires informed citizens, and informed citizens require media that supply them with factual information and knowledge.[7] A well-functioning representative democracy and a free press go hand in hand. The media are the fourth estate – a source of power or influence in addition to the executive, Parliament, and the judiciary. The role of the media is to act as a watchdog, to offer a platform for debate in an objective fashion, to act as a guardian for the broad public interest, and to assist in holding governments to account. The social media have, or should have, the same role and responsibilities.

Alexis de Tocqueville ranked the press as the leading instrument to ensure freedom and democracy: "I think that men living in aristocracies may, strictly speaking, do without the liberty of the press: but such is not the case with those who live in democratic countries ... [T]he press is the chiefest democratic instrument of freedom."[8] For Tocqueville, representative democracy without a free press was not possible. Natalie Fenton agrees: "News is [...] the life-blood of democracy," and the "vocation of journalism is embedded in a relationship with democracy and its practice."[9] Many politicians agree, too. Canada's Member of Parliament Mélanie Joly, for example, maintains that "journalism plays a central role in a healthy democracy."[10]

Tocqueville completed his treatise almost two centuries ago, while Fenton made her case only about a decade ago. If the news media had a golden age, it was during the years between Tocqueville and Fenton. During this period, the news media became less openly partisan, less tied to a political party, and more trusted as an objective source of information. Politicians came to respect the media, albeit grudgingly in many cases. Though Tocqueville regarded the press as the chief democratic instrument of freedom, the media in his day presented a combination of news and opinions, when there was "no concept of the objective unbiased journalist."[11]

By the turn of the twentieth century, however, many journalists concluded that to serve democracy better, they had to be objective. The print media encouraged their journalists to report "facts," to embrace objectivity, and to look beyond political spin and politically partisan information. The approach also made business sense. An objective and non-partisan newspaper could appeal to more readers and to more advertising clients. Both journalists and newspaper owners saw merit for their profession in presenting an impartial account of events and political development.[12] They set the stage for building institutions with norms, values, and editorial control to guide how news would be reported.

Canada recognized the link between the media and representative democracy in 1867. The new Parliament buildings were equipped with a press gallery to give journalists a ringside seat to the deliberations of MPs and government decision-making.[13] Political leaders wanted to make certain that what was debated in both Houses of Parliament would be reported back to Canadians.

Schools of journalism began to surface at the turn of the twentieth century. In 1912, Columbia University was the first university to introduce courses in journalism.[14] Canadian schools of journalism began to take shape at the end of the Second World War at Carleton University, the University of Western Ontario and Ryerson University. Journalism schools, then and now, stress the importance of objective reporting and the positive role the media need to play in supporting representative democracy.[15] Today, all universities have some capacity in the communications fields, with a number of them offering graduate programs.[16]

Schools of journalism have not, however, prevented the traditional media from fast losing ground to social media. Even twenty-four-hour cable channels are feeling the pressure, both in generating revenues and retaining viewers. Twitter and Facebook have become important sources of information and influential actors in the political process. The view that the traditional media are the champions of objectivity and quality is increasingly challenged.[17] And the question of better or not may not even matter. As Nic Newman at BBC observes, "Not better. Just inevitable that social media will change things."[18]

The new media are having a profound impact on the traditional media by threatening the existence of the printed newspaper and reshaping news, all with serious implications for representative democracy. Journalism has become wide open to novice journalists and is relatively free of editorial control. News can now surface from many points, not simply from the newsroom. Social media operate in a world of fragmented audiences and provide information to users at great speed. They are also interactive.[19] It seems that everyone who has a cellular phone can now be a journalist. The traditional media have been struggling to keep up with real-time information in a highly competitive environment. This has pushed them to cut costs by reducing oversight and fact-checking processes.

The debate among both journalists and students of journalism is whether the internet and social media are reinvigorating democracy or playing havoc with it. The central question: do social media "improve the quantity and quality of citizen participation in politics and mitigate the inequalities now found in the rates of participation of different social groups?"[20] The jury is still out, though more and more observers are making the case that social media are having a negative impact.

THE DEINSTITUTIONALIZATION OF THE MEDIA

In Madelaine Drohan's review of the state of Canadian media, she underlines the financial challenges confronting traditional media, pointing out that "news organizations in financial trouble rarely devote resources to costly investigations or the kind of deep dive into an issue that produces worthwhile journalism … They cut staff or entice senior journalists to take early retirement. The inevitable result is poorer journalism, fewer voices contributing to the public debate."[21] Cuts in staff are often made where they are easier to make – away from head office and the Ottawa office. For example, the *National Post* shut down operations in Atlantic Canada several years ago, and the *Globe and Mail* closed its Atlantic Canada correspondents' office, only to reopen it recently.

Provincial and local newspapers are struggling as well. Many have shut down in recent years. Those that are still in business are reducing staff and are much less likely to devote resources to in-depth studies as they did in the past. The traditional print media are feeling the pinch in their bottom line. A veteran Canadian journalist sums up the crux of the problem: "The disruption undermines democracy by gutting local reporting, removing journalists from legislatures and shifting money to non-Canadian news distributors, such as Google and Facebook."[22] The result is that the media in Canada are increasingly "global" and less "national," "regional," "provincial," or "local." Demography matters more than geography with the social media.

The *Globe and Mail* – self-proclaimed as "Canada's national newspaper" habitually overlooking French Canada in this claim – is a case in point. It is quietly shutting down regional offices. It shut down its print edition first in Atlantic Canada in the summer of 2017, with other regions likely to follow, pointing to the further urbanization of political news. In the same summer, the *National Post* eliminated its Monday print edition to all regions.[23] Phillip Crawley, the *Globe and Mail*'s publisher, explained his decision: "Unlike the CBC, which is State-funded, the Globe is an independently-owned company, and I make business choices ... to make sure we continue to have a viable business. We don't have a public duty to lose $1m per year on printing and distribution in the Maritimes."[24] The newspaper's focus is increasingly on national politics and the national economy, albeit now with less resources. Still, the *Globe and Mail*, like other daily newspapers, continues to have editors manage the process and ensure a level of integrity. It still has a strong presence in the head office in Toronto, its leading columnists and journalists in the Ottawa office, and until recently, voices from the regions, or from St John's to Victoria.

Regional and local newspapers are cutting their correspondents in the Ottawa press gallery. Sean Speer and Jamil Jivani explain the fallout: "These reporters played a critical role in both placing regional or local issues on the national agenda and conveying federal decisions in a way that connects to regional or local concerns."[25]

Three powerful voices from the print media and labour movement recently made a plea for help: "The situation is bad and getting worse. More and more newspaper jobs are disappearing – at least one in three since 2010 by our count – and newspaper closings in more than 200 federal ridings have loosened the social glue news provides to communities. These reporter-intensive organizations are the tributaries for much of the news about democratic institutions generated in Canada, both in print and online." They note the impact is keenly felt: "In Canada, the threat is more acute because the market is smaller. Canadian daily newspapers have seen more than half their ad revenues – about $1.5-billion – bleed away over the past decade, most of it going to Google and Facebook, which together served up more than eight out of 10 digital ads in Canada last year. Unfortunately, they don't invest in generating news."[26] There is no end to bleak news for the traditional print media. The *Toronto Star* has gone from a newsroom staff of 470 to 170 in ten years. Rogers Media killed the print editions of four of its magazines in 2015–16.[27] The *National Post* lost 25 staff to buyouts in late 2016, and Postmedia eliminated 90 journalists from its newsrooms in 2017.[28]

Allan Gregg reports that only 16 percent of adult Canadians now subscribe to a print version of a newspaper, and more and more of them now access news online rather than off-line. He notes that a significant majority of Canadians think that news available on nondigital media is "similar" to digital news and that "a plurality believe that the professionalism and objectivity of nondigital journalism are the 'same' as for journalism that is available online."[29] This view is being challenged. For instance, two students of Canadian journalism write that Canadians are critical of social media and point to a public opinion survey to report that only 24 percent of them believe that social media "help them distinguish fact from fiction."[30]

Andrew Potter goes to the heart of the issue when he writes about the "deinstitutionalization" of the media. He, and for that matter most of his colleagues, insist that Canadian journalism is confronting a "crisis." The crisis, he argues, goes beyond the dramatic loss in "newsroom headcounts" and the "number of layoffs."[31] The more important crisis, according to Potter, is that "journalism has been effectively de-institutionalized because those consumer protections are no longer in place. There is no longer any way of ensuring that we can trust the news."[32] He explains: "In some cases it's literally guys in sweatpants sitting on a couch making stuff up, writing their fabrications as a news story, complete with dateline, byline and quotes, and putting it on the internet ... And this is where the de-institutionalization starts to bite: online, every article, in a sense, is on an equal footing. In the great democracy of the worldwide web, a URL is like currency. Anyone's URL is as good as anyone else's."[33]

Some observers make the case that social media expand public debates by transcending territorial boundaries. The new media give everyone voice and the ability to extend political and economic debates beyond the elites.[34] However, how does one make sense of everything that is on social media? The *Economist* ran an article that asserts a contrary view: "Social media have been spreading poison" and they do "not cause division so much as amplify it."[35]

Edward Greenspon, a highly respected former journalist, contrasts social media with the underlying value of the traditional media: "I constantly challenged myself to ensure our conclusions were based on facts and analysis."[36] His point is that the social media fall short both on objectivity and on serving the broader public interest. They provide little more than a bubble, an echo chamber, where people who share the same political views can talk to one another and avoid contrary views to challenge their own thinking. Daily print newspapers, on the other hand, provide a great deal of material that the reader does not, or would not, have chosen.

The Canadian government is trying to walk a fine line between helping journalism and ensuring that it remains independent. In his 2018 fall fiscal update, Finance Minister Bill Morneau declared that it was important to protect the "vital role that independent news media play in our democracy and in our communities." He also unveiled a $600 million five-year package for Canadian journalism. The government decided to walk the fine line by turning to a series of tax incentives and tax credits to support local journalism. The Conservative Party was quick to denounce the initiative, accusing the government of using public funds to curry favour with journalists.[37]

WHY DOES THIS MATTER TO REPRESENTATIVE DEMOCRACY?

New media, from the twenty-four-hour news channels to social media, differ on several fronts from traditional media. They are more open to "citizen journalism" and, at the same time, global and able to link individuals to developments abroad in an unprecedented fashion. Social media are thus enabling people to become global citizens providing a front-row seat to developments abroad, such as the Arab spring, social tensions in Europe, and US presidential elections. This, among other factors, explains why advertisers are flocking to Facebook and other digital platforms.

Facebook and Twitter, for example, enabled Canadians to follow the 2016 US presidential election as closely as the Americans did. That election, in turn, served a number of lessons learned for the post-fact world. There was a constant stream of wild claims, from the pope had declared his support for Donald Trump to the pope was urging Roman Catholics not to vote for Trump. Michael Flynn, who Trump picked as national security adviser, retweeted a fake news story, claiming that the NYPD was investigating Hillary Clinton for money laundering and sex crimes with children.[38]

Some observers maintain that "fake news" on Facebook contributed to Donald Trump's victory. Facebook founder Mark Zuckerberg issued a statement shortly after the election to make the case that the 44 percent of Americans who get their news from social media are well served. He insists that "only a very small amount is fake news and hoaxes," and that "the hoaxes that do exist are not limited to one partisan view." He later acknowledged, however, that Facebook "has more work to do in combatting misinformation."[39] Later still, he went further in a pledge to overhaul Facebook's policy on political ads and to demand that, in future, political advertisers disclose who is paying for the advertisements.[40]

Shifting from traditional media to social media has important implications for representative democracy. Social media create platforms for sharing news, open lines of communication between users, and allow many to comment and add content without always ensuring its accuracy. They have brought the press to the people. Social media, however, do not lend themselves to in-depth studies and editorial control and, as a result, they are particularly vulnerable to fake news and a reliance on stereotypes.

Many politicians and observers have expressed deep concerns about the rise of social media. For example, President Obama made it an important theme in his farewell speech to Americans: "Increasingly, we become so secure in our bubbles that we accept only information, whether true or not, that fits our opinions, instead of basing our opinion on the evidence that's out there.'"[41] *The Economist* wrote: "Social media provide platforms for monomaniacs who previously raged in the privacy of their bedsits. People who might hesitate to berate their fellow citizens in person show no such qualms when it comes to sounding off against virtual targets. Bad-tempered tweets, dashed off in seconds, elicit bad-tempered responses, creating a culture of vitriol."[42] Brad Lavigne, a long-time political adviser to the NDP, writes that "Social media also amplifies the so-called bozo eruptions" in political discourse.[43] Taylor Owen asks, "Does Facebook threaten the integrity of Canadian democracy?" He delivers his answer: "Yes."[44]

Roberto Coloma, a bureau chief for Agence France Presse, argues that "The main risk of using social media for news gathering is accuracy. As for news distribution, you lose control over your information with each layer of transmission, as people condense, distort, interpret and comment on variations of the original report."[45] Social media are turning contributors into "jacks of all trades, masters of none." They are now expected to perform many tasks – reporter, editor, cameraman, soundman, photographer, photo editor, and monitor of social media with or without editorial oversight.

Today's journalists in traditional media are likewise expected to contribute to many platforms – newspapers, magazines, television, radio, and online. They are expected to produce news stories quickly with limited opportunities for in-depth analysis. Dan McHardie, a veteran print and CBC journalist, writes that "before the emergence of the minute-to-minute online news cycle, a journalist would be assigned a story in the morning, attend a news conference, work their sources throughout the day and produce a story for either the evening news or morning newspaper." Today, he notes, journalists "at a major mainstream news organization will likely be expected to bring [...] an iPhone to a news conference so they can send instant headlines out via Twitter, file short paragraphs to the organization's website, prepare radio or television hits that could go on cable networks or radio newscasts and then work on a longer story for the evening news or morning newspaper. There is an amazing pressure on journalists to get the story out accurately and quickly ... whatever means necessary. The media and politicians now operate in a news cycle that has quickly become nasty, brutish and short."[46] Natalie Fenton writes about the need to "speed it up and spread it thin."[47] News stories, even in traditional media, are increasingly pushed out before the usual checks for journalistic integrity are carried out.[48] Canada has not been immune to these developments.

Objective journalism requires balance between contending points of view – thus playing its traditional referee role. It should also promote pluralistic public debates and act as a watchdog on both private and public office holders. Pinar Gurleyen and Robert A. Hackett nicely sum up the importance of the matter: "Objectivity is embedded in an institutional framework. It presumes journalism is conducted by professionals with appropriate skills, employed within specialized institutions (news organizations, usually corporate-owned, but with separated editorial and marketing functions)."[49] When the institutional framework falls down, objectivity is not far behind.

Political scientists will continue to debate the merits of social media. Some argue that they make it easier for groups to organize, to give voice to people who had none, and to promote democratic activism. They are wide open to all participants able to voice views with little editorial oversight. Citizens are thus able to participate in public policy debates as equals, transforming representative democracy. Social media do provide new opportunities to challenge those who occupy positions of power and influence. The argument goes that citizens no longer have to be passive observers of political or government spin or traditional media.[50]

On one side of the debate, observers make the case that social media provide opportunities and structure for everyone, with access to the internet, to voice opinions and to participate in Canada's political life. As well, they force citizens from being simply passive consumers of the traditional media, political spin, or political party propaganda. Social media unleash citizens to participate in representative democracy by promoting citizens' participation in politics.

Others argue that social media are making politics more chaotic because they continue to inject more instability into politics.[51] Social media provide a home for trigger-happy observers who tend to debase informed discussions on public policy issues. Rather than provide a new tool to strengthen representative democracy, social media provide opportunities to all citizens to vent their frustrations, prejudices, and abuse without editorial and centralized control.

A good number of these observers insist that platforms like Facebook and Twitter enable fake news stories from unreliable sources to flourish. As already noted, there is evidence that fake news stories spread like wildfire during the 2016 US presidential and the

Brexit campaigns, and they had an impact. In addition, Facebook enables people of like mind to reinforce their views. Phil Howard explains: "When offered a choice of news stories, we prefer to read about the issues we already care about, from pundits and news outlets we've enjoyed in the past. Random exposure to content is gone from our diets of news and information. The problem is not that we have constructed our own community silos – humans will always do that. The problem is that social media networks take away the random exposure to new, high-quality information."[52] For instance, Canada's Liberal Party was involved in the Facebook-Cambridge Analytica scandal.[53] Social media are well suited to manipulating data and generating untruths, thus spreading "outrage, corroding voters' judgement and aggravating partisanship."[54]

To be sure, political and government institutions have challenges in coping with social media. Social media, by definition, are bottom up and can generate a multitude of controversial issues from several perspectives. They require a considerable time and resources to manage and the capacity to adapt privacy and security requirements.[55]

Governments have addressed some of these issues if only to enable them to look to social media to assist in program delivery. Federal government departments have relied on social media to advertise services and products and disseminate information to the public, including employment opportunities.[56] It has, however, been a one-way street with departments sending out information to citizens rather than soliciting information from them.

Canadian politicians have, for the most part, done the same. Tom Flanagan confirms as much: "By contrast [to the Americans] Canadian politicians use social media almost exclusively in a top-down way. They post pictures of themselves, their family members and their pets on their websites and Facebook ... They tweet to draw attention to their latest speech or to criticize opponents or just to tell their followers what they're doing today ... It's a top-down communication that doesn't energize political participation."[57] Justin Trudeau, as is well known, has made full use of selfies, Facebook, and Instagram to promote his political profile.[58]

In recent years, the federal government has shifted more and more of its purchased ads to social media. In 2011–12, Ottawa spent about 10 percent of its media placement on the internet. The number shot up to 25 percent by 2014–15, and the number keeps climbing. The ads cover a wide variety of issues, from asking Canadians to welcome new Canadians to promoting tourism at home.[59] A Treasury Board Secretariat official explains: "Whether it's Twitter, Facebook, Snapchat, Instagram ... it is important for our government to connect with Canadians on platforms with which they are increasingly familiar."[60] Ottawa, however, spends less on advertising in the print media. It came to the rescue of local journalism, in the 2018 budget, committing $10 million a year for five years to assist the newspaper industry. The funding was called "too little, too late," with one former journalist-turned-academic insisting that Ottawa has decided to let the "newspaper die."[61]

The federal government has not been successful in leveraging the internet to involve citizens in shaping new policies or in promoting public debate on issues. The bottom-up social media do not easily square with top-down government. Since 1867, governments in Canada have developed a well-honed capacity to manage from the top down with elected representatives intervening from time to time to adjust policies and programs. Citizens helping to shape public policies from the bottom up remain works in progress since participating democracy came in fashion in the 1960s.

The important point is that for social media the Canadian government works best when implementing programs and delivering services. Though politicians and senior public servants will turn to social media to push straightforward and non-controversial messages or to promote their work, everyone in government will tread carefully with social media when addressing policy issues, fearing that anything said could well kick-start the blame game. Because of the blame game that now permeates government, officials place a premium on controlling the message and have very little experience in dealing with voices from below that have, as they see it, a "sneering disregard for expertise."[62] In short, government hierarchical structure and its slow-pace decision-making process are not geared to managing information received in real time that may give rise to political controversies.

Social media can quickly generate a loud voice, but perhaps in reality it is little more than a small minority masquerading as a large popular movement. This poses a dilemma for government as Canadians become addicted to social media. Abacus Data reports that 21 percent of Canadians find things out first from Facebook versus 29 percent from television and only 1 percent from print newspapers. When combined, Facebook, news websites, news apps, and

Twitter account for 44 percent of where Canadians hear news first. More than half of Canadians check Facebook at least once every day and, at least one Canadian in three, now turns to Facebook to consult news daily. Moreover, the more active Facebook users in Canada now "feast on a diet of news and information that is catered specifically to their interests, values, and ideologies. The more active Canadians are on Facebook, the more limited their world view."[63]

Fully 84 percent of Canadians now believe that they could still get the news if their daily newspapers went out of business.[64] As a result, citizens no longer have to react to news coming from government or from the top down. News moulds itself around what people say or see on Facebook so that both the news industry and politicians, if not government departments, have to react to what bubbles up from social media. Esther Dyson, an internet pioneer, maintains that an important virtue of the internet is that it "erodes the power of institutions over people."[65] Therein lies the rub for representative democracy.

WHAT ABOUT REPRESENTATIVE DEMOCRACY?

Max Weber employed the term "elective affinity" to link capitalism and the Protestant ethic. The point is that there is an association between systems of belief operating in different spheres.[66] Social media have become a powerful force promoting elective affinity.

People prefer to associate with people and organizations they like. The Oxford Internet Institute looked at social media and democracy, concluding that it allows "fake news stories from untrustworthy sources to spread like wildfire over networks." He notes that social media outlets such as "Facebook and Twitter have been given a 'moral pass' on the obligations we hold journalists and civil society groups to."[67] They are spontaneous, sporadic, and much more unregulated, if regulated at all. They are not like traditional media, and they have a number of characteristics "that are particularly detrimental to man's ability to think for himself – the spread of fake news and conspiracy theories [...] and the passive activism it breeds." These social media platforms give rise to echo chambers and a capacity to avoid reading opposing points of view.[68]

Social democracy disconnects as much as it connects. They promote citizens of like mind and create communities of like mind. When everyone and every community of like mind speak, who actually listens? Like-minded communities tend to reinforce strong positions and create competing political realities and hyper partisanships.[69]

How, then, do social media square with the requirements of representative democracy? Representative democracy consists of a complex set of institutions that oversee a range of requirements – equality, the prevention of tyranny by the majority, citizen participation in various forms, resolution of conflicting agendas, a degree of control of government officials, and a capacity to hold them to account.[70] Many western countries, and Canada is no exception, are experiencing weak public confidence in political institutions, and social media have not been innocent bystanders.

BRAND AMBASSADORS

Cable and twenty-four-hour news channels have an important virtue: much like the local convenience store, they are opened all hours. Their products can also be consumed quickly. According to Justin Lewis, "The rolling news format is news at its most disposable, quick and easy to use, but designed to leave no lasting impression. It is built-in obsolescence by the hour, if not by the half-hour." The point is that twenty-four-hour news channels have squandered a great deal, all in the interest of immediacy and quick interviews. They favour "the instantaneous over the analytical" with the result that such news channels are more "disposable than democratic."[71]

No one, however, should underestimate the influence of twenty-four-hour news channels. Given the choice, a member of Parliament will opt for a five-minute interview on CBC's *Power and Politics* or CTV's *Question Period* rather than a lengthy speech in the House of Commons. There are four underlying reasons that explain the influence of twenty-four-hour cable news: broad appeal, long hours of programming, persuasiveness, and it is television.[72]

The twenty-four-hour cable news channels provide opportunities for party spokespeople to pursue never-ending election campaigns. All parties have spin doctors or "brand ambassadors" available to slug it out for one or two hours every day on Newsworld's *Power and Politics*, CTV's *Power Play*, or RDI's *Les coulisses du pouvoir*.[73] They even slug it out on weekends on these news channels. Their interventions are almost always predictable.

Brand ambassadors are there to make their party leaders look good and their political enemies look bad – end of story. They always have an eye out to spin developments to their party leader's advantage. They are ambassadors on television at supper hour on cable news network and often work as lobbyists in their day job. They are not there to be objective or to inform citizens on the merits of a proposed public policy. Rather, they are there to fuel or manage the blame game, to pursue gotcha journalism, and to position their political party and party leader to score points in a never-ending political campaign. If their party leader took a position on any issue, they will be certain to echo the leader's position, regardless of their own views or even what might have been their leader's position a year or two ago. One can predict what brand ambassadors will promote depending on the brand they represent.

Justin Trudeau, while in opposition, labelled anti-niqab laws as a "cruel joke." But once in power and after calculating that Quebec would be key for him to retain power in the next election, he argued that it is not "Ottawa's job to challenge such laws." As Adam Radwanski pointed out: "Small towns or Quebec City – could decide whether they [Trudeau's Liberals] win a second majority government."[74] Trudeau can count on his "brand ambassadors" to defend both sides of the argument on the twenty-four-hour news channels, which will focus on people and the news of the day.

Television lends itself better to people and political conflicts than to defining policy positions. Competition between the news channels to provide the latest news is intense, even when there isn't any news to report and an increase in the quantity of news is not invariably tied to quality.[75] A focus on people, political leaders and what their brand ambassadors have to say results in a failure to look at the big picture and avoid in-depth policy analysis; it also devalues the role of public institutions.[76] Leaving aside committed partisans, viewers can see political spin for what it is.

The goal of twenty-four-hour news channels is to hold the interest of viewers. The goal of brand ambassadors is to cast their political parties and their leaders in a positive light, no matter which side of an issue or argument. Focusing on personalities and conflicts, though well suited to television, has implications for our political institutions. It has led many Canadians to look to politics with "mistrust, skepticism and cynicism."[77] As Chris Waddell writes, it has "helped to alienate the public from politics and public policy."[78]

RIGHT-WING MEDIA: NO TRACTION IN CANADA

Some observers have linked the rise of right-wing movements to social media which provides an echo chamber to a new generation of right-wing populists to create a community of like minds.[79] Social media do lend themselves to "niche politics and non-mainstream representation."[80]

Canada has not been immune to the rise of right-wing groups. Barbara Perry and Ryan Scrivens authored *Right Wing Extremism in Canada* in which they document the presence of right-wing movements over the years and the recent rise of right-wing groups that are anti-Semitic, anti-Aboriginal, anti-immigrant, anti–government elite, and suspicious of centralized federal authority. They provide a "conservative estimate" of between eighty-two and one hundred such groups operating in Canada. The report's authors point to several developments that have fuelled the rise of these groups, identifying social media and the internet at the top of the list. They write that for members of right-wing movements, social media provide important support "to the extent that users typically find their views reinforced and mirrored by others rather than challenged by anti-racist sentiments." They add that the internet provides "a sense of belonging" and that it has been a "boon to the RWE[right-wing extremism] movement."[81] The internet is an excellent venue for extreme views because it has no limit, no one is there to challenge one's views, and it is free of hierarchical ranks.

Sun News – labelled Fox News North – launched an all-news channel in 2011. Staff at Sun News readily admitted that they were there to represent a right-of-centre perspective, if only to counterbalance what they saw as an oversupply of left-of-centre news outlets. They singled out television news channels, notably CBC's *Newsworld*. Sun News, however, shut down operations in February 2015, just five years after its launch. Sun News executive maintain that the channel's demise had little to do with the appetite of Canadians for a right-wing perspective on an all-news channel.[82] Senior Sun News executives pointed their fingers at Ottawa's regulatory agency, insisting that it was putting up roadblocks in Sun News's ability to grow. But others saw the situation differently. Jeffrey Dvorkin at the University of Toronto suggested that Sun News failed because Canadians were uncomfortable with right-wing views.[83]

Sun News made the case to the Canadian Radio-television and Telecommunications Commission (CRTC) that it needed "mandatory carriage" for five years, which would make it part of every basic cable subscription. This would have generated eighteen cents in revenue per subscriber per month. This, according to Sun News executives, would have assured the channel's survival. James Bradshaw, however, notes that Sun News was only able to attract "a few thousand viewers."[84]

Some staff members of Sun News went on to create a website to voice far-right of centre views. Ezra Levant suggests he launched The Rebel to report on stories that the mainstream media do not wish to cover because of their politically correct Liberal bias.[85] The Rebel was indeed known for voicing controversial views. One of its associates attended an alt-right rally in Charlottesville, Virginia, where a car ploughed into a crowd of counter-protestors, killing one and injuring nineteen other participants. She reported sympathetically on a growing "white racial consciousness." Other Rebel associates presented anti-Muslim and anti-Semitic views. Freed from the requirements of broadcasting authorities, Rebel associates are free to say whatever they want whenever they want, and they have made full use of this freedom. The goal is to present views to oppose what Rebel believes to be a left-wing bias in the media so that facts matter less than does presenting a right-wing perspective. The Rebel has met with relative success with about 840,000 followers on YouTube.[86]

Conservative Party members, however, appear uncertain in their dealings with The Rebel. Andrew Scheer, Conservative Party leader, hired Hamish Marshall, an associate with The Rebel, as his campaign manager in his run for party leadership. Marshall was later asked to run the next national election campaign for the Conservative Party.[87] At the same time, Scheer announced that he would not grant interviews to The Rebel, unless it changed its editorial direction.[88] He did not, however, explain what needed to change. Conservative MP Michael Chong publicly directed strong criticism at The Rebel: "I think it's clear that they're not a reputable news organization."[89] Reputable or not, it is widely consulted by people of like mind.

THE MEDIA AND CANADIAN REGIONALISM

The national media concentrated in Toronto, Ottawa, and Montreal tend to define national issues from an Ontario and Quebec perspective. They have a strong influence among Ottawa's political and bureaucratic elites. They read the *Globe and Mail*, the *Ottawa Citizen*, the *National Post*, *Le Devoir*, and *La Presse* if they are bilingual.

They do not read the *Regina Leader-Post* or the *Cape Breton Post*. The head offices of CBC, CTV, and *Radio-Canada*, as well as their leading journalists, all work out of Toronto-Ottawa-Montreal axis. They see Western or Atlantic Canada issues as regional issues, but the same is not true for Ontario or Quebec issues. Stephen Tomblin explains: "Regional stereotypes have drawn national attention to peripheral regions, rather than to central Canada."[90]

Glen Clark, a former British Columbia premier, pointed out that "for the national media, a Western Canadian statesman is someone who comes from Western Canada and takes the Ontario or central Canadian perspective."[91] One would also be hard-pressed to find a positive stereotype in the national (as in Looking for Bootstraps) media in recent years about the Maritime provinces. Harry Bruce's *Down Home* documented the "cultural imperialism" of CBC Toronto and the "insistence" that stories from the Maritimes deal with "Anne of Green Gables, Highland games, national parks, and fishermen in rubber boots."[92] Jeffrey Simpson, a widely respected observer of Canadian politics, wrote: "Atlantic Canada has a bit of an image problem. It's been down, economically speaking, for so long that people in the rest of Canada think of the region as nothing more than four provinces full of friendly people looking for handouts. You know the image. Unemployment insurance, seasonal workers, make-work projects, regional development agencies, pork-barrel politics, equalization."[93] Media stereotypes are like codes that give the reader a ready understanding a region.

Media stereotypes are self-fulfilling. No need to commit time and effort to gain a full understanding of the issue or the region. Once a media stereotype has been struck, it is difficult to change it. New media are unlikely to challenge regional stereotypes given that truths and untruths appear to co-exist on the internet with the same level of authority, and do not lend to in-depth studies.

LOOKING BACK

Trust in the institutions of representative democracy is declining, and the media have a lot to answer for. The traditional print media are fast losing currency, and with it objective criteria that they sought to promote for the past century. We are returning to partisan journalism and a world where facts are interwoven with alternate facts. The internet is a well-suited venue for "calling fake things true and true things fake."[94] Representative democracy, meanwhile, is founded on the idea that an informed citizenry will make informed decisions about who should have the power to lead.

Brian Loader and Dan Mercea write that the most obvious impact of the internet and social media on politics has been their "disruptive capacity for traditional political practices and institutions."[95] Social media rely on personal opinions, unlike traditional media that rely more on fact-checking and a balanced coverage of institutions. Social media ensure that all can participate as unrestricted equals – the informed and the ill-informed, the educated and the non-educated, and the economic elites and non-elites. Elites in the traditional media have much to lose from the emerging social media outlets. But so do institutions, and the political and bureaucratic actors that run them. Social media are by definition non-hierarchical, and for the most part, lack editorial control.

The first instinct of government institutions is to protect themselves. Nothing new here. Allan Levine looks to history to document the difficult relationship between prime ministers and the media in Canada.[96] However, it was a great deal easier for institutions to protect themselves before the arrival of access to information legislation, twenty-four-hour news cycles, and more importantly, social media. It is one thing for government officials to defend their institutions when dealing with traditional media and its bias toward fact-checking and attempts at objective reporting. It is quite another for them to address attacks from different quarters on Facebook, informed or ill-informed, valid or not, reporting facts or alternate facts. M.J. Crockett writes: "If your news feed is constantly making your blood boil, you may not have energy left for actions that make a difference, such as volunteering, marching or voting."[97]

We are, because of social media, witnessing an "unprecedented delegitimization of public institutions."[98] We know that when there is too much trust in institutions, problems can go on unchallenged, or even undetected. Too little trust, however, makes representative institutions difficult to function.[99] We are fast moving toward too little trust. There is ample evidence from public opinion surveys that trust in institutions tied to representative democracy from Parliament, political parties, and government bureaucracy is on the decline.

Parts of the media have made a full circle, looking more and more like their nineteenth-century predecessors. The difference is that today the media can follow politics and government activities in real time. Today's media, notably the social media, have become partisans and prone to creating an atmosphere of mudslinging. The twenty-four-hour news channels and social media have helped to promote permanent election campaigns. But our political and administrative institutions were not designed to operate under permanent election campaigns or to deal with a daily (or even minute by minute) soap opera atmosphere.

The traditional media, the social media, and what Andrew Chadwick labels the "hybrid media system" have contributed to information overload.[100] Noble prize laureate, Herbert A. Simon, wrote even before the rise of social media that we have a "wealth of information" that has created "a poverty of attention."[101] Information overload combined with a poverty of attention leads to citizens lacking the attention span, the critical judgment, and the knowledge to make competent political choices.

One thing is clear – there is no going back. Voters are living in a more complex, unsettled, and fragmented environment. Representative democracy, as the Speaker of the House of Commons in Britain once observed, "is a flexible creature."[102] Canada's representative democracy, and its institutions, need to be flexible and find a way to adapt or "[risk] being left behind."[103] A well-functioning representative democracy and a free press able to supply citizens with information and knowledge go hand in hand.

The risk of Canada's representative democracy being left behind is clear. We are witnessing the deinstitutionalization, denationalization, and de-regionalization of the media. Canadians are turning to various sources for their news, such as CNN, Facebook, and other internet channels. CBC, CTV, *Radio-Canada*, the *Globe and Mail*, *Le Devoir*, and the local print media are losing ground. Brenda O'Neill makes a persuasive argument that "the media play a role in shaping the political and civic engagement of Canadians."[104] She reports that the internet has a different impact on the level of civic engagement than traditional media and draws a distinction between the role the media play as an instrument of engagement as opposed to an instrument of information. This chapter makes the case that Canada's representative democracy is losing ground on both fronts. The deinstitutionalization of the media is not an isolated case. Canadians are witnessing the deinstitutionalization of other instruments that underpin representative democracy as the following chapters argue.

A Nowhere Man, in a Nowhere Land: Public Servants Now Operate in Two Institutions

Evoking the Beatles' song "Nowhere Man" is apt in a discussion of modern-day bureaucracy, which has been under sustained attack for the past forty years in Anglo-American democracies. It no longer enjoys the level of confidence it once had with both politicians and Canadians.[1] Public servants may well have come to believe that they have few friends outside of government, and at times, even inside.

The federal government initiative to overhaul its pay system turned into a series of costly blunders – it caused over 500,000 pay problems for federal public servants, taking on average over three months to rectify. It was widely believed in the public service that senior executives saw to it that their own pay problems, if any, were much more quickly resolved. What became known as the Phoenix pay fiasco was revealing on several fronts. Rank and file public servants did not sense any support from their senior or executives or Canadians, even though some of them went without pay for weeks.[2]

Public servants are asking fundamental questions about their role in government, some making the case that they are now sitting in a nowhere land. This is not, however, a Canada-only phenomenon – the public service in other Anglo-American democracies has been under attack since the early 1980s. Margaret Thatcher said that she disliked bureaucrats as a "breed." Ronald Reagan said that he went to Washington to "drain the swamp," and Brian Mulroney promised to give "pink slips and running shoes to bureaucrats if elected."[3] Politicians then and now, albeit with some notable recent exceptions, successfully continue to see votes in bashing bureaucracy. Donald Trump turned once again to the "drain the swamp" call, as he, too, successfully ran against Washington. Stephen Harper had a difficult relationship with the public service throughout his stay in office.[4] Derek Bok, former Harvard president, sums up the challenge for public servants: "Among the more affluent and better educated, one of the few things that unites the left and the right is their common disdain for bureaucrats."[5] .

MAX WEBER:
THE FATHER OF PUBLIC ADMINISTRATION

All governments require a bureaucracy to implement policy and deliver programs. Max Weber, one of the earliest students of public administration, saw government bureaucracy as a formalized and rigid institution capable of serving its political masters in an impersonal, detached manner. He strongly believed in hierarchy and that government managers should embrace rules and regulations as the hallmark of their institution. Weber saw a hierarchical division of responsibility, authority, and specialized knowledge as the best way to ensure that the higher office does not take over the work of the lower, and to provide the "government" a clear line for appealing "the decision of a lower office to the corresponding superior authority."[6] Weber's ideal public servants require that their values do not interfere with the evaluation of the research object.

As government expanded and assumed more and more responsibilities, more was expected of bureaucracy than delivering public services. It was easier for public servants to operate in the era of limited government – their work, as well as expectations and performance, were straightforward to assess.

Today, public servants are asked to provide policy advice to their political masters "without fear or favour," to formulate complex policy solutions to address wicked problems, and to impartially deliver programs and services.[7] A tacit bargain was struck between politicians and career public servants to guide their relations. Under the bargain, public servants exchanged overt partisanship, some political rights, and a public profile in return for permanent careers, or at least indefinite tenure, anonymity, selection by merit, and a promise of being looked after at the end of a career that does not require close attention to their own material self-interest while they serve. Meanwhile, politicians exchanged the ability to appoint or dismiss public servants and change their working conditions at will for non-partisan obedience to the government of the day.[8]

The bargain worked well in the immediate postwar period, until the late 1970s. If there was ever a golden period for bureaucracy, it was when the bargain was respected by both sides. However, both the Weberian perspective and the traditional bargain have been vilified for the past forty years, and tension between bureaucracy and politicians has intensified. And yet, Weber's conception of bureaucracy remains the starting point for many students of government and practitioners, if only because no one has defined anything better. However, in the eyes of many, the starting point no longer works.

Weber could not have possibly imagined the sprawling, complex bureaucracy that occupies such an important place in today's representative democracies. He saw a limited role for government, which was ideally suited for a hierarchical, rule-driven bureaucracy. His lasting value is how he positioned the role of bureaucracy in a representative democracy; he saw bureaucracy providing stability, impartiality, fairness, and standard administrative behaviour complementing a political process that saw politicians come and go, not to mention wars and revolutions. Because of hierarchy and the limited role of government, it was relatively easy for politicians to embrace a top-down approach, to direct the work of public servants, and to hold them to account.

After governments expanded on all cylinders in the 1960s and 1970s, politicians began to question their ability to direct, let alone control, bureaucracy. Thatcher, Reagan, and Mulroney were not the only politicians in the 1980s to voice critical opinions on the work of public servants. Politicians who had long promoted a stronger role for government in society, from Allan J. MacEachen in Canada to Shirley Williams in Britain, began to publicly voice their displeasure with government bureaucracies.

Canadian politicians had reasons to believe that the Weberian model and its accompanying traditional bargain no longer held. They were attempting to make executive federalism work while retaining control over shaping new initiatives and holding public servants to account. Ministers who served in both Liberal and Progressive Conservative governments began to make the case that public servants had undue influence in shaping both policies and programs, and that they were not paying sufficient attention to the proper management of government operations.[9]

The work of John Locke with his emphasis on legislative power as the centre of representative democracies and of Max Weber with his ideal-type bureaucratic model no longer resonated with politicians or even students of government by the 1980s. The search began on how best to reinvent bureaucracy. Politicians no longer accepted Weber's view that public servants were able to ensure their values would not interfere with their evaluations or their research. Some politicians looked to James Buchanan, who won the Nobel Prize in economics for his work on public choice theory, and to Michael Jensen and William Meckling's work on principal-agent theory, while others considered how private sector management practices could be introduced to government to make operations more efficient.

Richard Crossman dealt a serious blow to government bureaucracy when he published his book *Diaries of a Cabinet Minister*.[10] Crossman's diaries inspired Antony Jay and Jonathan Lynn to produce the BBC's *Yes Minister* series. *Yes Minister* was widely watched in Anglo-American democracies, particularly among the political and bureaucratic class and those keenly interested in government. Margaret Thatcher had each episode videotaped and urged senior public servants to watch the series. She subscribed to the caricature view of the senior civil service, and for many, the satire became a documentary on the work of government bureaucrats. The not-so-subtle message of *Yes Minister* was that public servants were running their country, their deference to politicians was pure pretence, and it was senior bureaucrats, not politicians, who had actual power inside government.[11]

Coincidence or not, it was around the time *Yes Minister* was airing that political leaders in Anglo-American democracies decided to reorient the work of public servants in the name of democracy. They wanted to exert greater control over the policy-making levers and shaping new initiatives, and have senior public servants focus more on management; however, the leaders' rhetoric spoke more to the problems than to solutions. Few of them came to office with a grand strategy to fix bureaucracy.[12]

Political leaders could turn to senior public servants for advice on how best to reform government. However, this posed challenges. Senior public servants were not convinced that the political rhetoric had it right. Though they provided policy advice, they pointed out that it was up to elected politicians to accept or reject it. If politicians were unhappy with the advice of senior public servants, then they should say so or turn to other sources, including a constantly growing array of think tanks and consultants. On the subject of management, many senior public servants felt that politicians should "heal thyself" before trying to heal bureaucracy. Senior public servants were, for the most part, convinced that management problems in government were rooted in political decisions, not in their work. The solution for many public servants was to batten down the hatches and wait for the latest political storm to pass.[13]

But the storm never passed. As Margaret Thatcher memorably put it, politicians "were not for turning," at least on this issue. Instead, they were set on getting hold of the steering wheel on policy and making senior public servants become better managers. They felt that government was too costly on the operations side, and they pointed their fingers at "bureaucrats."

Politicians were determined to rely less on the policy advice of senior public servants, convinced that they had their own policy agenda and self-interest to promote. Again, this was true for politicians at both ends of the political spectrum. Flora MacDonald, a red tory who served as minister of External Affairs in the short-lived Joe Clark government in 1979–80, went on the lecture circuit to denounce senior public servants, claiming that they employed clever ruses to push their own agenda and to circumvent Cabinet and ministerial directions.[14] Allan MacEachen, the veteran Cabinet minister and deputy prime minister in the Pierre Trudeau government, reported one thing the Liberal party had learned during their brief stay in opposition in 1979 was that the party would no longer rely as much as they had on the advice of senior public servants.[15]

Politicians who followed were even more determined to come to government with their own policy prescriptions. Paul Martin, former minister of finance and prime minister, was fond of telling his public servants, "If you want to run things, you will have to go in church basements across Canada and sell what you want to do."[16] The Stephen Harper government's uneasy relationship with bureaucracy is well documented. He explained the relationship this way: "Probably the most difficult job, practical difficult thing you have to learn as a prime minister and our ministers as well, is dealing with the federal bureaucracy. It's walking that fine line of being a positive leader of the federal public service but at the same time pushing them and not becoming captive to them."[17] Harper sent out a clear signal that he did not always value evidence-based policy advice from public servants when he decided to cancel the mandatory long-form questionnaire as part of the 2011 Canadian census and, again, when his government decided to reduce funding for Statistics Canada.[18]

Public servants adjusted. Andrew Griffith, a senior public servant, recalls: "Under the Harper government, one of the main challenges for the public service was having its knowledge and expertise put into question."[19] He remarked that adjusting to the new order "was existentialist, demoralizing, and even traumatic for many public servants."[20] They had to adjust to a world where politicians and their advisers were telling them not to bother with facts and evidence. The message from politicians, particularly from Prime Minister Harper and his close partisan advisers, was simple: we know what we want to do and your job is to help us do it, and you are not here to tell us what we should do but rather to explain why we are doing it.[21]

Senior public servants have had to deal with career politicians from all parties that have attenuated further their policy advisory role. Some politicians now get into politics at a younger age, and the successful ones try to make a career of it. Their expertise is politics and government, and they excel at surviving the gruelling twenty-four-hour news cycle. However, they lack the ability to test policy prescriptions against experiences gained outside of politics. Yet, when dealing with advice from public servants, they often know better – or, at least, they think they do – because they, too, have made work in government their life.

All of the above makes the point that, when it comes to their policy advisory role, senior public servants have been on the defensive for the past forty years or more. Since the early 1980s, public servants have been told repeatedly that with regard to management they do not measure up to their private sector counterparts. Those who hold political power today have a greater say in shaping policy and striking decisions than was held thirty years ago. In short, the verdict from politicians has been that public servants are not up to task on either policy or managing government operations. As one senior public servant said, "There is not much else for us to do."[22] Morale in government plummeted. Public servants stood accused of many things: being uncreative, lethargic, insensitive, and costly. The Weberian model was coming unglued, and politicians began to look for responsive competence to deliver their agenda rather than neutral policy advice.

Weber's ideal model had suited the time – until the post–Second World War period, when politicians through Parliament established highly prescriptive programs that laid out, in fairly concrete terms, what public servants could deliver, when, and how. The postwar period launched a new era of positive government, asking bureaucracy to be capable of addressing a wide range of issues. However, this gave bureaucracy more discretionary power, something that politicians began to resent, convinced that public servants were exerting too much influence over policy at their expense.[23]

A MODEL EMPLOYER IN A
COMPETITIVE GLOBAL ECONOMY

Positive government led the public sector to show the way in becoming a model employer. The Canadian Parliament in 1967 passed legislation introducing collective bargaining and gave public servants the right to strike.[24] Provincial governments followed one by one to embrace collective bargaining. The right to strike had proven effective in the private sector to settle disputes. However, in government the right to strike has to operate in an environment where there is no market to discipline either party's behaviour.[25] The decision to introduce collective bargaining shaped the behaviour of both managers and employees in the Government of Canada to a far greater extent than all the private sector, management-inspired measures combined introduced over the past thirty years or so.

Indeed, in spite of attempts to dress the public sector to look like the private sector, government departments remain monopolies or quasi-monopolies insulated from competitive pressure. The absence of market pressure means that the "self-interest of public officials does not include the efficient delivery of services."[26] It also instils inertia in government operations. There are still precious few incentives for government managers to go head-to-head with public sector unions and deal as well with non-performing employees. This has not, however, stopped politicians from pushing public servants to do more on the management front and trying to force their hand to manage like their private sector counterparts. Senior public servants have been trying to square that circle ever since, with limited success. The efforts have generated more reports and more work for consultants but little actual change, other than making government operations thicker, slower, and more expensive.

The public service does not operate in a vacuum. The global economy is not only highly competitive but it also reaches into all communities, large and small. Economic opportunities come and go quickly, as do businesses and jobs. Many private sector pension plans are collapsing and even large and highly profitable firms are moving away from defined pension plans, including Canada's banks.[27] For example, former Sears employees were told in June 2018 their pension cheques were being reduced by 20 percent in order to get their pension plans back to fully funded.[28] Sears Canada is only one of several large private sector employers that have left their pension plans underfunded, leaving thousands of former employees uncertain about their pensions.[29] Government employees, meanwhile, have been sheltered from the global economy. Jobs have not disappeared, public servants enjoy tenure with little to no chance of being let go for non-performance, and generous pension plans and other benefits, unavailable to those outside government, remain in place.

Non-government employees are asking, "Why the double standard?" Steve Bannon's call to "deconstruct the administrative state" resonated in some quarters in Canada.[30] Non-public servants are asking why *deux poids, deux mesures*, why their employment is subject to global competitiveness, and why they can no longer depend on defined pension plans while government employees have no such concerns. This, too, has contributed to bureaucracy bashing.

PUBLIC SERVANTS AS POLICY ADVISERS

Politicians are rarely elected for their intimate knowledge of policy issues. Career politicians, however, are able to gain a thorough understanding of the political process, the ways of Parliament, how to deal with the media and interest groups, how the machinery of government operates, and develop a keen appreciation for what their constituencies want. Public servants, meanwhile, are, or were, expected to provide policy advice free of partisan considerations, and the advice should not generate any advantage or disadvantage to the partisan political interests of a political party, including the party in power.[31]

That is the theory, at least, and senior public servants have attached a great deal of importance to this role, with management taking a back seat. As noted, Gordon Robertson, once described as the gold standard for the position of clerk of the Privy Council and head of the public service, did not discuss management issues in his memoirs – his interest and focus were on policy.[32] Al Johnson, former secretary to the Treasury Board, published an article in 1961, "The

Role of the Deputy Minister," and never employed the word "man-agement" once.[33] It was a sign of the time. The role of deputy minis-ters and other senior officials was to provide policy advice and steer ministers away from trouble. Johnson's view is worth underlining: "The role of the deputy minister is to make it possible for the minis-ter and the cabinet to provide the best government of which they are capable – even better if either of them happens to be weak."[34]

By the late 1970s, politicians wanted managers. Because they believed the expenditure budget was being mismanaged, they intro-duced new approaches in rapid succession to get a better handle on it.[35] Politicians essentially looked to bureaucracy as the problem to be solved. They found the policy capacity inside government to be lacking, suggesting that it was not addressing major economic and environmental challenges.[36] At the same time as politicians pushed senior public servants to become better managers, they began searching for other streams of policy advice, determined that they would not be captured by the bureaucracy like their predecessors were. Ronald Reagan expressed the view of many politicians when he argued that government bureaucracy was not "part of the solu-tion, but the problem."[37]

But change does not come easy inside government. The dom-inant culture among senior public servants, and those aspiring to the senior ranks, remains a focus on policy and on defining new measures while leaving management issues to the less ambitious and the less talented. Frankly put, they decided to leave management to a lower class, the less gifted, while they went about more import-ant things like developing policy proposals and whiz-bang ideas for politicians. There were centrally prescribed rules and regulations to guide the administrative class, thus enabling senior public servants to focus on policy issues. Politicians, meanwhile, wanted something different – a management class led by senior officials, not an admin-istrative class led by cautious bureaucrats more concerned with rules than results – to manage government operations, much like senior private sector executives would.

What to do? Senior public servants were not convinced there was a problem, at least a problem for which they were responsible. When politicians turned to them for advice on strengthening management in government operations, they drew a blank. Politicians then turned to the private sector for inspiration. Private sector executives were invited to participate in various task forces and review committees designed to overhaul government operations.[38] Two management consultants, with close ties to the private sector, coined a phrase that came in fashion throughout Anglo-American democracies, including Canada: governments should steer, not row.[39] Osborne and Gaebler made the case that government should steer in the direction it wants to go and let the private sector or empowered government managers do the rowing, looking after operations with a minimum of centrally prescribed rules.

Margaret Thatcher, once again, led the way, this time with sustained efforts to separate policy from government operations. This would allow politicians to make important policy decisions and, at the same time, force the hand of senior public servants to become better managers. She privatized government operations and empowered managers to enable them to perform like their private sector counterparts.[40] Political leaders in Canada, the United States, Australia, and New Zealand soon followed.[41]

There is no need to go into any detail about the efforts to reinvent government over the past thirty years or so. It has already been fully explored.[42] Suffice to underline the point that the efforts were designed to separate policy from operations, to empower managers, to instil a bias for action inside government, to introduce a competitive element in government operations, and to force the hand of senior public servants to become better managers. The thinking was that it was somehow possible to duplicate market forces inside government operations without changing how our political institutions work.[43]

The goal was nothing short of turning government administrators into managers. Even reluctant government managers would be told, in no uncertain terms, to manage like their private sector counterparts. Starting in the early 1980s to this day, we have seen a plethora of management reforms designed to reinvent government and to strengthen management practices. Though it has not been for want of trying, no one has been able to duplicate market forces inside government operations. We have seen numerous performance measurement schemes, management targets, and oversight bodies introduced, as well as an explosive growth in the program evaluation industry. Performance pay schemes have remained in vogue since the early 1980s. Neither program evaluation efforts nor pay-for-performance schemes, however, have ever lived up to expectations.[44] Indeed, there is evidence that both have given rise to gaming and attempts on the part of departments and public servants to distort government priorities.[45]

Notwithstanding the multitude of measures introduced over the past forty years, performance in government remains in the eye of the beholder – hardly an objective criterion on which to base a performance pay scheme. It may explain why whatever amount of money is allocated to performance pay schemes in Ottawa, it is invariably used up, and why, several years ago, well over 90 percent of public service managers in the Government of Canada received a performance award. This prompted the private sector chair on the advisory committee on retention and compensation of senior managers in government to observe that the committee "will refrain from recommending further increases ... until the government shows a commitment to ensuring the program does not reward poor performers."[46] However, the chair never explained how one could determine poor performance among the senior ranks of the public service, which remains work in progress. Performance bonuses continue to be awarded annually.

A number of centrally prescribed rules and regulations were abandoned to liberate government managers to manage as if they were in the private sector. While we have liberated senior public servants from some rules and regulations in managing human and financial resources, we still do not have the ability to assess objectively if managers are performing at a higher level. Consequently, the overhead cost of government has increased while the ability to hold managers to account has decreased.

The reform measures hold important implications for representative democracy. Many of the measures were based on an individual economic model. The thinking was that all management challenges are similar and should be approached in similar ways.[47] It assumes there is little difference between political and management accountability and between the public and private sector, at least when it comes to management. Representative democracies see things differently.

Changes on both the policy advisory and management fronts forced governments to juggle values tied to democracy – accountability, equity, and probity. As Guy Peters points out, "Choosing any one to maximize will tend to create problems for at least some of the others."[48] How far can government push senior public servants to be responsive while respecting the proper role for the public service in a Westminster-inspired representative democracy? How far can one go in pushing aside hierarchy while retaining strong accountability requirements? These questions matter in Canada perhaps more than in many other countries because, as Arend Lijphart points out in his *Patterns of Democracy*, a defining characteristic of Westminster democracy is a dominant executive.[49]

CANADA: PARTLY COMMITTED TO REFORM

The Canadian government, starting with Brian Mulroney's tenure, pursued a number of reform measures under the New Public Management (NPM) label. Mulroney, like Margaret Thatcher in Britain and Ronald Reagan in the United States, embraced NPM. Thatcher successfully hived off parts of the civil service and moved them to arm's length executive agencies. Some 133 agencies were created, employing 375,000 people – about 77 percent of the civil service. According to a British government official, they were created in part to "ensure more senior managers had experience of managing service delivery, and not just policy formulation" and to "focus attention on results achieved with resources (efficiency) rather than simply the amount of money spent by departments."[50]

Canada sought to follow Britain's lead but failed badly. Although the Canadian government embraced the agency concept, nothing much came of it. Initially, the government readily admitted that it looked to Britain for inspiration. The secretary of the Treasury Board explained that "Canadian interest in special operating agencies (SOAs) was spurred by the Executive Agency of *Next Step* in the United Kingdom."[51] Treasury Board Secretariat staff went to London to study the agency concept and returned with ideas on how to adapt it to Canada.

The Canadian SOAs remain an anemic iteration of the British version. Only a handful were established and, unlike those in Britain, they remain subordinate to their parent departments. Their leaders and personnel are selected much like those of a regular department, and their accountability requirements remain essentially the same as those in any government department. No one in Ottawa any longer speaks of SOAs as a model that should be pursued. And no one makes the case that SOAs are better managed than government departments.[52]

Unlike the Britain's example, no Canadian prime minister ever fully embraced the agency concept, and so it never enjoyed a determined commitment from the person that matters most in a Westminster-inspired parliamentary government. And, unlike Britain, the agency concept was never fully debated in a parliamentary committee, and no one took the lead at the bureaucratic level to promote the concept inside the public service.

Why? The prime minister of the day, Brian Mulroney, had more pressing issues to attend to than ensuring that the agency concept was fully implemented. Mulroney had to deal with the fallout of the proposed Meech Lake and Charlottetown constitutional accords. No Canadian prime minister will ever wish to see Quebec leave Canada under their watch. Mulroney, a Quebec MP, paid close attention to the economic interest of his province. Witness, for example, his decision to give the F-18 contract to a Montreal-based plant though a Winnipeg firm had a better proposal, and his determination to see Quebec endorse the 1982 constitutional amendment.[53] Chrétien, Harper, and Trudeau *fils*, who followed Mulroney in office, also showed no interest in pursuing the agency concept. Chrétien had to deal with pressing national unity problems, including a referendum that came close to seeing Quebec leave Confederation, as well as a difficult fiscal challenge in his first mandate. In Canada, national unity concerns easily override attempts to introduce management measures and make them stick.

Some governments have been better than others at pursuing the NPM reform measures.[54] Efforts have had a visible and lasting impact in Britain, Australia, and New Zealand, but the Government of Canada is at the back of the pack.[55] Indeed, NPM appears to have left the Canadian government without much of a trace, other than having generated many task forces and consultant reports.[56] As noted, SOAs petered out with very little impact, the introduction of the accounting officer concept has not changed operations in Ottawa, and other NPM measures in the Canadian government have fared no better.[57]

After thirty years of NPM, there is little evidence to suggest that senior public servants in Ottawa have shifted their focus away from policy to define new measures and offer innovative ideas to focus more on management. Yet, senior politicians and their partisan advisers have considerably extended their reach in shaping policy. In addition, there is ample evidence to suggest that senior public servants still view management as the preserve of a less gifted administrative class.

THE ACCOUNTING OFFICER

The Canadian government also sought to follow Britain's lead in introducing the accounting officer concept. Here, again, the effort fell far short off the mark. Accounting officers have occupied a key position in financial control and accountability in Britain for 150 years. They hold responsibility in their own right and are the "responsible" witnesses before Parliament's Public Accounts Committee. A memorandum, which outlines responsibilities for accounting officers, establishes the procedure to be followed when a minister overrules an accounting officer's advice on an issue of propriety and regularity. The memorandum makes it clear that accounting officers are responsible for delivering departmental objectives in the most economic, efficient, and effective manner.[58]

Jean Chrétien committed to introduce in Canada the accounting officer, patterned on the British model. But nothing came of his commitment.[59] Stephen Harper, meanwhile, rode the Chrétien-sponsorship scandal to power in January 2006 and made greater accountability a central theme of his election platform. Within weeks of assuming office, he brought forward legislation that provided for the introduction of the British accounting officer concept in the Government of Canada. What Harper envisaged while in opposition and what he incorporated in legislation were very different.

There is every indication that the PCO had serious reservations about Harper's proposal, which may well explain his decision to change his position once in power. For instance, the PCO produced a document for the use of deputy ministers that did not square with Harper's original position. The June 2003 document, *Guidance for Deputy Ministers*, which remains on the PCO's website, goes beyond the argument that the public service has no "constitutional personality" to state that public servants "do not have a public voice, or identity, distinct from that of their Minister, nor do they share in their Minister's political accountability." According to the same document, "In supporting the Minister's accountability, a Deputy Minister may find himself or herself before a parliamentary committee to explain what went wrong. He or she might say, for example, yes, an error was made. I am accountable to the Minister of the department and, with the support of the Minister, I have fixed the problem – this could include informing a committee that disciplinary action has been taken, but it would not extend to naming those concerned even if their identity had somehow been disclosed through the media or otherwise."[60] The PCO did not revise the document after Harper introduced the accounting officer concept to Canada. It saw no reason to, even though politicians had, since the early 1980s, stressed the need for senior public servants to fundamentally rethink their role and manage operations like their private sector counterparts.

Ralph Heintzman has labelled the Canadian version the "flawed implementation of the British concept." He argues that, in the end, it "changed nothing" and it "missed the opportunity" to fix the relationship between accounting officers and the executive.[61] As I noted earlier, one is hard-pressed to point to a single example where the Canadian version has had any impact either in Parliament or inside government since it was first introduced. Why? Certainly, public servants much prefer to see ministers accept full responsibility for both policy and administrative decisions. It explains, at least in part, why PCO officials pressed Harper and his advisers to dilute the accounting officer concept.

Senior public servants have several reasons for wanting to avoid turning management matters into political debates and to attenuate the accounting officer concept. Arthur Kroeger, a long-serving and widely respected deputy minister in the federal government, pointed to regionalism to make the case that the accounting officer concept is better suited for Britain than Canada. In an article titled "The Elected Should Have the Last Word," he observes: "A regional director could close local offices and lay off staff at will in areas of high unemployment. Any intervention by the responsible minister and local MPs would constitute political interference."[62] This does not, however, stop public servants from making the case, often with success, that elected politicians have no business in administrative matters. The merit principle, the Financial Administration Act, the Official Languages Act, among other statutes provide public servants ammunition to push elected politicians away from their offices and administrative responsibilities. These statutes give the public service a personality distinct from that of the ministers they serve. Regionalism in Canada, it seems, does not allow it fully.

MANAGEMENT MATTERS LESS

Notwithstanding numerous reform measures to strengthen management in government, the thinking that senior public servants should focus on policy and make the prime minister and ministers provide the best government of which they are capable remains the top priority for deputy ministers. For example, the PCO's *Guidance for Deputy Ministers* still ranks "supporting the ministers" at the top of the list of their responsibilities.[63] The Privy Council Office has a significant say in deciding who makes it to the top in the public service. This is one sign that management still takes a back seat to serving the prime minister and his courtiers, ministers, fixing problems and policy.

There are many others. As noted, the federal government's decision to overhaul its pay system soon ran into serious problems. Some public servants went unpaid for months and the government committed substantial financial and human resources to fix the issue. One of the senior public servants responsible for the Phoenix pay system pointed, to several key problems in hindsight – lack of planning, lack of training, and a lack of capacity to deal with the private sector contractor hired to design the system: all critical management issues. The responsible government department reported that the new pay system would not deliver the $70 million in savings that was promised to kick in by 2016, and it required another $45 to $50 million in September 2016 to fix the problems.[64] By 2017, still more financial resources were required to address the problem. In 2018, the government allocated another $431 million to the project and an additional $16 million to start the "process of replacing the troubled system."[65] The top public servant charged with implementing Phoenix was quietly shuffled to another senior position in government in October 2016.[66]

Public servants going unpaid is a highly visible problem that is sure to get media attention. We soon learned that public servants outside Ottawa were more affected by the failed Phoenix pay system than their Ottawa-based colleagues.[67] The blame game kicked in and the culprit in the eyes of many was regionalism. The *Globe and Mail* ran a story with the headline "Someone Should Take the Fall for Ottawa's Botched Phoenix Pay System" and argued that the move to locate the pay system in Miramichi, which "eliminated 700 jobs mainly in Ottawa," was a form of "political compensation."[68] It seems that for the *Globe and Mail* locating 700 jobs in Ottawa has nothing to do with "political compensation." The executive vice-president of the Public Service Alliance of Canada bluntly told the media, "I think it's clear. It was a mistake to move it to Miramichi."[69]

No one looked to the firm that sold the system to the government – IBM – as the source of the problem. No one looked to how the system was introduced or how management issues such as training and skills development were left unaddressed. No one looked at whether the proper funding level was put in place when introducing the system. No one looked to Australia, where a Phoenix-like pay system cost taxpayers $1.2 billion and was described as the "worst public policy failure in Australia's history."[70] No one in Australia blamed regionalism for the catastrophic failure.

The auditor general blamed three senior public servants for the Phoenix pay system problems. He labelled the situation as an "incomprehensible failure" and wrote about "pervasive cultural problems" in the federal public service. The accountability requirements were virtually non-existent and the three senior public servants were not fired, simply reassigned without losing rank or pay.[71]

The auditor general's report led to "an unprecedented feud" between him and the clerk of the Privy Council, which was widely reported in the media. The clerk dismissed the report as just "an opinion piece" full of "sweeping generalizations."[72] He acknowledged, however, that the federal public service was "risk-averse" and warned against "misdiagnosing" the problem and applying the wrong remedies, but had little to offer on either the diagnosis or possible remedies.[73]

Public opinion surveys report that only 6 percent of Canadians express "a lot of trust in senior public servants." Front-line public servants, meanwhile, fare better, with Canadians expressing a lot of trust in them.[74] This confirms the existence of the fault line separating senior public servants from front-line managers and their staff.

A Treasury Board–sponsored 2017 survey of public servants makes the same point and suggests that the clerk of the Privy Council is misdiagnosing what ails the public service. Based on the responses of 174,544 employees, only 17 percent of federal public servants report that "essential information flows effectively from senior management to staff," only 11 percent feel that "unsatisfactory employee performance is managed effectively," and only 25 percent feel they receive "meaningful recognition for work well done."[75] This suggests a pervasive cultural problem in the federal public service.

Three recent and similar cases to Phoenix make the point that regionalism is hardly to blame when new management measures go off the rails. The federal government launched a major effort in the mid-1990s to overhaul its classification and job evaluation system. The goal was to implement a standard government-wide approach to job classification. It invested approximately $200 million in studies and consultations and committed "tens of thousands of employees" to the task between 1998 and 2000.[76] The efforts failed, a verdict that the lead agency responsible for the initiative – the Treasury Board Secretariat – readily accepts. The one thing we learned was that between 1993 and 1999 about 28,000 promotions – at about one-third of all promotions – were awarded through a reclassification of positions. No one in central agencies or line departments knows how many of these positions were overclassified. The government has since launched other efforts at streamlining its classification and job evaluation processes but again has little success to show for these efforts. The effort to overhaul the classification system was strictly an Ottawa-driven exercise. The fact that it led to numerous reclassifications (essentially all winners and no losers, at least within the federal public service) and was inside the Ottawa system ensured that the endeavour did not generate media interest.

There have been a number of other and costlier administrative miscues. They have not been nearly as visible because they have had little impact on the lives of public servants and Canadians. Again, they have all been Ottawa-centric exercises. For example, the government made a mess of managing efforts to overhaul its IT infrastructure.[77] The government established Shared Services Canada to deliver email, data centre, and network services to forty-three departments and agencies. Before the agency was established, each department managed its own IT infrastructure and services. The Office of the Auditor General (OAG) took stock of the progress in 2015; the findings were nothing short of damning. The OAG discovered that basic management practices were lacking on several fronts: the government did not establish clear service expectations, did not document service agreements with departments, did not plan properly, and did not communicate clearly the objectives it wanted to pursue.[78]

There are still more costly management miscues associated with the initiative: office space was not secured for staff, the agency budget was subject to across-the-board cuts (the traditional method of reducing government spending), with the result that Shared Services Canada will now "end up costing taxpayers a fortune to set things right."[79] A Shared Services Canada employee put his finger on the problem: "I don't know how many times I heard from deputy ministers that they didn't understand information technology. They didn't like IT and they hoped never to have anything to do with IT for the rest of their career."[80] The culture among the most senior ranks of the public service that management issues are best left to others, to another class, and in many cases, to the less gifted, remains deeply ingrained. Again, the culprit in this case was not regionalism, given that the initiative was driven and managed in Ottawa.

A 2016 review of federal government buildings revealed that Ottawa spends over $40 million a year to maintain vacant ones.[81] And, in the same year, the Treasury Board once again launched a costly review of the government's job classification system, and once again the initiative involved many consultant reports, the establishment of many departmental and interdepartmental committees, and countless meetings. It, too, failed to deliver. The classification creep problem is largely an Ottawa phenomenon. A survey carried out by the Public Service Commission reveals that 60 percent of respondents from the National Capital Region (NCR) reported that they had been promoted during the past five years, compared with only 48 percent for "all other regions."[82]

Michael Ferguson, who served as Canada's auditor general, made a number of damning observations, at the midpoint of his ten-year term, in his November 2016 report. Borrowing a page from public choice theory, he writes: "What about programs that are managed to accommodate the people running them rather than the people receiving the services?" He argued that various "public accountability reports" failed to provide a clear picture of what is going on. He remarks further that "our auditors came across the same problems in different organizations time and time again ... [W]hen we come back to audit the same area again, we often find that program results have not improved – in the immortal words of Yogi Berra, it is *déjà vu* all over again."[83] However, the auditor general, like his predecessors, was short on solutions or on how to right the ship.

WHY HAS NPM FAILED IN CANADA?

Why has NPM had much more of an impact in Britain, Australia, and New Zealand than in Canada? Why do senior Canadian public servants continue to embrace the Max Weber view of bureaucracy and traditional administrative models? Why did senior public servants push to make the accounting officer concept ineffective? Why do the most senior cadre of public servants continue to attach a lower priority to management than their counterparts in other Westminster-inspired parliamentary systems?

There are few incentives for deputy ministers to focus on management. There is still a market in Ottawa for senior officials to come up with successful ideas, to help keep their ministers out of trouble, to define measures so that government can pursue commitments made in the last election campaign, and to impress senior officials in the PMO and the PCO. In brief, senior public servants prefer to look up, not down. Their next promotion – if you are an assistant deputy minister or a junior deputy minister – is tied to looking up, not down, to management issues or to regional offices. Kroeger's advice is not lost on ambitious public servants: tread very carefully on regional or national unity issues because they are often a political minefield. Best to let politicians deal with these issues and avoid structural change, like an effective accounting officer that could give life and visibility to regional issues. Dealing with national unity and addressing Quebec's place in the federation once again dominated the political agenda at critical moments when NPM issues were calling for attention from prime ministers and their courtiers.

Leading students of government have tried to reconcile path dependency theory with the implementation of NPM measures in the Canadian public service. They have to account for the fact that the public sector in most Anglo-American democracies looks very different than it did in 1980 in terms of size, scope of activities, and management practices. They argue that the "fundamental paradigm shift" occurred because leading politicians concluded the status quo was not working. They insist that path dependency theory still applies because it explains "extended periods of considerable stability ... interrupted by turbulent, formative moments."[84] Britain, New Zealand, and Australia witnessed "formative moments" in their national governments and introduced structural changes to their machinery of government. Canada did not because of concerns over national unity and regionalism.[85]

THE OTTAWA BUREAUCRACY

The federal bureaucracy remains a top-down institution. It has not been able to fully shake free from its limited role of regulatory enforcement, when government programs and directions were concrete, prescriptive, and designed to deliver narrowly defined measures that required little front-line discretion. The top-down model has held firm, even after the federal bureaucracy was delegated more abstract and prescriptive power to shape and deliver measures with the advent of executive federalism and modern government.[86] As we now know, even the flurry of NPM measures had little impact on Canada's bureaucracy.

The federal bureaucracy has been a top-down, Ottawa-centric institution since the country was born. If anything, it has become even more Ottawa-centric in recent years. Senior public servants much prefer working close to political power than away from it. I have written elsewhere about a fault line that separates policy-oriented public servants and front-line workers. Those above the line tend to look up to the political process and to PCO for guidance and accountability, while those below consider that they are accountable to a variety of actors from their immediate supervisor, oversight bodies to their clients.[87]

The federal Task Force on Public Service Values and Ethics later picked up on the theme in its report: "Our dialogue with public servants revealed to us a certain divide between levels in the public service, perhaps especially where public service values are concerned. Many at the middle and lower levels of the public service no longer feel connected to the senior levels, and they are not sure whether they necessarily share the same values as those at higher levels." The task force report notes that one "source of this fault line appears to be the confusion about accountability, and the tension between customer accountability and political accountability. Those closest to the front lines of accountability feel their primary accountability to citizen/clients while those farther up may feel primary accountability to citizen voters and taxpayers, as mediated by the political process."[88]

Deputy ministers, the top level in the public service, work out of Ottawa. Even when deputy ministers are appointed to head regional development agencies with head offices in the respective regions, they will have an office in Ottawa, and more often than not, their home as well, and spend most of the time there. They want to be in the loop, to be visible where it matters. Few ambitious federal public servants consider moving from Ottawa to a region to be a smart career move.

Ottawa is home to virtually all deputy ministers, associate deputy ministers, and assistant deputy ministers. They want to have the ears of ministers and the PCO. The culture is to look up to the PMO, to the PCO, to senior ministers, to the policy process, and to the most senior levels of the public service. Question period and the work of the national media matter a great deal in their work. Public servants in the regions, meanwhile, tend to look to citizens, program delivery, and to their departmental clients. Public servants in regions who move to Ottawa soon learn the ways of Ottawa, where public servants "have made their careers because of their skills in managing up. They have been valued and promoted because they were adept at providing superiors with what they needed, in a timely fashion."[89] They either blend in the Ottawa system, embracing its values and culture, or they are shunted aside with few prospects for promotion.

The Ottawa bureaucracy is defined by sectoral responsibilities assigned to their departments. The focus is on their sector, the goals of the department or agency, where they work, and where they live (i.e., Ottawa). They view things from a sectoral perspective (e.g., the manufacturing or natural resources sector) and from a "national" perspective. Leaving aside the federal regional development agencies, ministers, and members of Parliament, few in Ottawa think in regional terms other than their own region or the NCR.

PARTISAN ADVISERS

Jennifer Robson and Paul Wilson each document the growing influence of partisan political advisers on policy and government operations.[90] They look at the work of partisan advisers at the centre of government, in the PMO, and in ministerial offices. Jonathan Craft outlines how partisan advisers have been able to carve out an important role as a source of policy advice and how they act as "bridges" between senior public servants and elected politicians.[91] He singles out partisan advisers to the prime minister and their ability to shape "front-end" policy instruments through mandate letters and throne speeches.[92]

In the case of the federal government, partisan advisers can now attend Cabinet committee meetings in contrast to thirty years ago, when only ministers and career public servants could attend. Since the Mulroney government, chiefs of staff to ministers now occupy positions equal to the assistant deputy minister level.[93] The purpose of the change was to check the influence of career public servants, and as Jacques Bourgault argues, to strengthen political control and ensure that politicians are not captured by the "bureaucracy."[94]

Partisan advisers are by definition politically partisan. Their purpose is to promote the political interests of the prime minister, ministers, and the party in power. These advisers are former campaign workers or close associates of the politician they are asked to serve. Chiefs of staff are experienced hands in politics (some having served the party while in opposition), in law, and in public policy (some are former public servants). The majority of chiefs of staff in the Justin Trudeau government are from Toronto, many of them having served in similar positions in Liberal governments at Queen's Park. There were thirty chiefs of staff in February 2016: seventeen were from Ontario, seven from Quebec, five from Western Canada, and one from Atlantic Canada. As substantiated on several occasions herein, the political interest of the federal government lies in the more populous regions – Ontario, Quebec, and increasingly Western Canada. Partisan political advisers know this as well as the political masters they serve, which only added to concerns that Justin Trudeau's government would see issues through the Ontario-Quebec lens. The government won 80 of the 121 Ontario seats and 40 of the 78 Quebec seats, and MPs from the two provinces were appointed to all the senior Cabinet posts from prime minister, to finance, the environment and climate change, innovation, science and economic development, including all the regional agencies, transport, international trade, and health.[95]

Though little was said in the Ontario and Quebec media, the Western and Atlantic Canada media expressed concerns that twenty-four of the thirty chiefs of staff came from Ontario and Quebec, suggesting that the "power bloc" of ministers and their senior staffs would wield too much influence in Ottawa. Roger Gibbins, a long-time observer of Canadian politics, explains: "If you look at pipelines, if you look at resource development through the lens of metro Toronto, you come up with very different solutions than if you look at them from Calgary or even metro Vancouver."[96] Instead of looking to chiefs of staff from Western and Atlantic Canada to counterbalance the most senior Cabinet posts, they appointed them to reinforce the Ontario-Quebec bias or where the most votes are.

OTTAWA – WHERE THE ELITES MEET

There is an Ottawa perspective, Ottawa lens, and an Ottawa bubble under which the most senior politicians, public servants, and lobbyists operate. Prime Minister Justin Trudeau said that he was "excited to be getting out of the Ottawa bubble" as he left to attend a series of town hall meetings.[97] I lived the experience for several years in a line department and in two central agencies, my last appointment at the assistant deputy minister level. Roger Gibbins's point is valid: issues such as pipelines and measures to promote economic development have a different look, depending where one sits. Acquired beliefs, norms, values, and expectations that guide one's work in government depend on where one works. There are different expectations if one works in Ottawa, in the regions, as a partisan political adviser, as a career public servant, as a Cabinet minister, a government MP, or as an opposition MP. The Ottawa perspective is the key to understanding how the federal government policies and initiatives are shaped.

There are several reasons why the federal government has become even more centralized, more Ottawa-centric in recent years. Cabinet government is giving way to "governing from the centre." There is now a greater need to see government departments and agencies run on their tracks to avoid creating political controversies in the era of the twenty-four-hour news cycle and social media, to cope with the rise of the lobbyist class concentrated in Ottawa, and to work with a more centralized public service in the NCR.

Canada stands out among Anglo-American countries in locating public servants in its NCR. This has been true through the ages, and the pace has only accelerated in recent years. The Government of Australia publishes annually a *State of the Service Report*, which provides a breakdown of where public servants work. The latest report reveals that 38 percent work in the "Australian Capital Territory."[98] Britain also publishes an annual report, which contains data on civil service employment by region. The latest report reveals that 18.6 percent work in London.[99] In the United States, about 16 percent of federal government employees worked out of the Washington, DC, and area in September 2015.[100] France, a unitary state like Britain, has about 22 percent of public servants located in the Île-de-France region of Paris.[101]

In Canada, the Public Service Commission and the Treasury Board Secretariat no longer report on the location of federal public servants in their annual reports. However, Statistics Canada does, as did the Parliamentary Budget Office in 2015. Forty-five years ago, about one in four federal public servants worked in the NCR.[102] Since the early 1990s, we have seen a substantial shift away from the regions. In 2000, 35.5 percent of federal public servants worked in the NCR. Today, 41.1 percent of federal public servants work out of the NCR, a figure much higher than in other Anglo-American countries.[103] Ontario and Quebec are home to over 66 percent of federal public servants, though they represent 61.5 percent of the Canadian population.

Prime Minister Stephen Harper became concerned with the concentration of public servants in the NCR. He pledged in 2012 to look more to Ottawa-Gatineau than to the other regions in pursuing his commitment to eliminate 19,200 public service employees.[104] He failed to deliver his commitment. The Parliamentary Budget Office reported on 26 February 2015 that, after Harper made this commitment, "almost two-thirds of employment reductions have fallen outside of the NCR."[105] Given recent developments that enable public servants to connect between offices through teleconference and videoconference, one would expect the centralization of government employees to decline. What we are seeing is the opposite – their regional presence is declining.

It will be recalled that the federal government launched a program in the mid-1970s to "promote national unity, regional economic development, balanced urban growth and enhanced delivery of services to Canadians."[106] It pledged to move 10,000 jobs in 24 administrative units "to 24 cities outside of the NCR."[107] The federal government killed the program in 1979–80, although it has, from time to time, moved a unit to a region to address a political problem, for example, the closure of an air base in Summerside, Prince Edward Island.

A report from the Library of Parliament gives three reasons why the program was killed: cost, opposition MPs from the NCR, public servants and their unions. The last two reasons resonate but not the first. A strong case can be made that federal government units are less costly to operate in the regions. For one thing, the cost of office accommodation is less than in the NCR. For another, advances in information technology, from the internet and FaceTime to Skype, now enable easy and inexpensive communications between offices.

The cheque-redemption control unit of the Department of Supply and Services in Matane, located in the economically depressed Gaspé region, processes the same number of cheques with 275 employees that it processed with 300 employees when it was in Ottawa. The director of the unit explained that one reason for the increased productivity was that he was able to select the 275 employees from 3,500 applicants, while in Ottawa he had considerably fewer applicants to choose from. He added that staff turnover at Matane has been practically non-existent, compared to the high turnover experienced in Ottawa. The director of the Supply and Services unit in Shediac, New Brunswick, reported similar findings and claimed that his unit is also far more efficient than when it was located in Ottawa.[108] A manager told me that staff turnover is practically non-existent at the Shediac office. She said that someone who has a job in Shediac is not looking for a promotion with another government unit across the street because there is none, unlike in Ottawa.[109]

Neither central agencies in Ottawa nor public sector unions have ever calculated cost savings realized by having some administrative units operating in the regions, rather than Ottawa, when establishing the total cost of moving federal public service jobs to the regions. Ottawa-based senior public servants do not react well to even a hint that the mid-1970 decentralization program of government units might be relaunched. The Ottawa real estate markets matter to them, not the ones in Saskatoon or Sydney.[110] Dominic LeBlanc, an MP for New Brunswick, adds that "Deputy Ministers do not like to give bad news (cuts in employment or moving units out of Ottawa) to staff that were just laid off going up and down the elevator with them. It is easier for them to cut positions and staff in offices that they are unlikely to visit."[111]

Though far from the only factor, this explains the uneasy relations between at least some politicians and public servants. Politicians do not buy that the work of senior public servants is always evidence-based. When their own interest is at play, public servants will ignore evidence or not pursue it. Though senior public servants may still cling to Weber's ideal that public servants push aside their values so as not to interfere with the evaluation of a possible initiative, politicians no longer see it that way. In the case of centralization-decentralization of government units and public servants, however, prime ministers and their courtiers could have pushed senior public servants to produce a thorough cost-benefit analysis of Ottawa's decentralization program. There is no evidence that Mulroney, Chrétien, Harper, or Trudeau *fils* did. The political risk of alienating voters from the Montreal-Ottawa-Toronto corridor is too high. They could point to national unity concerns (e.g., ensuring that requirements of the Official Languages Act are respected when the unit is located in Saskatchewan, Newfoundland, or rural Quebec) and potential regional tensions are managed when selecting a community or a region over another.

Even governing from the centre, Harper could not deliver on his commitment to look more to the NCR when his government decided to eliminate nearly 20,000 public service jobs. Why? Prime ministers, given the constant pressure on their agenda, can only focus on a limited number of issues, and keeping a head count of where public servants are is not one of them. Ottawa and area MPs had every interest in downplaying Harper's commitment. There were no other voices in the Ottawa system to pursue it. The same can be said about the senior public service. Leaving aside the NCR real estate market, it is easier for central agencies and senior departmental officials to keep things running on their tracks when more and more public servants are located in Ottawa rather than Calgary or Halifax. The national media working out of Ottawa, Toronto, and Montreal have little interest in pursuing the issue. The Senate – the one national political institution that should have explored such matters – did not. The issue does not square with its "sober second thought" role.

LOOKING BACK

Canada's public service has developed the capacity to give the appearance of change while standing still. A multitude of consultant reports, task forces, NPM measures, and the introduction of the accounting officer concept have left hardly a trace. We have, however, seen the removal of many centrally prescribed rules and regulations, and this has only made government operations thicker, more expensive, and more risk-averse.

Politicians decided about forty years ago that they wanted senior public servants to focus more on management to become better managers. Politicians also wanted to have a stronger hold on policy levers by turning senior public servants into better managers. The shift, however, has had little impact on the work of senior public servants. Management in government remains the responsibility of a less gifted administrative class. Senior public servants still prefer to focus on policy and whiz-bang ideas to sell to prime ministers, their courtiers, the PCO, the Department of Finance, and their ministers.

We no longer have a public service with shared values. A fault line has divided the public service into two institutions – one that looks up to the most senior politicians on the government side and central agencies. Public servants operating above the fault line know how to navigate proposals on behalf of the prime minister or their ministers through the Ottawa approval process. Those below the fault line tend to look to their clients in delivering programs and services. The federal public service, meanwhile, is becoming more and more Ottawa-centric with 41 percent of federal public servants working out of the NCR, a percentage substantially higher than it was forty years ago and compared with other western democracies. This, at least in part, explains the deteriorating quality of federal government service to Canadians.

Canada's public service has slowly moved away from shared institutional values and norms. The rise in public servants looking out for themselves can be attributed to a range of factors: bureaucracy bashing, the removal of many centrally prescribed rules, the message that private sector managers are superior to government managers, the fault line dividing the public service, and governing from the centre with the prime ministers and their courtiers always on the lookout for individual senior public servants to promote their agenda. A former senior deputy minister summed up the situation well when he observed: "Politicians today dislike the public service but they like individual public servants."[112] Politicians of yesteryear may have disliked some individual public servants, but most of them liked and respected the public service as an institution. In short, politicians of yesteryear respected the public service, while today's politicians like individual public servants who "border on being promiscuously partisan" and who are willing to assist them in integrating permanent election campaigns into the art of governing.[113]

The Public Service:
An Institution with Six Goalies

Though I have spent the bulk of my career in academe, I was once a federal public servant starting fresh out of university as an assistant to Allan Gotlieb, then deputy minister of communications. I later served in a regional office in a line department and then at the assistant deputy minister level in a central agency in Ottawa. Later still, I was asked to serve at the deputy minister level (acting) for a year as head of the Canada School of Public Service while waiting for the permanent head to arrive.

My occasional forays in the federal public service – the first time in the 1970s and the last in 2004 – combined with my work as director of research for the Commission of Inquiry into the Sponsorship Program and Advertising Activities in the Government of Canada have given me important insights into both the workings of government and the evolution of the federal public service. I saw the public service evolve from a fairly confident proactive institution into a cautious, uncertain institution all too often at the ready to circle the wagons. In gathering material for this book, I asked Senator Peter Harder to share his views on the state of the federal public service. Before his appointment as government representative in the Senate, Harder had a distinguished career in the federal public service as deputy minister of Industry Canada and Department of Foreign Affairs respectively and secretary to the Treasury Board. Harder responded, "If the public service was now asked to ice a hockey team, it would ice six goalies."

Some of the problems in the federal public service are self-inflicted, but others are not. The Canadian public service is plagued by some of the same challenges found in all government bureaucracies in Anglo-American democracies. I recall meeting a senior departmental official while serving in government to say that, in my view, we had far too many employees in the department to carry out its role and responsibilities. The reaction was swift. I was told that I was showing disloyalty to the department, and if I truly believed what I had just said, then I should look for another job. I soon left the public service, but the message was clear: there is no room for discussion when looking at the department's interest.

I have watched the federal public service change over the past fifty years. Gotlieb was a highly regarded and widely respected public servant and for good reasons. He had a sharp mind and a strong working relationship with his minister; he was always on top of the more important departmental files and would get things done. His focus was on the department, on shaping new policy, and defining the department's mandate. I recall that he had some contacts with central agencies and other departments, but these never dominated his agenda. The minister, Gotlieb, and a handful of senior public servants from the department drove the policy agenda. I also recall, however, that he had little interest in administrative matters. The department had a staff to look after these things, and they came to brief him from time to time.

Today, things are different. In earlier publications, I made two points that resonated with public servants, former public servants, and journalists. As I noted earlier, in one instance I described the federal government bureaucracy as "a big whale that can't swim." In another, I described it as "too many federal public servants ... kept busy turning cranks not attached to anything." Many federal public servants and non-public servants, notably consultants, told me that both observations described very well the current state of the public service.

There are several important questions confronting the federal public service, which does not operate in isolation of political developments. It now has to cope with new media, the arrival of New Public Management, increased transparency requirements, an expanded audit system, the growth in partisan political staffers in the prime minister's and ministerial offices, and the shift away from Cabinet government to governing from the centre. These developments have largely occurred over the past fifty years and have reshaped how public servants interact with politicians, how they influence the policy-making process, and how they deliver programs and services to Canadians.

I recall, as a student, reading the Northcote-Trevelyan Report submitted in 1854 to the UK government on the state of the country's public service. The report paved the way for a merit-based public service in the United Kingdom and later in Canada. It sought to correct long-standing problems and to move the service away from partisan patronage appointments. It is an illuminating document, worth quoting at length:

> It would be natural to expect that so important a profession would attract into its ranks the ablest and the most ambitious of the youth of the country; that the keenest emulation would prevail among those who had entered it; and that such as were endowed with superior qualifications would rapidly rise to distinction and public eminence. Such, however, is by no means the case. Admission into the Civil Service is indeed eagerly sought after, but it is for the unambitious, and the indolent or incapable, that it is chiefly desired. Those whose abilities do not warrant an expectation that they will succeed in the open professions, where they must encounter the competition of their contemporaries, and those whom indolence of temperament or physical infirmities unfit for active exertions, are placed in the Civil Service, where they may obtain an honourable livelihood with little labour, and with no risk where their success depends upon their simply avoiding any flagrant misconduct, and attending with moderate regularity to routine duties; and in which they are secured against the ordinary consequences of old age, or failing health, by an arrangement which provides them with the means of supporting themselves after they have become incapacitated.[1]

The findings of the Northcote-Trevelyan Report still resonate today in certain parts of the federal public service at a time when other sectors are adapting to change. This chapter seeks to answer why.

The Northcote-Trevelyan Report reshaped the British civil service into arguably the best in the Western world.[2] Canada followed with the 1912 Murray Report. Murray concluded that the "business of a minister is not to administer, but to direct policy ... the carrying out of this policy should be left to his subordinates."[3] The Murray Report, and an earlier report on the state of the federal public service tabled in 1891–92, laid the basis for the merit principle in staffing the public service and the Civil Service Act in 1918.

The basis for the doctrine of ministerial responsibility was laid down during the Victorian era. Well into the twentieth century in both Britain and Canada, everyone knew their place, everyone knew their role, and everyone knew to whom they were accountable. The simplicity of government operations allowed ministers to secure information down the line and willingly accept responsibility for both policy and administration. Lord Palmerston, for example, took full responsibility in Parliament for "the disposal of one unserviceable horse."[4] John A. Macdonald explained the absence of three officials in his department – one who suffered from epilepsy, another who had lost his eyesight, and a third whose delicate health made attendance impossible.[5]

The simplicity of government, when the doctrine of ministerial responsibility first took shape, allowed ministers to pay attention to picayune detail. In 1867, there were only ten federal public servants for every MP in Canada. Today, there are about 800, and this does not include Crown corporations.[6] There were only a few newspapers with modest means, and there were no paid lobbyists walking the halls of government in Ottawa. There were no officers of Parliament and very few oversight bodies. The prime minister and ministers took care of oversight. The position of auditor general as an officer of Parliament was only established in 1875 in light of the Pacific Scandal. Until the late 1970s, the office was small and was only concerned with financial audits.[7]

To return to Harder's metaphor, the simplicity of government allowed for only one goalie on the ice. There were fewer referees watching players on the ice, dishing out penalties. There was also plenty of room on the ice for the players to break the rules with impunity.[8] As government grew thicker, the doctrine of ministerial responsibility gave way to confusion about accountability, an issue as important to government as market forces are to the private sector. Geoffrey Marshall summed up the problem well in his seminal work. He writes that it has become exceedingly difficult to provide "a clear and succinct account of the principle or convention of ministerial responsibility" because the convention is "somewhat vague and slippery." He further observes that "collective and individual responsibility are two doctrines, not one, and each divides in turn into a series of disparate topics."[9] The slipperiness has become even more evident in recent years, and the doctrine now provides cover for many in government. A former Cabinet minister in the Clark and

Mulroney governments, Elmer MacKay, said that no matter how hard he tried when he was in Cabinet, he could "never find the culprit" in the bureaucracy when things went wrong.[10]

THE DOCTRINE UNDER STRESS

The doctrine of ministerial responsibility held many advantages for both ministers and public servants. It enabled government to operate in relative secrecy and allowed public servants to operate under the radar screen. For a long time, the argument went that the public service had no legal personality of its own.[11] It was there to serve the government of the day. The doctrine even allowed ministers to reach back in time and secure answers to questions raised in Parliament, all the while protecting the anonymity of public servants.

In 1985, Robert Armstrong, then secretary to the Cabinet in Britain, in a carefully worded statement wrote: "Civil servants are servants of the Crown. For all practical purposes the Crown in this context ... is represented by the Government of the day ... The Civil Service has no constitutional personality or responsibility separate from the duly elected government of the day."[12] The Government of Canada adheres to the Armstrong view. A final submission to the Gomery Inquiry stated: "Public servants as such have no constitutional identity independent of their ministers."[13] The government warned that any "attempt to identify discrete areas of official accountability Parliament would likely result in the further blurring of lines of accountability to Parliament weakening the ability of the House to hold the minister responsible when it chooses for matters falling under his or her authority."[14] The Government of Canada goes even further than Britain with the no constitutional personality argument. In the government document titled *Guidance for Deputy Ministers*, the case is made that public servants "do not have a public voice, or identity distinct from that of their minister, nor do they share in their minister's political accountability."[15] To make it work, public servants need to operate under the cover of anonymity, otherwise the no personality thesis collapses.

Operating in secrecy became necessary as political parties fought to gain power. Norman Chester explains that the conflict over power "placed emphasis on government secrecy, not disclosing any information that might be of use to the opposition."[16] Public servants learned to provide advice under the cover of anonymity. That suited public servants well, however, because it would ensure their permanent status and the ability to work away from the public eye. If their views became public, they would be seen as political actors publicly favouring a policy position, in turn risking association with a political party's views. Public servants make the point that anonymity allows them to provide objective, evidence-based advice. The thinking is that politicians in return would protect their anonymity because it was in their interest.

This thinking no longer works, at least for ministers and the media. The view, outside of the public service, is that it is no longer appropriate to hold ministers responsible for their departments and allow public servants, who commit errors, to go unpunished publicly (and, more often than not, inside the system as well).[17] Ministers began to turn on their public servants in the 1980s by publicly singling them out for "their" mistakes. The Al-Mashat case, among others, makes the point that ministers are no longer willing to accept blame for decisions public servants make. Al-Mashat, Iraq's ambassador to the United States, was recalled by Baghdad. Canada provided him, and his wife's application to Canada, as ordinary landed immigrant status. The application was fast-tracked with public servants managing the process from start to finish. When the decision was made public, ministers refused to take responsibility and happily pointed at the responsible public servants.[18] By refusing to accept responsibility, ministers effectively gave the public service a personality distinct from the government of the day.

The Al-Mashat affair has hardly been the only case when ministers decided to shift responsibility to public servants.[19] For instance, Minister of National Revenue Diane Lebouthillier in the Justin Trudeau government pointed at her bureaucrats for the decision to tax employee benefits. Lebouthillier declared she was "disappointed" with her officials who would do this without her approval. The prime minister immediately declared his support for the minister, and he announced that she "has asked CRA[Canada Revenue Agency] to fix this."[20] A Fisheries and Oceans Canada director-level official told the media that his department's "risk tolerance is near zero regarding any entanglements or mortality of whales due to fishery," and added, "I can't say for sure, but there is a risk that the fisheries will be closed if an entanglement occurs." The director, unwittingly or not, was making the case that the public service has a personality. The minister of Fisheries and Oceans Canada was quick

to dissociate himself from his director's observations.[21] A senior
PCO official, meanwhile, made clear his views to the media about
problems with the prime minister's February 2018 visit to India. He
suggested that "rogue elements in the Indian government sabotaged
the prime minister's trip to India." The official was asked to appear
before a parliamentary committee but government MPs tried, initially at least, to block the request.[22] These are not isolated cases.[23]

BEST NOW TO HAVE SIX GOALIES ON THE ICE

Public servants have seen their world turned upside down over the
past fifty years. Consider the following that they have seen: the Official Languages Act implemented; the auditor general's role substantially expanded; several parliamentary officers established (many
with oversight responsibilities tied to the work of public servants);
Access to Information legislation implemented; arrival of twenty-
four-hour news channels and social media; a less deferential society;
affirmative action programs implemented for designated groups,
including women, Indigenous peoples, persons with disabilities,
and visible minorities; collective bargaining emerged; the Canadian
Human Rights Act introduced; Canadian Charter of Rights and
Freedoms adopted; growth of central agencies and shift to governing from the centre; a sharp fault line dividing public servants; and
the arrival of lobbyists (including some with strong ties to senior
politicians and a more activist judiciary).

Every single development above provides fuel for the blame
game. Combined, they become overwhelming forces that put public servants constantly on the defensive. They have to guard against
ministers unwilling to live by the requirements of ministerial responsibility, deal with the twenty-four-hour news cycle and the prime
minister's courtiers, and central agencies remain constantly on the
lookout to ensure that departments run on their tracks while officers
of Parliament are always looking for things that go off the tracks.

It is important to revisit the growth of central agencies over the
past fifty years. In 1969, the PCO and PMO employed 260 employees, Finance 372, and the Treasury Board 414.[24] Today, PCO-PMO
employ over 727 employees, Department of Finance 750, and
Treasury Board Secretariat 1,761.[25] I note that a number of large
Crown corporations were privatized twenty-five to thirty years ago,
including Air Canada, Canadian National Railways, Petro-Canada,

and airports, among others. This should have lessened the workload of central agencies.

Central agencies and officers of Parliament are like a shadow on the shoulders of public servants in line departments. One deputy minister told me that too many of his departmental officials spend too much time "feeding the beast" or providing information, reports, and performance assessments to central agencies.[26] As already noted, another line department deputy minister said that nearly 300 of his 700 employees were working on various accountability reports requested by central agencies and officers of Parliament.[27]

The above and never-ending calls for greater transparency in government and the arrival of new media have changed how government operates, placing public servants in difficult situations. It is in this environment that NPM measures were introduced, albeit in Canada with little success. NPM came in fashion throughout the Anglo-American democracies. Its central purpose was to introduce private sector management practices to government.[28] NPM ranks as one of the most misguided measure introduced to fix bureaucracy. In the case of Canada, at least, it only made things worse.[29]

The notion that we could make management in government look like management in the private sector has knocked government bureaucracies off their moorings. Those who still think that public sector management can be made to look like private sector management, and that it is possible for government managers to emulate their private sector counterparts, only need look to what legendary entrepreneur Harrison McCain said to a journalist when she said, "I would like to talk to you about your business." He responded, "My business is none of your business."[30] Imagine the reaction if a senior politician or a senior public servant made this statement to a journalist. McCain's point was that in the private sector you manage privately, while in the public sector you manage publicly.

Long-serving public servants knew intuitively that NPM measures were bound to fail. But they signed on because it was the fashion of the day, political leaders saw merit in the approach, and the measures would remove many centrally prescribed rules and regulations. They believed that, on the administrative side at least, NPM would make life easier. And so they did, but the drawbacks far outweighed the benefits for public servants, at least for those who would like to take risks. Central agencies kept piling on reporting requirements at the same time as some politicians became unwilling to accept the requirements of the doctrine of ministerial responsibility. Reporting requirements are no match for clearly defined rules and expectations. The result is that a number of senior public servants above the fault line have decided to identify with politicians in power and openly promote their political agenda. Others, notably those below the fault line, have decided to circle the wagons and avoid fuelling the blame game. This has served to further deinstitutionalize the public service.

The heart of the issue is Parliament. We have witnessed an important shift in how political accountability is achieved under our constitution. More to the point, "the focus of political competition has moved away from parliamentary contestation to the conflict between executive government and the more neutral, more specialist and more normatively driven agencies of accountability – the courts, regulatory agencies and oversight officers and commissions."[31]

Officers of Parliament are different from parliamentary committees. The latter have limited staff and Members of Parliament tend to focus on their constituencies, issues that matter to them, and on being cast in a favourable light in the media. Officers of Parliament, meanwhile, are generally well-educated professionals. They work out of Ottawa and can focus exclusively on their mandates free of political considerations. They need not worry about oversight bodies challenging the quality of their work. Sharon Sutherland argues, for example, that the role of the auditor general has been "flipped on its head" where parliamentary committees have become "stakeholders" and "clients" instead of "the source of [the office's] role and authority."[32]

Opposition MPs look to officers of Parliament for ammunition to attack the government, while government MPs and senior public servants see them as the leading voices of the blame game. Officers of Parliament recognize the problem. Seven officers of Parliament made an "unprecedented appeal" to the House of Commons to do "a better job of scrutinizing and overseeing" their work, but there has been no response.[33] Officers of Parliament go to work every morning, looking for errors and administrative miscues. Public servants know this, just as they know that the media, both old and new, will invariably focus on what is going wrong instead of what is going right in government. Best for them to play defence to avoid giving ammunition to the blame game.

IN BUSINESS IT IS BETTER TO ASK FOR FORGIVENESS, IN GOVERNMENT, BETTER NEVER TO SIN

Chuck Guité, the senior public servant at the centre of the Chrétien sponsorship scandal, has had a profound impact on the work of the federal public service. A sponsorship program was introduced to show Québécois the important role played by the federal government in their province. The program ran from 1996 to 2004, until corruption was discovered. Ottawa had spent $250 million on the program, with over $100 million going to Liberal-connected communications firms. Some of the firms were handsomely rewarded for little or no work. Chuck Guité was appointed to head the program.[34]

Guité bent the rules to get things done. He was later convicted of defrauding the government. Until the scandal erupted, Chuck Guité had been the poster boy for government efforts to introduce private sector management to government operations. Here was an individual who could get things done. He was an entrepreneur working in government, the kind that politicians and NPM promoted. He was told to cut red tape and to make things happen. This he did, and he was rewarded with several promotions over a relatively short period of time while being highly praised. Government officials told the media that Guité was "a man of action, a man of decisions, it did not take him 50 years to reach a decision. In terms of client services, there were few who could beat him."[35] The PMO and the minister responsible for the sponsorship initiatives all supported Guité's rapid promotions. He had done what he believed was expected of him, or what would be expected in the private sector. But when Canada's sponsorship scandal began to hit the front pages of the country's newspapers, the politicians and senior public servants ran for cover: the doctrine of ministerial responsibility be damned.

Prime Minister Chrétien said that he was not aware of all the shenanigans, the relevant minister, Alfonso Gagliano, pointed at public servants, the department's deputy minister said that Guité took direction from the PMO, while Guité confirmed that he looked to PMO for directions. The PMO deemed responsibility should lie with those who made decisions in the line department and the communications firms who defrauded the government. Justice Gomery pointed his finger at the PMO, Gagliano, Guité, and the communications firms.[36]

The sponsorship scandal is felt in government to this day. It has strengthened the hand of central agency officials to make sure that line departments do not provide fuel for the blame game. Public servants, who manage programs and services and understand that the doctrine of ministerial responsibility only applies when it suits ministers, came to also understand that they are on their own if things go off the rails. Consequently, the public service became more cautious and more bureaucratic in delivering programs.

The sponsorship scandal is only one of several high-profile scandals that have been linked to the federal government in recent years. Several flowed directly from public servants with no involvement or even knowledge of politicians. I am thinking, among others, of a senior Health Canada official who was caught setting up a fraudulent scheme and another at Department of National Defence who pleaded guilty of fraud.[37]

The federal public service has lost standing with Canadians in recent years. As already noted, this at a time when non-public sector workers are asking why government employees can remain isolated from the discipline and requirements imposed by the global economy. The socio-economic conditions of the 1960s and 1970s that gave rise to collective bargaining, to generous pension and healthcare plans, to job security and seeing government become the "model employer" are gone, but the benefits remain. Through collective bargaining, public servants continue to resist change when it comes to their benefits and job security. It is not uncommon for Canadians to read headlines reporting that "nobody is losing their jobs" in Ottawa when departments are reorganized.[38] All of the above has served to place the federal public service on the defensive.

DEALING WITH ACCESS TO INFORMATION LEGISLATION

Canada's constitution, notably the doctrine of ministerial responsibility, calls on the public service to operate from a closed world, under political direction and under the obligation of political accountability.[39] The doctrine is not solely in the interest of ministers. Max Weber insisted that the "official secret" is an invention of bureaucracy because it welcomes a poorly informed Parliament, media, and citizens since "ignorance somehow agrees with the bureaucracy's interests."[40]

Though many government officials are resisting it to this day, access to information legislation ensures that federal public servants are anonymous no more. The legislation has enabled the media, opposition parties, and interested Canadians to pin down what issues individual public servants are working on, even with whom they had lunch if taxpayers paid for it. The only way for senior public servants to remain anonymous is to avoid expense accounts and refrain from putting their views on paper or on their computers, since e-mails are accessible under the act. Recall that Prime Minister Stephen Harper led a $2 billion spending reduction effort by instructing public servants to do everything orally, with officials in at least one department directing consultants to deliver their findings through oral briefings.[41]

The impact of the legislation has been profound. For one thing, it has generated a demand for good political "firefighters" in Ottawa and has made public servants more cautious. As Giles Gherson, journalist and former policy adviser in the Department of Human Resources Development, explains, "To address the access to information issue ... I saw myself that officials are extremely leery of putting things on paper that they wouldn't like to see made public or find its way to the media, several months later, that could be embarrassing to the minister."[42] Conrad Winn, a pollster, argues that access to information has seriously inhibited the ability of government departments to ask the right questions when commissioning a survey: "The bottom line for the average public servant is don't embarrass the minister, that is the surest way to have your career stopped or slowed down. If you have polls that ask all kinds of questions that would reveal the truthful complexity of what people think ... [the polls] will inevitably show the public doesn't like something the government does."[43] Former political journalist Hugh Winsor readily admits the media often take advantage of access to information to get at a story. But, he argues, they do that "not so much to find out what the people dislike about the government ... but to try to get an advance look at what the government's agenda might be ... and at the next budget or the next Speech from the Throne by making an access to information request about a public opinion survey which is being commissioned."[44]

The legislation has also had a profound impact on career officials. In the case of Guité, at least, had it not been for a journalist working on a hunch, a tip, and an access to information request, Canadians would probably never have known about the sponsorship scandal, and Guité would have enjoyed his retirement in Arizona rather than serving a jail sentence. Senior departmental officials told the court that when the first access to information request on the sponsorship initiative came in, it plunged the department into a state of "crisis."[45] Access to information has enabled the media and others to turn their attention to public servants, not just to politicians. In response to criticisms that public servants were spending too much on hospitality and travel – including George Radwanski, the privacy commissioner, who spent $500,000 over a two-year period, staying at expensive hotels, travelling first class, and eating extravagant meals – in 2004 the government directed all senior managers to post their travel expenses on their departmental websites. As a result, two of Ottawa's most renowned restaurants – Café Henry Burger and Clair de Lune – closed their doors. The owner of one establishment said that the moment hospitality claims had to be disclosed on the internet, "they simply didn't come anymore." Another reported, "It wasn't necessarily the politicians, but it was the top civil servants that stopped coming."[46]

Public servants have long resisted expanding the scope of the access to information legislation, making the case that Max Weber had it right over one hundred years ago when he wrote that "official secret" is an invention of bureaucracy. Alasdair Roberts, a leading authority on access to information, documents how public servants have devised ways to minimize political damage to their departments and their ministers. Strategies to address the legislation include ways to delay responding or even thwart the request. Roberts explains that delay in processing information requests "can be very important, particularly for journalists, members of Parliament or other party representatives. The news cycle has its own rhythm – an issue will not remain in the foreground indefinitely and will soon be displaced by other topics."[47]

Public servants playing goalie on access to information legislation does not sit well with the access to information commissioner, who is an officer of Parliament. The hostility between senior public servants and the commissioner has been evident since the legislation was introduced.[48] Stephen Harper, on the advice of senior public servants, diluted commitments he made in the election campaign to strengthen access to information legislation. Justin Trudeau, on the same advice, watered down his commitments to strengthen the legislation. Trudeau had pledged to overhaul the access to information by introducing a number of measures to strengthen it, including provisions to enhance the power of the information commissioner. The proposed legislation his government tabled fell short in several key areas.[49] Suzanne Legault, the information commissioner, took aim at the legislation as she was taking her leave in February 2018. She remarked, "The government is sliding into more secrecy and actually not delivering on its promises," and added, "Bill C-58 is a bill for bureaucracy, it's not a bill for transparency."[50]

IT'S ABOUT PERMANENT ELECTION CAMPAIGNS

The PCO has guidelines on the role of public servants during election campaigns. The key words are "routine" and "non-controversial."[51] The PCO does not say how the guidelines apply in the era of permanent election campaigns, though one can appreciate that many public servants would see merit in continuing to apply them. Alex Marland, Thierry Giasson, and Anna Lennox Esselment go to the heart of the issue: "The requirements of election campaigns were once viewed as quite separate from the responsibilities of governing ... [T]he separation between campaigning and governing was relatively clear ... Nowadays, politicians are embroiled in constant electioneering – a nonstop competitive mindset to win the onslaught of media battles, to raise funds, to persuade public opinion, to push an agenda, and to generally maintain a state of election readiness."[52] If election campaigns are never-ending, then it follows that PCO guidelines for public servants during election campaigns should also never end. To be sure, it is safer for public servants.

The party in power now seeks continuous public approval and this has wide implications for public servants. Paul Thomas explains that "the techniques for winning power have been transferred increasingly to the processes of government."[53] The media have contributed greatly to the rise of permanent election campaigns. One does not have to go far back in history to see that there were only three evening news shows (CBC, CTV, and Radio-Canada), one daily newspaper (that at least claimed to be a national newspaper in English Canada), and a number of local newspapers. Today, the governing and opposition political parties have to keep feeding the internet and the twenty-four-hour cable news channels.

The great majority of public servants know the best way to survive and keep out of trouble is to keep their heads below the parapet. The sure way to see their careers take a downward spiral is to be

dragged into partisan political debates where even purely administrative miscues are fair game for highly charged political issues. They
know, whether in an election campaign or not, the doctrine of ministerial responsibility, as noted, now only applies when it is convenient
for ministers that it applies.[54]

Public servants know, better than anyone, that the media will give
visibility to errors large or small, political or administrative. They
know that their ministers will be held responsible and that there is
no benefit in taking risks unless someone at the centre of government gives them the green light to take risks. Those operating at the
centre are a world away from font-line managers. Best for front-line
managers to give the appearance of change while standing still, to
attend meetings that generate few, if any, decisions, and to commission and revise consultant reports.

However, some senior public servants at the highest level in the
public service see permanent election campaigns as opportunities.
Jonathan Craft is not alone in warning that permanent election campaigns are challenging public service impartiality.[55] Craft maintains
that the challenge for public servants at the highest level is to "align
policy-making with partisan aims with the traditional public service
norms."[56] There is evidence that the "detached competence" long
associated with public service values has lost ground in recent years.
Ralph Heintzman, a former senior federal public servant, maintains that senior officials in Ottawa have lost sight of maintaining a
"boundary between political and public service values."[57]

Peter Aucoin wrote about the pressure on senior public servants
in the Westminster parliamentary system to become "promiscuously
partisan." He saw a new approach to governance shaped by the rise
in numbers and influence of partisan political staffers tied to prime
ministers and their courtiers interpreting "public service loyalty"
with "support for the government." More to the point, he saw senior
public servants becoming "promiscuously partisan for the government of the day" no matter the political party in power. Aucoin
argued that the most trusted courtiers to the prime minister "can be
as influential, or even more influential, as senior ministers or senior
public servants." Aucoin focused on a cadre of senior public service
executives that numbers about eighty at the levels of deputy minister
and associate deputy minister. They are all appointed to this level by
the prime minister.[58] He could have added many at the assistant deputy minister level, or those aspiring to be appointed deputy minister

or associate deputy minister. Michael Keating, former secretary in the Department of the Prime Minister in Australia, puts it succinctly when he observes that there is a tendency among senior public servants looking for a promotion to be "excessively eager to please."[59]

A small layer of the most senior levels of the public service has been integrated with continuous election campaigns. The layer has become much more visible inside and outside of government. The most senior public servants are now expected to attend to stakeholders, the media, and parliamentarians, and to participate in public forums and public consultation exercises. The prime minister and ministers "sometimes explicitly, usually implicitly, expect these public servants who are seen and heard in countless public forums to support government policy, to go beyond mere description and explanation."[60] In an era of highly charged and volatile political environments of permanent election campaigns, it is no surprise that prime ministers and their courtiers will view the most senior public servants from the questioning perspective, are they with us or against us.

The rest of the public service, meanwhile, is expected to run their operations error free, or if there are errors, then they should be managed so that they do not draw the media's attention. It explains why the great majority of federal public servants have been turned into goalies. They are cautious, risk-averse, and will shy away from visibility outside of government circles. The Public Service Commission had this advice for public servants: "Although public servants are to be sensitive to partisan considerations, they are not actively to support or debate policy decisions. While they may be required to explain policy rationale, public servants are not to argue in favour of or against a particular policy." The Commission goes on to warn public servants: "Regardless of how the visibility of public servants has increased, the more visible public servants are the more vulnerable they become to partisan political attacks. If public servants are attacked publicly by one party and praised by another, this could undermine public service impartiality. This issue is further complicated when one considers the statutory authorities and responsibilities given to deputy heads."[61]

Having the bulk of the public service ensure that programs and services run on their tracks, having public servants trying as best they can to avoid making mistakes that may cast the prime ministers or ministers in a bad light, and telling them that their institution has no personality distinct from the government of the day are not without problems. There are signs that the public service is no longer able to attract the best and the brightest to their ranks.[62] We know that the federal public service has long been plagued by serious and stubborn morale problems.[63] We also know that the federal public service has been plagued by "soaring disability claims" with mental health disorders, led by depression and anxiety, accounting for nearly 50 percent of the claims.[64] The Global Business and Economic Roundtable on Addiction and Mental Health has described the federal government workplace as "an emotionally airless environment."[65] Statistics Canada has reported on "low morale" based on surveys.[66] The clerk of the Privy Council reports that there is a need to address a "disturbing level" of harassment in the federal public service such as bullying, intimidation, and conduct issues."[67]

In 2008, 150 "early career" federal public servants were invited to identify challenges confronting the federal public service and ways to meet them by the year 2017, Canada's 150th anniversary. They produced a revealing document, making the case that "as new public servants," they wanted more from their work than playing goal. They wrote, "We have identified some issues that, if not addressed, could result in an organization that has difficulty living up to citizens' expectations and fulfilling its mandate in 2017" and beyond. The challenges included

hierarchical structures that limit quick action and clear communication; a risk-averse culture that does not provide incentives for creativity or innovation; an intense focus on accountability that reinforces the emphasis on hierarchy and promotes a risk-averse culture, a focus on short-term results over long-term improvement, relationships based on contractual responsibilities rather than trust; poor relationships with stakeholders, citizens, other departments, and other order[s] of government that prevent partnerships and meaningful deliberations from taking shape; territorial in-fighting (both inter- and intra-departmentally) over who should take the "lead" on addressing an issue, creating an even more complex and hostile landscape; long-standing and unquestioned jurisdictional boundaries that discourage cooperation on shared problems; and regional animosity and declining trust in government that makes working together on how to frame and address our shared problems even more difficult.[68]

This is an illuminating list of challenges produced by young federal public servants who articulate their frustrations with being asked to play goal.

The above speaks to Canada's approach to governing and consists of political institutions that lack rules, instead relying heavily on loosely defined conventions.[69] The old bargain that guided relationships between politicians and public servants has broken down.[70] Successful deputy ministers, associate deputy ministers, and aspiring assistant deputy ministers "have developed a capacity to detect and manage emerging political crises,"[71] and to respond to both the partisan political and policy interests of prime ministers and their courtiers. These public servants know that the best way to survive and to remain upwardly mobile is to work with prime ministers and their courtiers to fend off opposition and media attack. Their desire to please is pervasive at the most senior level of the public service. They are, however, sacrificing the Westminster principle of public service impartiality for the political interest of the government of the day, and for their own personal and career interests. Some see themselves more capable than many ministers of identifying emerging political crises and managing them against the opposition and the media. They are the only ones in the public service not playing goal.

LOOKING BACK

The more senior federal public servants are resisting putting offensive players on the ice other than themselves. The risks are too high. The fear is that putting an offensive line on the ice could well generate new political crises feeding the insatiable appetite of opposition parties and the media – both new and old. All offensive players in the federal public service must play on Ottawa ice, where prime ministers and their courtiers, the media, ministers and their partisan staff, officers of Parliament, lobbyists and deputy ministers, associate deputy ministers, and ambitious assistant deputy ministers are located. What matters is the ability to promote the prime minister's brand and ensure errors, whether political or administrative, are properly managed to minimize any negative political impact on the government.

It is a world where perception, image-making, and political spins matter and evidence-based advice, all too often, takes a back seat. This message was brought home to me by a senior deputy minister, who pointed to Prime Minister Joe Clark's strategy to address

Quebec's sovereigntists. Clark held power for several months in 1979, three years after Quebec had elected the Parti Québécois to power. Quebec was aggressively promoting sovereignty-association at the time. Trudeau had made clear that he would fight sovereignty-association head-on in Quebec. Clark said that he would rather let Québécois decide and would keep federal interference in check. The deputy minister remarked that it was all "political spin" based on "political realities." The Clark government only elected two MPs from Quebec in 1979, Roch La Salle and Heward Grafftey. He explained, "Clark simply did not have the horses to mount a political fight in Quebec." La Salle, the only francophone minister from Quebec, was not known as a political heavyweight. In fact, he resigned from the Mulroney Cabinet in 1987, after being charged with accepting a bribe.[72] According to the deputy minister, Clark sought to spin the situation as best he could by denying reality. The deputy minister was making the point that political considerations dominate all aspects of governing; evidence-based advice only comes in when it is politically convenient. More to the point, one can rationalize any position in governing, and the more senior public servants are expected to help politicians do so as well as to manage delicate political situations, never in shortage given permanent election campaigns and twenty-four-hour cable news and social media.

Nothing has changed since high-profile deputy minister Al Johnson wrote in the 1960s that "the role of the deputy minister is to make it possible for the minister and Cabinet to provide the best government of which they are capable – even better if either of them happens to be weak."[73] This, even though politicians, since the early 1980s, were to change things through NPM and other reform measures. Senior public servants were to emulate their private sector counterparts and be transformed into better managers, while leaving politics and policy to politicians. The opposite has happened: public servants at the very top of the hierarchy are focusing more on politics and managing the day-to-day requirements of prime ministers and their courtiers as they navigate permanent election campaigns. Program managers, including the more senior ones, have been turned into goalies playing defensive so as not to provide grist to the media and opposition parties for the blame game mill. The permanent election campaign era is one thing. Senior program managers have to cope with a growing number of officers of Parliament looking over their shoulders and central agencies requiring more and more performance reports from those operating below the fault line.

The problem is strongly felt in regional offices, where programs and services are delivered. Not only are federal government regional offices bleeding staff to departmental head offices in Ottawa, but also regional offices are requiring flexibility and the ability to innovate, to attend to local circumstances and – in the words of the 150 "early career officials" – to address the "poor relationships with stakeholders and citizens" and deal with "regional animosity and declining trust in government." It is not possible to meet these challenges by only putting goalies on the ice. Playing defence is not the most promising way of attracting the best and brightest to the public service – a point the early career officials made. A recently retired clerk of the Privy Council expressed "concern about the ability of the public service to attract top students."[74]

Institutions live by rules, procedures, and norms, both formal and informal. When one of the most important norms – in this case, the doctrine of ministerial responsibility – is tossed aside or reinterpreted to meet the requirement of the day, the institution is left on shaky ground. This is what we are witnessing in Ottawa. The public service, in the absence of widely accepted norms and procedures, now consists of two institutions – one operating above the fault line with its own norms designed to please prime ministers and their courtiers, and another below the fault line populated by goalies.

New Forces above the Fault Line

There was a time, not long ago, when the courts took a back seat to Cabinet and Parliament. No more. There was a time, not long ago, when one would be hard-pressed to see more than a handful of lobbyists in Ottawa. No more. Though no one would want to draw a parallel between the work of the courts and lobbyists, both now wield power and influence. And their impact on Canada's national political and administrative institutions has been strongly felt in recent years.

Judges are independent. They are free to see truth as it is based on precedents and their best judgment. Lobbyists are different. They see truth as their customers see it. Politicians who do not see truth as pure, simple, or evidence-based can turn to lobbyists to challenge the views of their officials to hear the kind of truth they want to hear. However, when matters go before the courts, politicians have to accept truth as judges see it. Politicians do appoint judges, and they will seek to appoint those who have been identified with their political party. But that is as far as it goes, and once appointed, judges are free to see things for what they are, free of partisan political influence. The courts operate above the fray, whereas lobbyists are part of the fray. The reader may well ask why I would wish to deal with the judiciary and lobbyists in the same chapter. Both gained visibility and power at about the same time – in the mid-1980s – both, for the most part, deal with issues that are of concern in Ottawa to those operating above the fault line, both continue to have a profound impact on Canada's national political and administrative institutions, and both are strengthening the hand of prime ministers, their courtiers, and central agencies.

One year after Canada was born, a student of the judiciary in the Westminster setting observed that the first principle of the constitution was "the omnipotence of Parliament."[1] Three years later, Justice Willes said, "Acts of Parliament … are the law of the land; and we do not sit here as a court of appeal from parliament. We sit here as servants of the Queen and the legislature. The proceedings here are judicial, not democratic, which would be the case if we could make laws instead of administering them."[2] Canada got around to establishing its Supreme Court in 1875, and it dealt only with a few cases in its early years. Canada's courts were careful to preserve parliamentary supremacy for a century. The courts did not go beyond deciding how the constitution distributed power between the federal and provincial governments. When it came to government officials exceeding their authority, "the remedy was seen to be with parliament not the courts."[3] Things are very different today.

Forty-five years ago, one had to search far and wide for a lobbyist roaming the halls of power in Ottawa. Today, there are over 8,600 lobbyists in Ottawa. Some are well connected to the politicians in power, most are well paid, and many are experts in how government decides.[4]

THE COURTS

Trudeau would leave a far more important gift for future prime ministers: the Canadian Charter of Rights and Freedoms. It is often said in Ottawa circles that access to information legislation is a gift Pierre Trudeau gave to Brian Mulroney and other prime ministers that followed. In other words, Trudeau did not have to live with the consequences of the legislation produced by his government, except for several months before he left office.

Some prime ministers have had difficulties with the Supreme Court. As Emmett Macfarlane notes, some observers believe that "Harper became convinced that the Court had set itself up as the unofficial opposition."[5] It is not possible to overstate the impact the Charter of Rights and Freedoms has had on Canadian politics. The notion that Parliament is supreme now belongs to history books. The Charter and Canada's constitution both make it clear that any law inconsistent with the Charter is "of no force or effect."[6] In short, we now have constitutional supremacy.

The Supreme Court has carved out a role for itself that would have been unthinkable less than forty years ago. The courts did have an opportunity before to extend their scope, notably after 1960, when Parliament passed Diefenbaker's Canadian Bill of Rights.[7] Diefenbaker decided that he would not seek provincial agreement for entrenching his Bill of Rights into the British North America Act. Emmett Hall, a high-profile former Supreme Court justice, summed up the bill's impact when he wrote that it "went from a high point of great expectancy down a short steep slope to near oblivion."[8] The courts, however, have made up for lost time with the Charter of Rights and Freedoms.

Since the Charter's introduction, we have witnessed a remarkable transfer of power to the courts "from Parliament, Cabinet and the government."[9] They can tell Parliament or provincial legislative assemblies to act and then specify how long they have to act, as the Supreme Court did in 2015 in its decision on assisted suicide. Truth can be a moving target, even for the Supreme Court. In 1993, it denied Sue Rodriguez's request to end her life. She had a terminal disease and did not want a painful, prolonged death. The Supreme Court had a change of position in 2015 and ruled, in a unanimous decision, that Canadians did have a right to physician-assisted suicide.[10]

The Supreme Court and Supreme Court justices have become high-profile political actors. The court, in the eyes of many informed observers, has moved beyond Charter provisions to embrace Charter "values" decisions. The concern is that this shift enables the courts to "threaten the appropriate institutional division of labour between legislatures and the courts."[11] Canada's former chief justice Beverley McLachlin explains that Canadians can "now go to court to challenge laws and government acts not only on the grounds that they exceeded the grants of power, but also on the ground that they violate fundamental rights."[12] The Supreme Court now has the power to decide what constitutes fundamental rights and to shape laws, if not make laws.

Canadians have responded. They continue to appeal to the courts to secure their rights.[13] The Charter, as James B. Kelly argues, "has led to a further marginalization of parliament" on the one hand, and "deepened prime-ministerial government" on the other.[14] Kelly maintains that the Department of Justice has been drawn into the centre and has added to its power because it is tasked with coordinating rights scrutiny inside government.[15]

Senior Department of Justice (DOJ) officials are now part of the centre, operating above the fault line, when dealing with Charter issues. DOJ officials, in concert with senior central agency officials, have essentially pushed aside line departments and parliamentary scrutiny of legislation in the name of Charter vetting. Kelly explains that the emergence of DOJ as an important component of the centre was the moment "the clerk of the Privy Council, on the instruction of the prime minister, directed line departments to consult the DOJ when dealing with potential Charter issues."[16] The centre is where key decisions are now made to determine if proposed legislation squares with the Charter.

The courts, as they should, carefully guard their independence from the government and Parliament. Since the Charter was introduced, we have witnessed a lively debate between those who portray the Supreme Court as a powerful political force further weakening Parliament and Cabinet government and those who applaud judicial intervention in the name of assuring rights and freedoms for individuals.[17] The latter group argue that the Supreme Court has been the main agent responsible for fundamental and positive change in Canadian society. They add that the courts, including the Supreme Court, "are not self-starting institutions." They deal with individuals, associations and groups seeking answers.[18] In short, they do not initiate, they respond.

Both sides agree that the courts have become important policy actors. The Supreme Court has decided the fate of Senate reform and same-sex marriage, prohibited discrimination on the basis of sexual orientation, and established that Indigenous rights that pre-existed the Constitution Act, 1982 cannot be infringed without justification. But that is not all. Emmett Macfarlane's *Governing from the Bench* points to the growing importance of the Supreme Court and its impact both on Canada's political institutions and in shaping public policy. He remarks, "The Supreme Court of Canada's importance can be measured not only by its rulings on a country's law and immediate policy issues that come before it but also by the influence its decisions have on government, political culture, and public discourse."[19]

Macfarlane makes the case that the Supreme Court is hardly free of political considerations. He points to a number of cases dealing with contentious issues where the personal preferences of individual justices took over. In one case, the justices accepted the view of a single expert who maintained that allowing private health insurance would not hurt the public system and dismissed the views of six other experts who said it would.[20]

Prime ministers appoint judges, leaving aside provincially appointed judges. Many judges appointed by one prime minister, say, Jean Chrétien, would not likely be appointed by another, say, Stephen Harper. Judges bring to their work their values and political views, and prime ministers appoint judges whose judgments they prefer. Merit is in the eye of the prime minister and a past association with him or her, or with the political party in power, matters. In a recent study of the Supreme Court of Canada, Donald Songer observes a "moderately strong relationship" between the federal party that appointed a judge and his or her policy preferences. He writes that "notwithstanding disclaimers that judicial ideology is not actively considered in juridical selection," three of the Supreme Court justices whom he interviewed confirmed their belief that this is so.[21] Constance Backhouse, arguably Canada's leading student of the judiciary, has this to say: "Will we admit, finally, that politics, one's small-p politics, has an impact on the judicial rulings that one makes ... Because we've been all pretending that it never did. And of course in my view it always does, but it's muted."[22]

In an earlier publication, I wrote that Roméo LeBlanc, a senior minister in the Trudeau government and later governor general of Canada, once told me, "Lawyers are the only people in the world who can regain their virginity; all you have to do is appoint them judges." He explained that overnight some of them go from being fiercely partisan to having a disdain for politicians and for things political. "You meet them at airports, and they are eager to profess their complete loyalty to you and your party and their willingness to get involved and give a helping hand. You promote their nomination to the bench. Later, when you see them at airports, they will avoid you; some do not want even to make eye contact with you. Overnight, they change. Politics is suddenly unhealthy and to be avoided. I always find it quite amazing and amusing."[23]

A senior judge read my observation and later remarked that I should be careful not to "debase" the judiciary.[24] He recognized that Charter decisions have made judges more visible, and visibility is not without consequences. The more visible judges become, the more controversial they become. His point is that with visibility comes scrutiny, but judges are not politicians; they cannot defend themselves in public or respond to criticism.

Judges operate under different rules than politicians and public servants. They do not have to deal with access to information legislation in the name of maintaining judicial independence from politicians, the media, and taxpayers. Their employment benefits are rich, even by the standards of the federal public service. When judges reach retirement age, they have three choices: continue to sit as a full-time judge until age seventy-five, serve as a supernumerary judge, or retire. A supernumerary judge continues to receive the salary and all the benefits available to a full-time judge but is asked to perform only 40 percent of the caseload of a full-time judge.

Judges always keep a close eye on the requirements of judicial independence, which includes security of tenure, financial security, and administrative independence.[25] The Supreme Court ruled in 1997 that any provincial government attempt to address budget deficits by reducing judges' salaries violated judicial independence.[26] Governments could only do so by turning to independent judicial compensation committees for a decision. The Supreme Court has ruled that governments could not eliminate the position of supernumerary judge for fiscal considerations. Such a decision, if it were ever to be struck, needs to be made by an independent judicial compensation committee.[27]

The great majority of politicians in Canada appreciate the need for judicial independence, and few are prepared to challenge the judiciary, at least in public. They understand that the test of the rule of law in a democracy is whether a government can lose in its own court. Canada meets the test. Canada's former chief justice Beverley McLachlin once observed, "I am convinced that Canadian courts must become more administratively independent from the federal and provincial governments that regularly appear before them."[28] She noted, however, that "we live in an age of transparency and accountability. Our era is tinged with a sense of cynicism about our major social institutions and a certain pessimism about where we are going."[29]

As judges become more visible, so do calls increase for greater transparency in the work of the judiciary. Two judges acknowledge this: "Public confidence is the only source of authority for the judiciary. It is therefore imperative that the judiciary provide what is required in order to maintain that confidence. Expectations of the public have developed to where information on the judiciary's administrative function is required to maintain public confidence. This should not be resisted."[30] Public opinion is fickle, and as former chief justice McLachlin observed, "Our era is tinged with a sense of cynicism." There is evidence that some regions, notably

Alberta, "oppose the top court's power to make social justice through judicial interpretation."[31] As Lori Hausegger and Troy Riddell argue, Canada's Supreme Court does not operate in isolation of public opinion.[32]

Public opinion surveys reveal that, when compared with other institutions, Canadians have a favourable opinion of the Supreme Court. Jeffrey Simpson writes that the "courts are more popular than legislatures, judges more respected than politicians, and legal scholars themselves prefer the legalisms of courts to the hurly-burly of politics, 'dialogue' usually means for them that the courts should tell Parliament what to do, and Parliament should follow."[33] An Angus Reid survey, for example, reports that Canadians express more confidence in the Supreme Court than in Parliament. In this survey, 61 percent of Canadians express confidence in the Supreme Court compared with 25 percent in Parliament and only 13 percent in the political parties, and 12 percent in politicians. The Senate trailed everybody with only 10 percent reporting "a great deal" or "quite a lot" of confidence in the Upper House.[34]

The courts do not have to contend with opposition parties or deal with a prying media and access to information legislation. This is true regarding the expense accounts of judges. Supreme Court judges recently decided that documents dealing with their deliberations will not be revealed for fifty years, or during their lifetime and possibly forever. The fifty-year-rule applies from the time they rule on a case and the Supreme Court can, if it so wishes, keep the document forever confidential without providing justification. Judges do not have to compete against one another for an appointment, and they do not have to make difficult budgetary recommendations in striking decisions, even if their rulings require spending new public funds.

Every year, the Supreme Court produces decisions that have far-reaching implications for politics, for social policy, for economic policy, and for minorities' rights. The courts have become the main avenue for both individuals and groups in their pursuit of rights claims. Emmett Macfarlane writes about the rise of a "rights-infused political culture," and the courts have responded to that culture. In doing so, they have had a profound impact in several policy fields.[35] For example, the Macdonald-Laurier Institute named the Supreme Court Policy-Maker of the Year in 2014.[36]

As many observers have pointed out, the Supreme Court, going back to the mid-1980s, has reshaped relations between governments and minority groups. There is no need to go over the cases, even the more important ones. This has been done elsewhere.[37]

Our focus is on Supreme Court decisions with substantive policy content, of which there are many since the mid-1980s. Raymond Bazowski writes about the "judicialization of politics," suggesting that the courts have intruded into the policy-making arena and that political conflicts are transforming into legal issues that are now resolved "in an impenetrable institutional setting."[38] The setting may be particularly impenetrable to individual citizens, but much less so for groups and associations with financial resources. Some observers insist that "special interest" communities (such as feminist, LGBTQ, Indigenous, and minority-languages) have turned to the courts to secure rights they would not have been able to obtain through the political process.[39]

In some instances, the courts have gone beyond the Charter to stop the government from changing policy direction. For example, when the New Brunswick government decided to eliminate its early French immersion program in March 2008, some parents challenged the decision in court. Although the judge ruled that the government's decision did not violate the Canadian Charter of Rights and Freedoms, he did rule that the government had not allowed sufficient time for debate on the issue. He added that the minister's decision "was unfair and unreasonable," and on this basis "quashed" it.[40] The government decided not to appeal but to go back to the drawing board. It initiated a new round of public consultations and subsequently revised its plan by introducing early immersion in grade 3. The important point is that the court essentially ignored the substance of the issue but decided that a democratically elected government had adopted a wrong process in striking a policy decision. In other words, the court somehow knew better than the government how a public consultation process should work, and it forced the government to initiate a new one.

The New Brunswick government was in for another surprise when it decided to overhaul the delivery of health-care services in the province. Ostensibly to cut costs and eliminate duplication, it planned to reduce the number of regional health authorities from eight to two. A recently retired Supreme Court judge, known for being a strong advocate of minority-language rights while on the bench, agreed to be part of the citizens' group taking the provincial government to court. He dismissed out of hand the minister's claim that the decision belonged to the government. He insisted that no legislative body in Canada any longer has such power.[41]

The issue was a machinery-of-government matter, and the objective was to streamline operations and reduce spending. The courts, however, do not concern themselves with the finer points of machinery-of-government issues or where the money should come from. They do not concern themselves with how best to implement a program, thinking all that really matters is reaching the right decision, as they see it. Politicians and public servants are left to implement the decision, no matter the difficulty in doing so. In many cases, including this one, government has to pay all (or nearly all) of the legal costs for both sides. When the government pays legal costs for groups pursuing it in court, the groups have nothing to lose and everything to gain.

The Supreme Court, in a unanimous decision, ruled on 10 November 2012 that governments and school boards could not turn to budget constraints or other arguments to avoid providing special programs to help students with special needs access an education. Justice Rosalie Abella wrote, "Adequate special education is not a dispensable luxury. For those with severe learning disabilities, it is the ramp that provides access to the statutory commitment to education made to all children in British Columbia."[42] Representatives of the Learning Disability Association declared that they were "ecstatic ... Time and time [again], school divisions say: 'We can't afford this.' Well, now they can't afford not to."[43]

Once again, the courts had nothing to say about where the funding should come from or how the decision should be implemented. That was someone else's problem. Someone else will have to raise taxes or cut spending in other areas, and the court stayed clear of making any recommendation on this front. The court simply decided that providing special programs to help students with special needs was in the public interest. The court dealt with only one part of the equation, in many ways the easy part. It is no less in the public interest to determine how such initiatives can be financed from the public purse. Someone, not the courts, has to decide if other public services should be cut or reduced or which taxes should be increased. I note that leaving aside a few provincial premiers, prime ministers and parliamentarians have been reluctant to invoke section 33, the notwithstanding clause, to override Supreme Court decisions.

THE COURT AS A PUBLIC SECTOR MANAGER

The Supreme Court overturned a decision by the Nova Scotia Court of Appeal in 2003 and forced the provincial government to report on progress made in the province's school construction program for French-language students. The ruling served notice that delay in constructing schools for the linguistic minority constituted an infringement on their rights and would not be tolerated. The argument was that the linguistic minority was increasingly being assimilated into the English majority, and as a result, delays in implementing the court's decision would put the minority at risk. The Supreme Court ruling served notice that the court was not only satisfied in simply issuing a ruling without authority, it also wanted to assess the performance of the government in implementing the decision. Two justices of the Supreme Court (LeBel and Deschamps) wrote a dissenting opinion on the grounds that the courts should avoid becoming "managers of the public service."[44] They made the point that a duly elected government and MPs were able to think and act properly and be held accountable for their decisions, and that judges could never replace them.

The courts limited the government's ability to shape policies and programs when Justice Anne Mactavish ruled in July 2014 that cuts to health care for failed refugee claimants were "unconstitutional." She sounded like a politician from the opposition benches when she turned to section 12 of the Charter of Rights and Freedoms to declare that the government's decision was "cruel and unusual treatment." She gave the government four months to restore funding.[45] The responsible minister, Chris Alexander, explained that the move would have saved taxpayers "hundreds of millions at all levels of government."[46]

Adam Dodek warns that "judges cannot pick and choose which laws they like and which they do not. This undermines the rule of law and public confidence in the administration of justice." One judge recognizes that Dodek "is right," but adds that "the greater principle is one of justice, it's more important to stand up for what is just."[47] Judges, not politicians, now decide in certain circumstances what is the right public policy, and they now have the power, it seems, to decide to apply the law or not. It is no longer left to politicians to strike a proper balance between spending on guns versus butter. The courts now have an important say, albeit without the responsibility of squaring spending with revenues or levels of borrowing.

Those who enter the political arena soon realize governing is about making difficult decisions. One can – and many do – argue over whether politicians are competent or not at making these decisions, but it is their responsibility, or should be. The trade-offs are never easy, as Michael Ignatieff discovered in his relatively brief sojourn in politics. He writes: "Immigrant communities wanted more immigration and unionized workers wanted less; rich people wanted tax breaks and poor folks wanted a better deal. Gun control, of any kind, was poison in any small town or rural district, and yet it was the key to holding the vote in a downtown core. Everywhere people wanted more federal money, but everywhere people wanted the federal government to stay out of provincial jurisdictions."[48]

The courts are now full participants in the political arena without having to face the electorate or to reconcile a decision with another from a public policy and government spending perspective, or manage the difficult tasks of allocating scarce resources and actually figuring out how to implement the decision. The courts are increasingly leaving the art of political compromise out in the cold. Peter Russell warns that the "great bulk of the citizenry who are not judges and lawyers will abdicate their responsibility for working out reasonable and mutually acceptable resolutions of the issues which divide them."[49]

The Charter has shifted focus away from geography to individuals and their rights. The Supreme Court of Canada's decision in the 1999 *Marshall* case, which gave broad fishing rights to the Mi'kmaq nation, had far-reaching political and economic consequences for Atlantic Canada. For some unexplained reason, Atlantic Canada's representative on the Supreme Court was not invited by the chief justice to participate in the *Marshall* decision. By all accounts, the government of Canada had no contingency plan in place to address any political fallout resulting from *Marshall*. Contrast this example with the federal government establishing a special ad hoc unit in the PCO to deal with any political fallout when the Supreme Court tabled its decision on the Quebec referendum. Yet, Ottawa has jurisdiction over both the fishery and Aboriginal affairs.[50]

It was left to Department of Fisheries and Oceans officials operating below the fault line to pick up the pieces. They were left in the difficult position of both meeting expectations in Mi'kmaq communities with little experience in the commercial fishery, and selling and implementing the decision to long-established fishing communities. With little or no guidance from the Supreme Court or those operating above the fault line, they had to improvise, trying as best they could to manage expectations on both sides and the resulting tensions. The blame game soon kicked in. Kenneth Coates explains: "The only certainty about the *Marshall* decision is that it has created enormous uncertainty for the Maritimes. The Supreme Court judgement ... has created a variety of additional problems and challenges. The racial tensions created by the *Marshall* decision will likely linger."[51] When things go off the rails in the implementation, the blame does not fall on the Supreme Court or on central agencies. It falls on the "bureaucrats" operating below the fault line.

Since the Canadian Charter of Rights and Freedoms was introduced, the courts have further disconnected policy-making from those charged with implementing policies. It has made the fault line even more recognizable. The courts, inadvertently or not, have further strengthened the hand of the centre, in the federal government's dealings with line departments. The Charter, by design, has shifted focus away from geography or the regions to the rights of individuals and groups.

We now have a growing body of literature on the role of the Supreme Court in shaping public policy. What the literature all too often overlooks is that the Supreme Court has, through the Charter, carved out a role for itself as "managers of the public service" with an important say in how policies and programs should be implemented. It is said that the court's authority "– possessed of neither the purse nor the sword – ultimately rests on sustained public confidence in its moral sanction."[52] The Supreme Court in Canada has acquired the power of the purse in striking some of its decisions and the authority to instruct public servants on how to implement decisions. The implications are wide-ranging for public servants operating below the fault line.

LOBBYING: WHO YOU KNOW IS WHAT MATTERS

Former prime minister Paul Martin summed up the problem with the way the government works in the observation, "It's who you know in PMO if you want to get something done."[53] He pledged to address Canada's "democratic deficit by overhauling the centre of government and by empowering Members of Parliament and line ministers and their departments." However, as Susan Delacourt wrote, "It did matter who you knew in the PMO during the Martin years."[54] I would add that it matters even more now who in the PMO knows you.

Lobbyists, notably the ones well connected to prime ministers and their courtiers, are always in demand. Canada's governance structure is one of the most centralized political system in the world. Unlike the United States, where the separation of power can set the legislative branch against the executive, the federal government, with a majority in Parliament, does not have to worry about the opposition blocking its legislative, fiscal, and economic agendas. The result is that lobbyists in Ottawa can concentrate their efforts on the executive, in particular on prime ministers and their courtiers, in promoting the interest of their clients.

Lobbyists with access to the prime minister and the PMO have considerable influence, often more than a government MP and even a number of ministers. Canadian lobbyists have an advantage over their American counterparts: when they lobby members of the executive, they are at the same time lobbying members of the legislature.

There are two kinds of lobbyists in Ottawa: in-house lobbyists and consultant lobbyists.[55] Both have influence. This explains why Canada enacted legislation in the late 1980s and then moved to strengthen it by adding new regulations in 1995, 2005, and 2008. Thus, both Liberal and Conservative governments saw merit in regulating Canada's lobbying industry.[56] Lobbyists now have to register and disclose who they are lobbying for and provide a constant stream of information to the Commissioner of Lobbying, who oversees the public lobbying registry.

The introduction of the National Energy Program (NEP) in 1980 proved to be a seminal moment in the development and growth of Canada's lobbying sector. The NEP introduced a tax, in part, to fund Ottawa's energy company Petro-Canada. Foreign firms began to sell assets, which had a highly negative impact on Western Canada's energy sector. John Sawatsky writes that "the oil industry reacted with fury. Calgary wanted to know what had happened, which politicians and bureaucrats were the culprits and how to defeat them."[57] The NEP gave the lobby industry "a shot in the arm" and has grown and grown since the early 1980s.

Today, all major law firms in Canada have lobbyists on staff, as do all major industry associations. The largest private sector firms and industry associations also retain lobbyists as hired guns – lobbyists that are well connected to prime ministers and their courtiers – to look after their interest in Ottawa. Since the 1980s, all prime ministers have had close ties to some lobbyists. Pierre Trudeau and Bill Lee; Joe Clark and Bill Neville; Brian Mulroney and Frank Moores, the head of a major lobbying firm; Jean Chrétien and Edmond Chiasson, head of another major lobbying firm; Paul Martin and Michael Robinson; Stephen Harper and Ian Brodie; and Justin Trudeau and Sheamus Murphy.[58]

The life expectancy of hired guns is often tied to how long the prime minister remains in office. Frank Moores sold his lobbying firm when Mulroney left office, Chiasson's firm went out of business when Chrétien left office, and Ian Brodie is no longer a lobbyist. Any lobbyist consultant with access to prime ministers, or their close advisers, will be able to secure lucrative private sector contracts. One lobbyist consultant, who took satisfaction in having "three" meetings with Stephen Harper when he was prime minister, said so publicly: "A meeting with the prime minister is an accomplishment in itself for anyone in government relations. I would imagine he gets 500 requests a week, maybe more. I guess he's probably going to be pretty judicious in the ones that he picks."[59] He will invariably pick lobbyists who have close ties to his party, preferably ones who were part of his leadership campaign.

Hired guns with close ties to the centre of government are not the only ones whose successes are tied to the prime minister's continued success. Being well connected matters to all lobbyists. Bernard Lord, a former New Brunswick premier, co-chaired Stephen Harper's successful 2008 national campaign. A few weeks after the election, the Canadian Wireless Telecommunications Association appointed Lord as its CEO – essentially to lobby for the industry in Ottawa. When Harper left office, so did Lord. He was replaced by Robert Ghiz, former premier of Prince Edward Island, and a supporter and close friend of Justin Trudeau.[60]

A long-time lobbyist told me that not all lobbyists are created equal. Some are well known for getting things for their clients, others for briefing clients on latest developments in Ottawa that have an impact on their firms. He explained that those who "get things done" usually have close ties to the centre of government. He noted that other lobbyists are excellent at documenting efforts on behalf of their clients – how many meetings they attended, who they called, and who they met one-on-one.[61] This, he explained, speaks to plenty of activities, but not if the activities bore fruit. In other words, do not rely on the annual report of the Office of the Commissioner of Lobbying of Canada to see who wields power in Ottawa's lobbying industry.

The Commissioner of Lobbying's annual report discloses the government institutions that are lobbied. Combined the PMO and the PCO were the two most lobbied institutions in 2016–17, a total of 39,962. They are followed by the House of Commons at 30,748; Innovation, Science and Economic Development Canada at 25,265; and Finance Canada at 21,312. This makes clear that clients with economic issues dominate the agenda and why Industry Canada held the top spot in subject matter listed in the lobbyist register in 2016–17, followed by International Trade, Environment and Taxation, and Department of Finance. The commissioner's report reveals that there were 8,653 active lobbyists in 2016–17, over 1,700 more than in 2009.[62]

Do lobbyists have influence? Yes. Businesses are not in the habit of paying for nothing, and they expect something for their investments. The politically connected lobbyist can open doors, pitch messages at the highest level in government, search business opportunities inside government, challenge the advice of public servants, secure government funding for a project, and explain the finer points of a government policy to those with no experience on how government functions. Andrew Coyne reports on a conversation he overheard in an Ottawa restaurant between a lobbyist and his client. He reports that the lobbyist told the client he had a discussion with a ministerial staffer. The staffer explained to the lobbyist what the department required to flow money to the firm.[63]

Businesses have every reason to hire lobbyists to promote their interests. There are government regulations to review and public policy issues with implications for their firms to address. Ottawa also gives subsidies and grants to the private sector for a variety of purposes. John Lester, at the University of Calgary, published a study on business subsidies provided by Ottawa and the four largest provinces. He reports that Ottawa alone gave $14 billion in subsidies to businesses in 2014–15, an amount that represents half of the money raised from corporate income tax.[64]

Every year the *Hill Times*, a widely read publication in Ottawa, puts together a list of the top one hundred most influential lobbyists. The top lobbyists tend to have ties to the party in power, to have an appreciation of how the media operate, know how political spin works and have an intimate knowledge of politics and the policy process. The top lobbyists, in turn, tend to focus on the PMO, key ministers, policy advisers to senior ministers, and senior public servants.[65] Many of the top lobbyists were at one time former ministerial staffers, senior public servants, or public servants who operated above the fault line.

The above to make several points. First, all Canadians have the right to communicate with their governments, but it is far from a level playing field for everyone. Lobbyists have fundamentally changed how the more powerful in society deal with government. The average Canadian trying to communicate with the government through an MP or with a public servant, or more likely through a 1-800 number, is no match for a well-connected hired gun. Hired guns know who to meet in government, when to meet them, and how best to pitch the message.

Second, the lobby industry is Ottawa-centric. Lobbyists are part of the Ottawa community, and they are in constant communications with politicians and senior public servants. They know well Ottawa's political and bureaucratic culture. Many were part of it, and they remain a part of it but in a different capacity. They know that the key to success is to operate under the radar and to avoid involvement in public controversies. Their goal is to influence decision-makers on behalf of their clients, doing so quietly without being heard outside of Ottawa circles, particularly the media. In brief, their work is done in private, away from scrutiny.

The fact that the lobby is Ottawa-centric has strengthened the hand of prime ministers and their courtiers and weakened the hand of ministers and the public service. Lobbyists who try to set up a weekly meeting with the prime minister have an agenda, a proposal to sell. They rarely want to see the prime minister to say that all is well with their client's agenda. They often look to prime ministers and their courtiers as the last court of appeal for their clients to get their way. They know that access to the prime minister or his courtiers is the best way to challenge the position of ministers and public servants. Lobbyists, with the assistance of their clients, can marshal arguments and material in support of any position, and if the bureaucracy is not buying them, the prime minister might. The more competent lobbyists know that timing is critical, and that every effort should be made to align a proposal with the government's political agenda. One lobbyist reports that he sometimes tells his clients, "Don't waste your time and money" because the government is "not going to go there now. You might want to come back in a year or two or here is how you might want to get this on the agenda."[66] When all is said and done, private sector firms, industry associations, and their hired guns are there to promote their economic interest, not the broader public interest. It is worth underlining the point that there are very few lobbyists in Ottawa speaking on behalf of the regions or regional interests. There is no money in pursuing such interests.

Lobbyists, like the courts, have contributed to the shift away from Cabinet government to governing from the centre. Lobbyists, better than anyone, know that power lies at the centre of government with the prime minister and central agencies. They also know that the best guide for their activities and who is doing what are the "mandate letters" to ministers prepared by the PMO and the PCO. Greg MacEachern, a well-known Ottawa lobbyist, told the *Hill Times* that "lobbyists hoping to make headway with the government should use the mandate letters as a guideline."[67] If lobbyists cannot convince ministers and their departments, they know that they can always appeal to the centre.

LOOKING BACK

The courts and lobbyists operate in vastly different settings. Judges will wish to stay away from politicians. Lobbyists, meanwhile, will seek out politicians to make their case. The courts work in the interest of justice as defined by the constitution, statutes, and precedents, and the values that judges bring to their work. Lobbyists, meanwhile, work in the interest of their clients, however narrowly defined. Judges operate away from parliamentary and media scrutiny and are not subject to access to information legislation. Lobbyists have to respond to the demands from the Office of the Commissioner of Lobbying of Canada, and their dealings with government departments may become accessible to the media and others through access to information legislation.

Both the Supreme Court and lobbyists are Ottawa-centric, both deal either directly or indirectly with political and economic elites, and both have contributed to strengthening the hand of the centre in Canadian politics and public administration. Both downplay geography or the regional factor in their work. The Canadian Charter of Rights and Freedoms speaks to individuals' or communities' interests that transcend geography (for example, same-sex marriage, minority-language rights, and Indigenous peoples' rights). Lobbyists work for the economic or political interests of their clients, most of whom do not see things from a regional perspective.

Both the courts and the lobby industry favour the economic elites. Hired guns in Ottawa are expensive and out of reach to the average Canadian. The same can be said about accessing the justice system. Former chief justice Beverley McLachlin wrote: "We have wonderful justice for corporations and for the wealthy. But the middle class and the poor may not be able to access our justice system," and then she asks, "how can there be public confidence in a system of justice that shuts people out; that does not give them access?" She concludes with a warning: "That is a very dangerous road to follow."[68]

The book's introductory chapter makes the point that equality is a crucial element of representative democracy. In the opinion of many students of government, it is the most important element.[69] The courts and lobbyists, in particular, are now contributing more to the politics of inequality than to the politics of equality. This chapter makes the case once again that Canada's democratic deficit has a particular accent – it is tied to the inability of national institutions to accommodate regional circumstances and regional equality.

PART THREE

Why and What Now?

Is Canadian Democracy Failing?

The purpose of this chapter is to gain insights into how Canada's political institutions have changed or failed to change since 1867. More to the point, we need to determine the adaptability or inability of Canada's institutions to embrace change. We will need to revisit briefly points made in earlier chapters. We saw that Canada has changed dramatically since 1867 in terms of society, economic structure, population composition, as well as its urban-rural split, and politics. We saw that Canadian federalism turned to innovative approaches to deal with changes in society, and today it differs fundamentally from what it was, although Parliament looks much as it did. The public service went from a patronage-ridden to a non-partisan institution, the judiciary has been transformed, transparency and accountability requirements are immeasurably more demanding than they were, and today's media are a far cry from what they were. How then have Canada's institutions changed? And why?

IT ALL BEGAN IN 1867

The Fathers of Confederation had an impossible task, marrying a Westminster parliamentary system with federalism. They were breaking new ground with limited resources and little knowledge of federalism and its requirements. John A. Macdonald explained at the London Conference that the goal was to negotiate a treaty. The treaty was designed to tie together "two warring nations" that were still at it in the 1860s rather than to design new institutions to fit the country's socio-economic circumstances. Lord Durham had earlier argued that it was not possible to improve "institutions without

succeeding in extinguishing the mortal hatred which now divides
the inhabitants of Lower Canada into two hostile groups: French
and English."[1] The four leading architects of Confederation, all from
Lower and Upper Canada, had their hands full trying to attenuate
the animosity and strike a treaty to give the two Canadas a fresh
start. They were in awe of British institutions and unable, or unwilling, to define institutions to fit Canada's setting. They turned to
off-the-shelf British-designed institutional models to give life to the
treaty. In doing so, the Fathers of Confederation handcuffed political
leaders to follow by producing a constitution that did not reflect the
political and geographical requirements of the new country. As discussed, they were so confident that British-inspired institutions were
the answer for Canada that they did not even see any need to attach
an amending formula to the constitution.

It bears repeating that Walter Bagehot, credited for inventing
Britain's constitution, did not deal with geography in his classic
The English Constitution.[2] He warned that British-inspired institutions would have problems finding their footings in the colonies.
I note that in the preface of The English Constitution, he writes:
"The greatest difficulty in the colonies" was "geographical."[3] He had
nothing to offer to address this challenge; his constitution was for
England, not the colonies. He simply explained that "the principal
characteristics of the English Constitution are inapplicable in countries where the materials for a monarchy or an aristocracy do not
exist."[4] Bagehot was right.

The House of Lords had a place in 1867 Britain as the country
was tentatively moving toward representative democracy. Bagehot
was no democrat and feared extending the vote to the working class.
His biographer explains that Bagehot saw what was coming, disliked it intensely, and tried to "point out the dangers."[5] The point is
worth underlining once again that, in federations, an Upper House
is the key institution responsible for promoting the requirements of
intrastate federalism. As we saw earlier, this is the case, among others, in the United States, Australia, Germany, and Russia, but not
Canada. Canada's Senate has more in common with Britain's House
of Lords than with the Senate of the United States or Australia. It is an
appointed body, and one of its requirements is a net worth of $4,000,
an amount that in 1867 separated the have from the have-less.

Confederation's key architects from the two Canadas negotiating the treaty were more comfortable establishing an Upper House

patterned on Britain's House of Lords than one designed to give voice to the regions. We saw earlier that delegates to the Quebec Conference from the Maritime colonies pushed for an Upper House to represent the regions, but their calls were rejected. Prince Edward Island initially decided not to sign on to Confederation, and Western Canada had no voice at the Charlottetown, Quebec, or London conferences.

The Fathers of Confederation thought they had set in stone two key institutions – Parliament and federalism. Parliament, in the Westminster tradition, was to be supreme with absolute sovereignty over other institutions, including the courts, the executive, and provincial governments. Federalism was in name only at first, to the point that Ottawa had the right to disallow provincial government legislation. The public service in 1867, meanwhile, was regarded as an extension of the political party in power. The point is worth emphasizing, given its centrality to the book's thesis, that the Fathers of Confederation who drove the negotiations and established the terms of the treaty sought to downplay Canada's regional factor. Macdonald insisted that Cabinet was quite capable of dealing with Canada's regional factor, and there was no need to do anything else. But that was then.

WHAT ABOUT PARLIAMENT?

The broad outline of Canada's Parliament looks much like it did in 1867. For example, the government still needs the confidence of the House of Commons to remain in power. Form is one thing, but role is another. Parliament's role has been allowed to drift, and today – leaving aside prime ministers and their courtiers – no one is pleased with the status quo. Members of Parliament have, as we have seen in recent years, produced a series of reports calling for sweeping reform measures. Non-partisan think tanks, including Samara Centre for Democracy and Public Policy Forum, have made the same call.

The Senate remains unelected, and members still have to meet a wealth test before getting appointed. It, too, continues to be much maligned. Justin Trudeau's reform of the appointment process does not measure up to a transformative moment, at least thus far. As noted, the reform could be short-lived, given that the Leader of Opposition is committed to returning to partisan appointments. The Senate continues to generate negative headlines, and calls are still heard for its abolition.[6]

The heavily populated provinces have no interest in allowing a transformative moment for the Senate or in moving it off its sober second thought role because it is in their political and economic interests to let the Senate drift as is and to tolerate a modest version of its role. They have the political clout to stop Senate reform in its tracks. Justin Trudeau told senators there was even a limit to its sober second thought role and warned them not to go against Canadians' will expressed in the 2015 general election in favour of legalizing marijuana.[7]

The Senate still squares nicely with what John Macdonald and George Brown wanted. Macdonald saw only a limited role for the Senate on behalf of the regions. Indeed, he defined its sober second thought role and it continues to apply to this day; it remains trapped in a path-dependent trajectory. Even under new management and the reformed appointment process, as recently as March 2018, the Senate underlined the importance of its sober second thought role. Under the heading "Sober Second Thought in Action," the Senate reported that it had "improved several key government bills this session, including legislation on medical assisted dying, legislation that removes barriers to citizenship and legislation that helps tackle the opioid crisis." The Senate newsletter had nothing to say about its role on behalf of the smaller regions.[8]

The House of Commons has witnessed some change, but it can hardly be labelled transformative. The Commons did overhaul its approach to approving the government's expenditure budget. The change, however, only served to make it easier for the government to have its way on spending and to move funds around after Parliament approved the budget.[9]

The Commons grows every ten years, after a census in a year ending in the numeral one.[10] At the moment, there are 338 elected MPs, with a number of clauses in place that ensure it will continue to grow, including one that provides no province can have fewer MPs than it had in 1976. In addition, no province can have fewer elected members in the House of Commons than appointed senators. The Fathers of Confederation gave Quebec a constitutional guarantee of seats in the Commons. As a result of these clauses, there is about 1 elected MP in the Commons for every 102,000 Canadians, in contrast with 1 representative in Congress for every 750,000 Americans. The point is that any problem plaguing the Commons has nothing to do with a lack of members serving in it.

However, the House of Commons, through the benign neglect from those who could inject transformative change, has been allowed to slip backwards. Here is what two members of the House of Commons from different parties and one senator wrote in a report on Parliament: "The sense of alienation felt by many citizens and the remedies they propose, find an echo in the issues raised by Parliamentarians," they observed that Parliament has "lost its forum quality, lost its ability to scrutinize government activity," and "no longer contributes meaningfully to policy debates."[11]

There have been promises of transformative change from those who have the power to introduce it and make it stick. Paul Martin, Stephen Harper, and Justin Trudeau all made firm commitments before they became prime minister to change Parliament and its culture, to make it more relevant to Canadians, and to empower elected MPs. They soon discovered, once in power, that it was in their interest to stick with the status quo – and they all did.

Prime ministers and their courtiers all had a change of mind once in power. They insist that they not only have to manage an overloaded agenda, but also they see more than enough opposition voices and constraints in the way of getting things done. They see the twenty-four-hour news cycle and social media always at the ready to identify flaws in their agenda and on the lookout for scandals. They see opposition parties constantly looking to score political points against them and see no reason to give them more ammunition to do so. They see officers of Parliament always on the lookout for missteps as well. They see ten provincial premiers rarely, if ever, happy with them. They see interest groups with varying, and at times conflicting, agendas pushing them to do more or to do less, depending on their own agenda. All the while, they see global economic forces eroding their capacity to manoeuvre and get things done.[12] Why, then, would they add to their misery by upgrading the role of the House of Commons?

Prime ministers and their courtiers also soon learn that it is in their interest to control who has access to power – sharing power means less power for them. Best to hoard power rather than share it in order to move their agenda, to control the news cycle, and to manage political issues in the era of permanent election campaigns. If governing from the centre did not hold distinct advantages for them, they would reverse the trend of concentrating power.

There is never a shortage of debates in Parliament about reforming the House of Commons, ranging from borrowing a page from

Britain to strengthening question period and to control better omnibus bills. When a political party is in opposition, omnibus bills never
make sense, but somehow they do when the party sits on the government side of the House. Little usually comes from the debates
to change things because the one who holds all the cards to initiate
change – the prime minister – has no interest in change.[13]

We still elect MPs much like we did one hundred years ago. Justin
Trudeau broke one of his most important 2015 election promises:
electoral reform to make "every vote count" so that the "2015 election would be the last under the first-past-the-post voting system."[14]
The rationale for breaking his promise was that "broad support
needed among Canadians for a change of this magnitude does not
exist."[15] Trudeau did not explain how he was able to determine that
Canadians did not support a change of such "magnitude." The promise of transformative change made a great deal of sense during the
election campaign, but not when sitting in the prime minister's chair.
Trudeau rejected holding a referendum on the issue to assess first-hand
what Canadians wanted.[16] He blamed opposition parties because they
lacked "openness," and because "proportional representation would
be bad for our country."[17] He decided to consult Canadians through
a parliamentary committee – a much safer route than a referendum
when a prime minister with a majority mandate decides to look after
his party's interest.[18] More is said about this in the concluding chapter.
In short, transformative moments simply do not stand a chance unless
prime ministers and their courtiers see merit in them.

The purpose of an election is to elect a government and to give
every eligible voter the opportunity to be heard. Much more often
than not, the current electoral system elects majority governments
with a minority of votes. Canada's Law Commission argued in a 2014
report titled *Voting Counts: Electoral Reform for Canada* that the
current system should be scrapped because it gives artificial majorities
when a party wins significantly less than 50 percent of the vote. The
Law Commission argues that it promotes regional tensions, in part,
because "parties that enjoy strong support in a given region are more
likely to translate this support into a seat win."[19] A former leader of
the NDP teamed up with a former clerk of the Privy Council and a
former high-profile senator to pen an op-ed, calling for an end to first-
past-the-post voting system. They explained that it feeds "regional
discord. In a country as regionally diverse as Canada, the electoral
system must have the capacity of enabling a government to govern

effectively and the opposition's capacity to provide informed criticism. Regional representation is required for both. Our current system is seriously deficient in meeting this requirement."[20] They recommended a proportional voting system.

Trudeau realized after the 2015 general election that Canada's electoral system works just fine, at least for him and his party. It enabled him to win power with a sizeable majority mandate with only 39.5 percent of the popular vote. Trudeau has made the case that majority governments are good for Canada. However, Canada has had experience with minority governments (in twenty-nine elections since 1921, eleven resulted in minority governments) and, though short-lived – lasting on average less than two years – they have been productive. Minority governments would present a stronger check on the power of prime ministers and their courtiers, introduce a stronger spirit of co-operation between Parliament and government, and give MPs a greater say in shaping policy and in holding the government to account.[21] Minority governments also have a weak side, including a sharp increase of permanent election campaigning.

Regardless of the size of government, electoral reform requires the prime minister to give it a green light. Justin Trudeau, like many prime ministers before, had a change of mind about this and other measures that would attenuate his power after an election campaign. Winning is what matters. Keeping promises during the election campaign is another matter. When Jean Chrétien was asked, "What's a good politician?" he quickly replied, "One who wins."[22] Prime ministers know that they stand a better chance of winning a majority mandate with a first-past-the-post electoral system, transformative change be damned.

The lack of a transformative moment to set Parliament on a new trajectory may well explain why fewer than half of Canadians now have confidence in Parliament.[23] Surveys show that the trust of Canadians in public institutions is falling further behind from a comparative perspective. The Edelman Trust Barometer reveals that Canada "slipped in the distrusted category in 2017," ranking 49 behind Italy, Russia, Poland, and Turkey.[24] Governments in Canada now trail media and business in the trust factor. Edelman survey reveals a seventeen-point gap exists between "informed public" and "mass population" in trust in government.[25] The average Canadian has less trust in government than the more informed, more educated. Many Canadians believe that the public sector is tilted toward the economic elites and special interest groups and that too many politicians, public servants, and judges are there more to serve their own interests than the public interest.

Moreover, many Canadians do not believe that elections matter. The *Americas Barometer* on the study of democratic values reports that only one in five Canadians has a strong trust in elections. The survey reports as well that the involvement of Canadians in politics "tends to be more as spectators than as active participants."[26] It points to a disturbing trend that the confidence of Canadians in their political system is on a downward course under all three headings: 1) respect in political institutions; 2) pride in political system; and 3) should they support the political system.[27] But that tells only part of the story, and not the most important part at that. Canada falls short, even from a comparative perspective, in dealing with the regional perspective in shaping national policy.

FROM A QUASI-UNITARY STATE TO HYBRID FEDERALISM

John A. Macdonald, as we saw earlier, wanted a unitary state for Canada in 1867 and came very close to getting it. He hoped that Canada would in time be transformed into a unitary state. Canadian federalism has had transformative moments, but they moved the federation in an opposite direction than Macdonald wanted.

No country can survive for over 150 years without transformative moments, and Canada has seen its share of such moments. They have, however, taken root outside of the constitution and, to a degree, outside of political institutions. In refusing, at the outset, to equip the written constitution with an amending formula and failing to put in place a capacity within national institutions to promote intrastate federalism or ways to accommodate regional circumstances within national institutions, the Fathers of Confederation opened the door for provincial governments to eventually play this role, even though they are still not equipped to do so when it comes to shaping national policies. Those regions and individuals benefitting from a disproportionate access to the policy and decision-making levers have resisted fundamental change to the constitution and national political institutions. This, in turn, has served to fuel regional tensions rather than attenuate them.

Formative moments came when Quebec decided that it would speak for French Canada since no one else, including the federal government, could. Quebec also decided that it was best for the province to focus on activities within its geographical boundaries to pursue this goal.[28] Other provincial governments in Western and Atlantic Canada, meanwhile, decided that Macdonald's imperial model of federalism could not accommodate their interests. William Aberhart, for example, sought to promote Alberta's interests "by exploiting the power and position of the provincial legislature rather than by modifying national policy through securing legislative change in Ottawa."[29]

The Great Depression led to a formative moment. It made clear that the federal structure as defined in 1867 could not deal with a deep economic crisis. The constitution became a roadblock to what federal government policy-makers wanted to do to cope with the economic crisis and to build the welfare state. Unable to amend the constitution in a substantial manner to address the crisis, policy-makers in Ottawa turned to hybrid federalism to pursue policy prescriptions. Several provincial governments welcomed this approach. They gave rise to province-building. Ottawa's spending power became the new power of disallowance but with an important twist.[30] We saw that it made provincial governments stronger, louder, and the champion of regional interests.

This, too, speaks to Canada's experience. Hybrid federalism served to empower provincial governments because, not only do they now have access to federal government funding, but also they have a window into federal government operations through a vast network of federal-provincial committees. Hybrid federalism gave provincial governments a presence on the national stage, enabled them to play a proactive role in the provinces with federal government funds, and gave them opportunities and visibility in the media to champion regional interests.

Hybrid federalism gave public servants a presence and power in shaping new policies and shared-cost programs. It enabled public servants to promote their own interests, extend the scope of government activities, make government operations thicker, and muddy accountability. Traditional accountability requirements were tossed aside to make way for federal-provincial committees of public servants to plan and implement shared-cost programs needed to build the welfare state.

Historical institutionalism sheds light on the evolution of Canadian federalism. It identifies the policy option as the logical and rational choice at a given time.[31] Such is the case with Canada. The Rowell-Sirois Report gave policy-makers solutions to deal with the situation at hand. Historical institutionalism recognizes unintended consequences with formative moments, and again, such is the case with Canada. Rowell-Sirois and Ottawa policy-makers set out to address daunting economic challenges and uneven economic development. The traditional accountability requirements of Canada's political institutions were no match for the policy and program prescriptions needed to build the welfare state. In brief, the health of Canada's political institutions took a back seat to what was required to address the policy requirements of the day – hence, an unintended consequence of pursuing Rowell-Sirois policy prescriptions.

The fact that transformative moments in Canadian federalism took place outside the constitution and, to a large extent, outside of national political institutions, has also served to fuel regional tensions rather than attenuate them. Institutions have rules, constraints, and a logic of appropriateness.[32] Hybrid federalism tossed aside Westminster-inspired expected behaviour and introduced its own informal procedures and logic of appropriateness. It made federal-provincial committees of officials self-governing bodies. Hybrid federalism has also created processes that hold little meaning for those not directly involved in the decision-making process and has seriously blurred accountability requirements.[33]

The patch and spot-weld approach to intergovernmental relations has led to costly and misguided policies and moved governments away from their core responsibilities. Always aware that provincial governments are keeping a close watch on federal government spending, Ottawa has adopted a one-size-fits-all to address important public policy issues. This is the case, for health care, for example. But it is far from the only example. Shortly after the 2015 general election, Ottawa announced an ambitious infrastructure building program. The one-size-fits-all approach once again kicked in, which ignored that Canada is a country of regions with distinct diversity in terms of economic circumstances. To be sure, some of Canada's regions are in need of investments in infrastructure, notably large and growing urban centres such as Toronto, Montreal, and Vancouver. These centres do not have the infrastructure to accommodate a growing population, or put differently, they have too many people and not enough infrastructure.

Other regions, however, do not need more infrastructure. Some have more infrastructure than they need, or too much infrastructure, not enough people. In the case of New Brunswick, for example, adding infrastructure makes a bad problem even worse.[34] Ottawa's infrastructures program requires provincial government funding, which is very taxing for a small, financially strapped haveless province. But that is not all. Once the infrastructure is in place, provincial governments are fully responsible for the cost of maintaining it. If Canada had national institutions capable of addressing regional circumstances, Ottawa would have an infrastructure program for regions that require it, and other measures for regions that do not, that is, an infrastructure program for southern Ontario and measures designed to deal with a falling and aging population for New Brunswick.

Full-blown hybrid federalism has not been able to paper over Canada's linguistic and cultural divide and sharp regional economic differences. Hybrid federalism also leaves unattended an important requirement of federalism: the need for the federal government to look to its own policies and operations to accommodate Canada's regional economic circumstances. The chair of the House of Commons' Finance Committee explains that Canada "is really a country of economic regions, very diverse in terms of those economic regions, and as a result you just can't paint everything with the same brush."[35] Instead of looking to adjust its own policies and programs to meet the requirements of Canada's regions, Ottawa has turned things over to federal-provincial committees.

Prime Minister Justin Trudeau, exasperated over regional tensions, observed that Canadians "deserve better than a discussion in which leaders leap to capitalize on perceived regional slights, regardless of context or facts."[36] He is not the first prime minister to be overwhelmed by regional grievances. More than anything, regional frustrations and linguistic cleavage have shaped Canadian history.

One of Canada's leading journalists remarked: "A country that argues over such matters as federal-provincial relations and the shape and powers of the Senate is funnelling emotions into time-consuming but rather harmless pursuits." Jeffrey Simpson goes on to quote "an old friend" to describe Canada as having a "malignant sense of regional envy."[37] It is easy to dismiss the problem as simply "regional envy." The diagnosis does not require any changes to the country's national political institutions, just a change of attitude on the part of the regions other than Ontario and all will be well. This is a classic case of misdiagnosing the patient. A change in attitude that would matter can only take place in Canada's national political institutions, and that can only happen if the institutions themselves change.

FOR THE COURTS, THE TRANSFORMATIVE MOMENT CAME IN 1982

Pierre Trudeau had a purpose in going into politics: he wanted to secure Quebec's place in Canada, to patriate the constitution, and promote the rights of individuals.[38] Like John A. Macdonald and George-E. Cartier, and Lord Durham before, Trudeau saw Canada from a dual linguistic and cultural perspective: "The die is cast in Canada: there are two main ethnic and linguistic groups; each is too strong and too deeply rooted in the past, too firmly bound to a mother-culture to be able to engulf the other."[39]

Trudeau was appalled to see former Quebec premier Maurice Duplessis trample individuals' rights. The Duplessis government enacted the Padlock Act, designed to protect the province from "communist agitators." Duplessis also targeted Jehovah's Witnesses because of their anti-war attitudes and religious fervour.[40] Trudeau made his views clear in 1967: "If we reach agreement on the fundamental rights of the citizen, on their definition and protection in all parts of Canada, we shall have taken a major first step toward basic constitutional reforms."[41]

Once in power, Trudeau pursued his ideas with single-minded purpose. He sponsored the Victoria Constitutional Conference, where he proposed a rights document protecting freedom of thought, freedom of association, and language rights.[42] The effort failed when Quebec said no. Trudeau launched a new round of federal-provincial constitutional negotiations in 1978–79 and attached an entrenched Charter of Rights. These efforts also failed because many of the provinces were not ready to embrace a Charter of Rights in the constitution and because Trudeau's mandate was coming to end.[43]

Trudeau was returned to power with a majority mandate after a brief interlude in opposition, following the short-lived minority Joe Clark government that lost the confidence of the Commons in 1980. He set out to patriate the constitution and entrench a Charter of Rights with or without the support of the provinces. He called for a federal-provincial conference and tabled a "people's package."

As is well known, the debates that followed were acrimonious and divisive, and there is no need to go over those developments or this well-travelled territory once again.[44]

Trudeau was not for turning, even in the face of stiff opposition from eight provincial governments. He had just secured a majority mandate, and it was not to be wasted. If he could successfully pursue his agenda, he saw no need for another mandate, and the interest of his Liberal Party be damned. Trudeau had a more important agenda to deliver, a lifelong ambition to entrench the rights of citizens in the constitution. As it happened, the Liberal Party went down to a crushing defeat in the next election, winning only 40 seats to the Mulroney Progressive Conservative Party's 211.

However, Trudeau won the day in 1982. He successfully patriated the constitution with an amending formula and the Charter of Rights and Freedoms, described as his "magnificent obsession."[45] His purpose was to enshrine the rights of individuals in the constitution, so no need to change the constitution to deal with the capacity of national political institutions to attend to Canada's regional factor. Politicians from Ontario and Quebec going back to the era of Upper and Lower Canada do not see the problem as readily as Western and Atlantic Canadians do.

Trudeau's successful efforts to patriate the constitution speak to the power of a single man's will – at least if you happen to be prime minister – to launch a transformative moment and make it stick. That said, the Charter allows some rights to be overridden by the provinces. Some of the provincial premiers feared that the Charter would undermine the last vestige of Canada's Westminster-styled parliamentary government.[46] A notwithstanding clause was included, which allows Parliament or provincial legislatures the ability to override some portions of the Charter.

Quebec has yet to sign on to the constitution. On the twentieth anniversary of the Charter, the Quebec National Assembly unanimously passed the following motion: "That the National Assembly reaffirm that it never acceded to the Constitution Act 1982, whose effect was to lessen the powers and rights of Quebec without the consent of the Quebec Government, of the National Assembly, and this Act is still unacceptable to Quebec."[47]

The Constitution Act, 1982 was a transformative moment that has been deeply felt in Canadian society, in Parliament, in both orders of government, and in the federal public service. Canadians, from

Indigenous peoples and linguistic minorities to those seeking approval for same-sex marriage and members of the LGBTQ community, no longer have to look to Parliament for solutions. Two keen observers of the Charter maintain that it launched the courts, Parliament, and government on a new trajectory. F.L. Morton and Rainer Knopff go as far as arguing that Canada's "long tradition of parliamentary supremacy" has been compromised, and Canada is now looking at "judicial supremacy." They add that judges have become "active players in the political process" and "abandoned the deference and self-restraint that characterized their pre-Charter jurisprudence."[48] Emmett Macfarlane remarked on the relationship between the Harper government and the courts: "It is the only Charter period government to have policies specifically outlined in electoral platforms invalidated (and indeed, no fewer than five major promises were affected). It is also the only government to have lost every reference opinion issued by the Court. The Conservative government was unable to influence the Court's behaviour through the judicial appointments process or by other means, in large part due to the remaining elements of the previous long-standing Charter regime, including the Court itself."[49]

The Charter has had a profound impact inside government. It has strengthened the centre in its dealings with line departments (because of the need for Charter-proofing legislation). It has forced the hand of most departments to hire additional legal staff to handle Charter issues such as Indigenous peoples' rights and minority-language rights. We have seen that the Supreme Court has directed government departments not only to take a certain action but also how it should implement that action. In some instances, the decisions added cost to government; the courts simply walked away from these difficult decisions, leaving governments to deal with them. In brief, Trudeau's Constitutional Act, 1982 has established a new path dependency for institutions, politicians, and public servants.

The bitter federal-provincial negotiations of the early 1980s, followed by the failed Meech and Charlottetown accords, have left a bad taste in Ottawa and in provincial capitals – regardless of party affiliation – with regard to future efforts to amend the constitution.[50] The unanimous amending formula has never been employed, and the 7 and 50 formula was applied only once in dealing with Indigenous concerns shortly after the Charter came into force. We have seen bilateral constitutional change when Ottawa and a province agreed to amend the constitution to address a local issue. Such was the case when Ottawa and New Brunswick agreed in 1993 to linguistic equality between the English- and French-speaking communities.[51]

Canada will very likely continue to bypass the constitution when forced to act as it did in the aftermath of the Great Depression and in building its welfare state. Constitutional reform in Canada is now left to the Greek Calends, or the month that never arrives. It leaves unattended important constitutional issues such as Senate reform and the future admission of the territories as provinces.

Thinking that Canada can put off constitutional negotiations forever has tied the constitution and many policy-makers in knots. The Supreme Court decided in the *Comeau* case that Canada has no constitutional guarantees of free trade between provinces. The court ruled unanimously in 2018 that the Province of New Brunswick was within its right in imposing a fine on Comeau for importing fourteen cases of beer from Quebec.[52] Alberta and British Columbia were quick to look at the decision, given their conflicts over oil pipeline expansion. Some observers were quick to blame the courts for inhibiting free trade between provinces.[53] Trade barriers, however, are the product of provincial governments, not the courts. New Brunswick is not the only province to see national policies and the national interest as code words for the interest of only a few heavily populated provinces.

FOR THE PUBLIC SERVICE IT ALL BEGAN IN 1918–19

The Canadian public service came into its own about one hundred years ago. A series of reports and measures, some looking to Britain, others to the United States for inspiration, began to turn the Canadian public service into a non-partisan professional institution with a capacity to classify positions according to roles, responsibilities, and skill requirements. By looking to merit-based competitions rather than patronage to fill its ranks, the public service gained influence and a degree of independence from its political masters. It was a transformative moment brought about by a desire to develop a competent policy and administrative capacity and by motivation to look to developments in other jurisdictions pursuing the same objective.[54] If it made sense in Britain, the argument went that it should make sense in Canada in the early 1900s.

It is ironic that the attempt at a second transformative moment for the public service arrived some sixty years later because politicians felt that public servants had too much influence on policy and were not paying enough attention to management. The second attempt was tied to NPM initiatives. The first transformative moment launched the public service on a new sustained trajectory; the second has had no such impact. At best, it only accomplished 50 percent of what it sought to deliver.[55]

The first transformative moment was straightforward, turning the public service into a professional, non-partisan institution. The public service had every reason to make the moment stick and to launch a new path-dependent trajectory. Most politicians saw merit in the move since it gave rise to a bargain under which both they and public servants would benefit.[56] Politicians would still make all the important policy and some program decisions, while public servants provided policy advice without fear or favour and delivered programs according to prescribed rules designed to promote equality in delivery of government activities and services. Everyone was pushing in the same direction.

But the success created its own set of problems. In time, politicians felt that they were losing the ability to shape new policy. They became frustrated with a slow, rule-driven decision-making process and began to compare management in government with that found in the private sector. Thus began the effort to make management in government look like that found in the private sector. Later, politicians became convinced that public servants were thwarting their desire to introduce change to policy, programs, and government operations. Starting in the early 1980s, politicians decided to strengthen their resolve to push back public servants on policy while making them stronger managers.

The anticipated, or hoped for, transformative moment fell flat, at least in Canada. It did not, however, in other countries like Britain and Australia. This holds a very important message for Canadian political institutions. In Canada, at the same time as senior public servants were told to become stronger managers and to emulate their private sector counterparts, they were saddled with many new transparency and accountability requirements, the latter not always suited for government. And, at the same time they were told to emulate their private sector counterparts, they were also told to implement the Official Languages Act, promote employment equity, and cope with a growing number of oversight bodies.

Politicians believed that forcing senior public servants to focus on management would enable them to grab the levers of power in shaping new policy. However, they soon discovered that grabbing one policy lever could unearth surprises, not always positive ones, which had an impact far beyond their departments. They also learned that permanent election campaigns required the safe pair of hands that senior public servants can provide, given their intimate knowledge of government. We soon learned that management would continue to be the preserve of the less gifted. The impact of NPM in Canada has been modest, and if anything, has made matters worse.[57]

As noted, a fault line emerged that weakened front-line service and made public servants less accessible. It widened the divide between senior public servants with an interest in policy and in serving prime ministers and their courtiers and ministers, on the one hand, front-line public servants serving clients on the other. The fault line also considerably strengthened departmental head offices in Ottawa at the expense of regional and local offices, attenuating further the capacity of the federal machinery of government to accommodate Canada's regional factor.

What changed? In the eyes of several keen observers of public administration, the most senior public servants, have become promiscuously partisan as they are increasingly "being drawn into the limelight" by their political masters.[58] I recognize that public servants becoming promiscuously partisan is not new – prime ministers, going back to Mackenzie King, have always looked for deputy ministers who are sympathetic to their political agenda.[59] The difference is that today the most senior public servants, anxious to be counted among the prime minister's courtiers, are less and less concerned about the health of the public service below the fault line than were their predecessors.

The Canadian public service has been remarkably path dependent below the fault line. It has brushed aside NPM measures by giving the appearance of change while standing still. By my count, the public service has been subjected to at least eight ambitious renewal efforts over the past twenty-five years, with several led by the clerk of the PCO. A review of the efforts by a former senior public servant concluded that they have all "avoided the core issue,"[60] or avoided launching a transformative moment.

Together the government and public service have dismissed the suggestion that the public service should be restructured along regional rather than functional lines to more accurately reflect the country.[61] The argument is that better policies would emerge if the federal government would be explicitly organized around regional interests to shape national policy.[62] This would downplay the role of provincial governments speaking on behalf of the regions on the national stage. The one individual capable of addressing core issues is the prime minister and, from that vantage point, best to leave well enough alone. A path-dependent public service serves the interest of the prime minister.

Prime ministers and their courtiers have every reason to see the government and the public service run on their tracks in policy areas that do not hold their interest. A path-dependent public service is the answer if one wants to avoid controversies and surprises in departments that hold limited interest for prime ministers. Senior politicians have the advantage of access to lobbyists, many of them well-versed in the ways of government, if they need advice from outside the public service, or to get a sense of how government client groups are receiving government policies, programs, or decisions.

We saw in earlier chapters that national unity concerns and fear of fuelling regional tensions have inhibited the introduction of NPM measures, including such initiatives as the accounting officer concept. Both inhibiting factors continue to discourage the development of transformative moments for the public service. Prime ministers simply do not want to take their eyes off the national unity issue to focus on public sector management issues. The experience in Britain and Australia reveals that the prime minister must be continually engaged to ensure transformative moments in the public service and machinery of government take root.

MAKING SENSE OF IT ALL

I know of no student of government making the case that it is best to leave well enough alone or of many practitioners who insist that all is well with Canada's national institutions.[63] And yet, many observers argue that Canada operates one of the best democracies in the world.[64] This suggests that representative democracy is confronting important challenges everywhere. It explains why we are seeing, recently, a plethora of books with disquieting titles, including *Four Crises of American Democracy*, *The End of Whitehall?*, *Democracy in Decline*, and *How Democracies Die*.[65] That other countries are dealing with challenges in making their representative democracies operate does not suggest that Canadians should avoid dealing with weaknesses or deficiencies in their constitution and national institutions.

Robert Asselin, a former senior adviser to three Liberal Party leaders, including Justin Trudeau, to Finance Minister Bill Morneau, as well as a former public policy scholar at the Woodrow Wilson Centre, identified three fundamental problems with Canada's representative democracy: 1) political legitimacy, given the declining electoral participation rate; 2) how institutions hold decision-makers to account; and 3) declining trust in institutions.[66] Former prime minister Paul Martin often spoke about Canada's democratic deficit and pledged to pursue a fundamental change in Canada's parliamentary culture and to rebalance the relationship between the Cabinet and the House.[67] In his brief tenure as prime minister, he failed to have any impact on parliamentary culture or to rebalance any relationship inside or among institutions. Prime ministers who followed – Stephen Harper and Justin Trudeau – pledged to change the culture inside Parliament and the workings of Cabinet, with the latter insisting that he would bring back Cabinet government. He has not. If anything, he has concentrated even more power in his office: he has, as noted, done away with regional ministers.

Canada has witnessed the gradual deinstitutionalization of its national political institutions with the result that many Canadians do not believe those institutions now speak to their interest. Yet, institutions matter. Institutions lay down overt or implicit rules that guide human interaction and activity, and their durability lies in their capacity to establish stable expectations on the behaviour of individuals. Institutions enable "ordered thought, expectation and action by imposing form and consistency on human activities."[68] In short, institutions both constrain and enable behaviour through formal rules and processes. This study makes the case that Canada's national institutions are failing on this front. Overt or implicit rules are now made on the fly to suit the moment.

Do path dependency and historical institutionalism explain developments in Canada's national political institutions?[69] At its core, historical institutionalism speaks to institutions operating through extended periods of stability – characterized as path dependency – interrupted by turbulent new formative moments. It is during such turbulent formative moments that new goals are established, institutions adjust, and new extended periods of stability begin.[70] Historical institutionalism then identifies change as the most rational choice at a given time.[71] Once the change is in place, politicians and public servants will adjust their objectives to maximize their interest. Change can be abrupt and result in response to either exogenous or endogenous forces. Change, however, does not always alter who has power, and in some instances, power shifts hands. In other instances, those who have power will manoeuvre to hold on to it or expand it. I cannot possibly explain in any meaningful manner, in a few paragraphs, the rich and growing literature on path dependency and historical institutionalism. I note that the approach is problem driven and has been adopted in various national settings and from a comparative perspective.[72]

I argue that path dependency and historical institutionalism are well suited to account for the evolution of Canadian federalism and Canada's political institutions, albeit with important caveats. I maintain that in some instances, formative moments led to the disintegration of institutions because it allowed politicians and senior public servants to break free from the confines of institutions, their rules, and their procedures. In other instances, formative moments did not alter who has power in the federation. In still other instances, formative moments served to further concentrate power in the hands of prime ministers and their courtiers. In still more instances, formative moments enabled Canadian policy and decision-makers to rely on loosely defined, flexible conventions to get things done. In short, I argue that historical institutionalism, at least in the Canadian case, explains both the persistence of values and processes and the development of formative moments.

Historical institutionalism enables us to understand why and how Canadian federalism was remade over time. When new approaches are introduced, they are woven into existing processes rather than replace existing institutional forms. I hold that change is best understood by reviewing how institutions and organizations relate to one another over time rather than by focusing on only one institution or on any individuals. This is important, given Canada's complex institutional arrangement. The country's national political institutions distribute power unevenly across regions by giving some disproportionate access to the policy and decision-making levers.[73] This too, has strengthened their bias for path dependency.

My central argument is that path dependency and historical institutionalism explain both the nature of the transformative moments as well as the lack of developments in Canadian federalism, in Canada's national institutions, and in the public service. In brief, they explain why Canada's national institutions are highly path dependent, or unable to pursue fundamental change, unless they have to confront a situation that requires fundamental change, such as the Great Depression. These concepts also explain why Canada's most transformative moments in policy took place outside of its normal political institutions because they were not able to accommodate them. It is this that led to their gradual disintegration.

16

Looking Ahead

Historical institutionalism and path dependency explain a great deal about both the evolution and lack of it in Canada's Constitution and in national political and administrative institutions. They do not, however, explain everything. Historical institutionalism overstates the role of institutions and understates the role of ideas; historical institutionalists do not insist that institutions are the only force that matters in politics.[1] That said, transformational moments do happen – Canada is no exception – and such moments do set institutions on a new trajectory.

Leading Canadian politicians and senior public servants were able to initiate and manage transformative moments when confronting a crisis (e.g., the Great Depression) or when a prime minister pursued an initiative with a single-minded purpose (e.g., patriating the constitution). My purpose in situating historical institutionalism and path dependency in a Canadian context is to make the point that pursuing transformative moments is particularly difficult in Canada, given its constitution, its political institutions, and its regional character. If history is a guide, Canada's next transformative moment will be shaped either by a major political or economic crisis or by political leaders pursuing an idea with single-minded purpose. One cannot foresee the nature of the next crisis, whether political or economic, or its timing. One can predict, however, that the crisis will be somehow accommodated outside of the constitution.

Canada's Constitution remains rigid, at least, the written part. Regional differences, if not tensions, make it very difficult for provincial premiers to agree on what constitutes the national interest, let alone agreeing to amend the constitution. The Fathers of

Confederation assumed that Canada's Parliament and the federal Cabinet would define the national interest. However, the absence of a capacity to speak to the interests of all regions, including those of the smaller provinces, has made it very difficult for these governing bodies to define and pursue the national interest that resonates in all parts of Canada.

Canada has no shortage of issues that require transformative moments. However, the political environment is far more demanding today to navigate than it was when the Rowell-Sirois Report was tabled or when Pierre Trudeau pursued constitutional renewal. Political leaders will thus need strong resolve to pursue transformative change, no matter the issue.

The media, in all their forms, have more impact on politics than was the case thirty years ago. Politics is being "mediatized" to the point that it is changing not only what we are told but also what we know, how we know it, and how we think and act.[2] The twenty-four-hour news cycle has made an important difference and so have social media, accentuating discord and division. The relationship between new media and politics remains in transition, and early signs suggest that politicians are experiencing more difficulty now dealing with the media, both new and old.

Traditional media, with editorial oversight, were viewed as the champions of democracy, informing citizens, for the most part, in an objective fashion to equip them to make informed decisions.[3] The changing media represent a particularly daunting challenge for both politicians and for Canada, given the nation's regional divisions. The transition from politics that is local or regional to a social media environment where politics is social will be particularly difficult for future prime ministers. This, combined with incessant demands for greater transparency, will double the challenge for our political leaders wishing to pursue transformative moments. I remind the reader that both the implementation of the Rowell-Sirois measures and the patriation of Canada's Constitution predate Access to Information legislation, whereas the Fathers of Confederation were able, with no difficulty, to keep their negotiations away from media and public scrutiny.

Social media are making it very difficult, if at all possible, for Canadians to share a common baseline of facts. We saw in an earlier chapter that social media promote identity-group affinity, silos, the spread of fake news, and conspiracy theories. If you want to believe that climate change is a hoax, there are plenty of opportunities to "share, like, and retweet." If you want to believe that Sharia law is coming to North America, there is a website for you. Social media have served to dumb down society's wicked problems and have turned political and other government officials into easy targets. Doug Saunders reports that he asks political decision-makers in various Western countries, including Canada, "What scares you?" The typical response is, "We're losing touch with a huge number of voters who are getting all their news and information from posts and videos. We just can't reach those people anymore. They're abandoning normal politics."[4]

In contrast, the fading traditional media are better suited to draw citizens to politics. They provide an institutional framework, a baseline of facts, and act as an agent for cohesion in society by promoting and debating issues from different perspectives.[5] The traditional media respect hierarchy. Social media, meanwhile, have little patience for hierarchy – they are largely unregulated, unmonitored, and often anonymous. New media do not appear to promote wider civic engagement, as voter participation reveals.[6] In brief, supporters of transformative moments will need to confront new media that are unpredictable, uncontrollable, and not always connected to facts.

The media, new and old, are far from the only challenge that will make defining and pursuing transformational change difficult for political leaders. New Canadians will continue to impact Canada's political agenda. Canada has welcomed about five million new Canadians over the past twenty-five years, and today 22 percent of Canadians are foreign-born.[7] They arrive with little knowledge of past or even current regional tensions and how Canada's political institutions have ignored, from the start, the requirements of intra-state federalism. They came to Canada to pursue greater opportunities for their families. They are, for the most part, locating in already heavily populated regions, making politically strong regions even stronger. Given that they left their country of origin for better opportunities, they will not readily see flaws in Canadian national institutions or understand regional tensions, let alone their root causes. They may well wish to leave well enough alone when it comes to national political institutions. Any flaws in them likely pale in comparison to the ones in the political institutions they left behind. The challenge then for future prime ministers is to somehow square the expectations of new Canadians and heavily populated regions with deep-seated regional grievances in eight provinces. The challenge is beyond the grasp of a single individual, however powerful, including the prime minister.

WHAT TO DO?

Western countries are dealing with a democratic deficit. As noted in the introduction, Canada's democratic deficit has a particular bent. It lacks a capacity in its national institutions to accommodate the regional factor and promote regional equity, leaving aside the heavily populated provinces. In other words, the regional perspective has no political home in Canada's national political and administrative institutions – therein lies the problem. This is not, however, the only issue that speaks to Canada's democratic deficit. We saw earlier that Parliament, Cabinet, and the public service are all in a state of disrepair.

Leaving aside the Charter of Rights and Freedoms – albeit an important aside – Canada's transformative moments and developments in its national political institutions took place outside of the constitution. Canada has a lot of hidden wiring in its political and administrative institutions. Much of how Parliament and government operate is based on constitutional conventions or on "binding rules of behaviour" that are not legally enforceable by the courts, so they are only binding in a political sense, including the obligation to act in good faith.[8] Constitutional conventions in Westminster-inspired systems permeate the operations of both Parliament and government. It is worth underlining the point, once again, that the role of the prime minister, for example, is not even mentioned in Canada's written constitution.

The point is that important reform measures can be pursued without a formal constitutional amendment. There was nothing, for example, that prevented Prime Minister Justin Trudeau from appointing independent senators. There is nothing to prevent the Senate from restructuring itself along regional lines, as former senators Michael Kirby and Hugh Segal recommend.[9] There was nothing that prevented Prime Minister Justin Trudeau from doing away with regional ministers. There is also nothing to prevent a future prime minister from designating a minister responsible for a given region. The key to promoting important change is political will or the willingness to spend political capital. The one who decides if an issue warrants spending political capital is the prime minister – only the prime minister.

DEALING WITH THE DISINTEGRATION
OF PARLIAMENT

Everything in Ottawa revolves around prime ministers and their courtiers. I am not the only one making the case that they dominate all things in the federal government and that they govern from the centre.[10] We know that prime ministers now dominate election campaigns, Parliament, Cabinet, caucus, and the public service. Every new development, it seems, serves to strengthen further the hand of the prime minister, from the arrival of permanent election campaigns to new media. Things in Ottawa, however, should revolve around Parliament rather than the prime minister, and this is where we need to begin to address Canada's democratic deficit. Parliament is the one national institution that has direct ties to every community in Canada, large and small, through members elected to the House of Commons.

It is not possible, however, to put Parliament back on a pedestal above all other sources of authority. Unlike 1867, Parliament today has to coexist with other sources of authority, notably the courts and provincial legislatures. While it is not possible to remake our institutions to what they once were, it is possible to breathe new life into Parliament to strengthen both its ties to Canadians and its role. The challenge is to determine what Parliament can do and what it cannot do in today's political and legal environment. We can begin by accepting that all is not well with Parliament. A recent survey of sitting MPs reveals, once again, that a majority are "unsatisfied" with the level of debate and the workings of the Commons.[11]

There is no shortage of ideas on how to strengthen the role of Parliament. We have a multitude of studies produced by parliamentarians, think tanks, and leading academics with suggestions on how to improve Parliament. It is important to underline the point that Parliament does not take or implement decisions – this belongs to the government. Parliament does not, and should not, hold power in the day-to-day management of policies and programs. Parliament, rather, should have influence and be seen to have influence. Parliament's influence has waned in recent years – we have reached the point where even what is said in Parliament matters much less than what is said in many other settings, namely on twenty-four-hour television news channels. Too often, parliamentary democracy has become little more than an adjunct to the media, playing out the battle between electoral partisan machines.[12]

The challenge cannot be overstated. Politicians, individually and as a group, are not held in high esteem. The rise of new media has produced a "virulent strain of anti-politics" views.[13] Deference towards institutions has also declined in recent years. There is a widespread desire, in part because of social media, to assert the supremacy of popular judgment over the views of elected representatives and experts.[14] Still, Parliament remains the only source of consent to majority rule and the only authority to call to account those in power for their actions. This goes to the heart of representative democracy. I know of no plausible alternative to parliamentary government in the Westminster tradition.

Again, prime ministers are the only ones who hold the key to pursue transformative change in Parliament to make it more relevant to Canadians, to strengthen its capacity to influence, to enhance its ability to hold those in power to account, to provide the forum for debate about important issues confronting the nation, and to oversee how government carries out its responsibilities. Prime ministers have the power to decide how MPs are elected, to ensure that MPs represent more than the party's leader brand, to see that MPs can do more in Parliament than they currently do, and to put in place measures so that MPs play a stronger role in scrutinizing the raising and spending of public money.

What needs to be done? Prime Minister Justin Trudeau had it right when he pledged that 2015 would be the last federal election fought under the first-past-the-post voting system.[15] The House of Commons Special Committee on Electoral Reform was established in 2016 and delivered recommendations to replace the single-member plurality known as the first-past-the-post model with a proportional system of representation, where seats in the Commons are allocated to the proportion of votes each party receives. The committee recommended that its proposal be put to a referendum. Trudeau abandoned his commitment and dismissed the recommendation of the House Committee.

I recognize that proportional representation has drawbacks;[16] however, its advantages outweigh its drawbacks. For one thing, proportional representation operates successfully in many Western countries. Proportional representation makes every vote count, provides true representation in that different voices can be heard in Parliament, is more democratic by encouraging higher voter turnout, and assists in moving some of the power away from prime ministers

and their courtiers.[17] The first-past-the-post voting system exagger-
ates the winner's margin and is a disincentive to vote in what are
regarded as safe seats. I note that the Liberal Party won 54.4 percent
of the seats in the 2015 election after only winning 39.5 percent of
the votes, while the Green Party won 0.3 percent of the seats after
winning 3.4 percent of the votes. Conversely, the Conservatives won
53.9 percent of the seats in the 2011 election after only winning
39.6 percent of the votes, and the Green Party won 0.3 percent of
the seats after wining 3.9 percent of the votes.[18] Under proportional
representation, a party needs to win a majority of the vote to win a
majority of seats.

Prime ministers dominate Parliament in many ways. Leaving
aside question period, not much happens in the House of Commons
without the prime minister's blessing. Consider the following: prime
ministers appoint all chairs of parliamentary committees (except
the Public Accounts Committee); they set the tone for the work of
Parliament through the Speech from the Throne; they have the power
to declare all legislatures' proposals to be matters of confidence, they
can establish the level of financial resources for the operation of
House committees; they have an important say in scheduling the
business of the House of Commons; they have the power to approve
party candidates, and notwithstanding new legislation, prime ministers still hold the power to dissolve Parliament and call an election.
The Canadian prime minister has the power to prorogue Parliament,
to postpone a vote of non-confidence, or to sidestep being scruti-
nized for maladministration. Two prime ministers from different
political parties – Chrétien and Harper –exercised this power, which
has been called an "abuse of power."[19]

Before coming to office, prime ministers readily see the need to
strengthen the role and workings of Parliament. However, they soon
have a change of mind after they sit in the prime minister's chair.[20]
It is not possible to strengthen Parliament without restricting, to
some extent, the power of the prime minister. Some of the necessary
measures require amending the constitution, but many do not. In
addition, if amending the constitution is not possible, future prime
ministers need to refrain from enlarging the scope of their power
in the interest of strengthening Canada's parliamentary democracy. I note, however, that agreeing to constitutional amendments
to strengthen Parliament should be easier to accomplish since they
have no bearing on the legislative powers or rights of the provinces.

There are important measures that do not require constitutional amendments. What they require is the support of the prime minister. The Canada Elections Act should be amended to take away the power of party leaders to reject official party candidates. This power should be given to local party associations where representative democracy begins. This amendment would strengthen representative democracy by strengthening the role of rank-and-file party members. At the moment, party leaders can nudge candidates they do not like in favour of someone of like mind or a rising star in the eyes of party leaders and their courtiers, or conversely, refuse a candidate that the local party association prefers.

The requirement that the government needs to enjoy the confidence of the House of Commons in order to govern is a centrepiece of the Westminster parliamentary model. It needs to be respected. However, whether confidence should be engaged so frequently and routinely is an important question one can legitimately ask for loosening the power of prime ministers.[21] Canada should borrow a page from other jurisdictions and turn to a "constructive non-confidence system," which strips away the prime minister's power to declare any vote a matter of confidence. The constructive non-confidence system stipulates that confidence in the government can only be withdrawn through an explicit non-confidence motion. No other government legislation, including the Speech from the Throne, would constitute confidence matters. This would free MPs to vote as they see fit on proposed legislation. It would stop prime ministers and their courtiers from turning to a vote of confidence to bully government MPs to vote according to their wishes and to bully opposition MPs, in a minority situation, from voting against the government, thus triggering an election.[22]

The tendency to cram an entire parliamentary session's legislation into an omnibus bill not only severely limits debate, it also undermines the role of Parliament in scrutinizing proposed legislation. Parliament simply cannot conduct a proper review. Again, party leaders in opposition see many flaws in omnibus bills but soon have a change of heart when they come to power. When considering one omnibus bill, for example, MPs and interest groups had to have knowledge of a Canada-Poland agreement on social security, the implications of a proposal to do away with Canada Post monopoly over mail to be delivered outside of Canada, laws governing pensions, what it would entail when allowing credit unions to become banks, understand proposals to change the environmental process, and permission to sell off Atomic Energy of Canada Limited, and other financial measures.[23] This is not the only example of an omnibus bill that deals with several important and diverse issues. Justin Trudeau campaigned on a commitment to end omnibus bills, arguing that they force MPs to vote yes or no on a package of changes, though they might support parts of it and oppose others. This commitment did not stop Trudeau's minister of finance in 2017 from tabling a wide-ranging 300-page omnibus bill that again dealt with a multitude of issues.[24] There is nothing to prevent a prime minister from ending omnibus bills – all that is required is political will and respecting commitments made during an election campaign.

Anyone looking for evidence that Parliament has been on the "disintegration" trajectory need look no further than former senior Cabinet minister Lowell Murray's observation. He argued that Parliament, and particularly the House of Commons, "have allowed their most vital power, the power of the purse, to become a dead letter, their Supply and Estimates process an empty ritual."[25] Paul Thomas highlights the problem: "It is a long-standing problem that parliamentarians are stuffed with information and starved for understanding."[26]

The piles and piles of documents written in an obtuse impenetrable style hold little interest to MPs, as previous chapters make clear. If the goal is to discourage MPs from raising pointed questions about government spending in the era of permanent election campaigns, then the current approach is working. If the goal is to strengthen the ability of MPs to scrutinize government spending and to hold the government to account, then the estimate process needs to square better with their interest. MPs think in local and regional terms, not in departmental or sectoral terms. Public servants, meanwhile, think in departmental terms, not in spatial terms, unless the economic interest of their own community is under review. The current estimates process is tied to the interest of public servants, not MPs. The process also squares with the political interest of prime ministers and their courtiers. It enables them to keep things of little interest to their agenda running on their tracks, which in turn, helps to manage the blame game and permanent election campaigns.

The government's spending plans need a geographical breakdown or focus to capture MPs' attention. They will have a keen interest in knowing and debating what program funds go to their constituencies and regions, for what purpose and whether the funds would have a greater impact if reallocated to a different purpose. Senior public servants argue, as some have with me, that this approach runs the risk of fuelling further regional tensions. The risk is well worth taking if it turns "an empty ritual" into a meaningful role for MPs. I argue that shedding light on how government spends, where, and for what purpose will not only strengthen representative democracy by strengthening the role of all MPs but also go to the heart of what fuels regional tensions – a lack of evidence-based information available to Canadians on federal government spending at the regional level. Policy-makers should not be afraid of providing Canadians and their MPs with information that they can understand and debate. As noted in the preface, Tocqueville warned against an ill-informed public opinion. Canada's national institutions will not be able to serve as the central forum for reconciling regional and national interests unless there are provided with the information to do so. This starts with the government's expenditure budget.

Political parties need to launch a debate on how party leaders are selected and retained. They now leave it to rank-and-file party members. Two leading students of Canadian politics made an excellent contribution to the debate in their book *Politics at the Centre*.[27] They support the current approach, and while their contribution holds merit, we need a thorough assessment from Parliament's perspective. Christopher Moore provides a different view that challenges the wisdom of leaving the responsibility of selecting and retaining leaders to rank-and-file party members. He suggests that turning the responsibility to MPs would ensure they would no longer be called "nobodies."[28] William Hague, former leader of the British Conservative Party, is worth quoting on this issue, for he says it all:

Having the leader elected in parliament strengthens parliament itself. Without the power to change the leader, to elect the prime minister, backbench MPs would have less influence, would have less power over their party leader. All of us who are constituency MPs, trying to represent our constituents and our interests in different parts of the country, know that we are strengthened by having this colossal power at our disposal. In other systems, where party conventions do the choosing of the leader, individual members of Parliament have less influence throughout most of the life of the parliament. And it can very clearly be argued that democracy suffers as a result because the ability of members of Parliament to bring influence to bear is fundamental to democracy.[29]

The Senate should embrace the Kirby-Segal suggestion that it be organized along regional lines, consisting of four regional convenors. They correctly argue that this would give the Senate greater political legitimacy.[30] The recommendation went nowhere in light of criticism from Quebec senators. We saw earlier that Senator Paul Massicotte expressed strong reservations about the Kirby-Segal report. Another, André Pratte, warned that "this approach ... carries the risk that senators will come to see all the issues coming before the Senate only from the perspective of their region ... Canada does not need yet another institution fostering regional tensions. Powerful provincial governments already promote local needs."[31] It is not clear which other institution Pratte had in mind that fosters regional tensions.

Provincial governments are absent when federal government policies and programs are taking shape, a point developed fully in earlier chapters. Pratte's argument ignores the requirements of intra-state federalism, which are also outlined earlier. While his argument has carried weight in Quebec and Ontario since 1867, it has not in Western and Atlantic Canada. The argument ignores the debate that raged in Western Canada over the merits of a Triple-E Senate considered much better equipped to speak on behalf of the regions. It ignores the fact that other federations – Australia, the United States, Germany, and Russia – have an Upper House that speaks for the regions. Pratte does not explain why such an Upper House is good for all other federations but not for Canada.

DEALING WITH THE DISINTEGRATION OF CABINET

In *Governing from the Centre* (1999), I wrote that "Cabinet has joined Parliament as an institution being bypassed." Twenty years later, governing from the centre has only gained strength. The book generated a great deal of comments, some positive, others less so.[32] A point I made earlier bears repeating here. Those who wish to challenge the thesis in *Governing from the Centre* need to explain how the following squares with Cabinet government: "Cabinet government, by way of a far from atypical illustration, two key decisions regarding Canada's deployment in Afghanistan – one by a Liberal government, one by a Conservative government – were made in the PMO with the help of a handful of political advisers and civilian and military officials. The relevant ministers – of National Defence and Foreign Affairs – were not even in the room."[33] Cabinet was simply informed of the decision. I know many former federal Cabinet ministers, both Liberals and Conservatives, as well as senior public servants who told me that I had it right in *Governing from the Centre*. I accept, however, that those who disagree with the book may well have avoided raising it with me.

There is no need to revisit the book's findings or the discussions in earlier chapters on a prime ministerial–centric government. Much of the power of the prime minister comes from a long-established position as the first minister of the Crown to carry on the business of government. The power to appoint ministers, senior public servants, heads of Crown corporations, parliamentary secretaries, senators and judges, and various appointments to public bodies is long-standing and gives the prime minister immense power. The profile of prime ministers has risen in recent years, while that of ministers has declined. Prime ministers now exert greater control over the whole of the government. They often circumvent full Cabinet and its committees to strike understandings with key ministers in bilateral meetings and conversations. They often strike deals and inform Cabinet as a *fait accompli*. The media, both traditional and new, are making the prime minister the only voice that matters in Ottawa. Nevil Johnson remarks: "The cabinet has become a much more fluid and elusive component in the structure of British government than it used to be."[34] The same applies to Canada.

Prime ministers now enjoy the support of well-staffed central agencies to exert control on the whole of government and to ensure that ministers and their departments run on their tracks. The PMO is immeasurably larger and better staffed than it was in the Pearson years and before. The same is true for other central agencies, from the PCO and Department of Finance to the Treasury Board.

Permanent election campaigns have changed the dynamics of governing, which is felt everywhere in government, from the PMO to front-line employees. A government cannot navigate permanent election campaigns without being able to manage the blame game. The blame game is not a temporary condition. There are now blame-makers and blame-takers inside and outside government. The makers are the opposition parties, the media, officers of Parliament, and interest groups. There are several layers of blame-takers from the prime minister, ministers, and senior public servants to front-line managers and their staff. There are also both blame-avoidance strategies and credit-claiming strategies.

The central player is the prime minister, and everyone in government needs to avoid creating instances that would generate blame in that direction. Knowledge of how to navigate in a "blame world" and the fear of being blamed push government officials at all levels to shy away from taking risks.[35] Ministers are important blame targets. They have to be managed by the centre – one more reason why governing from the centre is now *de rigueur* in Ottawa, no matter which prime minister is in office. The centre has to keep a close eye on all matters, even those that once clearly belonged to ministers. I recall, for example, during the Pierre Trudeau era when ministers had a free hand in hiring their own political exempt staff. No more. The PMO now has a direct hand in staffing ministerial offices, and has had since Jean Chrétien's time in office.

It is up to prime ministers to make Cabinet the centrepiece of the government policy-making process. After all, there are only a few, if any, constitutional impediments if prime ministers decide to concentrate more and more power in their hands. However, prime ministers can provide better government if they are challenged by Cabinet colleagues and rely on them to define, shape, and implement policies. Prime ministers can make Cabinet more than a sounding board, and much more than a ratifying body. They can make Cabinet a forum for ministers to discuss issues of major concern for Canada or the government as a whole. Ministers should feel free to raise any matter of concern to the nation, their regions, and their departments, and more than anything, prime ministers must want it. Cabinet ministers have direct ties to Canadians; they are visible and accountable in a way that courtiers to prime ministers can never be.[36]

If they want it, prime ministers can empower both Cabinet and their ministers simply by changing a few things. For one, ministers should be free to staff their own offices. This would send an important signal to them and others. Prime ministers should substantially reduce the size and role of central agencies, starting with the PMO and the PCO. Both have been going in the opposite direction since Pierre Trudeau. The prime minister could simply announce that central agencies, including PMO, will be reduced by 25 percent and make it stick. By any international comparison, the Government of Canada has more and better-staffed central agencies than the other governments in Anglo-American democracies.[37] Reducing staff in central agencies would reduce central agency meddling in the work of line ministers and their departments and would empower ministers, at least within their departments.

Justin Trudeau, as we saw earlier, embraced deliverology in coming to office. This is the latest step by prime ministers to extend the ambit of their influence. They have the capacity not only to intervene directly in developing policies in most spheres of government activities, but also they have yet another unit in central agencies to monitor what is done and how it is done. Justin Trudeau asked no one, including his Cabinet or senior public servants, about the merit of taking this measure. He and his courtiers simply decided that this would make for better government, enabling them to exert stronger control on the government's direction and agenda. The jury is still out on its merit. However, one thing is certain: it made government thicker and imposed still more reporting requirements on line departments.[38] Future prime ministers can undo the deliverology unit as quickly as it was introduced.

DEALING WITH THE DISINTEGRATION
OF THE PUBLIC SERVICE

The public service has been knocked off its moorings. It is costly, over-staffed, and risk-averse. It is unsure of its policy advisory role and does not measure up in managing financial and human resources. It is an increasingly Ottawa-centric institution with a fault line separating senior public servants from front-line managers. The institution needs to develop a much stronger capacity to deal with Canada's regional reality. I can do no better than quote from the report prepared by the 150 early-career public service employees to identify the challenges Canada was facing at its 150th anniversary: "Although 60 percent of the Public Service work outside the National Capital, it often feels like 100 percent of the opportunities and anything of value are in the National Capital Region. By and large, Ottawa tends to do a poor job of disseminating policy discussions to regions, as well as not fully considering advice that comes from the regions."[39]

The acrimonious debate that raged between the auditor general and the clerk of the Privy Council over the failed Phoenix pay system already discussed is pertinent here. The auditor general argued that the system's "incomprehensible failure stemmed from a broken culture in government." The clerk quickly dismissed the auditor general's report as an "opinion piece" unsupported by evidence.[40] This was a cheap shot responding to a report that tried to make sense out of a failed management initiative that is costing Canadians over a billion dollars. The clerk of the Privy Council needs to answer the question, If the failure is not from a broken culture in government, then what is the cause?

I read every annual report to the prime minister on the public service of Canada submitted by the clerk of the Privy Council. These are classic opinion pieces that never explain why, at times, things go off the rails in government, let alone how to fix why things go off the rails or who is responsible.[41] Ralph Heintzman, a former senior federal public servant and the main author of the Tait Report on values and ethics in the federal service, wrote that the auditor general was right to say that the Phoenix pay "fiasco points to a serious problem," and that the management consultants brought in to review the botched pay system were also right when they explained the failings were "partly rooted in a public service culture that does not reward speaking truth to power."[42]

The clerk's message to federal public servants – there is no broken culture in the federal public service – also does not square with the findings of a report prepared by 150 early-career federal public servants to identify the challenges they are confronting. They wrote about a "risk-averse culture," "territorial-infighting" (turf), "regional animosity and declining trust in government," and an inability of the system to deal with "poor performers."[43] These factors, too, speak to a broken culture in government.

The federal public service is not living up to expectations on two fronts: providing timely policy advice and solid management. It is a cultural problem that stems from its relations to prime ministers and their courtiers, permanent election campaigns, the blame game, a fault line that divides the public service, failed attempts to make the public sector management look like the private sector management, and a chronic inability to establish who is responsible for what. There is no need to revisit points made in earlier chapters on these issues.

On policy, senior public servants have lost standing and must compete with several sources of policy advice that senior politicians can now turn to – partisan or exempt status advisers, think tanks,

associations, consultants, and lobbyists. It has become more difficult
for senior public servants to draw the line between serving the government of the day and the partisan interest of the governing party.[44]
Permanent election campaigns have pushed senior public servants
to become "promiscuously partisan" rather than being neutral and
providing objective evidence-based advice in carrying the government's agenda.[45] They look to prime ministers and their courtiers to
make it to the top because the power of appointment is concentrated
in the hands of prime ministers.[46] Permanent campaigns have also
increasingly drawn public servants into politicized communication
activities, turning non-partisans into cogs of a partisan machinery.[47]

On management, the federal public service has been described as
a "big whale that can't swim." It is Ottawa-centric, has far too many
management layers, has too many employees, and has been told to
manage like the private sector, knowing that the differences between
the two sectors are immeasurably different. Public servants have to
contend with a wide array of oversight bodies and a fault line dividing it in two. In an earlier publication, I wrote that in government, it
was possible to "let the manager manage so long as it squares with
RPPS, DPRS, MAF, OCG, PCO, TBS, OAG, OLA, IBP, PSC, ATIP, CIEC,
OPSICC, DAGS, QFR and that it does not create problems for the
minister and deputy minister or draw attention of the prime minister and his advisors."[48] Not much has changed since I wrote this in
2013, and observers need not ponder long to appreciate why public
servants are risk-averse.

WHAT TO DO?

The public service needs to rediscover its role as an independent
source of authoritative policy advice. The starting point is to change
how deputy ministers are appointed. Other Western countries under
the Westminster model have revised their approach to appointing
deputy ministers or permanent secretaries.[49] Canada has not. As
long as prime ministers hold the power to appoint deputy ministers
without an open, transparent, and competitive process, court government will remain in place.

The federal government should borrow a page from the Alberta
government, where the deputy ministers of the Executive Council
(the equivalent of the clerk of the Privy Council) chair an interview
panel, which includes a representative of client groups that makes

recommendations to the relevant minister. The final recommendation is made to Cabinet by the minister with the premier holding a
veto power.[50] The last point is important: the prime minister would
retain the right to say no but only on the basis of competition and
transparent process.

The federal government needs to give teeth to the accounting
officer concept, a point made earlier. I recall senior public servants
telling me that the accounting officer concept was a "train wreck
in the making" by pitting ministers against their public servants or
vice versa. We have not even seen a fender bender since the concept
was introduced in Canada, let alone a train wreck. The concept was
diluted to the point where one former senior federal public servant
described it as a "fraud." He argued that the government adopted
the concept in name only, and that despite the accounting officer
title, deputy ministers "still have neither the obligation nor the tools
to draw a line, where needed, between political and public-service
accountability. This must be corrected."[51] The accounting officer
provisions, properly structured, would allow deputy ministers to
draw a line in the sand that establishes those matters for which they
can and cannot be called to account before Parliament.[52] The concept has worked well in Britain, and there is no reason why it cannot work as well in Canada. Properly designed, the concept would
strengthen accountability on management issues, if not management
itself in government operations.

There is a need to reduce management levels, which stifle creativity,
make government operations costlier, and help to grow a fault line
separating senior management from front-line managers. Reducing
management levels is in the interest of the public service by improv-
ing morale, a point once made by the Treasury Board Secretariat. It
would also give the public service greater credibility with taxpayers.
There are currently in the federal government at least six management levels between the deputy minister and front-line workers. I am
not including the number of "associate" positions such as associate
deputy ministers and associate assistant deputy ministers. I note that
the Roman Catholic Church has only five layers between the Vatican
and the parish priest in a small Canadian town.

I recall that the Treasury Board announced with great fanfare in
1989 that it was launching a new initiative to "cut executive-level
jobs in a bid to improve morale and operations."[53] In 1989, there
were 2,562 executives, a number that the Treasury Board Secretariat

argued was too high: "If you take a whole layer out of the management pyramid, then the managers below automatically gain greater
control over operations."[54] A management layer was not taken out in
1989. If anything, new ones have been added, along with the prolif-
eration of senior associate positions. In 2000, there were 3,293 senior
public servants in the executive group, or the senior management
group that lies between the deputy minister and the mid-level management working levels. In March 2011, there were about 6,000.[55] In
March 2017, there were 6,480.[56] The initiative failed badly and the
number of executives in the federal government has kept climbing.
The failure to delayer management levels has never been mentioned in
the numerous performance evaluation reports submitted annually to
Parliament. No one in Parliament or elsewhere has taken the Treasury
Board to task for not delivering what it set out to do.

The only thing the federal government needs to do with respect
to reducing management levels is declare that it will reduce them
and make it stick. The federal government can also announce that it
wishes to decentralize the operations, making the point that decentralization strengthens the capacity to serve Canadians and it makes
economic sense to move federal government units to regions (because
of lower staff turnover and lower rental and other operations costs).
It could add that having 41.1 percent of its public service located in
the National Capital Commission (NCC) in a country as large and
diverse as Canada is not in the interest of Canadians, national unity,
or the public service itself. As we saw earlier, other jurisdictions,
including countries that have the Westminster system and much less
geographic area to deal with, have a greater percentage of their public servants located in the regions. Recent advancements in information and communications technologies make it a much easier for
offices to connect to one another than was the case as recently as
the late 1970s, when an ambitious decentralization program was
launched, only to be terminated a few years later.

The federal public service is too large for the responsibilities the
federal government holds. Provincial governments hold responsibility for the employee-intensive sectors such as health care, education,
and social services. There are too many federal public servants in
policy, coordination, and evaluation units. The government needs to
reduce the number of policy positions and upgrade its operational
delivery capacity. Canadians are asking for a better program delivery, not more policy or other staff positions. I once suggested to a

deputy minister that we could reduce the size of the public service by 25 percent, and we would have a more efficient and less costly government, while at the same time, improve morale in government. He responded, "Do you have a basis for saying this?" To which I answered: "No more than you have a basis for suggesting that the government requires 262,696 public servants to carry out the responsibilities assigned to it by the constitution."

There is evidence to make the case that federal servants are under-employed. A senior analyst in a line department spent more than half his working day looking at news, sports, and porn websites from his desk while working at head office. This is not an isolated case. The department took the unusual step of firing him for committing "time theft," claiming that he was accepting pay for surfing the internet. The employee appealed to the Public Service Labour Relations Board (PSLRB). He argued that he was not given enough work to keep him busy, and made the point that he had met every deadline and received positive performance appraisals. PSLRB ruled in favour of the employee and ordered the department to reinstate him immediately. The board argued in its ruling that it was surprised "that an employee could spend the amount of time that he did on non-work-related activities for months without his supervisors noting a lack of production or engagement."[57] Again, this ruling was not lost on other public sector managers: Why bother trying to discipline or fire an employee?

The federal public service needs a stronger capacity to deal with non-performers to regain credibility with Canadians, notably the many that do not enjoy the kind of employment benefits that public servants do. It has never been easy to deal with non-performers in the Government of Canada, and it appears that the challenge is greater still today. The clerk of the Privy Council told the Standing Senate Committee on National Finance in June 2018 that it was hard to fire people who work for the federal government. He called for changes to the Public Service Employment Act "to make it easier to fire public servants for misconduct, poor performance or mismanagement."[58] The 150 early-career public service employees' report also called for a stronger capacity to deal with non-performers to improve morale and to avoid tarnishing the public service when no one is accountable.[59] The head of the second largest federal union took the clerk of the Privy Council to task for calling for stronger measures to deal with non-performers.[60]

Senior public servants report that dealing with non-performers is too often time-consuming, too difficult, and too uncertain of outcomes to try. It is easier, they add, to simply sideline non-performers or move them to another branch or to other departments. They point to their dealings with public sector unions as an important stumbling block. From a dead start in the mid-1960s, government workers now have collective bargaining and union membership throughout the federal public service. Today, 70 percent of public sector workers in Canada belong to a union, compared with only 14 percent for private sector workers. Managers know full well that employees and their union representatives will go to court if management initiates any action to remove anyone for non-performance. To avoid the hassles, managers will focus on things over which they have more control. In any event, they have little incentive to engage in what would likely be a two-year process to terminate an employee for non-performance. Even if they think they have a solid case, there is no guarantee of success.[61]

To be sure, prime ministers could accept the advice of the clerk of the Privy Council and go to Parliament to amend the Public Service Employment Act. It would require political will, as the government would meet with vocal opposition from union leaders. But there is more to the issue then revising the relevant legislation.

It is easy for the clerk of the Privy Council and other senior public servants to point their finger at the Act and at Parliament, claiming the problem lies there. We know that the great majority of font-line managers and workers do not take annual performance evaluations seriously. Barbara Wake Carroll and David Siegel write that "virtually everyone" laughed when they asked public servants in the field about the performance appraisal system. They report that performance appraisal is largely a matter of going through the motions; neither supervisor nor subordinates take it very seriously. They quote one front-line worker as follows: "There hasn't been anyone in the last seven years come and tell me I've ever done anything wrong. Nobody ever comes to look ... They don't tell you you've done something right; and they don't tell you you've done something wrong. There's no review of the operation."[62] Taking annual performance evaluations seriously does not require political will or changing legislation – it only requires managers to do what is expected of them.

CANADA'S REPRESENTATIVE DEMOCRACY
NEEDS HEALTHY INSTITUTIONS

Members of Parliament sitting in the Commons are the product of universal suffrage by secret ballot. Canada has a competitive party system, a free press, a professional public service, and an independent judiciary. In short, Canada has what is required to make representative democracy work. The question is whether these institutions – the building blocks of representative democracy – are up to the task. I argue that they are not; we have allowed them to drift for too long. We should no longer regard the work of our national institutions to be "whatever happens," happens.[63]

I argue that what is needed to repair our institutions is political will, a willingness to accept that we have concentrated too much power in the hands of a single individual and a handful of courtiers. Canada's vast geography and its regional differences require a capacity in national institutions to reflect the regional factor and accommodate better those regional circumstances when shaping national policies and programs. Political will, not constitutional amendments, can reinstate the House of Commons's role as the "legitimator," or the only legitimate voice that can speak for all of Canada's communities, and can turn the Senate into the voice of the regions. Political will is all that is needed to make the Cabinet the government's policy-making body, where all important issues are brought for resolution rather than serving as a body to simply ratify decisions taken by prime ministers and their courtiers. Political will is all that is required to give the public service authoritative judgment, a renewed capacity to develop and put forward evidence-based advice, as well as a capacity to deliver programs and services efficiently.

In the preface, I quoted Robertson Davies: "Canada is not a country you love. It is a country you worry about." Canadians have reasons to worry about the state of their national political and administrative institutions. Canada's future is tied to their capacity to represent the views of all Canadians and all regions, to show Canadians that they are able to speak beyond the interest of elites, and to establish who is responsible for what. What is needed is a prime minister who is as firmly committed to fixing our political institutions as Pierre E. Trudeau was in patriating Canada's Constitution. Nothing less will succeed, as history demonstrates.

Notes

PREFACE

1 C.B. Macpherson, *The Real World of Democracy* (Toronto: House of Anansi Press, 1992), 3.

2 Howard A. Doughty, review of *Participatory Democracy: Prospects for Democratizing Democracy* by Dimitrios Roussopoulos and C. George Benello, eds, *College Quarterly* 9, no. 4 (2006), www.collegequarterly. ca/2006-vol.9,num4-fall/reviews/doughty3.html.

3 See, among others, Donald J. Savoie, *What Is Government Good At? A Canadian Answer* (Montreal: McGill-Queen's University Press, 2015).

4 Bob Hepburn, "Why Canada's Democracy Rates a Sad 'C' Grade," *Toronto Star*, 25 March 2015.

5 R. Davies quoted in David Olive, *Canada Inside Out: How We See Ourselves – How Others See Us* (Toronto: Doubleday, 1996), 41.

6 Barack Obama, "Farewell Speech" (Washington, DC: Executive Office of the President, 10 January 2017), 9.

INTRODUCTION

1 John Dunn, *Setting the People Free: The Story of Democracy* (London: Atlantic Books, 2005), 16.

2 See, for example, A.C. Grayling, *Towards the Light: The Story of the Struggles for Liberty and Rights That Made the Modern West* (London: Bloomsbury, 2007), 159.

3 William Cross, "Canada: A Challenging Landscape for Political Parties and Civil Society in a Fragmented Polity," in *Political Parties and Civil*

Society in Federal Countries, ed. Klaus Detterbeck, Wolfgang Renzsch, and John Kincaid (Don Mills: Oxford University Press, 2015), 71.

4 James Madison, "The Utility of the Union as a Safeguard against Domestic Faction and Insurrection," *The Federalist Papers*, No. 10, *Daily Advertiser* (New York), 22 November 1787.

5 Cheryl Simrell King and Camilla Stivers, "Citizens and Administrators: Roles and Responsibilities," in *Public Administration and Society: Critical Issues in American Governance*, ed. Richard C. Box (London: M. E. Sharpe, 2004), 272.

6 William Doyle, *The Oxford History of the French Revolution* (Oxford: Oxford University Press, 2002).

7 Phillip A. Buckner, "Rebellions of 1837–38," in *The Canadian Encyclopedia*, Historica Canada, 15 July 2013, www.thecanadianencyclopedia.ca/en/article/rebellions-of-1837/.

8 The Act of Settlement 1701 established that Parliament could control the identity of the monarch by altering the line of succession.

9 Dunn, *Setting the People Free*, 26.

10 Ibid., 13.

11 Ibid., 18.

12 Stephen Brooks, *Canadian Democracy*, 8th ed. (Toronto: Oxford University Press, 2014), 15

13 Forrest Vern Morgeson III, "Reconciling Democracy and Bureaucracy: Towards a Deliberative-Democratic Model of Bureaucratic Accountability," PhD dissertation, mimeo 10, University of Pittsburgh, 2005.

14 "Apple against Pie: How Liberal Democracy Fell Apart," *The Economist*, 17 March 2018, 81.

15 Marc Mayrand, "Maintaining Trust and Engagement in Canadian Elections: A Call to Action," speech of the Chief Electoral Officer of Canada at the Economic Club of Canada, 25 September 2012, Toronto, 1.

16 Thomas S. Axworthy, *Addressing the Accountability Deficit: Why Paul Martin's Minority Government Must Pay More Attention to the Three A's* (Montreal: Institute for Research on Public Policy, Working Paper Series no. 2004–11, October 2004), 1.

17 Alison Loat and Michael MacMillan, *Tragedy in the Commons: Former Members of Parliament Speak Out about Canada's Failing Democracy* (Toronto: Random House, 2014), 33.

18 Andrea Lawlor, Alex Marland, and Thierry Giasson, "Emerging Voices, Evolving Concerns," in *Political Elites in Canada: Power and Influence in Instantaneous Times*, ed. Alex Marland, Thierry Giasson, and Andrea Lawlor (Vancouver: UBC Press, 2018), 269.

19 See, among others, Peter Aucoin, Mark Jarvis, and Lori Turnbull, *Democratizing the Constitution: Reforming Responsible Government* (Toronto: Emond Montgomery Publications, 2011).

20 *Samara's Democracy 360: Talk, Act, Lead* (Toronto: Samara, 2015).

21 See, among others, Donald J. Savoie, *What Is Government Good At? A Canadian Answer* (Montreal and Kingston: McGill-Queen's University Press, 2015); and Fareed Zakaria, *The Future of Freedom: Illiberal Democracy at Home and Abroad* (New York: W.W. Norton, 2007).

22 I am in debt to a colleague, Professor Gabriel Arsenault, who underlined this point when reading the manuscript.

23 Francis Fukuyama makes this very point in his *Political Order and Political Decay: From the Industrial Revolution to the Globalization of Democracy* (New York: Farrar, Straus and Giroux, 2015), 548.

24 Richard Nadeau and André Blais, "Accepting the Election Outcome: The Effect of Participation on Losers' Consent," *British Journal of Political Science* 23, no. 4 (October 1993): 553–63.

25 Bill Browder, *Red Notice: A True Story of High Finance, Murder, and One Man's Fight for Justice* (New York: Simon and Schuster, 2015), 6.

26 Ibid., 10, 11, and 24.

27 Kelly Blidook, *Constituency Influence in Parliament: Countering the Centre* (Vancouver: UBC Press, 2012), 1.

28 Daniel J. Levitin, *A Field Guide to Lies: Critical Thinking in the Information Age* (London: Allen Lane, 2016), 41.

29 Michael Harris, "Feels Like," *Globe and Mail*, 3 September 2016, R8.

30 Cass R. Sunstein, *#Republic: Divided Democracy in the Age of Social Media* (Princeton: Princeton University Press, 2017), 1–4, 9, and 259.

31 Joel Stein, "Millennials: The Me, Me, Me Generation," *Time*, 9 May 2013, time.com/247/millennials-the-me-me-me-generation/

32 Savoie, *What Is Government Good At?*, chapter 2.

33 Bob Rae, *What's Happened to Politics?* (Toronto: Simon and Schuster Canada, 2015), 108.

34 Richard Simeon, "Regionalism and Canadian Political Institutions," *Queen's Quarterly* 82, no. 4 (Winter 1975): 504.

35 See, among others, ibid., 33.

36 Guy Lawson, "Trudeau's Canada, Again," *New York Times*, 8 December 2015.

37 Margaret Atwood, *Survival: A Thematic Guide to Canadian Literature* (Toronto: McClelland and Stewart, 1972), 58.

38 Quoted in "Searching for a Canada of the Soul Not the Census," *Globe and Mail*, 18 June 2016, F3.

39 Ramsay Cook quoted in Northrop Frye, *The Bush Garden: Essays on the Canadian Imagination* (Toronto: Anansi, 1971), i–ii.

40 Don Desserud, "The Senate Residency Requirement and the Constitution – He Shall Be Resident in the Province," *Journal of Parliamentary and Political Law* 11, no. 1.

41 See, for example, Michael Kirby and Hugh Segal, *A House Undivided: Making Senate Independence Work* (Ottawa: Public Policy Forum, 2016).

42 Guy Laforest, *Trudeau and the End of a Canadian Dream* (Montreal: McGill-Queen's University Press, 1995), 46.

43 Gregory S. Mahler, "Canada: Two Nations, One State?" in Daniel P. Franklin and Michael J. Baun, eds, *Political Culture and Constitutionalism: A Comparative Approach* (London: M.E. Sharpe, 1995), 62.

44 Arthur Lower quoted in Neil Reynold, "Quebec a Nation? In a Dominion of Canada," *Globe and Mail*, 3 November 2006.

45 Gordon T. Stewart, *The Origins of Canadian Politics: A Comparative Approach* (Vancouver: University of British Columbia, 1986), 7.

46 See, among others, Elisabeth Gidengil, André Blais, Richard Nadeau, and Neil Nevitte, "Making Sense of Regional Voting in the 1997 Canadian Federal Election: Liberal and Reform Support Outside Quebec," *Canadian Journal of Political Science* 32, no. 2 (June 1999): 247–72.

47 See, among others, Donald J. Savoie, *Looking for Bootstraps: Economic Development in the Maritimes* (Halifax: Nimbus, 2017).

48 See, among others, Alan Cairns, "The Governments and Societies of Canadian Federalism," *Canadian Journal of Political Science* 10, no. 4 (December 1977): 695–725.

49 Peter Leslie, *Rebuilding the Relationship: Quebec and Its Confederation Partners* (Kingston: Institute of Intergovernmental Relations, 1987).

50 Nelson Wiseman, *In Search of Canadian Political Culture* (Vancouver: UBC Press, 2007).

51 Andrew Coyne, "New Senate Activism Undermines the Very Principle of Democracy," *National Post*, 6 June 2016.

52 See, among others, Colin Crouch, *Post-Democracy* (Cambridge: Polity Press, 2004).

53 Guy Lodge and Glenn Gottfried make this point in "Introduction," in *Democracy in Britain: Essays in Honour of James Cornford* (London: IPPR, 2014), 8.

54 Ganesh Sitaraman, *The Crisis of the Middle-Class Constitution: Why Economic Inequality Threatens our Republic* (New York: Alfred A. Knopf, 2017), 3.

5 Donald J. Savoie, *Breaking the Bargain: Public Servants, Ministers and Parliament* (Toronto: University of Toronto Press, 2003).

6 See, Gidengil, Blais, Nadeau, and Nevitte, "Making Sense of Regional Voting"; and Stéphane Paquin, *L'invention d'un mythe: Le pacte entre deux peuples fondateurs* (Montreal: VLB éditeurs, 1999).

7 Peter H. Russell, *Canada's Odyssey: A Country Based on Incomplete Conquests* (Toronto: University of Toronto Press, 2017).

8 Richard Simeon and Luc Turgeon, "Federalism, Nationalism and Regionalism in Canada," *Revista d'Estudis Autonòmics i Federals* 3 (2006): 19.

9 B. Guy Peters, "Institutional Theory: Problems and Prospects" (Vienna: Institute for Advanced Studies – Political Science Series, 2000), 3.

10 There is a growing body of work on path dependency and historical institutionalism. See, for example, J.G. March and J.P. Olsen, *Rediscovering Institutions: The Organizational Basis of Politics* (New York: Free Press, 1989).

11 For an excellent study of historical institutionalism, see P.A. Hall, *Governing the Economy: The Politics of State Intervention in Britain and France* (Oxford: Oxford University Press, 1986).

12 B. Guy Peters, Jon Pierre and Desmond S. King, "The Politics of Path Dependency: Political Conflict in Historical Institutionalism," *The Journal of Politics* 67, no. 4 (November 2005): 1282 and 1283.

13 See, for example, David E. Smith, *Federalism and the Constitution of Canada* (Toronto: University of Toronto Press, 2010).

14 Ibid., 2.

15 Richard Simeon, "Conflicts and Contradictions: Contemporary Strains in Canadian Federation," Conference on Social Development in a Pluralist Society, Proceedings (Ottawa: The Canadian Council on Social Development, 1977), 9.

16 Nicholas d'Ombrain, "Cabinet Secrecy," *Canadian Public Administration* 47, no. 3 (Fall 2004): 353.

17 See, for example, March and Olsen, *Rediscovering Institutions*.

18 See, among others, Donald J. Savoie, *Visiting Grandchildren: Economic Development in the Maritimes* (Toronto: University of Toronto Press, 2006).

19 J.E. Hodgetts, "Challenge and Response: A Retrospective View of the Public Service of Canadas," *Canadian Public Administration* 7, no. 4 (December 1964): 410, 414, and 415.

20 Alan C. Cairns, "From Interstate to Intrastate Federalism in Canada" (Kingston: Institute of Intergovernmental Relations, Paper No. 5, 1979), 8.

21 Savoie, *Breaking the Bargain*.

72 See, for example, Andrew Griffith, "Resetting Citizenship and Multiculturalism," *Optimum Online* 43, no. 2 (June 2013): http://www. optimumonline.ca/article.phtml?&id=436.

73 Remarks of the Right Honourable Beverley McLachlin, PC, Chief Justice of Canada, University of Western Ontario, Faculty of Law, London, Ontario, 6 November 2002, 4 and 5.

74 Peter Russell, "The Effect of a Charter of Rights on the Policy-Making Role of Canadian Courts," *Canadian Public Administration* 25, no. 1 (March 1982): 1–33.

75 John Sawatsky, *The Insiders: Government, Business, and the Lobbyists* (Toronto: McClelland & Stewart, 1987).

CHAPTER ONE

1 Plato, *Plato: Complete Works*, ed. John M. Cooper and D.S. Hutchinson (Indianapolis: Hackett Publishing Company, 1997).

2 Rod Jenks, *Plato on Moral Expertise* (New York: Lexington Books, 2008), 53.

3 Alexander Hamilton, John Jay, and James Madison, *The Federalist* (New York: McGraw-Hill, 1987), 313.

4 Josiah Ober, *Mass and Elite in Democratic Athens: Rhetoric, Ideology and the Power of the People* (Princeton: Princeton University Press, 1989), 7.

5 John Thorley, *Athenian Democracy* (Abingdon: Taylor and Francis, 2004).

6 A.H.M. Jones, *Athenian Democracy* (Oxford: Basil Blackwell, 1957).

7 Plato, *The Republic*, trans. Desmond Lee (London: Penguin, 1955).

8 Thomas Paine, *Rights of Man* (Mineola: Dover Publications, 1999).

9 See, among many others, Hans Julius Wolff, *Roman Law: An Historical Introduction* (Norman: University of Oklahoma Press, 1951).

10 S.E. Finer, *The History of Government from the Earliest Times*, vol. 1 (Oxford: Oxford University Press, 1997), 1: 542.

11 Ibid.

12 Ibid., 543.

13 Ibid., 583–5.

14 Thomas Jefferson, "Letter to Henry Lee," 9 May 1825, in Morton Frisch and Richard Stevens, eds, *The Political Thought of American Statesmen* (Itasca: F.E. Peacock Publishers, 1973), 12.

15 Mortimer N.S. Sellers, "The Roman Republic and the French and American Revolutions," in *The Cambridge Companion to the Roman*

Republic, ed. Harriet I. Flower (Cambridge: Cambridge University Press, 2004), 347–64.

6 Anthony Everitt, *Cicero: The Life and Times of Rome's Greatest Politician* (New York: Random House, 2002).

7 The Act of Settlement 1701 established that Parliament could control the identity of the monarch by altering the line of succession.

8 See, among others, Jeffrey Goldsworthy, *The Sovereignty of Parliament: History and Philosophy* (Oxford: Oxford University Press, 2001), 16–18.

9 A.C. Grayling, *Toward the Light of Liberty: The Struggles for Freedom and Rights That Made the Modern Western World* (London: Bloomsbury, 2007), 111.

10 Quoted in Joyce Lee Malcolm, "Doing No Wrong: Law, Liberty, and the Constraint of Kings," *Journal of British Studies* 38, no. 2 (April 1999): 161.

11 New World Encyclopedia contributors, "Magna Carta," *New World Encyclopedia*, 28 August 2014, www.newworldencyclopedia.org/p/index. php?title=Magna_Carta&oldid=983998.

12 Barry Coward, *The Cromwellian Protectorate* (Manchester: Manchester University Press, 2002).

13 Goldsworthy, *The Sovereignty of Parliament*, 140–1.

14 Alfred, Lord Tennyson, "You Ask Me, Why, Tho' Ill at Ease," *Poems*, 2 vols. (Boston: W.D. Ticknor, 1842), rpo.library.utoronto.ca/poems/ you-ask-me-why-tho-ill-ease.

15 Finer, *The History of Government*, 1: 1340.

16 John Miller, *James II* (New Haven: Yale University Press, 2000).

17 Bryan Bevan, *King William III: Prince of Orange, the First European* (London: Rubicon Press, 1997).

18 L.G. Schwoerer, "The Contributions of the Declaration of Rights to Anglo-American Radicalism," in *The Origins of Anglo-American Radicalism*, ed. M.C. Jacob and J.R. Jacob (London: George Allen and Unwin, 1984), 112.

19 Adam Tomkins, *Public Law* (Oxford: Oxford University Press, 2003), 44.

30 Walter Bagehot, *The English Constitution* (London: Chapman and Hall, 1867), 270 and 83.

31 L.G. Schwoerer, "Locke, Lockean Ideas, and the Glorious Revolution," *Journal of the History of Ideas* 51, no. 4 (October–December 1990): 538.

32 Alex Tuckness, "Locke's Political Philosophy," *The Stanford Encyclopedia of Philosophy* (Spring 2016), plato.stanford.edu/archives/spr2016/entries/ locke-political/.

33 John Locke, "Second Treatise of Government," *The Gutenberg Project* (1690), www.gutenberg.org/files/7370/7370-h.htm.

34 John Locke, with an introduction by David Wootton, *Locke: The Political Writings* (Cambridge: Hackett Publishing, 2003).

35 Joanna Innes and Mark Philp, eds, *Re-imagining Democracy in the Age of Revolutions: America, France, Britain, Ireland 1750–1850* (Oxford: Oxford University Press, 2013).

36 Janet Ajzenstat, *The Canadian Founding: John Locke and Parliament* (Montreal: McGill-Queen's University Press, 2007).

37 Anne M. Cohler, Basia C. Miller, and Harold S. Stone, eds, *Montesquieu: The Spirit of the Laws* (Cambridge: Cambridge University Press, 1989).

38 For an excellent discussion of Thomas Paine, his work, and his impact, see Grayling, *Toward the Light of Liberty*, chapter 4.

39 Thomas Paine, *Common Sense* (1776), Constitution Society, www.constitution.org/tp/comsense.htm.

40 Ibid.

41 W.A. Speck, *A Political Biography of Thomas Paine* (London: Routledge, 2013).

42 Ian Ward, *The English Constitution: Myths and Realities* (Oxford: Hart Publishing, 2004).

43 See, for example, P.B. Waite, ed., *The Confederation Debates in the Province of Canada, 1865* (Montreal: McGill-Queen's University Press, 2006).

44 Barbara Silberdick Feinberg, *The Articles of Confederation: The First Constitution of the United States* (Brookfield: Twenty-First Century Books, 2002).

45 George M. Wrong, "The Creation of the Federal System in Canada," in George M. Wrong et al., *The Federation of Canada 1867–1917: Four Lectures Delivered at the University of Toronto in March 1917 to Commemorate the Fiftieth Anniversary of the Federation* (Toronto: Oxford University Press, 1917), 19.

46 Cohler, Miller, and Stone, *Montesquieu*.

47 K.C. Wheare, "Walter Bagehot: Lecture on a Master Mind," *Proceedings of the British Academy 60*, read on 27 February 1974 (Oxford: Oxford University Press, 1975), 197.

48 Walter Bagehot, *The English Constitution* (London: Chapman and Hall, 1867), 13.

49 Ibid., 21.

50 Ibid., 51.

51 Ibid., 221.

52 Ibid., 80–1.
53 Ibid., 258 and 255.
54 Vernon Bogdanor, "Britain: The Political Constitution," in Vernon Bogdanor ed., *Constitutions in Democratic Politics* (Aldershot: Gower, 1988), 54.

CHAPTER TWO

1 J.M.S. Careless, *The Union of the Canadas: The Growth of Canadian Institutions, 1841–1857* (Toronto: McClelland and Stewart, 1967).
2 Ibid. See also Gordon Stewart, *The Origins of Canadian Politics: A Comparative Approach* (Vancouver: University of British Columbia Press, 1986), 59.
3 Richard Gwyn, *John A.: The Man Who Made Us, Volume 1, 1815–1867* (Toronto: Vintage Canada, 2008), 271.
4 Stephen Harper, "Sir Wilfrid Laurier Was One of the Greatest Prime Ministers of All Time," *National Post*, 9 September 2016.
5 Canada, "Constitution Act, 1867," 30 Victoria, c. 3 (UK), Government of Canada: Justice Laws Website, http://laws-lois.justice.gc.ca/eng/Const/page-1.html.
6 Quoted in J.K. Johnson and P.B. Waite, "Macdonald, Sir John Alexander," in *Dictionary of Canadian Biography, Volume 12: 1891–1900* (University of Toronto/Université Laval, 1990), www.biographi.ca/en/bio/macdonald_john_alexander_12F.html.
7 Gwyn, *John A.*, 321–2.
8 C.M. Wallace, "Smith, Sir Albert James," in *Dictionary of Canadian Biography, Volume 11: 1881–1890* (University of Toronto/Université Laval, 1982), http://www.biographi.ca/en/bio/smith_albert_james_11E.html.
9 J.M.S. Careless, *Canada: A Story of Challenge*, 2nd ed. (Cambridge: Cambridge University Press, 2012).
10 Donald Creighton, *John A. Macdonald: The Young Politician* (Toronto: Macmillan, 1952).
11 Quoted in Gwyn, *John A.*, 398.
12 Quoted in Joseph Pope, *Memoirs of the Right Honourable Sir John Alexander Macdonald, G.C.B., First Prime Minister of the Dominion of Canada*, volume 1 (London: Edward Arnold, 1894), 229.
13 Goldwin Smith, quoted in Ged Martin, "Faction and Fiction in Canada's Great Coalition of 1864," the Winthrop Pickard Bell Lecture (mimeo, Mount Allison University, Sackville, NB, November 1991), 1.

14 Ibid., 8.

15 George F.G. Stanley, "Act or Pact: Another Look at Confederation" (mimeo, presidential address to the Canadian Historical Association, 1956), 7.

16 Martin, "Faction and Fiction in Canada's Great Coalition of 1864," 3.

17 Gwyn, *John A.*, 292 and 439.

18 Ibid., 311.

19 *Parliamentary Debates on the Subject of the Confederation of the British North American Provinces*, 3rd Session, 8th Provincial Parliament of Canada (Quebec Hunter, Rose & Co. Parliamentary Printers, 1865), 984.

20 Donald Creighton, *The Road to Confederation: The Emergence of Canada, 1863–1867* (Toronto: Macmillan, 1964), 130.

21 M.O. Hammond, "Sir Samuel Leonard Tilley," in *Canadian Confederation and Its Leaders* (New York: George H. Doran, 1917), www.electriccanadian.com/makers/confederation/chapter12.htm.

22 See, among others, Gwyn, *John A.*, 271.

23 Creighton, *The Road to Confederation*, 330.

24 Ibid., 342.

25 Wallace, "Smith, Sir Albert James."

26 Ibid.

27 Quoted in ibid.

28 Wallace, "Smith, Sir Albert James."

29 Creighton, *The Road to Confederation*.

30 Ronald Rees, *New Brunswick: An Illustrated History* (Halifax: Nimbus, 2014), 142.

31 Ed Whitcomb, *A Short History of Nova Scotia* (Ottawa: From Sea to Sea Enterprises, 2009), 29.

32 Quoted in Peter Burroughs, "MacDonnell, Sir Richard Graves" *Dictionary of Canadian Biography, Volume 11: 1881–1890* (University of Toronto/ Université Laval, 1982), www.biographi.ca/en/bio/macdonnell_richard_graves_11E.html.

33 Creighton, *The Road to Confederation*, 350.

34 Ibid., 368.

35 Ibid.

36 Ibid.

37 See, among others, Jack Stilborn, *Senate Reform: Issues and Recent Developments* (Ottawa: Library of Parliament, 2008).

38 Gwyn, *John A.*, 319.

39 Quoted in Jennifer Smith, *Federalism* (Vancouver: UBC Press, 2004), 49.

40 G.P. Browne, ed., *Documents on the Confederation of British North America: London Conference, 13 December 1866* (Montreal: McGill-Queen's University Press, 2009), 211.

41 Creighton, *The Road to Confederation*, 153.

42 See the Honourable Noël A. Kinsella, *Forewords: The Senate Report on Activities, 2010*, undated, https://sencanada.ca/portal/AnnualReports/2009-2010/forewordhnk-e.htm.

43 Margaret Conrad, "150? Canada's Sticky, Messy History," *Atlantic Books Today*, 5 June 2017, http://atlanticbookstoday.ca/150-canadas-sticky-messy-history/.

44 Philip Girard, "The Atlantic Provinces and the Confederation Debates of 1865," 28 June 2016, http://activehistory.ca/2016/06/the-atlantic-provinces-and-the-confederation-debates-of-1865/.

45 Richard Foot, "Senate of Canada," in *The Canadian Encyclopedia*, Historica Canada, 7 February 2006, http://www.thecanadianencyclopedia.ca/en/article/senate/.

46 See, among many others, Lysiane Gagnon, "A Senate Still Searching for Sober Second Thought," *Globe and Mail*, 13 February 2013.

47 Stilborn, *Senate Reform*.

48 Chris Wattie, "It Gets Large-H Harder to Say Just What the Senate's For," *Globe and Mail*, 5 May 2016.

49 Canada, 2014 SCC32, case number 35203 (Ottawa: Supreme Court of Canada, 25 April 2014), 11–12.

50 Michael Kirby and Hugh Segal, *A House Undivided: Making Senate Independence Work* (Ottawa: Public Policy Forum, 2016), 5.

51 Ibid., 8.

52 Ibid., 13.

53 Ibid., 15.

54 See Paul Thomas, "Transforming Senate Will Take Soft Power," *Winnipeg Free Press*, 29 December 2016.

55 Senator Paul J. Massicotte, "Why the Senate Shouldn't Organize by Region," *Hill Times*, 24 November 2016.

56 Matthew Mendelsohn, "Abolish the Senate? Forget It: Change the Senate? Maybe," *Globe and Mail*, 24 May 2013.

57 Stéphane Dion, "Institutional Reform: The Grass Isn't Always Greener on the Other Side," in Hans J. Michelmann, Donald C. Story, and Jeffrey S. Steeves eds., *Political Leadership and Representation in Canada: Essays in Honour of John C. Courtney* (Toronto: University of Toronto Press, 2007), 185.

58 Roger Gibbins, *Regionalism: Territorial Politics in Canada and the United States* (Toronto: Butterworth, 1982), 195.

59 Quoted in Colby Cosh, "Roger Gibbins against Senate Reform? The Hell You Say!" *Maclean's*, 14 May 2012, http://www.macleans.ca/authors/Colby-cosh/roger-gibbins-against-senate-reform-the-hell-you-say/.

60 Ibid.

61 "Abolish the Senate Because Reform Is Never Going to Happen, Saskatchewan Premier Brad Wall," *National Post*, 23 July 2013.

62 Preston Manning, "Senate Reform, Not Abolition, Is in the East's Interests," *Globe and Mail*, 10 June 2013, A13.

63 Donald J. Savoie, *Looking for Bootstraps: Economic Development in the Maritimes* (Halifax: Nimbus, 2017).

64 Ibid.

65 Ibid., 86.

66 Quoted in Stanley, "Act or Pact."

67 MacNutt, *New Brunswick: A History*, 456.

68 Ibid., 457.

69 Creighton, *The Road to Confederation*, 444.

70 Phillip Buckner, "CHR Dialogue: The Maritimes and Confederation: A Reassessment," *Canadian Historical Review* 71, no. 1 (Toronto: University of Toronto Press, 1990): 3.

71 Whitcomb, *A Short History of Nova Scotia*, 31.

72 Gwyn, *John A.*, 372.

73 See, for example, Donald Creighton, *Towards the Discovery of Canada: Selected Essays* (Toronto: Macmillan of Canada, 1972), 295.

74 "A Hard-Won Century," *The Economist*, 7 October 2017, 86.

75 Johnson and Waite, "Macdonald, Sir John Alexander."

76 Gwyn, *John A.*, 279–81.

77 Creighton, *Towards the Discovery of Canada*, 295.

78 Gwyn, *John A.*, 390.

79 "Nova Scotia (1867)," *Canadian Confederation* (Ottawa: Library and Archives Canada), undated, http://www.bac-lac.gc.ca/eng/discover/politics-government/canadian-confederation/Pages/nova-scotia-1867.aspx.

80 Quoted in Douglas How, *A Very Private Person: The Story of Izaak Walton Killam and His Wife Dorothy* (Halifax: Trustees of the estate of the late Dorothy Killam, 1976).

81 Hammond, "Sir Samuel Leonard Tilley."

82 Kenneth McNaught, *The Pelican History of Canada* (London: Penguin Books, 1976), 131.

83 Johnson and Waite, "Macdonald, Sir John Alexander."

84 I consulted two leading students of Canadian political institutions – Professor David E. Smith and Richard Gwyn – and they, too, report that they are not aware of any published material on the issue.

85 Ganesh Sitaraman, interview with Rebecca Rosen, "Can the Country Survive without a Strong Middle Class?," *The Atlantic*, 21 March 2017, https://www.theatlantic.com/business/archive/2017/03/middle-class-constitution/519909/.

86 Ganesh Sitaraman, *The Crisis of the Middle-Class Constitution* (New York: Alfred A. Knopf, 2017), 4.

87 Claude Bélanger, "The Powers of Disallowance and Reservation in Canadian Federalism" (Montreal: Marianopolis College), 19 February 2001, http://faculty.marianopolis.edu/c.belanger/quebechistory/federal/disallow.htm.

88 Ibid.

89 Ibid.

90 Ibid.

91 Ronald Watts, "Final Comments," in *Regionalism: Problems and Prospects*, ed. Bertus de Villiers and Jabu Sindane (Pretoria: HSRC Publisher, 1993), 197.

92 Nelson Wiseman, *In Search of Canadian Political Culture* (Vancouver: UBC Press, 2007).

93 Richard French, "The Future of Federal-Provincial Relations ... If Any" (paper presented to IPAC, National Capital Region, June 1990), 2.

94 Linda Cardinal and Sébastien Grammond, *Une tradition et un droit: Le Sénat et la représentation de la francophonie canadienne* (Ottawa: Les Presses de l'Université d'Ottawa, 2016).

95 "Canadian Confederation," Library and Archives Canada, https://www.collectionscanada.gc.ca/confederation/023001-2700-e.html.

96 "Second Reform Act 1867," Living Heritage, n.d., http://www.parliament.uk/about/living-heritage/evolutionofparliament/houseofcommons/reformacts/overview/furtherreformacts/.

97 Canada, "Constitution Act, 1867," 30 Victoria, c.3 s.18.

98 Walter Bagehot, *The English Constitution* (London: Chapman and Hall, second edition, 1873), 14.

99 Ibid., 15.

100 Ibid., 43.

101 Claude Bélanger, "Supremacy of Parliament and the Canadian Charter of Rights and Freedoms," *Quebec History* (Montreal: Marianopolis College, 19 February 2001), http://faculty.marianopolis.edu/c.belanger/quebechistory/federal/parl.htm.

102 Bagehot, *The English Constitution*, 76.

103 Ibid., 68.

104 Ibid., 99.

105 Ibid., 17.

106 Ibid., 19.

107 Ibid., 9.

108 Bagehot, *The English Constitution*, 107.

109 David E. Smith, *The People's House of Commons: Theories of Democracy in Contention* (Toronto: University of Toronto Press, 2007), 8.

110 See, for example, William C. MacPherson, *The Baronage and the Senate: Or, the House of Lords in the Past, the Present, and the Future* (London: John Murray, 1893).

111 G. Lowes Dickinson, *The Development of Parliament during the Nineteenth Century* (London: Longmans, Green, 1895), 181–2.

112 Zsuzsanna C. Krakker, *Golden Age of the British Aristocracy: Methods of Preserving Traditional Leader Position in the Industrial Society* (Saarbrucken, Germany: VDM Publishing, 2008).

113 Ibid.

114 James Allan, *Democracy in Decline: Steps in the Wrong Direction* (Montreal and Kingston: McGill-Queen's University Press, 2014), 25 and 26.

115 Bagehot, *The English Constitution*, 197.

116 Ibid., 196.

117 Ibid., 171.

118 See, for example, Seymour Martin Lipset, "The Value Patterns of Democracy: A Case Study in Comparative Analysis," *American Sociological Review* 28, no. 4 (August 1963): 517.

119 David E. Smith, "Coming to Terms: An Analysis of the Supreme Court Ruling on the Senate – 2014" (mimeo, Toronto: Ryerson University, 3 December 2015), 17.

120 Quoted in Lipset, "The Value Patterns of Democracy," 523.

121 Bagehot, *The English Constitution*, 50.

122 B. Guy Peters, Carl Dahlstrom, and Jon Pierre, eds, *Steering from the Centre: Strengthening Political Control in Western Democracies* (Toronto: University of Toronto Press, 2011).

123 Smith, "Coming to Terms," 16.

124 Ibid., 18–19.

125 Ibid., 4.

126 Ibid., 15.

CHAPTER THREE

1 See Herbert Spencer, *The Man versus the State* (Caldwell, ID: The Caxton Printers, 1960).
2 John Stuart Mill, *Considerations on Representative Government* (London: Parker, Son, and Bourn, West Strand, 1861), 112.
3 Norman McCord and Bill Purdue, *British History 1815–1914* (Oxford: Oxford University Press, 2007), 11.
4 J.A. Cannon, "Aristocracy," *The Oxford Companion to British History*, 2002, http://www.encyclopedia.com/social-sciences-and-law/political-science-and-government/political-science-terms-and-concepts-80.
5 Janet Ajzenstat, *The Canadian Founding: John Locke and Parliament* (Montreal and Kingston: McGill-Queen's University Press, 2007), 119.
6 See, for example, V.H.H. Green, *A History of Oxford University* (London: B.T. Batsford, 1974).
7 Joe Nimmo, "Why Have So Many Prime Ministers Gone to Oxford University?" *BBC News*, 5 October 2016, http://www.bbc.com/news/uk-england-37500542.
8 Karen Seidman, "McGill University Loses Title of 'Harvard of the North' to U of T: Rankings," *Global News*, 5 March 2013, https://globalnews.ca/news/403400/mcgill-university-loses-title-of-harvard-of-the-north-to-u-of-t-rankings/.
9 M.L. Bush, *The English Aristocracy: A Comparative Synthesis* (Manchester: Manchester University Press, 1984), 151.
10 David Cannadine, *The Decline and Fall of the British Aristocracy* (New Haven: Yale University Press, 1990).
11 Alexis de Tocqueville, *Democracy in America: English Edition*, ed. Oliver Zunz, tr. Arthur Goldhammer, volume 2 (New York: Library of America, 2012), 185.
12 Donald J. Pierce, "The Rebellion of 1837 and Political Liberty: The Meaning and Value of Responsible Government in Canada," *CCHA Reports* 4 (1936): 73.
13 "A Responsible Government," *CBC Learning*, 2001, http://www.cbc.ca/history/EPISCONTENTSE1EP7CH5PA4LE.html.
14 See, for example, J.M.S. Careless, *Careless at Work: Selected Canadian Historical Studies* (Toronto: Dundurn Press, 1996), 67–77.
15 Quoted in J.-C. Bonenfant, "Cartier, Sir George-Étienne," *Dictionary of Canadian Biography, Volume 10: 1871–1880* (University of Toronto/

Univeristé Laval, 1972), http://www.biographi.ca/en/bio/cartier_george_etienne_10F.html?revision_id=7587.

16 Careless, *Careless at Work*, 72.

17 Donald Creighton, *The Road to Confederation: The Emergence of Canada, 1863–1867* (Don Mills: Oxford University Press Canada, 2012).

18 Michael Nolan, "Political Communication Methods in Canadian Federal Election Campaign 1867–1925," *Canadian Journal of Communication* 7, no. 4 (1981): 32.

19 Norman Ward, *The Public Purse: A Study in Canadian Democracy* (Toronto: University of Toronto Press, 1951), 80.

20 See, among others, Richard Gwyn, *John A.: The Man Who Made Us, Volume 1, 1815–1867* (Toronto: Vintage Canada, 2008), 303.

21 See, for example, Donald J. Savoie, *Looking for Bootstraps: Economic Development in the Maritimes* (Halifax: Nimbus, 2017).

22 James H. Marsh, "Railway History," *The Canadian Encyclopedia*, 25 March 2009, http://www.thecanadianencyclopedia.ca/en/article/railway-history/.

23 Jean-Pierre Kesteman, "Sir Alexander Tilloch Galt – Canada's First Finance Minister," *Financial Post*, 3 November 2008.

24 Pierre Berton, *The Last Spike: The Great Railway 1881–1885* (Toronto: Anchor Canada, 2001).

25 Laura Neilson Bonikowsky, "The First Telegraph in Canada," in *The Canadian Encyclopedia*, Historica Canada, 18 October 2013, http://www.thecanadianencyclopedia.ca/en/article/the-first-telegraph-in-canada-feature/.

26 George M. Wrong, "The Creation of the Federal System in Canada," in George M. Wrong, Sir John Willison, Z.A. Lash, and R.A. Falconer, *The Federation of Canada 1867–1917: Four Lectures Delivered in the University of Toronto in March, 1917, to Commemorate the Fiftieth Anniversary of the Federation* (Toronto: University of Toronto Press, 1917), 32.

27 Escott Reid, "The Rise of National Parties in Canada," in *Party Politics in Canada*, ed. Hugh Thorburn and Alan Whitehorn (Toronto: Prentice-Hall, 2001), 15.

28 Khayyam Paltiel, *Political Party Financing in Canada* (Toronto: McGraw-Hill, 1970), 76.

29 Canada, "Canadian Statistics in 1867," undated, https://www65.statcan.gc.ca/acybo7/acybo7_0002-eng.htm; and Warren E. Kalbach, "Population of Canada," in *The Canadian Encyclopedia*, Historica Canada, 7 February 2006, http://thecanadianencyclopedia.ca/en/article/population/.

30 Sir John A. Macdonald, quoted in "The Indian Act," *Indigenous Foundations*, undated, https://indigenousfoundations.arts.ubc.ca/the_indian_act/.

31 William B. Henderson, "Indian Act," in *The Canadian Encyclopedia*, Historica Canada, 7 February 2006, www.thecanadianencyclopedia.ca/en/article/indian-act/.

32 Jean-Charles Bonenfant, *The French Canadians and the Birth of Confederation* (Ottawa: Canadian Historical Association, 1984), http://www.collectionscanada.gc.ca/cha-shc/008004-119.01-e.php?&b_id=H-21&ps_nbr=1&brws=y&&PHPSESSID=s72pjvaac26t-2n55f5d52as7t4.

33 Ibid., 16, 18, and 19.

34 Quoted in ibid., 16.

35 Sir John Bourinot, *The Story of Canada* (New York: G.P. Putnam, 1896), 439.

36 J.P. Beaulieu, *Province of Quebec Industrial Expansion Publication* (Quebec: Office provincial de publicité pour le ministère de Commerce et Industrie, 1952).

37 Justin Trudeau, *Common Ground* (Toronto: HarperCollins Publishers, 2014), 92.

38 Ian McKay and Robin Bates, *In the Province of History: The Making of the Public Past in Twentieth-Century Nova Scotia* (Montreal and Kingston: McGill-Queen's University Press, 2010), 23.

39 Canada, *First Nations in Canada*, Indigenous and Northern Affairs Canada, 2 May 2017, https://www.rcaanc-cirnac.gc.ca/eng/1307460755710/1536862806124.

40 Canada, *A History of Indian and Northern Affairs Canada*, Indigenous and Northern Affairs Canada, 2 September 2011, https://www.aadnc-aandc.gc.ca/DAM/DAM-INTER-HQ/STAGING/texte-text/ap_htmc_inaclivr_1314920729809_eng.pdf.

41 Canada, "Constitution Act, 1867," 91 (24) Victoria, c.3 (UK), http://laws-lois.justice.gc.ca/eng/Const/page-1.html.

42 Stephen Brooks, *Canadian Democracy*, 8th ed. (Toronto: Oxford University Press, 2015), 503.

43 Desmond Morton, *A Short History of Canada* (Toronto: McClelland and Stewart, 2006).

44 Creighton, *The Road to Confederation*, 123.

45 Ibid., 147.

46 Ibid., 159.

47 *Canadian History of Women's Rights*, The Nellie McClung Foundation, undated, http://www.ournellie.com/womens-suffrage/canadian-history-of-womens-rights/.

48 Richard Gwyn, "How Macdonald Almost Gave Women the Vote," *National Post*, 14 January 2015.

49 Canada, "Canada Remembers Women in the Canadian Military," Veterans Affairs Canada, 28 November 2017, http://www.veterans.gc.ca/eng/remembrance/those-who-served/women-and-war/military.

50 Reverend Mather Byles was a well-known Boston clergyman. It is believed that he said: "Which is better ..." but there is no written record. See J.L. Bell, "Mather Byles, Sr., and 'three thousand tyrants,'" *Boston 1775: History, Analysis and Unabashed Gossip about the Start of the American Revolution in Massachusetts*, 11 March 2007, http://boston1775.blogspot.ca/2007/03/mather-byles-sr-and-three-thousand.html.

51 Ruth Holmes Whitehead, *Black Loyalists: Southern Settlers of Nova Scotia's First Free Black Communities* (Halifax: Nimbus, 2013).

52 W.S. MacNutt, *New Brunswick: A History, 1784–1867* (Toronto: Macmillan, 1963), 83.

53 Barry Cahill, "The Black Loyalist Myth in Atlantic Canada," *Acadiensis* vol. 29, no. 1 (Autumn 1999): 82.

54 Ed Whitcomb, *A Short History of Nova Scotia* (Ottawa: From Sea to Sea Enterprises, 2009), 13.

55 See, among others, Norman Knowles, *Inventing the Loyalists: The Ontario Loyalist Tradition and the Creation of Usable Pasts* (Toronto: University of Toronto Press, 1997).

56 John Milloy, *Indian Act Colonialism: A Century of Dishonour, 1869–1969* (Ottawa: National Centre for First Nations Governance, 2008) 2.

57 Canada, "British North America Act, 1867," 30–31 Victoria, c.3 (UK), Section 133, http://www.justice.gc.ca/eng/rp-pr/csj-sjc/constitution/law-reg-loireg/p1t15.html.

58 Quoted in Creighton, *The Road to Confederation*, 98.

59 Paul Pierson, *Politics in Time: History, Institutions, and Social Analysis* (Princeton: Princeton University Press, 2004).

60 George F.G. Stanley, "Act or Pact: Another Look at Confederation," presidential address to the Canadian Historical Association, 1956, https://cha-shc.ca/_uploads/4zubg8j1d.pdf.

61 Milloy, *Indian Act Colonialism*, 8.

62 E.B. Titley, *A Narrow Vision: Duncan Campbell Scott and the Administration of Indian Affairs in Canada* (Vancouver: UBC Press, 1986).

63 K.C. Wheare, *Federal Government*, 4th ed. (Oxford: Oxford University Press, 1963), 20.

64 I could not complete this chapter without a reference to John Porter's classic *The Vertical Mosaic: An Analysis of Social Class and Power in Canada* (Toronto: University of Toronto Press, 1965).

CHAPTER FOUR

1 C.M. Wallace, "Smith, Sir Albert James," *Dictionary of Canadian Biography, Volume 11: (1881–1890)* (University of Toronto/Université Laval, 1982), http://www.biographi.ca/en/bio/smith_albert_james_11E. html.

2 Jennifer Smith, *Federalism* (Vancouver: UBC Press, 2004), 49.

3 Quoted in C.M. Wallace, "Albert Smith, Confederation and Reaction in New Brunswick: 1852–1882," *The Canadian Historical Review* 44, no. 4 (December 1963): 298–9.

4 "Not Satisfied and Why," *Daily Telegraph* (Saint John), 29 April 1870, 4.

5 Donald J. Savoie, *Looking for Bootstraps: Economic Development in the Maritimes* (Halifax: Nimbus, 2017).

6 David E. Smith, *Federalism and the Constitution of Canada* (Toronto: University of Toronto Press, 2010), 24.

7 Ashley Csanady, "Quebec Premier Couillard Addresses Ontario Legislature, First Premier to Do So in Over 50 Years," *National Post*, 11 May 2015; and Tristin Hopper, "Central Canada Still 'a Force to be Reckoned With,' Quebec Premier Tells Surging West," *National Post*, 11 May 2015.

8 Madeline Kotzer, "'This Is a Sad Day for Our Country,' Premier Brad Wall Slams Montreal Mayor," CBC *News*, 22 January 2016, http://www.cbc.ca/ news/canada/saskatchewan/montreal-mayor-fires-back-feisty-tweet-at-sask-premier-1.3415474, translation.

9 Janine Brodie, *The Political Economy of Canadian Regionalism* (Toronto: Harcourt Brace Jovanovich, 1990), 143; and Richard Starr, *Equal as Citizens: The Tumultuous and Troubled History of a Great Canadian Idea* (Halifax: Formac, 2014), 30.

10 Patrice Dutil, *Prime Ministerial Power in Canada: Its Origins under Macdonald, Laurier, and Borden* (Vancouver: UBC Press, 2017), 52–3.

11 Quoted in Smith, *Federalism and the Constitution of Canada*, 47.

12 Senate of Canada, "List of Committees," n.d., https://sencanada.ca/en/ committees/; and House of Commons/Chambre des Communes Canada,

"List of Committees of the House of Commons," n.d., https://www.ourcommons.ca/Committees/en/Home.

13 Smith, *Federalism and the Constitution of Canada*, 92.

14 See, among many others, Sean Fine, "Court's Permission Necessary for Assisted Dying, Ontario Judge Rules," *Globe and Mail*, 15 June 2016.

15 "Top Judge Rejects Allegation of Activism," *Globe and Mail*, 23 November 2004, A10.

16 Quoted in Richard Gwyn, *Nation Maker: Sir John A. Macdonald – His Life, Our Times, Volume Two: 1867–1891* (Toronto: Vintage Canada, 2012), 37.

17 Quoted in Robert F. Nixon, "Democracy in Ontario," an address to the Empire Club of Canada, Toronto, 20 April 1967, 1.

18 Gwyn, *Nation Maker: Sir John A. Macdonald ..., Volume Two*, 43.

19 See Donald J. Savoie, *Governing from the Centre: The Concentration of Power in Canadian Politics* (Toronto: University of Toronto Press, 1999).

20 David E. Smith, *The People's House of Commons: Theories of Democracy in Contention* (Toronto: University of Toronto Press, 2007), 58.

21 Statistics Canada, "Census Program," n.d., https://www12.statcan.gc.ca/census-recensement/index-eng.cfm.

22 Randy William Widds, "Saskatchewan Bound: Migration to a New Canadian Frontier," *Great Plains Quarterly* 12, no. 4 (Fall 1992): 257, https://digitalcommons.unl.edu/cgi/viewcontent.cgi?article=1648&context=greatplainsquarterly.

23 Quoted in "Only Farmers Need Apply: Sir Clifford Sifton – The Immigrants Canada Wants," *Maclean's*, 1 April 1922, 32–4.

24 Ibid.

25 Anthony H. Richmond, *Post-War Immigrants in Canada* (Toronto: University of Toronto Press, 1967).

26 Ted McDonald, Elizabeth Ruddick, Arthur Sweetman, and Christopher Worswick, eds, *Canadian Immigration: Economic Evidence for a Dynamic Policy Environment* (Kingston: School of Public Studies, Queen's University, 2010).

27 Statistics Canada, "Immigration and Ethnocultural Diversity in Canada," 2013, http://www12.statcan.gc.ca/nhs-enm/2011/as-sa/99-010-x/99-010-x2011001-eng.cfm.

28 Ibid.

29 World Bank Group, "Exports of Goods and Services (% of GDP)," accessed on 13 February 2018, https://data.worldbank.org/indicator/NE.EXP.GNFS.ZS?locations=CA.

30 Statistics Canada, "Canadian Statistics in 1867," 26 August 2009, https:// www65.statcan.gc.ca/acybo7/acybo7_0002-eng.htm.

31 Statistics Canada, "Employment, by Industry, Annual," accessed 1 May 2018, https://www150.statcan.gc.ca/t1/tbl1/en/tv.action?pid=1410020201.

32 Daniel Workman, "Canada's Top Trading Partners," *World's Top Exports*, accessed 1 February 2018, http://www.worldstopexports.com/ canadas-top-import-partners/.

33 Daniel Workman, "Canada's Top 10 Exports," *World's Top Exports*, accessed 1 February 2018, http://www.worldstopexports.com/ canadas-top-exports/.

34 Canada, *Statutes of Canada, Passed in the Session Held in the Thirty-First Year of the Reign of Her Majesty Queen Victoria: Being the First Session of the First Parliament of Canada, Begun and Holden at Ottawa, on the Sixth Day of November, and Adjourned on the Twenty-First December, 1867, to the Twelfth March Following; Reserved Acts, Part Second* (Ottawa: Malcom Cameron, 1868), 21–35.

35 Ibid.

36 Canada, "150 Years and Counting: History of the Department of Finance Canada" (Ottawa: Department of Finance, undated), https://www.fin. gc.ca/afc/index-eng.asp.

37 J.E Hodgetts, "Privy Council Office," in *The Canadian Encyclopedia*, Historica Canada, 7 February 2006, http://www.thecanadianencyclopedia. ca/en/article/privy-council-office/.

38 Norman Ward, *The Public Purse: A Study in Canadian Democracy* (Toronto: University of Toronto Press, 1962), 3–4.

39 Canada, *House of Commons Debates – 1869, Session 2* (Ottawa: Information Canada, 1975), 48.

40 Mélanie Brunet, *Out of the Shadows: The Civil Law Tradition in the Department of Justice Canada, 1868–2000* (Ottawa: Department of Justice, 2000), 15.

41 R.M. Punnett, *The Prime Minister in Canadian Government and Politics* (Toronto: Macmillan of Canada, 1977), 75.

42 J.L. Granatstein, *The Ottawa Men: The Civil Service Mandarins, 1935– 1957* (Toronto: Oxford University Press, 1982), 11–12.

43 Costas Melakopides, *Pragmatic Idealism: Canadian Foreign Policy, 1945– 1955* (Montreal and Kingston: McGill-Queen's University Press, 1998).

44 J.E. Hodgetts, *Pioneer Public Service: An Administrative History of the United Canadas, 1841–1867* (Toronto: University of Toronto Press, 1955).

45 Quoted in Ward, *The Public Purse*, 57.

46 Ibid., 44.

47 Ibid., 47.

48 J.E. Hodgetts, *The Canadian Public Service: A Physiology of Government 1867–1970* (Toronto: University of Toronto Press, 1973), 49.

49 Sir George Murray, *Report on the Organization of the Public Service of Canada* (Ottawa: King's Printer, 1912), 7.

50 Hodgetts, *The Canadian Public Service*, 18.

51 Ibid., 51.

52 Ward, *The Public Purse*, 169.

53 Ibid.

54 Luther Gulick, "Notes on the Theory of Organization," in *Papers on the Science of Administration*, ed. Luther Gulick and L. Urwick (New York: Institute of Public Administration, 1937).

55 John Stuart Mill, *Considerations on Representative Government* (New York: Harper, 1869), 100.

56 Hodgetts, *Pioneer Public Service*, 55.

57 Quoted in Henry Parris, *Constitutional Bureaucracy* (London: George Allen and Unwin, 1969), 80.

58 See, for example, Ward, *The Public Purse*.

59 J.R. Mallory, "Canada," in *Sovereigns and Surrogates: Constitutional Heads of State in the Commonwealth*, ed. David Butler and D.A. Low (London: Macmillan, 1991), 43.

60 Quoted in Pradeep K. Chhibber and Ken Kollman, *The Formation of National Party Systems: Federalism and Party Competition in Canada, Great Britain, India and the United States* (Princeton: Princeton University Press, 2004), 108.

61 J.K. Johnson and P.B. Waite, "Macdonald, Sir John Alexander," *Dictionary of Canadian Biography, Volume 12: (1891–1900)* (University of Toronto/ Université Laval, 1990), http://www.biographi.ca/en/bio/macdonald_john_alexander_12E.html.

62 Chhibber and Kollman, *The Formation of National Party Systems*, 108.

63 Johnson and Waite, "Sir John Alexander Macdonald."

CHAPTER FIVE

1 See, among others, Donald J. Savoie, *Governing from the Centre: The Concentration of Political Power in Canada* (Toronto: University of Toronto Press, 1999).

2 Richard Gwyn, *Nation Maker: Sir John A. Macdonald: His Life, Our Times, Volume 2: 1867–1891* (Toronto: Vintage Canada, 2012), 46.

3 Ibid.

4 J. Murray Beck, *The Government of Nova Scotia* (Toronto: University of Toronto Press, 1957).

5 Quoted in Gwyn, *Nation Maker*, 365 and 366.

6 K.C. Wheare, *Federal Government*, 4th ed. (Oxford: Oxford University Press, 1963), 10.

7 W.H. Riker, *Federalism: Origin, Operation, Significance* (Boston: Little, Brown and Company, 1964), 11.

8 Ronald L. Watts, *New Federation: Experiments in the Commonwealth* (Oxford: Clarendon Press, 1966), 9.

9 "Creation and Beginnings of the Court," Supreme Court of Canada, n.d., https://www.scc-csc.ca/court-cour/creation-eng.aspx.

10 G.P. Browne, *The Judicial Committee and the British North America Act: An Analysis of the Interpretative Scheme for the Distribution of Legislative Powers* (Toronto: University of Toronto Press, 1967).

11 Gwyn, *Nation Maker*, 361.

12 Alan C. Cairns, "The Judicial Committee and Its Critics," *Canadian Journal of Political Science* 4, no. 3 (September 1971): 302. Cairns himself held a much more favourable view of the committee's work.

13 Ibid., 305–7.

14 Canada, "The History of the Persons Case" (Ottawa: Status of Women Canada, n.d.), https://www.swc-cfc.gc.ca/commemoration/pd-jp/history-histoire-en.html.

15 Since 1982, most amendments can be enacted if identical resolutions are passed by the House of Commons, the Senate and two-thirds of the provincial legislative assemblies.

16 Peter W. Hogg, "Formal Amendment of the Constitution of Canada," *Law and Contemporary Problems*, 55, no. 1 (Winter 1992), 254.

17 Bora Laskin, "'Peace, Order and Good Government,' Re-examined," in *The Courts and the Canadian Constitution*, ed. W.R. Lederman (Toronto: McClelland and Stewart, 1964), 92.

18 James Struthers, "Great Depression," in *The Canadian Encyclopedia*, Historica Canada, 11 July 2013, https://www.thecanadianencyclopedia.ca/en/article/great-depression/.

19 Editors of Encyclopedia Britannica, "New Deal," *Encyclopedia Britannica*, 26 April 2018, https://www.britannica.com/event/New-Deal.

20 Canada, *Report of the Royal Commission on Dominion-Provincial Relations: Book I – Canada 1867–1939* (Ottawa: King's Printer, 1940), 14.

21 Quoted in Barry Ferguson and Robert Wardhaugh, "'Impossible Conditions of Inequality': John W. Dafoe, the Rowell-Sirois Royal

Commission, and the Interpretation of Canadian Federalism," *The Canadian Historical Review* 84, no. 4 (December 2003): 564.

22 Ibid., 571.

23 Ibid., 574.

24 Robert Bothwell, Ian Drummond, and John English, *Canada 1900–1945* (Toronto: University of Toronto Press, 1987), 275.

25 Ferguson and Wardhaugh, "'Impossible Conditions of Inequality,'" 598.

26 Canada, *Report of the Royal Commission on Dominion-Provincial Relations: Book II – Recommendations* (Ottawa: Queen's Printer, 1954) and Richard Simeon, "Royal Commission on Dominion-Provincial Relations," in *The Canadian Encyclopedia*, Historica Canada, 7 February 2006, https://www.thecanadianencyclopedia.ca/en/article/royal-commission-on-dominion-provincial-relations/.

27 BNA Act, s.91 (2A).

28 Ferguson and Wardhaugh, "'Impossible Conditions of Inequality,'" 564.

29 W.A. Mackintosh, *The Economic Background of Dominion-Provincial Relations* (Ottawa: Printer to the King, 1939), 3. Among the other studies is one by the renowned Harvard economist Alvin Hansen on Canadian monetary policy.

30 Ferguson and Wardhaugh, "'Impossible Conditions of Inequality,'" 575.

31 Keith Banting, *The Welfare State and Canadian Federalism*, 2nd ed. (Montreal: McGill-Queen's University Press, 1987).

32 Donald V. Smiley, "Public Administration and Canadian Federalism," *Canadian Public Administration* 7, no. 3 (September 1964): 377.

33 Ibid., 372.

34 Ronald L. Watts, *The Spending Power in Federal Systems: A Comparative Study* (Kingston: Queen's University, Institute of Intergovernmental Relations, 1999).

35 See, for example, Donald J. Savoie, *Federal-Provincial Collaboration: The Canada-New Brunswick General Development Agreement* (Montreal: McGill-Queen's University Press, 1981).

36 Peter Hogg, chapter 33, *Constitutional Law of Canada* (Toronto: Carswell, 2007), 174–5.

37 See, among many others, Jacqueline Ismael, ed., *Canadian Social Welfare Policy: Federal and Provincial Dimensions* (Montreal: McGill-Queen's University Press, 1985).

38 Donald V. Smiley argues that "the term 'cooperative federalism' has had a wide although somewhat uncritical acceptance in Canada," in Smiley, "Public Administration and Canadian Federalism," 373.

39 Anthony Sayers and Andrew Banfield, "The Dispersal of Power in Federal States: Canada and Australia," (mimeo, paper prepared for the Canadian Political Science Association Annual General Meeting, 1–3 June 2010, Concordia University, Montreal).

40 Richard Simeon, "Plus ça change … Intergovernmental Relations Then and Now," *Policy Options* 1 (March 2005).

41 Quoted in Mark Sproule-Jones, "An Analysis of Canadian Federalism," *Publius* 4, no. 4 (Autumn 1974): 111.

42 Pierre Elliott Trudeau, *Federalism and the French Canadians* (Toronto: Macmillan, 1968), 79.

43 Pierre Elliott Trudeau, *Federal-Provincial Grants and the Spending Power of Parliament* (Ottawa: Queen's Printer, 1969), 4.

44 See, among many others, Banting, *The Welfare State and Canadian Federalism*.

45 Watts, *The Spending Power in Federal Systems*, 51.

46 Sproule-Jones, "An Analysis of Canadian Federalism," 135.

47 See, among others, Savoie, *Federal-Provincial Collaboration*.

48 Andrew Petter, "The Myth of the Federal Spending Power Revisited," *Queen's Law Journal* 34, no. 1 (Fall 2008): 165.

49 Savoie, *Federal-Provincial Collaboration*.

50 Donald V. Smiley, "An Outsider's Observations of Federal-Provincial Relations among Consenting Adults," in *Confrontation and Collaboration: Intergovernmental Relations in Canada Today*, ed. Richard Simeon (Toronto: Institute of Public Administration of Canada, 1979), 112.

51 Savoie, *Federal-Provincial Collaboration*.

52 Smiley, "Public Administration and Canadian Federalism," 379.

53 Savoie, *Federal-Provincial Collaboration*.

54 The agreements were, in fact, labelled first-, second-, and third-generation agreements. See ibid.

55 Savoie, *Federal-Provincial Collaboration*.

56 See, among others, Jack Stillborn and Robert B. Asselin, *Federal-Provincial Relations* (Ottawa: Library of Parliament, May 2001).

57 See, for example, Iain McLean, *Fiscal Federalism in Canada* (Oxford: Nuffield College, working paper 2003, W17).

58 Jean-Francois Nadeau, *2014–2015 Federal Transfers to Provinces and Territories* (Ottawa: Office of the Parliamentary Budget Officer, 19 June 2014), 1.

59 Janine Brodie, *The Political Economy of Canadian Regionalism* (Toronto: Harcourt Brace Jovanovich, 1990), 145.

60 Canada, Table 2-1: Provincial CHT Cash Entitlements, Millions of Dollars, *2014–2015 Federal Transfers to Provinces and Territories* (Office of the Parliamentary Budget Officer, 19 June 2014), 1.

61 See, among others, Stephen Duckett and Adrian Peetoom, *Canadian Medicare: We Need It and We Can Keep It* (Montreal: McGill-Queen's University Press, 2013).

62 See, for example, Richard Saillant, *A Tale of Two Countries: How the Great Demographic Imbalance Is Pulling Canada Apart* (Halifax: Nimbus, 2016).

63 I owe this point to Gabriel Arsenault, my colleague at l'Université de Moncton.

64 I benefited greatly from a luncheon I had with Hon. Michael Wilson, Toronto, 13 September 2016.

65 Canada, Table 051-0004: Components of Population Growth, Canada, Provinces and Territories, Statistics Canada, accessed on 3 November 2017.

66 See, for example, Donald J. Savoie, *Looking for Bootstraps: Economic Development in the Maritimes* (Halifax: Nimbus, 2017).

67 Éric Grenier, "21.9% of Canadians Are Immigrants, the Highest Share in 85 Years: StatsCan," CBC *News*, 25 October 2017, https://www.cbc.ca/news/politics/census-2016-immigration-1.4368970.

68 Frank Graves, *The Reinstatement of Progressive Canada*, Ekos Politics (Ottawa: Ekos, January 2016), 21.

69 ICC, *Ballots and Belonging: New Citizens on Political Participation* (Toronto: Institute for Canadian Citizenship, 2015), 32.

70 Ibid.

71 Donald V. Smiley and Ronald L. Watts, *Intrastate Federalism in Canada* (Toronto: University of Toronto Press, for the Royal Commission on the Economic Union and Development Prospects for Canada, 1985), xv.

72 Graves, *The Reinstatement of Progressive Canada*, 21.

73 See, among others, Alec Castonguay, "Kenney, le missionnaire de Harper," *L'Actualité*, 22 November 2012.

74 Neil Nevitte, Nevitte Research Inc., "World Values Survey (Canada) Immigrant and Native Born Respondent Comparisons," Citizenship and Immigration Canada, June 2008, https://www.canada.ca/en/immigration-refugees-citizenship/corporate/reports-statistics/research/world-values-survey-canada-immigrant-native-born-respondent-comparisons.html.

75 Ibid.

76 Ibid.

77 Donald J. Savoie, *Visiting Grandchildren: Economic Development in the Maritimes* (Toronto: University of Toronto Press, 2006).

78 Alain Noël, "How Do You Limit a Power That Does Not Exist?" *Queen's Law Journal* 34, no. 1 (2008): 391–412.

79 David Herle, "Poll-driven Politics – the Role of Public Opinion in Canada," *Policy Options*, 1 May 2007.

CHAPTER SIX

1 Mia Rabson, "Nellie McClung Won't Appear on Canadian Bank Note," *Winnipeg Free Press*, 25 November 2016, https://www.winnipegfreepress.com/local/nellie-mcclung-wont-appear-on-canadian-bank-note-403051206.html.

2 Ingrid Peritz, "Maritimers, Quebeckers Denounce CBC Series as Historically Inaccurate," *Globe and Mail*, 4 April 2017.

3 Ibid.

4 Campbell Clark, "Justin Trudeau Clinches Climate Deal Despite Christy Clark's Balk," *Globe and Mail*, 9 December 2016.

5 *Pan-Canadian Framework on Clean Growth and Climate Change: Canada's Plan to Address Climate Change and Grow the Economy* (Ottawa: Environment and Climate Change Canada, 8 December 2016), 52–78.

6 Andy Blatchford and Kristy Kirkup, "Provinces, Territories Take a Pass on Trudeau Government's Health Care Funding Offer," *Global News*, 19 December 2016.

7 Canadian Press, "Newfoundland, Nova Scotia Reach Health-Care Funding Deals," *The Toronto Star*, 23 December 2016.

8 Adam Huras, "Fed Budget 2018: N.B. Lands $75M Seniors Pilot Project," *Telegraph Journal*, 27 February 2018.

9 Philip Resnick, *The Politics of Resentment: British Columbia Regionalism and Canadian Unity* (Vancouver: UBC Press, 2000), 11.

10 Michael Ornstein, "Regionalism and Canadian Political Ideology," in *Regionalism in Canada*, ed. Robert J. Brym (Toronto: Irwin, 1986), 80.

11 Resnick, *The Politics of Resentment*, 11.

12 Jeffrey Simpson, "State of the Nation," *Globe and Mail*, 1 July 2016, 1 and A11.

13 Ibid., A11.

14 Erich Hartmann and Jordann Thirgood, *Mind the Gap: Ontario's Persistent Net Contribution to the Federation* (Toronto: Mowat Centre, 2017).

15 Quoted in Alain Gagnon and James Tully, eds, *Multinational Democracies* (Cambridge: Cambridge University Press, 2001), 155.

16 Donald J. Savoie, "All Things Canadian Are Now Regional," *Journal of Canadian Studies* 35, no. 1, (Spring 2000): 203–17.

17 See, among others, Bruce Anderson and David Coletto, "How Big Are Canadian Regional Differences on Questions of Morality?" *Abacus Data*, 10 July 2016, http://www.abacusdata.ca/how-big-are-canadian-regional-differences-on-questions-of-morality/.

18 Canadian Press, "Kevin O'Leary Wants to 'Finish Task' with Bernier Team After Failing to Get Rival to Drop Out of Race," *National Post*, 27 April 2017.

19 David Herle, "Poll-Driven Politics – the Role of Public Opinion in Canada," *Policy Options*, 1 May 2007, http://policyoptions.irpp.org/magazines/the-arctic-and-climate-change/poll-driven-politics-the-role-of-public-opinion-in-canada/.

20 Campbell Clark, "Conservatives Can't Win without Support from Quebec," *Globe and Mail*, 8 January 2017.

21 Donald J. Savoie, *Looking for Bootstraps: Economic Development in the Maritimes* (Halifax: Nimbus, 2017).

22 Richard Simeon and Luc Turgeon, "Federalism, Nationalism and Regionalism in Canada," *Revista d'Estudis Autonòmics i Federals* 3 (October 2006).

23 See, among many others, David J. Elkins and Richard Simeon, *Small Worlds: Provinces and Parties in Canadian Political Life* (Toronto: Methuen, 1980); and Mildred A. Schwartz, *Politics and Territory: The Sociology of Regional Persistence in Canada* (Montreal and Kingston: McGill-Queen's University Press, 1974).

24 Richard Simeon, "Regionalism and Canadian Political Institutions," *Canadian Federalism: Myth or Reality*, ed. J. Peter Meekison, 3rd ed. (Toronto: Methuen, 1977), 293.

25 Éric Montpetit, Erick Lachapelle, and Simon Kiss, "Does Canadian Federalism Amplify Policy Disagreements? Values, Regions and Policy Preferences" (paper prepared for the Institute for Research on Public Policy, Montreal, Quebec, no. 65, September 2017), 1 and 8.

26 Canada, "Historical Boundaries of Canada," 11 August 2017, https://www.canada.ca/en/canadian-heritage/services/historical-boundaries-canada.html.

27 See *The Report on Maritime Union*, better known as the Deutsch Report (Fredericton: Maritime Union Study, 1970).

28 Quoted in Alan C. Cairns, "The Governments and Societies of Canadian Federalism," *Canadian Journal of Political Science* 10, no. 4 (December 1977): 701.

29 R. Cole Harris, "Regionalism," in *The Canadian Encyclopedia*, Historica Canada, 7 February 2006, https://www.thecanadianencyclopedia.ca/en/article/regionalism.

30 Alexander Hamilton, James Madison, and John Jay, *The Federalist Papers* (Mineola: Dover Publications, 2014), 3–4.

31 Ganesh Sitaraman, *The Crisis of the Middle-Class Constitution: Why Economic Inequality Threatens Our Republic* (New York: Alfred A. Knopf, 2017), 5.

32 Ibid., 236.

33 Cairns, "The Governments and Societies of Canadian Federalism," 718.

34 See, for example, Savoie, *Looking for Bootstraps.*

35 See, for example, Richard Simeon, "The Federal-Provincial Decision-Making Process," in *Intergovernmental Relations: Issues and Alternatives* (Toronto: Ontario Economic Council, 1977), 26.

36 For a description of the Equalization Program and its criteria, see Canada, "Equalization Program" (Ottawa: Department of Finance, n.d.), https://www.fin.gc.ca/fedprov/eqp-eng.asp.

37 Jean-Francois Nadeau, *2014–2015 Federal Transfers to Provinces and Territories* (Ottawa: Office of the Parliamentary Budget Officer, 19 June 2014), 1.

38 Ibid., 2.

39 Ontario, *Public Services for Ontarians: A Path to Sustainability and Excellence* (Toronto: Commission on the Reform of Ontario's Public Services, 2012), chapter 20.

40 Richard Saillant, *A Tale of Two Countries* (Halifax: Nimbus, 2016), 107.

41 Hartmann and Thirgood, *Mind the Gap.*

42 The study, confidential at the time, was titled "A Perspective on the Regional Incidence of Federal Expenditures and Reserves and Revenues," Ottawa, Department of Regional Economic Expansion, n.d. I also reported on this study in Savoie, *Looking for Bootstraps.*

43 Savoie, *Looking for Bootstraps.*

44 Donald J. Savoie, *Regional Economic Development: Canada's Search for Solutions* (Toronto: University of Toronto Press, 1986).

45 Canada, *Report of the Royal Commission on Dominion-Provincial Relations: Book II – Recommendations* (Ottawa: Queen's Printer, 1954), 232.

46 Robert C. Brown, "National Policy," in *The Canadian Encyclopedia*, Historica Canada, 7 February 2006, https://www. thecanadianencyclopedia.ca/en/article/national-policy.

47 Quoted in Dirk Meissner, untitled article, Canadian Press, reporting on Hon. Paul Martin's trip to Vancouver, accessed 9 July 2003, http://www. canada.com.

48 "Martin to Emphasize Regions," *National Post*, 23 September 2003, A1.

49 "Stephen Harper's Next Move," *National Post*, 12 July 2004, A11.

50 I note, however, that McGuinty later apologized. See Steven Chase, "Liberal MP McGuinty Apologizes for Comments; Resigns as Energy Critic," *Globe and Mail*, 21 November 2012, A3.

51 Kenneth Harold Norrie and Doug Owram, *A History of the Canadian Economy*, 2nd ed. (Toronto: Harcourt Brace, 1996), 419.

52 See Canada, Economy of Canada, https://www.cia.gov/library/ publications/resources/the-world-factbook/geos/ca.html. See also Canada, *Recent Trends in Canadian Automotive Industries* (Ottawa: Statistics Canada, 20 June 2013).

53 See Canada, Statistics Canada, Total Manufacturing Jobs – Motor Vehicle and Motor Vehicle Parts, Table 2810024.

54 Ontario, Canada: Open for Business, Automotive, *Ontario, Canada: Open for Business*, accessed 7 May 2015, www.investinontario.com/automotive.

55 See, among many others, "Project Would Secure about 4,000 Jobs at Plant," *Globe and Mail*, 8 September 2004, B18.

56 Paul Vieira, "Canada Auto-Bailout Funds Issued with Limited Research: Watchdog," *Wall Street Journal*, 17 February 2015.

57 Greg Keenan, "Canadian Taxpayers Lose $3.5 billion on 2009 Bailout of Auto Firms," *Globe and Mail*, 7 April 2015.

58 Steven Chase, "Davie Shipyard Suspected Scott Brison of Favouring Irving in Dispute: Affidavits," *Globe and Mail*, 23 August 2017.

59 Jeffrey Jones, "Energy East Pipeline: Best-Laid Backup Plan Goes Away," Globe and Mail, 5 October 2017.

60 Canadian Press, "Montreal-Area Mayors' Energy East Criticisms 'Short Sighted,' Notley Says," CTV *News Atlantic*, 22 January 2016.

61 "Trudeau Warns Against 'National Divisions' After Energy East Pipeline Decision," *Huffington Post* (Canada), 7 October 2017.

62 Jean-Marc Léger, Jacques Nantel, and Pierre Duhamel, *Cracking the Quebec Code: The 7 Keys to Understanding Quebecers* (Montreal: Juniper Publishing, 2016); and Derek Abma, "Quebec Sovereignty Could Be Ignited by Pipeline Decision, PQ Win, Says Léger," *Hill Times*, 17 October 2016.

63 Gary Mason, "Why a Pipeline Could Cost Justin Trudeau the Next Election," *Globe and Mail*, 13 April 2018.

64 Daniel Leblanc, "Trudeau Adviser Mathieu Bouchard More Than Just PMO's Quebec Guy," *Globe and Mail*, 29 January 2016.

65 I attended a briefing in Ottawa on 28 November 1989, where the proposal was outlined in detail.

66 Richard Brennan, "Beatty Baffled by Millions in Bear Head Lobby Fees," *Toronto Star*, 29 April 2009.

67 "Mulroney Didn't Promote Bear Head, Exec Testifies," *Kingston Whig-Standard*, 22 April 2009.

68 See Steven Chase, "Ottawa Aims to Keep Lid on Details of Saudi Arms Deal," *Globe and Mail*, 27 May 2015; and Steven Chase, "Canada's Arms Deal with Saudi Arabia Shrouded in Secrecy," *Globe and Mail*, 21 January 2015.

69 Steven Chase, "Amnesty Wants Ottawa to Reveal Details of $15-billion Saudi Arms Deal," *Globe and Mail*, 29 May 2015.

70 Steven Chase, "Foreign Affairs Found No Red Flags for Israel in Saudi Arms Deal," 27 August 2015.

71 Steven Chase, "Critics Push Ottawa to Explain Justification for Saudi Arms Deal," 5 January 2016.

72 Ibid.

73 Richard Blackwell, "London, Ont. Defends Saudi Arms Deal as Integral to Region's Economy," *Globe and Mail*, 7 January 2016.

74 Steven Chase, "Liberals Committed to Saudi Arms Deal Even after Concerning UN Report, Dion Says," *Globe and Mail*, 28 January 2016.

75 Steven Chase, "Liberals Mum on Dion's Rationale for Not Cancelling Saudi Arms Deal," *Globe and Mail*, 19 February 2016.

76 Steven Chase, "Saudi Arms Deal Exempt from Global Treaty, Ottawa Says," *Globe and Mail*, 9 February 2016.

77 Steven Chase, "The Big Deal," *Globe and Mail*, 5 February 2016.

78 Steven Chase, "Cancelling Saudi Arms Deal Would Have No Effect on Human Rights: Dion," *Globe and Mail*, 29 March 2016.

79 Steven Chase, "Trudeau Says Canada Trying to End Arms Contract with Saudi Arabia," *Globe and Mail*, 16 December 2018.

80 Consultation with Paul LeBlanc, former president-deputy minister of ACOA, Moncton, various dates.

81 Howard Pawley, "Mulroney, Me and the CF-18," *Winnipeg Free Press*, 19 March 2011.

82 See, among others, Canadian Press, "East vs. West: Canadian Regional Differences on Display at TPP Trade Talks," *National Observer*, 2 October 2015.

83 See, for example, Vassy Kapelos, "5 Things to Know about Canada's Softwood Lumber Trade War with US," *Global News*, 12 October 2016, accessed 2 September 2017, www.globalnews.com.

84 See, for example, Normand Lafrenière, *The Ottawa River Canal System* (Ottawa: Parks Canada, 1984), 41–3.

85 See Savoie, *Looking for Bootstraps.*

86 Percy Downe, "No Tolls on Champlain Bridge – $46.00 Toll on Confederation Bridge – Why?" *National Newswatch*, 31 August 2016, https://www.nationalnewswatch.com/2016/08/31/no-tolls-on-champlain-bridge-46-00-toll-on-confederation-bridge-why/#.WtTZF3_A-70; and John Ivison, "Ask Not for Whom the Bridge Tolls (It Tolls for Thee, P.E.I)," *National Post*, 15 May 2017.

87 Konrad Yakabuski, "When the CBC Broadcasts History, Politics Is Sure to Follow," *Globe and Mail*, 5 April 2017.

88 Harris, "Regionalism," accessed on 29 December 2016.

89 Charlotte Gray, "Canada 150, Doomed from the Start, Now Ends with a Whimper," *Globe and Mail*, 20 December 2017. See also Jonathan Kay, "Why Our Intellectual Class Made Canada 150 the Worst Birthday Ever," *National Post*, 28 December 2017.

90 "Reform, Not Abolition, Is in the East's Interest," *Globe and Mail*, 10 June 2013, A13.

91 J.M.S. Careless, "'Limited Identities' in Canada," *Canadian Historical Review* 50, no. 1 (March 1969): 6.

92 Herle, "Poll-Driven Politics," 1 May 2007.

93 See, among many others, Resnick, *The Politics of Resentment.*

94 Jonathan Lemco and Peter Regenstreif, "The Fusion of Powers and the Crisis of Canadian Federalism," *Publius* vol. 14, no. 1 (Winter 1984): 111.

95 Richard Simeon, "The Future of Federal-Provincial Relations," in *The Future of North America: Canada, the United States and Quebec Nationalism*, ed. Elliott J. Feldman and Neil Nevitte (Cambridge: Center for Intergovernmental Affairs, Harvard University and Montreal: The Institute for Research on Public Policy, 1979), 149.

96 Richard Simeon, "Scenarios for Separation," in *Must Canada Fail*, ed. Richard Simeon (Montreal: McGill-Queen's University Press, 1977), 147.

97 See, among others, Bob Plamondon, "Blue Thunder: The Truth about Conservatives from Macdonald to Harper," *Policy Options*, 1 July 2009, http://policyoptions.irpp.org/magazines/canadas-water-challenges/blue-thunder-the-truth-about-conservatives-from-macdonald-to-harper-book-excerpt/.

98 *The Task Force on Canadian Unity – A Future Together* (Ottawa: Minister of Supply and Services, 1979).

99 Frank Davey, "Towards the End of Regionalism," in *A Sense of Place: Re-Evaluating Regionalism in Canadian and American Writing*, ed. Christian Riegel and Herb Wyile (Edmonton: University of Alberta Press, 1998), 6.

100 Ibid., 11.

101 Donald V. Smiley, "Territorialism and Canadian Political Institutions," *Canadian Public Policy* 3, no. 4 (Autumn 1977): 453.

102 Canada, "A Transformational Infrastructure Plan," Infrastructure Canada, Fall 2016, https://www.budget.gc.ca/fes-eea/2016/docs/themes/ infrastructure-en.html.

103 Guy Caron, MP, quoted in Marco Vigliotti, "Opposition Slams Government for Removing Regional Development Cabinet Posts," *Hill Times*, 10 August 2016.

104 Bill Curry, "Canada Should Take Regional Approach to Address Housing Problems: IMF Chief," *Globe and Mail*, 13 September 2016.

105 John Ibbitson, "East vs. West: Political Success Involves Pitting Group against Group," *Globe and Mail*, 16 May 2012.

CHAPTER SEVEN

1 Telephone consultations with Hon. Raymond Garneau, 20 November 2016.

2 Canada, "Policy on Conflict of Interest and Post-Employment," n.d., https://www.tbs-sct.gc.ca/pol/doc-eng.aspx?id=25178.

3 Rem C. Westland, *Running for the People: How Canadian Elections Favour the Career Politician*, e-book (Polarbear Lane Editions, 2015).

4 Ibid., 3.

5 Ibid., 4.

6 Ibid., 7–12.

7 Ibid., 34.

8 See Canada, "Elections Canada Official Voting Results," n.d., www. elections.ca.

9 See, among others, Donald J. Savoie, *Power: Where Is It?* (Montreal and Kingston: McGill-Queen's University Press, 2010).

10 Alison Loat and Michael MacMillan, *Tragedy in the Commons: Former Members of Parliament Speak Out about Canada's Failing Democracy* (Toronto: Random Canada, 2014), 55–6.

11 Brent Rathgeber, *Irresponsible Government: The Decline of Parliamentary Democracy in Canada* (Toronto: Dundurn, 2014), 140.

12 Westland, *Running for the People*, 36.

13 See, for example, Jason Roy and Christopher Alcantara, "The Candidate Effect: Does the Local Candidate Matter?," *Journal of Elections, Public Opinion and Parties* 25, no. 2 (2015): 195–214.

14 Elisabeth Gidengil and André Blais, "Are Party Leaders Becoming More Important to Vote Choice in Canada?," in *Political Leadership and Representation in Canada: Essays in Honour of John C. Courtney*, ed. Hans J. Michelmann, Donald C. Story, and Jeffrey S. Steeves (Toronto: University of Toronto Press, 2007), 39.

15 Gidengil and Blais, "Are Party Leaders Becoming More Important to Vote Choice in Canada?."

16 Peter Aucoin, "Prime Minister and Cabinet," in *Canadian Politics: An Introduction to the Discipline*, ed. James Bickerton and Alain-G. Gagnon (Toronto: Broadview Press, 1994), 268.

17 Michael Ornstein and H. Michael Stevenson, *Politics and Ideology in Canada* (Montreal and Kingston: McGill-Queen's University Press, 1999), 248.

18 See, for example, Donald Blake, "Division and Cohesion: The Major Parties," in *Party Democracy in Canada: The Politics of National Party Conventions*, ed. George Perlin (Scarborough: Prentice Hall, 1988), 23–53.

19 Janine M. Brodie and Jane Jenson, "Piercing the Smokescreen: Brokerage Politics and Class Politics," in *Canadian Parties in Transition: Discourse, Organization and Representation*, ed. Alain-G. Gagnon and A. Brian Tanguay (Scarborough: Nelson, 1991), 33.

20 Richard Johnston, "The Ideological Structure of Opinion on Policy," in *Party Democracy in Canada: The Politics of National Party Convention*, ed. George Perlin (Scarborough: Prentice Hall, 1988), 54–70 and 57.

21 I owe this insight to an anonymous reviewer of the manuscript with McGill-Queen's University Press.

22 Richard Johnston, *The Canadian Party System* (Vancouver: UBC Press, 2017), 3.

23 David Herle, "Poll-Driven Politics – the Role of Public Opinion in Canada," *Policy Options*, 1 May 2007, http://policyoptions.irpp.org/ magazines/the-arctic-and-climate-change/poll-driven-politics-the-role-of-public-opinion-in-canada/.

24 William Cross, "The Increasing Importance of Region to Canadian Election Campaigns," in *Regionalism and Party Politics in Canada*, ed. Lisa Young and Keith Archer (Toronto: Oxford University Press, 2002), 117.

25 See, among others, Donald J. Savoie, *Governing from the Centre: The Concentration of Power in Canadian Politics* (Toronto: University of Toronto Press, 1999).

26 Herle, "Poll-Driven Politics."

27 Margaret Conrad makes this point by quoting Philip Girard in "150? Canada's Sticky, Messy History," *Atlantic Books Today* 83 (Spring), 5 June 2017, www.atlanticbookstoday.ca/150.

28 Sharon Sutherland, "Does Westminster Government Have a Future?" (Ottawa: Institute on Governance, Occasional Paper Series, 11 June 1996), 5.

29 Andrew Perez, "Regional Strengths (and Weaknesses) Key to Electoral Success in Campaign in 2015," *National Newswatch*, 15 August 2015, https://www.nationalnewswatch.com/2015/08/15/regional-strengths-and-weaknesses-are-key-to-electoral-success-in-campaign-2015/#. XFTucVVKiUk.

30 Bob Rae, *What's Happened to Politics?* (Toronto: Simon and Schuster, 2015), 8.

31 R. Kenneth Carty, William Cross and Lisa Young, *Rebuilding Canadian Party Politics* (Vancouver: UBC Press, 2000), 185.

32 Herle, "Poll-Driven Politics."

33 Ibid.

34 A. Paul Pross, "Parliamentary Influence and the Diffusion of Power," *Canadian Journal of Political Science* vol. 18, no. 2 (June 1985): 256.

35 Ibid.

36 Herman Bakvis provides an excellent review of the role of regional ministers in his *Regional Ministers: Power and Influence in the Canadian Cabinet* (Toronto: University of Toronto Press, 1991).

37 Mia Rabson, "Trudeau Doing Away with Regional Cabinet Ministers," *Winnipeg Free Press*, 18 November 2015.

38 Consultations with a Government of Canada senior official, Moncton, 10 May 2017.

39 William Cross, "Policy Study and Development in Canada's Political Parties," in *Policy Analysis in Canada: The State of the Art*, ed. Laurent Dobusinskis, Michael Howlett, and David Laycock (Toronto: University of Toronto Press, 2007), 425.

40 Ibid.

41 R. Kenneth Carty and William Cross, "Political Parties and the Practice of Brokerage Politics," in *The Oxford Handbook of Canadian Politics*, ed. John C. Courtney and David E. Smith (Toronto: Oxford University Press, 2010) 204.

42 Robert Young, "Effecting Change: Do We Have the Political System to Get Us Where We Want to Go?" in *Canada at Risk? Canadian Public Policy in the 1990s*, ed. G. Bruce Doern and Byrne B. Purchase (Toronto: C.D. Howe Institute, 1991), 77.

43 Jennifer Lees-Marshment, *Political Marketing: Principles and Applications* (London: Routledge, 2014).

44 Alex Marland, *Brand Command: Canadian Politics and Democracy in the Age of Message Control* (Vancouver: UBC Press, 2016), 3.

45 Ibid., 365.

46 Alex Marland, Anna Lennox Esselment, and Thierry Giasson, "Welcome to Non-Stop Campaigning," in *Permanent Campaigning in Canada*, in ed. Alex Marland, Thierry Giasson, and Anna Lennox Esselment (Vancouver: UBC Press, 2017), 5.

47 Alex Marland, "Political Communication in Canada: Strategies and Tactics," in *Canadian Politics*, ed. James Bickerton and Alain-G. Gagnon (Toronto: University of Toronto Press, 2014), 322.

48 Aaron Wherry, "Every Day is Election Day in Canada," *Maclean's*, 9 January 2012, https://www.macleans.ca/news/canada/every-day-is-now-election-day/.

49 John Swaine, "Donald Trump's Team Defends 'Alternative Facts' after Widespread Protests," *Guardian*, 23 January 2017.

50 David McLaughlin, "In Canada's Damaged Democracy Partisanship Has Taken the Place of Trust," *Globe and Mail*, 25 June 2013, A8.

51 R. Kenneth Carty, "The Shifting Place of Political Parties in Canadian Public Life," *Choices* 12, no. 4 (June 2006): 5 and 9, http://irpp.org/wp-content/uploads/assets/research/strengthening-canadian-democracy/the-shifting-place-of-political-parties-in-canadian-public-life/vol12no4.pdf.

52 William Cross, "Canada: A Challenging Landscape for Political Parties and Civil Society in a Fragmented Polity," in *Federalism, Political Parties and Civil Society*, ed. Klaus Detterbeck, Wolfgang Renzsch, and John Kincaid (Toronto: Oxford University Press, 2015), 71.

53 Alan C. Cairns, *From Interstate to Intrastate Federalism in Canada* (Kingston: Institute of Intergovernmental Relations, paper no. 5, 1979), 5.

54 E.E. Schattschneider, *Party Government* (London: Transaction Publishers, 2009).

55 John Meisel, "The Stalled Omnibus: Canadian Parties in the 1960s," *Social Science Research* vol. 30, no. 3 (Autumn 1963): 370.

56 Canadian Association of Former Parliamentarians, "Survey: The Political Nomination Process in Canada," 8 March 2005, (Ottawa), 2.

57 William Cross, "Candidate Nomination in Canada's Political Parties," in *The Canadian Federal Election of 2006*, ed. Jon H. Pammett and Christopher Dornan (Toronto: Dundurn Press, 2006), 172.

58 Liberal Party of Canada, *Interim National Rules for the Selection of Candidates for the Liberal Party of Canada* (Ottawa: Liberal Party of Canada, ratified 13 September 2016).

59 Conservative Party of Canada, *Candidate Nomination Rules and Procedures* (Ottawa: Conservative Party – Candidate Nomination Rules and Procedures, adopted on 29 October 2017).

60 Graham Fox, *Rethinking Political Parties* (Ottawa: Public Policy Forum – discussion paper, November 2005), 4.

61 Carty, "The Shifting Place of Political Parties in Canadian Public Life," 5.

62 R. Kenneth Carty, *Big Tent Politics: The Liberal Party's Long Mastery of Canada's Public Life* (Vancouver: UBC Press, 2015), 1.

63 Ibid., 30.

64 See Canada, *Elections Canada*, http://www.elections.ca.elections-current-and-past-elections.

65 See, among others, Carty, Young, and Cross, *Rebuilding Canadian Party Politics*.

66 Janine Brodie, *The Political Economy of Canadian Regionalism* (Toronto: Harcourt Brace Jovanovich Canada, 1990), 145.

67 Donald J. Savoie, *Looking for Bootstraps: Economic Development in the Maritimes* (Halifax: Nimbus, 2017).

68 Maurice Duverger, *Political Parties: Their Organization and Activity in the Modern State* (New York: Wiley, 1954).

69 Andrew Coyne, "Harper Made Bigger Mark as Party Leader Than as Prime Minister," *National Post*, 27 May 2016.

70 Carty, "The Shifting Place of Political Parties in Canadian Public Life," 8.

71 Joseph Schull, *Laurier, the First Canadian* (Toronto: Macmillan, 1965).

72 Stephen Clarkson, *The Big Red Machine: How the Liberal Party Dominates Canadian Politics* (Vancouver: UBC Press, 2005), 9 and 10.

73 Donald J. Savoie, chapter 10, in *The Politics of Public Spending in Canada* (Toronto: University of Toronto Press, 1990).

74 Ernest R. Forbes, *Challenging the Regional Stereotype: Essays on the 20th Century Maritimes* (Fredericton: Acadiensis Press, 2012), 174.

75 Ibid., 180.

76 Ibid., 181.

77 Canada, *The Budget Plan: 1999 Including Supplementary Information and Notices of Ways and Means Motions* (Ottawa: Department of Finance, 16 February 1999).

78 Canada, *Budget 2000: Making Canada's Economy More Innovative* (Ottawa: Department of Finance, 28 February 2000).

79 Roger Gibbins, *Prairie Politics and Society: Regionalism in Decline* (Toronto: Butterworths, 1980), 41.

80 See, among others, Terry Milewski, "Stephen Harper's Legacy: Good, Bad and a Dose of Ugly," CBC *News*, 20 October 2015, https://www.cbc.ca/news/politics/canada-election-2015-harper-political-obit-1.3273677.

81 John Ibbitson, "In Wake of Tory Loss, Questions Remain about Harper's Legacy," *Globe and Mail*, 19 October 2015.

82 Consultations with a senior federal public servant, Moncton, 11 October 2016.

83 Jessica Asato makes this point in "Tomorrow's Political Parties," in *Democracy in Britain: Essays in Honour of James Cornford*, ed. Guy Lodge and Glenn Gottfried (London: Institute for Public Policy Research, 2014), 82. For Canadian data, see Martin Turcotte, *Civic Engagement and Political Participation in Canada* (Ottawa: Statistics Canada, 14 September 2015), 8.

CHAPTER EIGHT

1 Kelly Blidook, *Constituency Influence in Parliament: Countering the Centre* (Vancouver: UBC Press, 2012), 2.

2 Gordon Aiken, *The Backbencher: Trials and Tribulations of a Member of Parliament* (Toronto: McClelland and Stewart, 1974); and Pierre Elliott Trudeau, *Memoirs* (Toronto: McClelland and Stewart, 1993), 41.

3 C.E.S. Franks, *The Parliament of Canada* (Toronto: University of Toronto Press, 1987), 79.

4 John Ibbitson, "Few Countries Can Claim Such a Pathetic Parliament," *Globe and Mail*, 8 January 2010.

5 Walter Bagehot, *The English Constitution* (Oxford: Oxford University Press, 2001), 142.

6 Ibid., 159.

7 A. Paul Pross, *Group Politics and Public Policy* (Toronto: Oxford University Press, 1992).

8 Michael M. Atkinson and Paul G. Thomas, "Studying the Canadian Parliament," *Legislative Studies Quarterly* 18, no. 3 (August 1993): 415.

9 Andrew Coyne, preface to *Irresponsible Government: The Decline of Parliamentary Democracy in Canada*, by Brent Rathgeber (Toronto: Dundurn, 2014), 12.

10 Rebecca Lindell, "Backbenchers Point to Less Party Discipline as a Fix for Parliament," *Global News*, 10 February 2013, https://globalnews.ca/news/391008/backbenchers-point-to-less-party-discipline-as-a-fix-for-parliament/.

11 Rathgeber, *Irresponsible Government*, 62.

12 David C. Docherty, *Mr. Smith Goes to Ottawa: Life in the House of Commons* (Vancouver: UBC Press, 1997).

13 See, among others, Donald J. Savoie, *Court Government and the Collapse of Accountability in Canada and the United Kingdom* (Toronto: University of Toronto Press, 2008).

14 Carolyn Bennett, Deborah Grey, and Yves Morin, *The Parliament We Want: Parliamentarians' Views on Parliamentary Reform* (Ottawa: Library of Parliament, 2003), 13.

15 Consultation with a Member of Parliament, 21 October 2016.

16 Frank McKenna made this observation on several occasions during golf games.

17 See, among others, Brian Laghi, "Mulroney Says Leaders Must Take Good Care of Caucus," *Globe and Mail*, 20 August 2002.

18 A Week in the House of Commons, www.parl.gc.ca, n.d.

19 Abbas Rana, "Upcoming Gun Bill 'Scaring the Hell Out of the Liberal Caucus,' and Trudeau's Response to Harvey's Concerns Puts a Chill on Backbenchers, Say Liberals," *Hill Times*, 12 March 2018.

20 Gloria Galloway, "Finance Committee Chair Wayne Easter Denounces His own Government's Rollout of Tax Changes," *Globe and Mail*, 13 September 2017.

21 Joan Bryden, "Liberal Caucus Retreat to Focus on Small Business Tax, Other Hot-Button Topics," *Global News*, 5 September 2017.

22 Sue Bailey, "Trudeau Won't Commit to a Supreme Court Judge from Atlantic Canada," CBC *News*, 15 August 2016, https://www.cbc.ca/news/politics/justin-trudeau-supreme-court-judge-atlantic-canada-1.3721255.

23 Canadian Press, "Atlantic Canada Lawyers Challenge Trudeau on Changes to Supreme Court Appointment Process," CBC *News*, 19 September 2016, https://www.cbc.ca/news/politics/atlantic-lawyers-supreme-court-1.3769108.

24 Peter Cowan, "Ottawa Stripped Atlantic Canada of Inclusion on Supreme Court with Barely a Peep," CBC *News*, 10 August 2016, https://www.cbc.ca/news/canada/newfoundland-labrador/supreme-court-appointments-justin-trudeau-policy-atlantic-canada-1.3713759.

25 Katie Simpson, "MPs Unanimously Support Regional Representation for Supreme Court," CBC *News*, 27 September 2016, https://www.cbc.ca/news/

politics/mps-vote-in-favour-of-regional-representation-scc-custom-
1.3781520.

26 Ibid.

27 Adam Huras, "Updated: War of Words Reignites Debate over Why a
Central Canadian MP Heads ACOA," *Telegraph Journal*, 26 October 2016.

28 Jean-François Godbout and Bjørn Høyland, "The Emergence of Parties in
the Canadian House of Commons (1867–1908)," *Canadian Journal of
Political Science* 46, no. 4 (December 2013): 773–97.

29 F.H. Underhill, "The Development of National Parties in Canada,"
Canadian Historical Review 16, no. 4 (December 1935): 367–75.

30 Jonathan Lemco, "The Fusion of Powers, Party Discipline, and the
Canadian Parliament: A Critical Assessment," *Presidential Studies
Quarterly* 18, no. 2 (Spring 1988): 287.

31 Roman March, *The Myth of Parliament* (Scarborough: Prentice-Hall,
1974), 59.

32 Paul Thomas, "The Role of National Party Caucuses," in *Party
Government and Regional Representation in Canada*, ed. Peter Aucoin
(Toronto: University of Toronto Press, 1985), 81.

33 Godbout and Høyland, "The Emergence of Parties in the Canadian House
of Commons," 773.

34 Michael Ignatieff, *Fire and Ashes: Success and Failure in Politics* (Toronto:
Random House Canada, 2013), 147.

35 Gloria Galloway, "Is Canada's Party Discipline the Strictest in the World?
Experts Say Yes," *Globe and Mail*, 7 February 2013.

36 Blidook, *Constituency Influence in Parliament*, 27.

37 David Kilgour, MP, John Kirsner, and Kenneth McConnell, "Discipline
versus Democracy: Party Discipline in Canadian Politics," published in
Crosscurrents: Contemporary Political Issues, 2nd ed., ed. Mark Charlton
and Paul Barker (Toronto: Nelson, 1994), www.david-kilgour.com/mp/
discipline.htm.

38 Gloria Galloway, "Tory MP Kicked Out of Caucus Over Budget Vote,"
Globe and Mail, 6 June 2007.

39 E. Kaye Fulton, "Nunziata Expelled from Liberal Caucus," in *The
Canadian Encyclopedia*, Canada Historica, 17 March 2003, www.
thecanadianencyclopedia.ca/en/article/
nunziata-expelled-from-liberal-caucus.

40 David Kilgour, "Parliamentary Democracy in Canada" (mimeo, Ottawa,
September 2012), 2.

41 An anonymous reviewer with McGill-Queen's University Press brought
these cases to my attention.

42 "Party Discipline and Free Votes" (Ottawa: Library of Parliament, 2006), 3.

43 Doreen Barrie, "Parliamentary Reform Could be Progress," *Times Colonist*, 12 May 2017, 3.

44 Rafe Mair, "What the UK Can Teach Canada about Democracy," *National Observer*, 9 May 2015.

45 See, for example, Paul E.J. Thomas, "Measuring the Effectiveness of a Minority Parliament," *Canadian Parliamentary Review* 30, no. 1 (Spring 2007): 22–31.

46 Jonathan Malloy, "High Discipline, Low Cohesion? The Uncertain Patterns of Canadian Parliamentary Party Groups," *The Journal of Legislative Studies* vol. 9, no. 4 (Winter 2003): 116–29.

47 I recognize that others may have a different perspective. See, for example, Lemco, "The Fusion of Powers, Party Discipline, and the Canadian Parliament," 283–302.

48 Kilgour, "Parliamentary Democracy in Canada," 2.

49 Ibid.

50 Lemco, "The Fusion of Powers, Party Discipline and the Canadian Parliament," 294.

51 Robert W. Jackman, "Political Parties, Voting and National Integration: The Canadian Case," *Comparative Politics* 4, no. 4 (July 1972): 512.

52 Lemco, "The Fusion of Powers, Party Discipline, and the Canadian Parliament," 289.

53 Anthony Sayers and Andrew Banfield, "The Dispersal of Power in Federal States: Canada and Australia" (mimeo, paper presented to the Canadian Political Science Association Annual General Meeting, 1–3 June 2010, Concordia University, Montreal), 4.

54 Hon. Brian Tobin quoted in William P. Cross, *Political Parties: Canadian Democratic Audit* (Vancouver: UBC Press, 2004), 55.

55 Joan Bryden, "Incumbent Liberals Who Meet New Conditions Won't Have to Face Nomination Challenge," *Globe and Mail*, 28 January 2018.

56 Samara, *'It's My Party': Parliamentary Dysfunction Reconsidered* (Ottawa: Samara, 2011), 6.

57 Robert Marleau, "Legislative Process," *Hill Times* (Ottawa), 18 February 2002.

58 *Appropriations and the Business of Supply* (Ottawa: Library of Parliament, 2004), 7.

59 Robert F. Adie and Paul G. Thomas, *Canadian Public Administration: Problematical Perspectives* (Scarborough: Prentice-Hall, 1980), 141.

60 See, among many others, *The Parliament We Want*.

61 See Laura Ryckewaert, "Hill Journalists Say There's Too Much Government Information Control and Parliament Has Lost Its Power," *Hill Times*, Ontario, 1 March 2014, 5.

62 See, for example, *Meeting the Expectations of Canadians: Review of the Responsibilities and Accountabilities of Ministers and Senior Officials* (Ottawa: Treasury Board Secretariat, 2005), 15.

63 Grant Purves and Jack Stilborn, *Members of the House of Commons: Their Role* (Ottawa: Library of Parliament, 1988), 14, http://publications.gc.ca/Collection-R/LoPBdP/BP/bp56-e.htm.

64 Ibid., 21.

65 Donald J. Savoie, *The Politics of Public Spending in Canada* (Toronto: University of Toronto Press, 1990), preface.

66 Quoted in "Scrutinize Spending Estimates," *Hill Times*, 20 June 2011, 8.

67 Canada, House of Commons, *Debates*, 7 February 1994, 961.

68 Donald J. Savoie, *What Is Government Good At? A Canadian Answer* (Montreal and Kingston: McGill-Queen's University Press, 2015), 66.

69 Lowell Murray, "Souper homage à Donald J. Savoie," speech, Bouctouche, NB, 8 June 2011.

70 See *National Post*, 25 December 2016, https://nationalpost.com/news/over-350-million-spent-to-clean-up-abandoned-mine-in-yukon-and-not-an-inch-has-been-remediated.

71 "140 Years and Counting – History of Department of Finance" (Ottawa: Department of Finance, n.d.).

72 Brian Pagan, "Connecting the Dots between Resources and Results" (paper presented to the CPA Canada Public Sector Conference, November 2016), 6.

73 Mark Schacter, *A Step toward Common Sense* (mimeo, Ottawa, December 2016), 1, https://www.schacterconsulting.com/.

74 *Policy on Results* (Ottawa: Government of Canada, 1 July 2016), www.tbs-sct.gc.cva, 3.1.1, 3.1.2, and 3.2.4.

75 Ibid., 3.2.3.

76 Canada, Treasury Board, C.M. Drury, President, *Planning, Programming, Budgeting Guide*, July 1968.

77 For a discussion on this point, see Donald J. Savoie, *Breaking the Bargain: Public Servants, Ministers and Parliament* (Toronto: University of Toronto Press, 2003).

78 Pagan, "Connecting the Dots between Resources and Results," 3.

79 William Robson, "Government Budgets: Why It's So Difficult to Follow the Money," *Globe and Mail*, 16 April 2016.

80 Doug Hartle, "The Role of the Auditor General of Canada," *Canadian Tax Journal* 23, no. 3 (1975): 197.

81 Savoie, *What Is Government Good At?*

82 Warren Kinsella, "Big Political Graves Are Dug with Tiny Shovels," *Hill Times*, 29 August 2016.

83 Editorial, "When It Comes to the Money That Politicians Spend, We Worry about the Wrong Stuff," *Globe and Mail*, 23 August 2016.

84 David E. Smith, "A Question of Trust: Parliamentary Democracy and Canadian Society," *Canadian Parliamentary Review* 27, no. 1 (Spring 2004): 25.

85 This information was provided to me as a member of the agency's Strategic Review Committee, Moncton, 18 May 2010.

86 Consultations with a senior department official, Ottawa, 20 October 2011.

87 An excellent case in point is the Parliamentary Budget Office established by the Harper government following commitments made in an election campaign. Harper dismissed out of hand advice from Parliament's budget officer as "dumb," and his government launched efforts to restrict the scope of the officer's work. See, among others, "Harper Rejects 'Dumb' Budget Advice," *National Post*, 11 July 2009.

88 Liberal Party of Canada, *Creating Opportunity: The Liberal Plan for Canada (Red Book)*, chapter 6 (Ottawa: Liberal Party of Canada, 1993).

89 Ibid.

90 See, for example, Andrew MacDougall, "Why the Ethics Commissioner Did Wrong by Nigel Wright," *Maclean's*, 26 May 2017, https://www.macleans.ca/politics/ottawa/why-the-ethics-commissioner-did-wrong-by-nigel-wright/.

91 See Sharon Sutherland, "Parliament's Unregulated Control Bureaucracy," *Briefing Notes* (Kingston: Queen's University School of Policy Studies, 2002), 9. It should be noted, however, that the Office of the Auditor General has statutory authority to launch comprehensive or value-for-money audits.

92 "The Woman Who Enraged Voters," *Ottawa Citizen*, 9 June 2004, B1.

93 See "Week of Heavy Job Losses Puts Pressure on Flaherty to Open Stimulus Taps Wider," *Globe and Mail*, 6 February 2009, A1.

94 "Why Canada's Budget Watchdog Is So Good at Dropping the Gloves," *Globe and Mail*, 31 January 2009, F3.

95 "Put Tether on Budget Watchdog, MPs Urge," *Toronto Star*, 17 June 2009.

96 See, for example, "It's Finance Minister Flaherty versus Budget Officer Page," *Hill Times*, 24 October 2011, 1 and 20.

97 "On PBO Reform, Liberals Make the Right Call," *Globe and Mail*, 29
    May 2017.
98 Andrew Coyne, "Bloated, Glossy $212,000 Federal Budget Cover a Fitting
    Symbol of Modern Government," *National Post*, accessed on 8 December
    2017.

CHAPTER NINE

 1 Percy Mockler, "As NAFTA Talks Near Collapse, Scrapping Energy East
    Especially Tragic for New Brunswick," *Telegraph Journal* (Saint John), 4
    November 2017, A12.
 2 Supreme Court of Canada, *Reference re: Legislative Authority of
    Parliament in Relation to the Upper House* [1980], SCR 54 at 10.
 3 Canada, *Reference re Senate Reform*, 2014 SCC32, File no. 35203.
 4 Alan C. Cairns, "From Interstate to Intrastate Federalism in Canada"
    (discussion paper no. 5, Kingston: Institute of Intergovernmental
    Relations, 1979), 5.
 5 "NDP Leader Tom Mulcair Says He'll Seek Mandate for Senate Abolition,"
    CBC News, 10 June 2015, https://www.cbc.ca/news/politics/ndp-leader-
    tom-mulcair-says-he-ll-seek-mandate-for-senate-abolition-1.3107870.
 6 Canada, *Report of the Royal Commission on the Economic Union and
    Development Prospects for Canada*, vol. 2 (Ottawa: Minister of Supply
    and Services Canada, 1985), 72.
 7 "Why the Senate Should Be Abolished," *Maclean's*, 8 March 2013, https://
    www.macleans.ca/politics/why-the-senate-should-be-abolished/.
 8 David C. Docherty, "The Canadian Senate: Chamber of Sober Reflection
    or Loony Cousin Best Not Talked About," *The Journal of Legislative
    Studies* 8, no. 3 (Autumn 2002): 27–8 and 38.
 9 David E. Smith, *Coming to Terms: An Analysis of the Supreme Court
    Ruling on the Senate, 2014* (Toronto: Ryerson University, 2014), 7.
10 See, among others, "Le poids du Québec et le Sénat," *Devoir*, 12 June
    2013.
11 See, among others, Dr. Roger Gibbins and Roger Roach, "Four Arguments
    for Senate Reform in Canada," *Troy Media*, 21 February 2010, www.troy-
    media.com; and "Alberta Says Provinces Must Be Consulted on Senate
    Reform," *Calgary Herald*, 30 August 2013.
12 Quoted in Serge Joyal, ed., *Protecting Canadian Democracy: The Senate
    You Never Knew* (Montreal: McGill-Queen's University Press, 2003).
13 Janet Ajzenstat, "Bicameralism and Canada's Founders: The Origins of the
    Canadian Senate," in ibid., 18.

14 See, among many others, David E. Smith, *The Canadian Senate in Bicameral Perspective* (Toronto: University of Toronto Press, 2003), 114; and "Canada's Senate Speaker Pierre Claude Nolin Dies," *Toronto Star*, 24 April 2015.

15 *Out of the Shadows at Last: Transforming Mental Health, Mental Illness and Addiction Services in Canada* (Ottawa: the Senate, 2006).

16 See, among others, "Mental Health in Canada: Out of the Shadows Forever," CMAJ-JAMC 178, no. 10 (6 May 2008): 1320–2; and "Ten-Year Anniversary of the Kirby Report," *British Columbia Medical Journal* 54, no. 10 (December 2012).

17 Smith, *The Canadian Senate in Bicameral Perspective*, 181.

18 Supreme Court of Canada, *Reference re Senate Reform*, SCC32, File no. 35203 (Ottawa: Supreme Court of Canada, [2014]).

19 John F. Conway, *Debts to Pay: The Future of Federalism in Quebec* (Toronto: James Lorimer, 2004), 154.

20 Éric Grenier, "Canadians Want to Reform or Abolish Senate: Polls," *Globe and Mail*, 30 May 2013.

21 Canada, *Census of British North America*, Statistics Canada, accessed on 12 February 2019, https://www66.statcan.gc.ca/eng/1867/186700160016_The%20Census.pdf.

22 Smith, *The Canadian Senate in Bicameral Perspective*, 4.

23 R.A. Mackay, *The Unreformed Senate of Canada* (Toronto: McClelland and Stewart, 1963), 38.

24 Supreme Court of Canada, *Reference Re: Senate Reform* SSC32, File no. 35203 (Ottawa: Supreme Court of Canada, [2014]), par. 16, 13.

25 Ibid.

26 Ibid.

27 David E. Smith, *The Constitution in a Hall of Mirrors: Canada at 150* (Toronto: University of Toronto Press, 2017), 63.

28 Canada, *Reference Re: Senate Reform*.

29 I am thinking of senators Mike Duffy, Pamela Wallin, Patrick Brazeau, and Andrew Thompson. The latter only attended the Senate forty-seven times over a fourteen-year period, spending most of his time in Mexico. He was subsequently suspended.

30 See, among others, C.E.S. Franks, *The Parliament of Canada* (Toronto: University of Toronto Press, 1987).

31 Smith, *The Canadian Senate in Bicameral Perspective*, 159–60.

32 See MacKay, *The Unreformed Senate of Canada*; and Colin Campbell, *The Canadian Senate: A Lobby from Within* (Toronto: Macmillan, 1978).

33 Canada, *A Future Together – Observations and Recommendations* (Ottawa: Department of Supply and Services, 1979), 97.

34 *Regional Representation: The Canadian Partnership* (Calgary: Canada West Foundation, September 1981).

35 Canada West Foundation, *Re-inventing Parliament … A Conference on Parliamentary Reform*, 25–6 February 1994 (Calgary: Canada West Foundation, 1994), 2.

36 Keith G. Banting, "Royal Commission on Economic Union and Development Prospects for Canada," in *Canadian Encyclopedia*, Historica Canada, 7 February 2006, https://www.thecanadianencyclopedia.ca/en/ article/royal-commission-on-economic-union-and-development-prospects-for-canada.

37 Canada, *Report of the Royal Commission on the Economic Union and Development Prospects for Canada* vol. 3 (Ottawa: Department of Supply and Services, 1985).

38 See Roger Gibbins, "Senate Reform: Always the Bridesmaid, Never the Bride," in Ronald L. Watts and Douglas Brown, eds, *Canada: The State of the Federation 1989* (Kingston, On: Institute of Intergovernmental Relations, 1989), 193–210.

39 Kenneth McRoberts and Patrick Monahan, eds, *The Charlottetown Accord, the Referendum and the Future of Canada* (Toronto: University of Toronto Press, 1993).

40 *Reforming the Senate of Canada: Frequently Asked Questions* (Ottawa: Library of Parliament, 2011).

41 See, for example, *Bill C-7-Senate Reform Act* (Ottawa: The Canadian Bar Association, 2012).

42 Danielle Pinard, "The Canadian Senate: An Upper House Criticized Yet Condemned to Survive Unchanged?," in *A World of Second Chambers: Handbook for Constitutional Studies on Bicameralism*, ed. Luther Jörg, Paola Passaglia, and Rolando Tarchi (Milano: Giuffrè, 2006).

43 Roger Gibbins, "When Pigs Fly?" *Dialogues*, a Canada West Foundation Publication, vol. 2, no. 3 (Summer 2006): 32.

44 Canada, *The Constitution of Canada: A Brief History of Amending Procedure Discussions* (Ottawa: Publications Canada, 1992).

45 See, for example, Claude Bélanger, "Quebec, the Constitution and Special Status," Quebec History, Marianopolis College, 23 August 2000, www. faculty.marianopolis.edu.

46 Howard Cody, "Parliamentary Reform: Some Implications for Western Canada," *American Review of Canadian Studies* 22, no.1 (1992), 11–27.

47 Adam Dodek, "The Politics of the *Senate Reform Reference*: Fidelity, Frustration, and Federal Unilateralism," *McGill Law Journal* 60, no. 4 (2015): 624.

48 Canada, *Reference Re: Senate Reform.*

49 Canada, *Speech from the Throne to Open the First Session*, Thirty-Ninth Parliament of Canada, First Session (4 April 2006).

50 Jane Taber, "Tory Resistance to Senate Reform Puts Harper in Bind, Pollster Says," *Globe and Mail*, 16 June 2011; and consultations with Senator Percy Mockler, various dates.

51 Canadian Press, "Harper Senate Reform Bill Rejected by Quebec Appeal Court," CBC *News*, 24 October 2013, https://www.cbc.ca/news/politics/harper-senate-reform-bill-rejected-by-quebec-appeal-court-1.2223975.

52 Canada, *Reference Re: Senate Reform*, par. 3, 85, 86.

53 Ibid.

54 Ibid.

55 Ibid., par. 4.

56 See, among others, Randall Palmer, "Canada Court Kills Off Government's Senate Reform Plan," Reuters, 24 April 2014, https://ca.reuters.com/article/topNews/idCABREA3O1BN20140425; and "After the Supreme Court Decision is Senate Reform Off the Table?," CBC *News*, 24 July 2015, www.cbc.ca.

57 Emmett Macfarlane, "Did the Supreme Court Just Kill Senate Reform?" *Maclean's*, 25 April 2014, https://www.macleans.ca/politics/did-the-supreme-court-just-kill-senate-reform/.

58 Liberal Party of Canada, *Real Change: A New Plan for a Strong Middle Class* (Ottawa: Liberal Party of Canada, 2015), 29.

59 Canada, *Independent Advisory Board for Senate Appointments*, www.canada.ca, undated.

60 Michael Wernick, the Clerk of the Privy Council, made this observation over dinner in Moncton, New Brunswick, May 2017.

61 Prime Minister Justin Trudeau quoted in "What Do We Do about Fools in the Senate," *iPolitics*, 28 March 2017, www.ipolitics.ca.

62 Peter Zimonjic and Rosemary Barton, "Andrew Scheer Says He Will Not Appoint Independent Senators if Elected Prime Minister," CBC *News*, 28 June 2017, https://www.cbc.ca/news/politics/andrew-scheer-interview-barton-1.4182567.

63 Editorial, "Senate Reform Is No Reform at All, and Could Have Unintended Consequence," *Globe and Mail*, 3 December 2015.

64 Editorial, "Senate Showing Its Undemocratic Side with Delay of Bills," *Globe and Mail*, 29 October 2017.

65 "Le Québec ne veut pas de la réforme du Sénat," *Le Devoir*, 2 June 2007.

66 See, for example, Mylène Crète, "Justin Trudeau: 'on ne rouvre pas la constitution,'" *Presse*, 1 June 2017.

67 Andrew Coyne, "Who Asked for This Kind of Senate Reform?," *National Post*, 14 December 2015.

68 Jesse Kline, "Canada Needs Triple-E Senate Reform," *National Post*, 28 May 2013.

69 Tony Keller, "Mr. Trudeau's FrankenSenate: It's Alive, and It's Dangerous," *Globe and Mail*, 14 June 2017.

70 Canada, "Assessment Criteria – Independent Advisory Board for Senate Appointments," www.canada.ca, n.d.

71 Canada, *Reference Re: Senate Reform*, par. 16.

72 Canada, *Independent Advisory Board for Senate Appointments*, www.canada.ca, undated.

73 Tony Dean, "Senate in Transition: Observations from a Rookie Senator," *Toronto Star*, 3 April 2017.

74 Adam Huras, "Gay N.B. Senator: Dark Facet of Our History Repaired," *Telegraph Journal* (Saint John), 9 February 2018.

75 Gloria Galloway, "Increasingly Independent Senate Injecting Uncertainty into Parliamentary Process," *Globe and Mail*, 4 February 2018.

76 Michael Kirby and Hugh Segal, *A House Undivided: Making Senate Independence Work* (Ottawa: Public Policy Forum, 2016), 2, 7, and 8.

77 Ibid., 15–21.

78 Michael Kirby in conversations with the author, Bradenton, Florida, March 2017.

79 Hugh Segal, "We Can't Return to a Senate Ruled by Partisan Politics," *Globe and Mail*, 27 June 2018, https://www.theglobeandmail.com/opinion/article-we-cant-return-to-a-senate-ruled-by-partisan-politics/.

80 Canada, *Working Sessions on Senate Modernization Report* (Ottawa: Senate, 11 December 2015).

81 The Honourable V. Peter Harder PC, "Complementarity: The Constitutional Role of the Senate of Canada" (Ottawa: The Senate, 12 April 2018), 5 and 6.

82 "FAQs about Government Representation in a Changing Senate," 10 November 2017, https://senate-gro.ca/senate-renewal/faqs-government-representation-changing-senate/.

83 Marie-Danielle Smith, "Six-Fold Increase in Senate Lobbying under Trudeau, with Independents Taking Most Meetings," *National Post*, 22 January 2018.

84 Paul G. Thomas, "The 'New' Improved Senate," *Policy Options*, 26 January 2018.

85 Zimonjic and Barton, "Andrew Scheer Says He Will Not Appoint Independent Senators if Elected Prime Minister."

86 Quoted in Kirby and Segal, *A House Undivided*, 14.

87 Editorial, "It Gets Large-H Harder to Say Just What the Senate's For," *Globe and Mail*, 5 May 2016.

88 Dean, "Senate in Transition."

89 Docherty, "The Canadian Senate," 38.

90 Andrew Coyne, "Our Unelected Senate Has No Business Rewriting Federal Budgets," *National Post*, 12 June 2017.

91 See, for example, Senator Diane Bellemare, "Let's Adopt a Sober Second Thought Checklist," 3 November 2017, https://senate-gro.ca/senate-renewal/lets-adopt-sober-second-thought-checklist-senator-bellemare/.

92 Douglas C. North, "Economic Performance through Time," *American Economic Review* 84, no. 3 (June 1994): 361.

93 Brian Lee Crowley makes this point in "Canada Needs a Senate and Our Senate Needs To Be Fixed. Here's How," *National Post*, 10 June 2015.

94 Donald Dennison, a former deputy minister of Intergovernmental Affairs in New Brunswick, wrote this in a memo to me dated 22 February 2013.

CHAPTER TEN

1 Jean Blondel, "Cabinet Government and Cabinet Ministers," in *The Profession of Government Minister in Western Europe*, ed. Jean Blondel and Jean-Louis Thiébault (London: Palgrave Macmillan, 1991).

2 Walter Bagehot, *The English Constitution*, 2nd ed. (Boston: Little, Brown and Company, 1873), 67.

3 Ibid., 53.

4 See, for example, Ian Brodie, former chief of staff to Prime Minister Stephen Harper in *At the Centre of Government: The Prime Minister and the Limits on Political Power* (Montreal: McGill-Queen's University Press, 2018).

5 Chris Hall, "Justin Trudeau Begins His Bold Experiment in 'Government by Cabinet,'" *CBC News*, 5 November 2015, https://www.cbc.ca/news/politics/government-cabinet-chris-hall-1.3304812.

6 Ryan Maloney, "At Different Pressers, Trudeau Fields Questions for His Finance Minister, While Scheer Ends Things Abruptly," *Huffington Post* (Canada), 16 October 2017.

7 See, among others, Donald J. Savoie, *The Politics of Public Spending in Canada* (Toronto: University of Toronto Press, 1990), 189–93.

8 Alex Marland, "Studying Message Control in Canadian Politics and Beyond" (presentation to the Atlantic Provinces Political Science Association, Moncton, NB, 12 October 2017).

9 Doug Saunders, "The World Needs Canada Back in the Democracy Export Business," *Globe and Mail*, 29 December 2017.

10 See, for example, Éric Grenier, "Post-Election Polls Suggest Reasons behind Trudeau Win," CBC *News*, 23 October 2015, https://www.cbc.ca/news/politics/grenier-election-poll-change-oct24-1.3286044.

11 See, for example, Eric Andrew-Gee, "How the Trudeau Liberals Won a Majority in the 2015 Federal Election," *Globe and Mail*, 30 October 2015.

12 Patrice Dutil, *Prime Ministerial Power in Canada: Its Origins under Macdonald, Laurier, and Borden* (Vancouver: UBC Press, 2017).

13 John Boyko, "Seeking Stephen Harper Historically," *Globe and Mail*, 27 August 2013.

14 See, for example, Michael Foley, *The British Presidency* (Manchester: Manchester University Press, 2000).

15 Alan C. Cairns, *From Interstate to Intrastate Federalism in Canada* (Kingston: Institute of Intergovernmental Relations, 1979), 6.

16 The term "big beasts" of Cabinet was coined in Britain to identify ministers who were "unsackable." See, for example, "Executives – Prime Minister, Cabinet and the Core Executive," Ashbourne College, Government and Politics, n.d., 1, www.ashbournecollege.co.uk.

17 See Herman Bakvis, *Regional Ministers: Power and Influence in the Canadian Cabinet* (Toronto: University of Toronto Press, 1991).

18 Elizabeth Thompson, "Trudeau Government Sets New Record for Vacant Appointments," CBC *News*, 1 December 2017, https://www.cbc.ca/news/politics/trudeau-appointments-government-jobs-1.4427307.

19 "Trudeau Commits to Largest Infrastructure Investment in Canadian History," 27 August 2015, https://www.liberal.ca/trudeau-commits-to-largest-infrastructure-investment-in-canadian-history/; and Jordan Press, "Bill Morneau Wants Slow and Steady Approach to Infrastructure Funding," *Globe and Mail*, 24 March 2017.

20 See, for example, Donald J. Savoie, *Governing from the Centre: The Concentration of Power in Canadian Politics* (Toronto: University of Toronto Press, 1999).

21 R.M. Punnett, *The Prime Minister in Canadian Government and Politics* (Toronto: Macmillan, 1977), 75.

22 See, among others, "Span of Control," *The Economist*, 9 November 2009, https://www.economist.com/news/2009/11/09/span-of-control.

23 Elliott Jaques, *Requisite Organization: A Total System for Effective Managerial Organization and Managerial Leadership for the 21st Century* (Arlington: Cason Hall, 1996), 97.

24 David Mulroney, "Trudeau's China Setback Was a Self-Inflicted Wound," *Globe and Mail*, 6 December 2017.

25 Gordon Robertson, "The Changing Role of the Privy Council Office," *Canadian Public Administration* 14, no. 4 (Winter 1971): 497.

26 Canada, *Responsibility in the Constitution* (Ottawa: Privy Council Office, 1993).

27 Gordon Robertson, *Memoirs of a Very Civil Servant: Mackenzie King to Pierre Trudeau* (Toronto: University of Toronto Press, 2000).

28 Trudeau quoted in George Radwanski, *Trudeau* (Toronto: Macmillan, 1978), 146.

29 Tom Kent, *A Public Purpose: An Experience of Liberal Opposition and Canadian Government* (Montreal: McGill-Queen's University Press, 1988), 225.

30 Peter Aucoin, "Organizational Change in the Machinery of Canadian Government: From Rational Management to Brokerage Politics," *Canadian Journal of Political Science* 19, no. 1 (March 1986): 22.

31 Richard Brennan, "Gomery Challenges Harper and the All-Powerful PMO," *Toronto Star*, 14 March 2008.

32 Staff, "8 of the Most Scathing Quotes about the Former PMO in the Duffy Judgement," CTV *News*, 22 April 2016, https://www.ctvnews.ca/politics/8-of-the-most-scathing-quotes-about-the-former-pmo-in-the-duffy-judgment-1.2870429.

33 See David Johnson, *Thinking Government: Public Administration and Politics in Canada* (Toronto: University of Toronto Press, 2011).

34 Quoted in Charlie Gillis, "The Case for Decentralizing Power in the PMO," *Maclean's*, 18 September 2015, https://www.macleans.ca/politics/ottawa/the-case-for-decentralizing-power-in-the-pmo/.

35 Michael Barber et al., *Deliverology 101: A Field Guide for Educational Leaders* (London: Sage Publications, 2011).

36 Kathryn May, "Delivering the Goods: Why Matthew Mendelsohn is Trudeau's Go-To Guy," *Ottawa Citizen*, 15 January 2016.

37 Savoie, *The Politics of Public Spending in Canada*.

38 See, for example, Allan M. Maslove, "Budgetary Process," in *Canadian Encyclopedia*, Historica Canada, 6 February 2006, https://www.thecanadianencyclopedia.ca/en/article/budgetary-process.

39 Adam Radwanski, "Trudeau's 'Deliverology' on the Verge of Becoming Punchline," *Globe and Mail*, 17 November 2017.

40 Aaron Wherry, "How Justin Trudeau Plans to Deliver on 'Deliverology,'" CBC *News*, 27 August 2016, https://www.cbc.ca/news/politics/ wherry-trudeau-deliverology-1.3735890.

41 See, for example, Radwanski, "Trudeau's 'Deliverology' on the Verge of Becoming a Punchline."

42 François Petry, "To What Extent Do Parties Fulfill Their Campaign Promises?" (mimeo, Quebec: Laval University, n.d.); and Aaron Wherry, "Promises, Promises: The Liberals Made a Lot, Maybe too Many," CBC *News*, 16 November 2017, https://www.cbc.ca/news/politics/ liberals-trudeau-promises-tracker-analysis-wherry-1.4401614.

43 Treasury Board of Canada Secretariat, www.Canada.ca, n.d.

44 Richard French, "Trudeau's Challenge: Turning Promises into Policy," *Globe and Mail*, 20 July 2016, A11.

45 Canada, "Departmental Plan 2017–18 for central agencies," 2017, https:// www.canada.ca/en/public-service-commission/services/publications/2017- 18-departmental-plan.html.

46 See, for example, Maslove, "Budgetary Process."

47 Savoie, *Governing from the Centre*.

48 "Trudeau PMO Tightening Control over Ministerial Staffing, 'Identical' to Harper Approach, Says Ex-Liberal MP," *Hill Times*, 25 October 2017.

49 Ibid.

50 Philippe Lagassé, "The Crown and Prime Ministerial Power," *Canadian Parliamentary Review* 39, no. 2 (June 2016): 22.

51 Mark Bevir and R.A.W. Rhodes, "Prime Ministers, Presidentialism and Westminster Smokescreens," *Political Studies* 54, no. 4 (2006): 671–90.

52 Ibid.

53 Don Russell, "The Role of Executive Government in Australia," papers on Parliament no 41 (Canberra: Parliament of Australia, December 2003), 2.

54 See chapters 5, 7, and 8 in Carl Dahlström, B. Guy Peters, and Jon Pierre eds., *Steering from the Centre: Strengthening Political Control in Western Democracies* (Toronto: University of Toronto Press, 2011).

55 Canada, *The Role and Structure of the Privy Council Office* (Ottawa: Privy Council Office, October 1997), 1.

56 See the mandate discussion in Canada, *Privy Council Office 1997–98 Estimates*.

57 Sharon Sutherland, "The Role of the Clerk of the Privy Council," in *Restoring Accountability – Research Studies*, vol. 3 (Ottawa: Commission

of Inquiry into the Sponsorship Program and Advertising Activities, 2006), 65.

58 Senator Lowell Murray, "Power, Responsibility and Agency in Canadian Government," in *Governing: Essays in Honour of Donald J. Savoie*, ed. James Bickerton and B. Guy Peters (Montreal: McGill-Queen's University Press, 2013), 27; and Janice Gross Stein and Eugene Lang, *The Unexpected War: Canada in Kandahar* (Toronto: Viking Canada Press, 2007), 2.

59 Jean Chrétien, *Straight from the Heart* (Toronto: Key Porter, 1994), 85.

60 Abbas Rana et al., "The List: The Top 100 Most Powerful and Influential People in Federal Government and Politics in 2018," *Hill Times*, 8 January 2018, 14.

61 John Ibbitson, "Trudeau's Shuffle Reveals Two Truths about Liberal Cabinet," *Globe and Mail*, 29 August 2017.

62 Canada, Robert Marleau, and Camille Montpetit, eds, "Responsible Government and Ministerial Responsibility," in *House of Commons Procedure and Practice*, 2nd ed. (Ottawa: House of Commons, 2009), http://www.ourcommons.ca/procedure-book-livre/Document. aspx?sbdid=73cc891e-0676-4773-850b-ccdcb472ad8c&sbpid=be842475-5632-4969-835b-fc015ce50169#.

63 Felicity Matthews, "The Coalitioninsing of Collective Responsibility," a paper prepared for the Annual PSA Conference, 14–16 April 2014, Department of Politics, University of Sheffield, 1.

64 Nicholas D'Ombrain, "Cabinet Secrecy," *Canadian Public Administration* 47, no. 3 (Fall 2004): 334.

65 Bryce to St-Laurent, 14 June 1957, quoted in ibid., 353.

66 See *Confidences of the Queen's Privy Council for Canada (Cabinet Confidences)*, undated, https://www.canada.ca/en/treasury-board-secretariat/services/access-information-privacy/privacy/confidences-queen-privy-council-canada-cabinet-confidences. html.

67 Canada, The Governor General of Canada, "Oaths of Office," n.d., http://www.gg.ca/document.aspx?id=316.

68 D'Ombrain, "Cabinet Secrecy," 333.

69 Tonda MacCharles, "Tory Minister Quits over Quebec Vote," *Toronto Star*, 28 November 2006, A1.

70 David E. Smith, "Clarifying the Doctrine of Ministerial Responsibility as it Applies to the Government and Parliament of Canada," in *Restoring Accountability* – Research Studies, vol.1, *Parliament, Ministers and Deputy Ministers*, Commission of Inquiry into the Sponsorship Program

and Advertising Activities, (Ottawa: Public Works and Government Services, 2006), 111.

71 D'Ombrain, "Cabinet Secrecy," 352.

72 Ibid., 352–3.

73 Ibid.

74 Richard Dicerni made this observation at a luncheon in Ottawa when he was deputy minister of industry in 2011.

75 Alpheus Todd, *On Parliamentary Government in England: Its Origin, Development, and Practical Operation* (London: Longmans, Green, 1889), 130–40.

76 See, for example, W.T. Stanbury, *Accountability to Citizens in the Westminster Model of Government: More Myth Than Reality* (Vancouver: The Fraser Institute, February 2003), 8.

77 Savoie, *Governing from the Centre.*

CHAPTER ELEVEN

1 "Yes, I'd Lie to You," *The Economist,* 10 September 2016.

2 Jacob Schroeder, Tyler Sommers, Dana Wagner, "365 Days of Lies: The Year in Canadian Political Claptrap," *iPolitics,* 4 January 2016, https://ipolitics.ca/2016/01/04/365-days-of-lies-the-year-in-canadian-political-claptrap/.

3 See in general www.factscan.ca, 2015.

4 "Word of the Year 2016 Is …," in "Word of the Year", *English Oxford Living Dictionaries,* n.d., https://en.oxforddictionaries.com/word-of-the-year/word-of-the-year-2016.

5 Ibid.

6 Lawrence Martin, "Canada's Media: A Crisis that Cries Out for a Public Inquiry," *Globe and Mail,* 2 February 2016, F2.

7 Doris Graber, "The Media and Democracy: Beyond Myths and Stereotypes," *Annual Review of Political Science* 6, no. 2, (June 2003): 139–60.

8 Alexis de Tocqueville, *Democracy in America, Volume II,* ed. Bruce Erohnen (Boston: John Allyn), 401.

9 Natalie Fenton, "Drowning or Waving? New Media, Journalism and Democracy," in *New Media, Old News: Journalism and Democracy in the Digital Age,* ed. Natalie Fenton (London: Sage, 2010), 1.

10 Quoted in "Democracy Warning as Canadian Media Outlets Merge and Papers Close," *Guardian,* 23 February 2016.

11 Ted McAllister, *Liberty and a Free Press* (Princeton: Witherspoon Institute, 2012), 2.

12 See, among others, Richard L. Kaplan, *Politics and the American Press: The Rise of Objectivity, 1865–1920* (Cambridge: Cambridge University Press, 2002).

13 "The Future of Canadian Journalism," *Policy Options*, 23 January 2017.

14 James Boylan, *Pulitzer's School: Columbia University's School of Journalism, 1903–2003* (New York: Columbia University Press, 2003).

15 See, among others, Andrew Osler, "The Beginnings of Communication Studies in Canada: Royal Commissions, Journalism, and Communication Studies," *Canadian Journal of Communication*, 25, no. 1 (2000).

16 For an excellent overview of the study of journalism in Canada, see Osler, "The Beginnings of Communication Studies in Canada."

17 Charlie Beckett, *SuperMedia: Saving Journalism So It Can Save the World* (London: Wiley-Blackwell, 2008).

18 Nic Newman, quoted in Jennifer Alejandro, *Journalism in the Age of Social Media* (Oxford: Reuters Institute for Study of Journalism, 2010), 26.

19 Ibid., 6.

20 F. Christopher Arterton asked this question with respect to cable television in his book *Teledemocracy: Can Technology Protect Democracy?* (London: Sage, 1987), 7.

21 Madelaine Drohan, *Does Serious Journalism Have a Future in Canada?* (Ottawa: Public Policy Forum, 2016), 5.

22 Edward Greenspon quoted in Dean Beeby, "Squeeze Cash from Facebook, Google, Say Canadian News Media Leaders," CBC *News*, 11 January 2017,https://www.cbc.ca/news/politics/newspapers-news-media-digital-public-policy-forum-google-facebook-tax-1.3929356.

23 Canadian Press, "National Post to Eliminate Monday Print Edition," CBC *News*,19June2017,https://www.cbc.ca/news/business/national-post-monday-1.4167247.

24 Email from Phillip Crawley to J.W. "Bud" Bird, 24 August 2017. Mr Bird made the email available.

25 Sean Speer and Jamil Jivani, "The Urban/Rural Divide and a More Inclusive Canada," *Policy Options*, 5 June 2017, 5.

26 Bob Cox, Jerry Dias, and Edward Greenspon, "Journalism Matters More than Ever. We Need Help to Save It," *Globe and Mail*, 14 September 2017.

27 Michael Den Tandt, "Do Something, or We'll Have the CBC – and Nothing Else," www.thenationalpost.com, 2 October 2016.

28 "Postmedia to Cut *National Post*'s Monday Print Edition," www.theglobeandmail.com/report-on-business, 19 June 2017.

29 Allan R. Gregg, "What Canadians Think of the News Media," *Policy Options*, 10 February 2017.

30 Sébastien Charlton and Colette Brin, "Traditional Media Still Most Trusted," Policy Options, 22 June 2017, 3.

31 Andrew Potter, "De-institutionalization, Fake News and the Crisis of Journalism," *Policy Options*, 6 February 2017, 2.

32 Ibid.

33 Ibid., 3.

34 Barend Lutz and Pierre du Toit, *Defining Democracy in a Digital Age: Political Support on Social Media* (New York: Palgrave Macmillan, 2014).

35 "Do Social Media Threaten Democracy?" *The Economist*, 4 November 2017.

36 Edward Greenspon, "Shoring Up the Civic Function of Journalism in Canada," Policy Options, 26 January 2017, 3.

37 See, among others, "Morneau's Update Bolsters Struggling Media with $66M in Tax Measures," CBC *News*, 21 November 2018, https://www.cbc.ca/news/politics/news-industry-economic-update-1.4915113.

38 "Washington Gunman Motivated by Fake News 'Pizzagate' Conspiracy," *Guardian*, 5 December 2016.

39 Andrew Liptak, "Mark Zuckerberg Outlines How Facebook Will Tackle Its Fake News Problem," *The Verge*, 19 November 2016; and Samuel Burke, "Zuckerberg Will Develop Tools to Fight Fake News," CNN Business, 19 November 2016; and Michael Nunez, "Facebook's Fight Against Fake News Was Undercut by Fear of Conservative Backlash," GIZMODO, 14 November 2016.

40 David Ingram, "Facebook to Overhaul Policy on Political Adverts after Regulation Threats," *Independent*, 22 September 2017.

41 "Read the Full Transcript of President Obama's Farewell Speech," *Los Angeles Times*, 10 January 2017, https://www.latimes.com/politics/la-pol-obama-farewell-speech-transcript-20170110-story.html.

42 "Bagehot – Get Stuffed," *The Economist*, 22 July 2017, 46.

43 Brad Lavigne, "The Whole New Ballgame of Social Media," *Policy* magazine, January/February 2015, http://www.policymagazine.ca/pdf/11/PolicyMagazineJanuaryFebruary-2015-Lavigne.pdf.

44 Taylor Owen, "Is Facebook a Threat to Democracy?," *Globe and Mail*, 19 October 2017.

45 Roberto Coloma quoted in Alejandro, Journalism in the Age of Social Media.

46 Daniel McHardie, "How the Media Influences Public Policy: A Case Study on the New Brunswick Government's Failed Attempt to Sell NB Power" (master's thesis, University of New Brunswick, 2014), 27.

47 Fenton, "Drowning or Waving?," 7.

48 Barrie Gunter, *News and the Net* (Mahwah: Lawrence Erlbaum, 2003).

49 Pinar Gurleyen and Robert A. Hackett, "Who Needs Objectivity? Journalism in Crisis, Journalism for Crisis," *Journalism in Crisis: Bridging Theory and Practice for Democratic Media Strategies in Canada*, ed. Mike Gasher et al. (Toronto: University of Toronto Press, 2016), 9.

50 See, for example, Chris Atton, *An Alternative Internet: Radical Media, Politics and Creativity* (Edinburgh: Edinburgh University Press, 2004).

51 For an excellent review of the issues, see Helen Margetts, Peter John, Scott Hale, and Taha Yasseri, *Political Turbulence: How Social Media Shape Collective Action* (Princeton: Princeton University Press, 2016).

52 Phil Howard, "Is Social Media Killing Democracy?," Culture Digitally, 14 November 2016.

53 Andy Blatchford, "Canadian at Centre of Facebook Data Scandal Cut Political Teeth with Liberals," CBC *News*, 19 March 2018, https://www.cbc.ca/news/politics/christopher-wylie-canada-libeals-cambridge-analytica-1.4582190.

54 "Do Social Media Threaten Democracy?" *The Economist*, 4 November 2017, 11.

55 Amanda Clarke, *Social Media, Volume 4: Political Uses and Implications for Representative Democracy*, Publication no. 2010-10-E (Ottawa: Library of Parliament, 22 March 2010), 8.

56 Ibid., 3.

57 Tom Flanagan, "Will Social Media Change Canadian Politics? Hasn't Happened Yet," *Globe and Mail*, 6 May 2013.

58 See, for example, Chantal Hébert, "Trump, Meet Trudeau, King of the Selfie: Hébert," *Toronto Star*, 23 January 2017.

59 Jason Fekete, "Liberals Have Spent More on Facebook Ads than Total Amount Spent between 2006 and 2014," *National Post*, 10 October 2016.

60 R. Aiello, "Trudeau Government Spent $13.6M on Sponsored Social Media," CTV *News*, 25 September 2017, https://www.ctvnews.ca/politics/trudeau-government-spent-13-6m-on-sponsored-social-media-1.3607104.

61 Paul Adams quoted in Bruce Campion-Smith, "Federal Budget Fails to Provide Real Help to Canadian Media, Industry Officials Warn," *Toronto Star*, 27 February 2018.

62 Dhruva Jaishankar, "Brexit: The First Major Casualty of Digital Democracy," Brookings, 29 June 2016.

63 Bruce Anderson and David Coletto, "Newspapers in Peril: Canadians Unworried," Abacus Data, 16 June 2017, 7.

64 Ibid., accessed 18 October 2017.

65 Esther Dyson, "Imagining the Internet," in Eli Pariser, *The Filter Bubble: How the New Personalized Web Is Changing What We Read and How We Think* [e-book] (London: Penguin, 2001), n.p.

66 Richard H. Howe, "Max Weber's Elective Affinities: Sociology within the Bounds of Pure Reason," *American Journal of Sociology* 84, no. 2 (September 1978): 366–85.

67 Philip Howard, "Is Social Media Killing Democracy?" (video of inaugural lecture, Oxford Internet Institute, 15 June 2017).

68 Boryana Ilyova, "Social Media: Do They Enhance or Erode Democracy?" American University in Bulgaria, Spring 2017, 2–3.

69 See, for example, Omidyar Group, "Is Social Media a Threat to Democracy?," 1 October 2017, https://www.omidyargroup.com/wp-content/uploads/2017/10/Social-Media-and-Democracy-October-5-2017.pdf.

70 Christopher Weare, "The Internet and Democracy: The Causal Links between Technology and Politics," *International Journal of Public Administration* 25, no. 5 (2002): 662.

71 Justin Lewis, "Democratic or Disposable? 24-Hour News, Consumer Culture, and Built-in Obsolescence," in *The Rise of 24-Hour News Television: Global Perspectives*, ed. Stephen Cushion and Justin Lewis (New York: Peter Lang, 2010), 86–7.

72 Brenda O'Neill, "The Media's Role in Shaping Canadian Civic and Political Engagement," *The Canadian Political Science Review* 3, no. 2 (June 2009): 105–27.

73 I owe the term "brand ambassadors" to Alex Marland at Memorial University.

74 Adam Radwanski, "Why Trudeau Has Incentive to Go Easy on Quebec's Controversial Niqab Law," *Globe and Mail*, 25 October 2017.

75 Fenton, "Drowning or Waving?," 9.

76 Rodney Tiffen, "The Media and Democracy: Reclaiming an Intellectual Agenda," in *Not Just Another Business: Journalists, Citizens, and the Media*, ed. J. Shultz (Leichhardt: Pluto Press, 1994), 64.

77 See, among others, Gary Mason, "Our political discourse has become belligerent, cynical and un-Canadian," *Globe and Mail*, 16 October 2015.

78 David Taras and Christopher Waddell, eds, *How Canadians Communicate IV: Media and Politics* (Edmonton: Athabasca University Press, 2012), 111.

79 John McCoy and David Jones, "Look Beyond Trump to Explain the Rise of Right Wing Extremist," *Globe and Mail*, 17 August 2017.

80 Majid Khosravinik, "Right Wing Populism in the West: Social Media Discourse and Echo Chambers," Commentary, *Insight Turkey* 27, no. 3 (2017): 63.

81 Barbara Perry and Ryan Scrivens, *Right Wing Extremism in Canada: An Environmental Scan* (Toronto: University of Ontario Institute of Technology, 2015), 45–51.

82 News Staff, "Demise of Sun News Not Due to Canadian Tastes: Bureau Chief," City*News* (Toronto), 14 February 2015.

83 Quoted in ibid.

84 James Bradshaw, "Five Fatal Flaws that Led to Sun News Network's Demise," *Globe and Mail*, 13 February 2015.

85 Tabatha Southey, "Some Conservatives Have Denounced The Rebel. What Took So Long?" *Globe and Mail*, 25 August 2017.

86 For an in-depth review of The Rebel, see "Inside Rebel Media," *National Post*, 21 August 2017.

87 Catherine Cullen, "Conservatives Name Former Rebel Media Director as 2019 Campaign Chair," CBC *News*, 17 October 2017, https://www.cbc.ca/news/politics/hamish-marshall-andrew-scheer-conservative-campaign-1.4358811.

88 Aaron Wherry, "Andrew Scheer Won't Grant Interviews to The Rebel under Current 'Editorial Direction,'" CBC *News*, 17 August 2017, https://www.cbc.ca/news/politics/andrew-scheer-rebel-interviews-1.4251070.

89 Quoted in "Inside Rebel Media," *National Post*, 21 August 2017.

90 Stephen G. Tomblin, *Ottawa and the Outer Provinces: The Challenge of Regional Integration in Canada* (Toronto: Lorimer, 1995), 16.

91 Quoted in Philip Resnick, *The Politics of Resentment: British Columbia Regionalism and Canadian Unity* (Vancouver: UBC Press, 2000), 28.

92 Harry Bruce, *Down Home: Notes of a Maritime Son* (Toronto: Key Porter Books, 1988).

93 Jeffrey Simpson, "The Truth about Atlantic Canada's Economy," *Globe and Mail*, 20 June 2001, A7.

94 Jeff Flake made this point in his speech announcing that he would not run again for the Senate. See "Full Transcript: Jeff Flake's Speech on the Senate Floor," *New York Times*, 24 October 2017.

95 Brian D. Loader and Dan Mercea, "Networking Democracy? Social Media Innovations in Participatory Politics," *Information, Communication and Society* 14, no. 6 (2011): 762.

96 Allan Levine, *Scrum Wars: The Prime Ministers and the Media* (Toronto: Dundurn Press, 1996).

97 M.J. Crockett, "Modern Outrage Is Making It Harder to Better Society," *Globe and Mail*, 2 March 2018.

98 Deborah Coyne, "Does Social Media Save or Sour Politics?" *Huffington Post* (Canada), 23 November 2013.

99 Peter Dahlgren, *Media and Political Engagement: Citizens, Communication and Democracy* (Cambridge: Cambridge University Press, 2009).

100 Andrew Chadwick, *The Hybrid Media System: Politics and Power*, 2nd ed. (Oxford: Oxford University Press, 2017).

101 Herbert A. Simon quoted in "How the World Was Trolled," *The Economist*, 4 November 2017, 20.

102 John Bercow, "Representative Democracy in a Digital Age: Fact or Fiction?," http://www.parliament.uk/business/commons/the-speaker/speeches/speeches/representative-democracy-in-a-digital-age, accessed 11 December 2017.

103 Gillian Wong Miswardi, "Digital Media: A Double-Edged Sword for Representative Democracy," (mimeo, IDEA Essay Prize Winner, 2017), 16.

104 O'Neill, "The Media's Role in Shaping Canadian Civic and Political Engagement," 121.

CHAPTER TWELVE

1 See, among many others, Donald J. Savoie, *Breaking the Bargain: Public Servants, Ministers and Parliament* (Toronto: University of Toronto Press, 2003).

2 See, among many others, a series of articles under the heading "Phoenix Falling," CBC *News*, 24 October 2017, https://www.cbc.ca/news/canada/topic/Tag/Phoenix%20Falling.

3 See, among others, Donald J. Savoie, *Thatcher, Reagan, Mulroney: In Search of a New Bureaucracy* (Pittsburgh: University of Pittsburgh Press, 1994).

4 See, for example, Susan Delacourt, "The Harper Government vs. the Public Servants," *Toronto Star*, 12 July 2013, A6.

5 Derek Bok, "A Daring and Complicated Strategy," *Harvard Magazine*, May–June 1989, 49.

6 Max Weber, *The Theory of Social and Economic Organization* (New York: Oxford University Press, 1947), 333–7.

7 See, among others, Savoie, *Breaking the Bargain*.

8 Bernard Schaffer, *The Administrative Factor* (London: Frank Cass, 1973).

9 See, for example, Donald J. Savoie, *The Politics of Public Spending in Canada* (Toronto: University of Toronto Press, 1990).

10 Richard Crossman, *The Diaries of a Cabinet Minister*, 3 vols (New York: Holt, Rinehart and Winston, 1976).

11 Savoie, *Thatcher, Reagan, Mulroney.*

12 See, among others, Hugo Young and Anne Sloman, *No, Minister: An Inquiry into the Civil Service* (London: British Broadcasting Corporation, 1982), 19.

13 See, among many others, Christopher Pollitt and Geert Bouckaert, *Public Management Reform: A Comparative Analysis*, 3rd ed. (Oxford: Oxford University Press, 2011).

14 Flora MacDonald, "The Minister and the Mandarins," *Policy Options* 1, no. 3 (September–October 1980), 29–31.

15 Savoie, *The Politics of Public Spending in Canada*, 144.

16 Paul Martin shared this very observation with me while I consulted him in Ottawa in January 1998 for my book *Governing from the Centre*.

17 Quoted in Susan Delacourt, "Tory Government Takes Aim at Bureaucracy," *Toronto Star*, 17 January 2008.

18 See, among others, Jeffrey Simpson, "From Census to Wireless: A Lesson in Intransigence," *Globe and Mail*, 14 September 2013.

19 Quoted in Delacourt, "The Harper Government vs the Public Servants."

20 Andrew Griffith, "Resetting Citizenship and Multiculturalism," *Optimum Online* 43, no. 2, June 2013.

21 Based on conversations with Richard Saillant, a former director general at Industry Canada, various dates.

22 Consultations with a senior federal government official, 10 May 2016, Halifax.

23 See, for example, Richard A. Harris and Sidney Milkis, *The Politics of Regulatory Change: A Tale of Two Agencies* (New York: Oxford University Press, 1996).

24 Ruth Hubbard, "Performance, Not Model Employer," *Optimum Online* 43, no. 2, June 2013.

25 Treasury Board Secretariat, *Expenditure Review of Federal Public Sector Compensation* (Ottawa: Treasury Board Secretariat, 2007), 15–24.

26 Mark Bevir, *Governance: A Very Short Introduction* (Oxford: Oxford University Press, 2012), 73.

27 Bob Plamondon, "Look in the Mirror, MPs, Before Reforming Pensions," *Globe and Mail*, 3 January 2012.

28 Michael Staples, "Disgusted: Ex-Sears Worker Fuming over Pension Hit," *Telegraph Journal* (Saint John), 22 June 2018.

29 Daniel Tencer, "Trudeau Suggests E.I. for Sears Workers Who Risk Losing Pensions," *Huffington Post* (Canada), 25 January 2018.

30 See, for example, Charlie Spierling, "Steve Bannon Details Trump Agenda: Deconstruction of the Administrative State," Breitbart, 23 February 2017.

31 See Peter Aucoin, "New Political Governance in Westminster Systems: Impartial Public Administration and Management Performance at Risk," Governance, 25, no. 2 (April 2012), 178.

32 Gordon Robertson, Memoirs of a Very Civil Servant (Toronto: University of Toronto Press, 2001), 38.

33 A.W. Johnson, "The Role of the Deputy Minister," Canadian Public Administration 4, no. 4 (1961): 363.

34 Ibid.

35 See Savoie, The Politics of Public Spending, and David Good [incomplete?]

36 Peter Aucoin, Introduction: Restructuring the Canadian Government (mimeo, Ottawa: Canadian Centre for Management Development, 1995), 5.

37 Ezra Suleiman, Dismantling Democratic States (Princeton: Princeton University Press, 2005), 34.

38 See, among many others, Savoie, Thatcher, Reagan and Mulroney.

39 David Osborne and Ted Gaebler, Reinventing Government: How the Entrepreneurial Spirit Is Transforming the Public Sector (Boston: Addison-Wesley, 1992).

40 Savoie, Thatcher, Reagan, Mulroney.

41 See, for example, Jerome B. McKinney and Lawrence C. Howard, Public Administration: Balancing Power and Accountability (London: Praeger, 1998).

42 See, among others, Pollitt and Bouckaert, Public Management Reform.

43 See, for example, Christopher Hood, "A Public Management for All Seasons," Public Administration vol. 69 (Spring 1991): 3–19.

44 See Savoie, Breaking the Bargain.

45 See Gwyn Bevan and Christopher Hood, "Have Targets Improved Performance in the English NHS?," British Medical Journal 332 (18 February 2006): 419–22.

46 "Senior Civil Servants Use Up Entire Budget for Bonuses," National Post, 29 August 2002, A1 and A9.

47 See, for example, B. Guy Peters and Jon Pierre, "Governance without Government? Rethinking Public Administration," Journal of Public Administration Research and Theory 8, no. 4. (1998): 227–43.

48 B. Guy Peters, "Still the Century of Bureaucracy? The Role of Public Servants," Public Policy and Administration no. 30 (2009): 8.

49 Arend Lijphart, Patterns of Democracy: Government Forms and Performance in Thirty-Six Countries, 2nd ed. (Yale University Press, 2012).

50 See report prepared by Andrew Limb, seconded from the Cabinet Office of the UK to Statskontoret, *What Lessons Can Be Learned from the UK's Next Steps Agencies Model?* (London: Statskontoret), 2001, 10.

51 I.D. Clark, "Special Operating Agencies: The Challenges of Innovation," *Optimum* 22, no. 2 (1991): 13.

52 Donald J. Savoie, *Court Government and the Collapse of Accountability in Canada and the United Kingdom* (Toronto: University of Toronto Press, 2008).

53 See, among others, Ian Stewart, *Just One Vote* (Winnipeg: University of Manitoba Press, 2009).

54 See, for example, Chris Hood, "The New Public Management in the 1980s: Variations on a Theme," *Accounting, Organizations and Society* 20, no. 2 (1995): 93–109.

55 See, among others, Donald J. Savoie, *Whatever Happened to the Music Teacher? How Government Decides and Why* (Montreal and Kingston: McGill-Queen's University Press, 2013).

56 See, among others, Kate McLaughlin, Stephen P. Osborne, and Ewan Ferlie, eds, *New Public Management: Current Trends and Future Prospects* (Abingdon: Routledge, 2002); and Savoie, *Thatcher, Reagan, Mulroney*.

57 Donald J. Savoie, *Court Government and the Collapse of Accountability in Canada and the United Kingdom* (Toronto: University of Toronto Press, 2008).

58 UK Treasury, *Responsibilities of an Accounting Officer Memorandum* (London, undated).

59 Canada, Office of the Prime Minister, "Prime Minister Announces New Ethics Guidelines for the Ministry and the New Appointment Procedure for Ethics Counsellor," news release, 11 June 2007.

60 Canada, Privy Council Office, Section 4, Accountability for Addressing Errors in Administration, in *Guidance for Deputy Ministers* (Ottawa: 2003), 4.

61 Ralph Heintzman, "Establishing the Boundaries of the Public Service: Toward a New Moral Contract," in *Governing: Essays in Honour of Donald J. Savoie*, ed. James Bickerton and B. Guy Peters (Montreal: McGill-Queen's University Press, 2013), 102.

62 Arthur Kroeger, "The Elected Should Have the Last Word," *Globe and Mail*, 7 February 2006, A15.

63 *Guidance for Deputy Ministers* (Ottawa: Privy Council Office), accessed 5 January 2017, www.pco-bcp.gc.ca.

64 Kathryn May, "Price Tag to Fix Phoenix Pay System Nearly Doubles, Expected to Cost up to $50 Million," *Ottawa Citizen*, 7 September 2016.

65 Susan Burgess, "Phoenix Fix Approaching $1B as Feds Look at Scrapping System," CBC News, 27 February 2018, http://www.cbc.ca/news/canada/ottawa/phoenix-eventually-replaced-federal-budget-2018-1.4554399.

66 Kathryn May, "Bureaucrat Who Led Phoenix Project Shuffled Aside in Executive Shakeup," Ottawa Citizen, 12 October 2016.

67 Marie-Danielle Smith, "Public Servants outside Ottawa More Often Affected by Phoenix Pay Fiasco: Documents," National Post, 31 January 2018.

68 Barrie McKenna, "Someone Should Take the Fall for Ottawa's Botched Phoenix Pay System," Globe and Mail, 26 February 2017.

69 Nathalie Sturgeon, "Miramichi Mayor Wants Apology for Payroll Centre Comments," CBC News (New Brunswick), 27 August 2017, https://www.cbc.ca/news/canada/new-brunswick/miramichi-pay-centre-apology-pheonix-pay-system-1.4264367.

70 See, among others, Blair Crawford, "Phoenix Down Under: Auditor Likens Bungled Payroll System to 'Catastrophic' Australian Experience," Ottawa Citizen, 21 November 2017.

71 Canada, Report 1 – Building and Implementing the Phoenix Pay System (Ottawa: Office of the Auditor General, 2018), 25–38.

72 See, for example, John Ivison, "Canada's Senior Bureaucrat and Top Auditor Are Having an Unprecedented Feud over the Public Service," National Post, 14 June 2018.

73 Kathryn May, "Clerk Defends Bureaucracy against Accusations of a Broken Culture," iPolitics, 12 June 2018, https://ipolitics.ca/2018/06/12/clerk-defends-bureaucracy-against-accusations-of-a-broken-culture/.

74 Kathryn May, "Canadians Lack Faith in Upper Ranks of Public Service: Survey," Ottawa Citizen, 7 September 2016.

75 Canada, 2017 Public Service Employee Survey (Ottawa: Treasury Board Secretariat, 2017); and Jake Cole, "The Latest Public Service Survey Shows Us What to Fix," Ottawa Citizen, 26 June 2018.

76 Chapter 6 – Reform of Classification and Job Evaluation in the Federal Public Service (Ottawa: Office of the Auditor General, 2003); and Canada, Directive on Classification (Ottawa: Treasury Board Secretariat, 2015).

77 Monique Scotti, "Government Email Project Still Stalled after Five Years, $100 Million Spent," Global News, 10 September 2017, https://globalnews.ca/news/3709736/canadian-government-email-project-stalled/.

78 Report 4 – Information Technology, Shared Services (Ottawa: Office of the Auditor General, Fall 2015).

79 Editorial, "Built to Crash: The Ugly, Sputtering Beginning of Shared Services and How Politics Conspired Against It," Ottawa Citizen, 14 November 2016.

80 Ibid.

81 Laura Ryckewaert, "Feds Paid More than $40-million in 2016 to Maintain Vacant, Partially Vacant Buildings," *Hill Times*, 19 December 2016.

82 *Survey on Bureaucratic Patronage in the Federal Public Service, Final Report* (Ottawa, 2005), www.psc-cfg-gc.ca.

83 Canada, *Message from the Auditor General – 2016 Fall Report of the Auditor General* (Ottawa: Office of the Auditor General, November 2016).

84 B. Guy Peters, Jon Pierre, and Desmond S. King," The Politics of Path Dependency: Political Conflict in Historical Institutionalism," *The Journal of Politics* 67, no. 4 (November 2005): 1276.

85 Pollitt and Bouckaert, *Public Management Reform.*

86 Theodore J. Lowi makes this point in his book *The End of Liberalism* (New York: Norton, 1969), 98–9.

87 Savoie, *Whatever Happened to the Music Teacher?*, 112–13.

88 Canada, Task Force on Public Service Values and Ethics, *Discussion Paper* (Ottawa: Privy Council Office, 1996), 57.

89 Ibid., 45.

90 Jennifer Robson, "Spending on Political Staffers and the Revealed Preferences of Cabinet: Examining a New Data Source on Federal Political Staff in Canada," *Canadian Journal of Political Science* 48, no. 3 (September 2015): 675–97; and Paul Wilson, "Research Note: Profile of Ministerial Policy Staff in the Government of Canada," *Canadian Journal of Political Science* 48, no. 2 (June 2015): 455–71.

91 Jonathan Craft, *Backrooms and Beyond Partisan Advisors and the Politics of Policy Work in Canada* (Toronto: University of Toronto Press, 2016).

92 Ibid, 249.

93 Donald J. Savoie, *Breaking the Bargain: Public Servants, Ministers, and Parliament* (Toronto: University of Toronto Press, 2003).

94 Jacques Bourgault, "The Role of Deputy Ministers in Canadian Government," in *The Handbook of Canadian Public Administration*, ed. C. Dunn (Toronto: Oxford University Press, 2002).

95 Sean Kilpatrick/Canadian Press, "Trudeau's 2017 Cabinet: Read the Full List of Who's In, Who's Out and Who Keeps their Job," *Globe and Mail*, 10 January 2017.

96 Roger Gibbins, quoted in "Trudeau Says He Won't Be Ruled by His Massive Eastern Power Block," *Calgary Herald*, 21 October 2015. See also Ashely Csanady, "Top Queen's Park Staffers Heading of Ottawa to Work for Trudeau's New Government," *National Post*, 26 November 2015.

97 Aaron Wherry, "Trudeau Goes Again to the People, but Spare a Thought for the Ottawa Bubble," CBC *News*, 10 January 2018, http://www.cbc.ca/news/politics/trudeau-town-halls-ottawa-bubble-wherry-1.4480775.

98 Australian Public Service Commission, *State of the Service Report 2014–15* (Canberra: Commonwealth of Australia, 2015), 13.

99 Civil Service Statistics, 2015, www.officefornationalstatistics.

100 Data, Analysis and Documentation, Federal Civilian Employment by Major Geographic Area, Office of Personnel Management, 2015, www.opm.gov.

101 Savoie, *Whatever Happened to the Music Teacher*, 201.

102 There are various ways in the Government of Canada to establish size of the federal public service. First, there is the core public administration, including separate employees for which the Treasury Board is the employer; second is the broader public service that includes Crown corporations, military personnel, the RCMP, and other entities not included in schedules I, 4, and 5 of the Financial Administration Act.

103 "Employment Trends in the Core Public Administration: A Geographical Profile," Statistics Canada, www.statcan.gc.ca; and Population of the Federal Public Service by Province, n.d., www.canada.ca/en/reasury-boardsecretariat.ca.

104 "Federal Job Cuts to Hit Ottawa-Gatineau Hardest," *Ottawa Citizen*, 29 March 2012.

105 *Supplementary Estimates (2) 2014–15* (Ottawa: Parliamentary Budget Office, 26 February 2015).

106 Ibid.

107 "Moving Public Servants to the Regions" (Ottawa: Library of Parliament, 31 March 2006), 1.

108 "Productivité accrue," *Le Soleil* (Quebec), 5 August 1978. The director at Shediac made his observation at a meeting of federal officials to which I was invited. The meeting was chaired by the FEDC for New Brunswick.

109 The manager made the observation as a student in my Master Public Administration course at the Université de Moncton, November 2008.

110 See, among others, Donald J. Savoie, "Le programme federal de decentralisation – un réexamen," *Canadian Public Policy* 12, no. 3 (1986); and Donald J. Savoie, "La bureaucratie représentative: une perspective régionale," *Canadian Journal of Political Science* 20, no. 4 (1987).

111 Dominic LeBlanc made these comments on *The House*, CBC Radio, 30 August 2011.

112 Gérard Veilleux made this observation to me on several occasions.

113 See, among others, Peter Aucoin, "New Political Governance in Westminster Systems: Impartial Public Administration and Management Performance at Risk" (mimeo, Halifax: Dalhousie University, 2010), 2.

CHAPTER THIRTEEN

1 *Report on the Organisation of the Permanent Civil Service* (London: House of Commons, printed by George E. Eyre and William Spottiswoode, 1854).

2 See, among others, Donald J. Savoie, *Thatcher, Reagan, Mulroney: In Search of a New Bureaucracy* (Pittsburgh: University of Pittsburgh Press, 1994).

3 See Robert C. Brown, *Robert Laird Borden: A Biography, 1854–1914*, vol. 1 (Toronto: Macmillan, 1975), 215.

4 Henry Parris, *Constitutional Bureaucracy* (London: George Allen and Unwin, 1969), 106.

5 Ibid., 127.

6 Donald J. Savoie, *Court Government and the Collapse of Accountability in Canada and the United Kingdom* (Toronto: University of Toronto Press, 2008), 30.

7 Donald J. Savoie, *The Politics of Public Spending in Canada* (Toronto: University of Toronto Press, 1990).

8 I owe this observation to an anonymous reviewer with McGill-Queen's University Press.

9 Geoffrey Marshall, *Constitutional Conventions: The Rules and Forms of Political Accountability* (Oxford: Clarendon Press, 2001), 54.

10 Based on consultations with Elmer MacKay.

11 Donald J. Savoie, "The Canadian Public Service Has A Personality," *Canadian Public Administration* 49, no. 3 (September 2006): 261–81.

12 R. Armstrong, *The Duties and Responsibilities of Civil Servants in Relation to Ministers: Note by the Head of the Civil Service* (London: Cabinet Office, 1985), 2.

13 Canada, *Final Submissions of the Attorney General of Canada to the Commission of Inquiry into the Sponsorship Program and Advertising Activities* (Ottawa, June 2005), par. 72, 16.

14 Canada, Privy Council Office, *Responsibility in the Constitution: Constitutional Responsibility and Accountability,* section 7 (Ottawa: Accountability in Parliamentary Government, 1993).

15 Canada, "Section 4, Accountability for Addressing Errors in Administration," *Guidance for Deputy Ministers* (Ottawa: Privy Council Office, 2003).

16 Norman Chester, *The English Administrative State: 1780–1870* (Oxford: Clarendon Press, 1981), 22.

17 Christopher Kam, "Not Just Parliamentary Cowboys and Indians: Ministerial Responsibility and Bureaucratic Drift," *Governance* 13, no. 3 (July 2000): 380.

18 S.L. Sutherland, "The Al-Mashat Affair: Administrative Accountability in Parliamentary Institutions," *Canadian Public Administration* 34, no. 4 (December 1991): 573–603.

19 See, for example, Veterans Affairs Minister Seamus O'Regan who told a military widow that a decision was made by public servants and he could not overturn it. Jeff Rose-Martland, "Veteran Affairs Still Acts Like It Doesn't Owe Canadian Soldiers a Thing," *Huffington Post* (Canada), 10 November 2017.

20 Bill Curry, "Trudeau Rules Out Taxing Employee Discounts," *Globe and Mail*, 11 October 2017.

21 Tom Bateman, "Fishery Closure Threat 'Categorically False,'" *Telegraph Journal* (Saint John), 2 March 2018.

22 Laura Stone, "Liberal MPs Block Tory Bid to Hear from Trudeau's National Security Advisor on India," *Globe and Mail*, 1 March 2018.

23 I could provide a list of similar cases. See, among others, David Pugliese, "Seamus O'Regan – Here Is an Example of How Screwed Up Your Veterans Affairs Department Really Is," *Ottawa Citizen*, 13 October 2017.

24 Canada, *Budget des dépenses pour l'année financière se terminant le 31 mars 1969* (Ottawa: Imprimerie de la Reine, 1969), 106, 109, 349, 365, 436, and 438; and *Part III Estimates, 1996–97*.

25 Canada, "Population of the Federal Public Service by Department," n.d., www.canada.ca.

26 Consultations with the deputy minister of Industry Canada, Ottawa, 20 October 2011.

27 For a more detailed assessment of the role of central agencies and officers of Parliament, see Donald J. Savoie, *Whatever Happened to the Music Teacher? How Government Decides and Why* (Montreal: McGill-Queen's University Press, 2013), 144–6.

28 See, among many others, Donald J. Savoie, *Thatcher, Reagan, Mulroney: In Search of a New Bureaucracy* (Pittsburgh: University of Pittsburgh Press, 1994).

29 Donald J. Savoie, "What Is Wrong with the New Public Management," *Canadian Public Administration* 38, no. 1 (March 1995): 112–21.

30 Donald J. Savoie, *Harrison McCain: Single-Minded Purpose* (Montreal: McGill-Queen's University Press, 2013).

31 David E. Smith, *The Constitution in a Hall of Mirrors: Canada at 150* (Toronto: University of Toronto Press, 2017), 125.

32 Sharon L. Sutherland, "The Office of the Auditor General of Canada: Government in Exile" (Kingston: Queen's University School of Policy Studies, 2003), 2.

33 Kathryn May, "Parliamentary Watchdogs Still Wait for Reply on Call for Better Accountability from MPs," *Ottawa Citizen*, 20 December 2011.

34 Canada, *Commission of Inquiry into the Sponsorship Program and Advertising Activities* (Ottawa, 25 January 2005).

35 "Before You Clamour for Results-Based Management in the Civil Service, Remember Chuck Guité Could Be Its Poster Boy," *Globe and Mail*, 23 November 2005.

36 Canada, *Commission of Inquiry into the Sponsorship Program and Advertising Activities*.

37 See Savoie, *Whatever Happened to the Music Teacher?*, 209–11.

38 Peter Mazereeuw, "Inside the Indigenous Affairs Split: 'Nobody Is Losing Their Job' During the Transition, Feds Say," *Hill Times*, 6 September 2017.

39 The Fulton report made this point in 1986. See D.N. Chester, "The Report of the Fulton Committee on the Civil Service," *Australian Journal of Public Administration*, 27, no. 4 (1968), 295–310.

40 Max Weber, C. Wright Mills, introduction, *Essays in Sociology*, tr. H.H. Gerth (New York: Oxford University Press, 1946), 231.

41 Donald J. Savoie, *Court Government and the Collapse of Accountability in Canada and the United Kingdom* (Toronto: University of Toronto Press, 2008), 267.

42 Giles Gherson, "Public Opinion," *This Morning*, CBC Radio broadcast, 3 December 1997.

43 Ibid.

44 Ibid.

45 "Globe Request Caused Crisis, Guité Trial Told," *Globe and Mail*, 11 May 2006, A1.

46 "Big Spending Days Over for Ottawa," *National Post*, 24 April 2004, RB1.

47 Alasdair S. Roberts, "Spin Control and Freedom of Information: Lessons for the United Kingdom from Canada," *Public Administration*, 82, no. 2 (2005), 4.

48 See, among others, Alasdair Roberts, "'Two Challenges in Administration of the Access to Information Act,' in Canada, Commission of Inquiry into the Sponsorship Program and Advertising Activities," *Restoring Accountability: Research Studies, Volume 2, The Public Service and Transparency* (Ottawa, 2006).

49 See, for example, Shawn McCarthy, "Trudeau Needs to Deliver on His Access-to-Information Promises," *Globe and Mail*, 18 September 2017.

50 Daniel Leblanc, "Information Watchdog Blasts Liberals Ahead of Her Retirement," *Globe and Mail*, 21 February 2018.

51 Canada, *Guidelines on the Conduct of Ministers, Ministers of State, Exempt Staff and Public Servants During an Election* (Ottawa: Privy Council Office, August 2015).

52 Alex Marland, Thierry Giasson, and Anna Lennox Esselment, eds, "Welcome to Non-Stop Campaigning," in *Permanent Campaigning in Canada* (Vancouver: UBC Press, 2017), 3 and 4.

53 Paul G. Thomas, "Communications and Prime Ministerial Power," in *Governing: Essays in Honour of Donald J. Savoie*, ed. B. Guy Peters and Jim Bickerton (Montreal: McGill-Queen's University Press, 2013).

54 Donald J. Savoie, *Breaking the Bargain: Public Servants, Ministers, and Parliament* (Toronto: University of Toronto Press, 2003).

55 Jonathan Craft, "Governing on the Front Foot: Politicians, Civil Servants, and the Permanent Campaign in Canada," in *Permanent Campaigning in Canada*, ed. Alex Marland, Thierry Giasson, and Anna Lennox Esselment (Vancouver: UBC Press, 2017), 30.

56 Ibid., 41.

57 Ralph Heintzman, "Renewal of the Federal Public Service: Toward a Charter of Public Service," policy paper Canada 2020 series (Ottawa, 2014), 11.

58 Peter Aucoin, "New Political Governance in Westminster Systems: Impartial Public Administration and Management Performance at Risk," *Governance* 25, no. 2 (April 2012): 177–99.

59 Michael Keating quoted in ibid., 189.

60 Aucoin, "New Political Governance in Westminster Systems," 191.

61 Canada, *Public Service Impartiality: Taking Stock* (Ottawa: Public Service Commission of Canada, 2008), 18 and 21.

62 Savoie, *Breaking the Bargain*.

63 Hugh Winsor pointed to this issue back in 2010 in "A New Style for the Public Service" (Kingston: Queen's University News Centre, 2010), 8.

64 "PS Disability Claims Soaring," *Ottawa Citizen*, 28 June 2011.

65 Quoted in ibid.

66 *Public Employee Survey* (Ottawa: Statistics Canada, 12 May 2009).

67 Emily Haws, "'Disturbing Level' of Bullying, Intimidation in Public Service Must Be Rooted Out, Says PCO Clerk," *Hill Times*, 2 May 2018.

68 Canada, *Canada's Public Service in 2017* (Ottawa: Policy Horizon, n.d.).

69 Dennis C. Grube and Cosmo Howard also draw this conclusion from my work. See their article, "Promiscuously Partisan? Public Service Impartiality and Responsiveness in Westminster Systems," *Governance* 29, no. 4 (October 2016): 528.

70 Savoie, *Breaking the Bargain.*

71 Ibid., 19.

72 See Robert Bothwell, Ian Drummond, and John English, *Canada since 1945: Power, Politics and Provincialism* (Toronto: University of Toronto Press, 1989), 332.

73 A.W. Johnson, "The Role of the Deputy Minister," *Canadian Public Administration* 4, no. 4 (1961): 363.

74 Canada, "2017 Manion Lecture – Strengthening Trust in Canada: the Role of the Public Service" (Ottawa: Canada School of Public Service, 2017), 4.

CHAPTER FOURTEEN

1 C.D. Yonge, *The Life and Administration of Robert Banks, the Second Earl of Liverpool,* 3 vols (London: Macmillan, 1868), 3:340.

2 Ibid.

3 Carl Baar, "The Courts in Canada," in *The Political Role of Law Courts in Modern Democracies,* ed. Jerold L. Waltman and Kenneth M. Holland (New York: St Martin's Press, 1988), 79.

4 Canada, *Annual Report 2016–2017* (Ottawa: Office of the Commissioner of Lobbying of Canada, 2017), 5.

5 Emmett Macfarlane, "You Can't Always Get What You Want: Regime Politics, the Supreme Court of Canada, and the Harper Government," *Canadian Journal of Political Science* 51, no. 1 (September 2017): 479.

6 William Conklin, Chapter 5, in *Images of a Constitution* (Toronto: University of Toronto Press, 1989).

7 W.H. McConnell, "Canadian Bill of Rights," in *Canadian Encyclopedia,* Canada Historica, 7 February 2006.

8 Dennis Gruending, *Emmett Hall: Establishment Radical* (Toronto: Macmillan of Canada, 1985), 164.

9 Emmett Macfarlane, *Governing from the Bench: The Supreme Court of Canada and the Judicial Role* (Vancouver: UBC Press, 2013), 12.

10 "Supreme Court of Canada Ruling," Bill C-14, 17 June 2016, www. justice.gc.ca.

11 Mark S. Harding and Rainer Knopff, "Charter Values vs. Charter Dialogue," *National Journal of Constitutional Law* 31, no. 2 (2013): 161–81.

12 Remarks by Beverley McLachlin, Chief Justice of Canada, University of Western Ontario, Faculty of Law, London, Ontario, 6 November 2002, 4 and 5.

13 Daniel Schwartz, "6 Big Changes the Charter of Rights Has Brought," CBC *News*, 17 April 2012, https://www.cbc.ca/news/canada/6-big-changes-the-charter-of-rights-has-brought-1.1244758.

14 James B. Kelly, *Governing with the Charter: Legislative and Judicial Activism and Framers' Intent* (Vancouver: UBC Press, 2005), 223.

15 Ibid., 222.

16 Ibid., 224.

17 See, for example, F.L. Morton and Rainer Knopff, *The Charter Revolution and the Court Party* (Peterborough: Broadview Press, 2000); Christopher P. Manfredi, *Judicial Power and the Charter* (Don Mills, ON: Oxford University Press, 2001); and Lorraine Eisenstat Weinrib, "Canada's Constitutional Revolution: From Legislative to Constitutional State," *Israel Law Review* 33, no. 1 (1999): 13–50.

18 Alan C. Cairns, "The Judicial Committee and Its Critics," *Canadian Journal of Political Science* 4, no. 3 (1971), 319–20.

19 Macfarlane, *Governing from the Bench*, 12.

20 Ibid., chapter 1. See also Bob Tarantino, "Court Politics," *Literary Review of Canada*, January–February 2014, 8.

21 Donald R. Songer, *The Transformation of the Supreme Court of Canada: An Empirical Examination* (Toronto: University of Toronto Press, 2008), 109–10.

22 Quoted in Sean Fine, "Retired Supreme Court Justice Claire L'Heureux-Dubé's Biography Uncovers Secret History of Court," *Globe and Mail*, 27 August 2018.

23 I had numerous conversations with the Right Honourable Roméo LeBlanc, various dates between 1982 and 2004 in Ottawa and Grande-Digue, New Brunswick.

24 I do not have permission to reveal his identity.

25 Kelly, *Governing with the Charter*, 150.

26 Ibid.

27 Ibid., 151.

28 Chief Justice Beverley McLachlin quoted in Donald J. Savoie, "Machinery of Government and the Canadian Judicial Council (Ottawa: Canadian Judicial Council, 2017), 17.

29 Remarks by the Chief Justice of Canada the Right Honourable Beverley McLachlin, PC, at the Hutcheon Papers dinner, Vancouver, British Columbia, 1 March 2017, 1.

30 Judge Jan-Marie Doogue, Judge Colin Doherty, and Jeff Simpson, "Accountability for the Administration and Organisation of the Judiciary," a discussion paper, n.d., 11.

31 Brian Laghi, "Rage Finds Its Voice in Alberta," *Globe and Mail*, 11 April 1998, A4.

32 Lori Hausegger and Troy Riddell, "The Changing Nature of Public Support for the Supreme Court of Canada," *Canadian Journal of Political Science* 37, no. 1 (March 2004): 23–50.

33 Jeffrey Simpson, "Medically Assisted Dying: How Not to Make a Law," *Globe and Mail*, 2 June 2016.

34 BJ Siekierski, "Vast Majority of Canadians Trust Supreme Court, Including Tories," *iPolitics*, 16 August 2015, https://ipolitics. ca/2015/08/16/vast-majority-of-canadians-trust-supreme-court-including-most-tories/.

35 Emmett Macfarlane, "The Supreme Court of Canada and the Judicial Role: An Historical Institutionalist Account," a thesis submitted to the Department of Political Studies, Queen's University, 2009, 3.

36 *The Supreme Court of Canada: Policy-Maker of the Year* (Ottawa: Macdonald-Laurier Institute, November 2014).

37 Raymond Bazowski, "The Judicialization of Canadian Politics," in *Canadian Politics*, ed. James Bickerton and Alain-G. Gagnon (Peterborough: Broadview, 2004), 203.

38 Ibid.

39 See, among others, F.L. Morton and Rainer Knopff, *The Charter Revolution and Court Party* (Peterborough: Broadview, 2000).

40 Chris Morris, "NB Holds More Talks on Early French Immersion after Losing Court Case," *Canadian Press*, 12 June 2008, http://hamlit2008. blogspot.ca/2008/06/wow-lots-to-report-from-press-in-nb.html.

41 "Michel Bastarache reprend du service," *L'Acadie Nouvelle*, 23 August 2008, 3.

42 D.F. Philpott and C.A.M. Fiedorowicz, *The Supreme Court of Canada Ruling on Learning Disabilities* (Ottawa: Learning Disabilities Association of Canada, 2012), 2.

43 Quoted in Steve Mertl, "Supreme Court Decision in Favour of Dyslexic B.C. Students Has Wide Implications for School Boards across Canada," Yahoo News, 10 November 2012, https://ca.news-yahoo.com/blogs/ dailybrew/supreme-court-decision-favour-dyslexic-b-c-student-224858176. html.

44 Marilyn L. Pilkington, "Enforcing the Charter: The Supervisory Role of Superior Courts and the Responsibility of Legislatures for Remedial Systems," *Supreme Court Law Review* 25 (2004), 77–99. See also full text of the Supreme Court of Canada decision at Lexum, http://scc-csc.lexum. com/scc-csc/scc-csc/en/item/2096/index.do, and http://www.canlii.org/en/ ca/scc/doc/2003/2003scc62/2003scc62.html.

45 Sean Fine, "Ottawa's Refugee Health-Care Cuts 'Cruel and Unusual,' Court Rules," *Globe and Mail*, 4 July 2014.

46 Debra Black, "Court Strikes Down Conservatives' Cuts to Refugee Health-Care Coverage," *Toronto Star*, 5 July 2014.

47 Quoted in ibid.

48 Michael Ignatieff, *Fire and Ashes: Success and Failure in Politics* (Cambridge: Harvard University Press, 2013), 63–4.

49 Peter Russell, "The Political Purposes of the Canadian Charter of Rights," *Canadian Bar Review* 61 (1983): 52.

50 Donald J. Savoie, *Visiting Grandchildren: Economic Development in the Maritimes* (Toronto: University of Toronto Press, 2006), 288–9.

51 Kenneth S. Coates, *The Marshall Decision and Native Rights* (Montreal: McGill-Queen's University Press, 2000), 187.

52 Justice Frankfurter quoted in Hausegger and Riddell, "The Changing Nature of Public Support for the Supreme Court of Canada," 23.

53 See, among others, Peter Aucoin and Lori Turnbull, "The Democratic Deficit: Paul Martin and Parliamentary Reform," *Canadian Public Administration* 46, no. 4 (December 2003): 427–49.

54 Susan Delacourt, "What Canada's 21st and 23rd Prime Ministers Have in Common," *Toronto Star*, 13 May 2016.

55 W. Scott Thurlow, "Some Observations on the State of Lobbying in Canada," *Canadian Parliamentary Review* 33, no. 2 (2010).

56 Alexander Furnas, "Transparency Case Study: Lobbying Disclosure in Canada," Sunlight Foundation, 5 May 2014.

57 John Sawatsky, *The Insiders: Government, Business and the Lobbyists* (Toronto: McClelland and Stewart, 1987), 140.

58 "Here Are a Few Liberal Lobbyists that Boast Close Connections to the Trudeau Government," *Ottawa Citizen*, 16 December 2016.

59 Quoted in Derek Abma, "Energy, Tech Sectors Dominate List Lobbying Prime Minister Trudeau," *Hill Times*, 25 April 2016, 1 and 20.

60 Kevin Yarr, "Former P.E.I. Premier Robert Ghiz to Lead Wireless Industry Group," CBC *News*, 28 November 2016, https://www.cbc.ca/news/canada/prince-edward-island/pei-robert-ghiz-cwta-1.3871003.

61 Consultations with Gerry Doucet, formerly with GCI – Ottawa, various dates.

62 Canada, *Annual Report 2016–2017* (Ottawa: Office of the Commissioner of Lobbying of Canada, n.d.).

63 Andrew Coyne, "The Bonanza of Buying Subsidies," *National Post*, 5 December 2015, A4.

64 John Lester, *Business Subsidies in Canada: Comprehensive Estimates for the Government of Canada and the Four Largest Provinces*, SPP Research Paper 10, no.1 (Calgary: University of Calgary – The School of Public Policy, January 2018).

65 Derek Abma, "Lobbyists' Communications Up by More than 100 Percent over Last Year, Liberals More Open to Lobbying," *Hill Times*, 6 June 2016, 4.

66 Tim Powers quoted in Derek Abma, "The Hill Times' Top 100 Lobbyists: Elite Players Know How to 'Align Interests' with Government," *Hill Times*, 20 February 2017.

67 Derek Abma, "Bains, MacAulay Two Most Lobbied Cabinet Ministers during Summer Months," *Hill Times*, 12 September 2016.

68 Justice Beverley McLachlin quoted in Kirk Makin, "Access to Justice Becoming a Privilege of the Rich Judge Warns," *Globe and Mail*, 10 February 2011.

69 See, among others, James Bickerton, Stephen Brooks, and Alain-G. Gagnon, eds, *Freedom, Equality and Community: The Political Philosophy of Six Influential Canadians* (Montreal: McGill-Queen's University Press, 2006).

CHAPTER FIFTEEN

1 Lord Durham, Chapter 3, in *Report on the Affairs of British North America* (Oxford: Clarendon Press, 1912).

2 K.C. Wheare, "Walter Bagehot," *Proceedings of the British Academy* 60 (1974): 105–6.

3 Walter Bagehot, *Bagehot: The English Constitution*, ed. Paul Smith and Raymond Geuss (Cambridge: Cambridge University Press, 2001), 196.

4 Ibid., 43.

5 Alastair Buchan, *The Spare Chancellor: The Life of Walter Bagehot* (London: Chatto and Windus, 1959), 31.

6 See, for example, Chris Selley, "Listening to Senators Debate Marijuana Bill Convinced Me We Need to Abolish the Senate," *National Post*, 23 March 2018.

7 Cormac MacSweeney and Canadian Press, "Trudeau Warns Senators Not to Thwart Will of Canadians on Marijuana Bill," City*News*, 22 March 2018.

8 Canada, "Sober Second Thought in Action," SenateGRO/SénatBRG, 20 March 2018, https://senate-gro.ca/news/sober-second-thought-in-action/.

9 Donald J. Savoie, *The Politics of Public Spending in Canada* (Toronto: University of Toronto Press, 1990).

10 Eli Yarhi and Robert J. Jackson, "Member of Parliament (MP)," in the *Canadian Encyclopedia*, Historica Canada, 17 June 2010, https://www.thecanadianencyclopedia.ca/en/article/member-of-parliament.

11 Carolyn Bennett, Deborah Grey, Hon. Yves Morin, *The Parliament We Want* (Ottawa: Library of Parliament, 2003), 6 and 7.

12 Guy Lodge and Glen Gottlieb, "Introduction," in *Democracy in Britain: Essays in Honour of James Cornford*, ed. Guy Lodge and Glen Gottlieb (London: Institute for Public Policy Research, 2014), 10–29.

13 See, for example, Aaron Wherry, "Liberals' Latest Attempt at Parliamentary Reform Remains a Tale of Woe, for Now," CBC *News*, 24 March 2017, https://www.cbc.ca/news/politics/wherry-parliament-reform-chagger-1.4037813.

14 Laura Stone, "Trudeau Abandons Electoral Reform, Breaking Key Campaign Promise," *Globe and Mail*, 1 February 2017.

15 Ibid.

16 "Electoral Reform: It's Complicated," *Globe and Mail*, 12 May 2016.

17 See, among others, "PM Trudeau Blames Opposition for Electoral Reform Failure, Budget Deficit," CTV *News*, 27 June 2017, https://www.ctvnews.ca/politics/pm-trudeau-blames-opposition-for-electoral-reform-failure-budget-deficit-1.3478395; and Brian Platt, "'There Was No Path' to Bring in Electoral Reform, Trudeau Says about Breaking His Promise," *National Post*, 27 June 2017.

18 Paul Thomas, *Comparing Electoral Systems: Criteria, Advantages and Disadvantages, and the Process for Finding a Consensus on Which System Is Best for Canada* (mimeo, Winnipeg: University of Manitoba, 2 March 2016), 25.

19 Canada, *Voting Counts: Electoral Reform for Canada* (Ottawa: Law Commission of Canada, 2004), 69.

20 Ed Broadbent, Alex Himelfarb, and Hugh Segal, "Only Proportionality Will Fix Our Democratic Malaise," *Globe and Mail*, 10 May 2016.

21 See, among others, Maxwell Cameron, "Minority Government Could Be Good for Our Democracy," *Globe and Mail*, 12 October 2015.

22 Paul Wells, *The Longer I'm Prime Minister: Stephen Harper and Canada, 2006–* (Toronto: Random House Canada, 2013), 405.

23 *Confidence in Parliament* (Ottawa: Conference Board of Canada, 2013).

24 "2017 Edelman Trust Barometer – Canadian Results," https://www. slideshare.net/EdelmanInsights/2017-edelman-trust-barometer-canadian-results.

25 Ibid.

26 *Americas Barometer: Citizens across the Americas Speak on Democracy and Government* (Ottawa: Environics Institute and Institute on Governance, 2014), 5.

27 Ibid., 27.

28 William Morton, "Confederation 1870–1896," in *Contexts of Canada's Past: Selected Essays of William Morton*, ed. A.B. McKillop (Toronto: Macmillan, 1980), 217.

29 James Mallory, *Social Credit and the Federal Power in Canada* (Toronto: University of Toronto Press, 1976), 57.

30 Jörg Broschek, "Federalism and Political Change: Canada and Germany in Historical-Institutionalist Perspective," *Canadian Journal of Political Science* 43, no. 1 (2010): 17.

31 B. Guy Peters, Jon Pierre, and Desmond S. King, "The Politics of Path Dependency: Political Conflict in Historical Institutionalism," *The Journal of Politics* 67, no. 4 (November 2005): 1277.

32 See, among others, Donald J. Savoie, *Federal-Provincial Collaboration: The Canada-New Brunswick General Development Agreement* (Kingston and Montreal: McGill-Queen's University Press, 1981).

33 Donald Smiley makes this point in his essay "An Outsider's Observations of Federal-Provincial Relations among Consulting Adults," in *Confrontation and Collaboration: Intergovernmental Relations Today*, ed. Richard Simeon (Toronto: Institute of Public Administration, 1979), 105–13.

34 "New Brunswick, Federal Government Sign Infrastructure Agreement," *Sackville Tribune-Post*, 15 March 2018.

35 Rachel Aiello, "Budget Should Respect Regional Economic Differences, Says Finance Committee Chair Wayne Easter," *Hill Times*, 31 October 2016, 1.

36 See, for example, Wherry, "Liberals' Latest Attempt at Parliamentary Reform Remains a Tale of Woe, for Now."

37 Jeffrey Simpson, "State of the Nation," *Globe and Mail*, 1 July 2016, A2 and A5.

38 John English, *Just Watch Me: The Life of Pierre Trudeau – 1968–2000* (Toronto Knopf, 2009).

39 Pierre E. Trudeau, *Federalism and the French Canadians* (Toronto: Macmillan of Canada, 1968), 178.

40 See, among others, Eugene A. Forsey, "Padlock Act," in *The Canadian Encyclopedia*, Canada Historica, 7 February 2006, https://www. thecanadianencyclopedia.ca/en/article/padlock-act; and William Kaplan, *State and Salvation* (Toronto: University of Toronto Press, 1989).

41 Trudeau, *Federalism and the French Canadians*, 35.

42 Claude Bélanger, "The Victoria Charter: Constitutional Reform and Quebec (1971)," in Quebec History, Marianopolis College, 23 August 2000, www.faculty.marianopolis.edu.

43 Peter H. Russell, *Constitutional Odyssey: Can Canadians Become a Sovereign People?* (Toronto: University of Toronto Press, 1993).

44 See, among others, Roy Romanow, Howard Leeson, and John Whyte, *Canada Notwithstanding: The Making of the Constitution 1976–1982* (Toronto: Carswell-Methuen, 1984).

45 Andrew Cohen, "The Last Act: Pierre Trudeau, the Gang of Eight, and the Fight for Canada," *Globe and Mail*, 6 May 2011.

46 Romanow, Leeson, and Whyte, *Canada Notwithstanding*.

47 David Akin, "Analysis: Canada's Charter Remains a Flawed Document that No Politician Dares to Fix," *Global News*, 18 April 2017, https:// globalnews.ca/news/3385359/analysis-canadas-charter-flawed-document-no-politician-dares-try-to-fix/.

48 F.L. Morton and Rainer Knopff, *The Charter Revolution and the Court Party* (Peterborough: Broadview Press, 2000), 13.

49 Emmett Macfarlane, "You Can't Always Get What You Want: Regime Politics, the Supreme Court of Canada, and the Harper Government," *Canadian Journal of Political Science* 50, no. 1 (March 2018): 18.

50 Peter W. Hogg, "The Difficulty of Amending the Constitution of Canada," *Osgoode Hall Law Journal* 31, no. 1 (Spring 1993): 41–61.

51 Canada, *The Constitution of Canada: A Brief History of Amending Procedure Discussions* (see section 43), Ottawa: Library of Parliament, 1992.

52 Canada, *Supreme Court Judgments*, 2018 SCC15, Case number 37398, 19 April 2018.

53 Andrew Coyne, "Supreme Court Beer Ruling Ties the Constitution in Knots, and the Economy with It," *National Post*, 20 April 2018.

54 John E. Hodgetts, *The Canadian Public Service: A Physiology of Government 1867–1970* (Toronto: University of Toronto Press, 1973).

55 See, among others, Savoie, *Thatcher, Reagan and Mulroney*.

56 See, among others, Savoie, *Breaking the Bargain*.

57 See, among others, Donald J. Savoie, *Whatever Happened to the Music Teacher? How Government Decides and Why* (Montreal and Kingston: McGill-Queen's University Press, 2013).

58 See, for example, Peter Aucoin, "The New Public Governance and the Public Service Commission," *Optimum Online* 36, (2006): 33–49. However, see also Dennis C. Grube and Cosmo Howard, "Promiscuously Partisan? Public Service Impartiality and Responsiveness in Westminster Systems," *Governance* 29, no. 4 (October 2016): 517–33.

59 J.L. Granatstein, *Mackenzie King: His Life and World* (Toronto: McGraw-Hill Ryerson, 1976).

60 Ralph Heintzman, "Renewal of the Federal Public Service: Toward a Charter of Public Service," a policy prepared for Canada 2020 (Ottawa: Canada 2020, 2016), 6.

61 Richard Simeon, "Regionalism and Canadian Political Institutions," *Queen's Quarterly* 82 (Winter 1975), 504.

62 Ibid., 507

63 See, among others, Savoie, *Whatever Happened to the Music Teacher?*

64 I owe this observation to an anonymous reviewer with McGill-Queen's University Press.

65 Alasdair Roberts, *Four Crises of American Democracy: Representation, Mastery, Discipline, Anticipation* (Oxford: Oxford University Press, 2017); Patrick Diamond, *The End of Whitehall? Government by Permanent Campaign* (London: Palgrave Macmillan, 2018); James Allan, *Democracy in Decline: Steps in the Wrong Direction* (Montreal: McGill-Queen's University Press, 2014); and Steven Levitsky and Daniel Ziblatt, *How Democracies Die* (New York: Crown, 2018).

66 Robert Asselin, *An Agenda for Democratic Reform in Canada* (Ottawa: Canada 2020, 2014), 5.

67 James Bickerton, "Parties and Democracy in Canada: Regional Fragmentation, Institutional Inertia, and Democratic Deficit," in *Political Parties and Democracy: The Americas*, ed. Kay Lawson and Jorge Lanzaro (Oxford: Praeger, 2010), 23.

68 Geoffrey M. Hodgson, "What Are Institutions?" *Journal of Economic Issues* 40, no.1 (March 2006): 2.

69 See, among others, Peter A. Hall and Rosemary C.R. Taylor, "Political Science and the Three New Institutionalism," *Political Studies* 44, no. 5 (1996): 936–57; and James March and Johan Olsen, "The New Institutionalism: Organizational Factors in Political Life," *The American Political Science Review* 78, no. 3 (1984): 734–49.

70 Peters, Pierre, and King, "The Politics of Path Dependency: Political Conflict in Historical Institutionalism," 1276.

71 Ibid., 1277.

72 I am thinking here of Peter A. Hall's widely read *Governing the Economy: The Politics of State Interventions in Britain and France* (New York: Oxford University Press, 1986).

73 Peter A. Hall and Rosemary C.R. Taylor, "Political Science and the Three New Institutionalisms," *Political Studies* 44, no. 5 (1996): 941.

CHAPTER SIXTEEN

1 Peter A. Hall and Rosemary C.R. Taylor, "Political Science and the Three New Institutionalisms," *Political Studies* 44, no. 5 (1996): 941.

2 John Street, *Mass Media, Politics and Democracy* (London: Palgrave Macmillan, 2011), 2–3 and 8.

3 Alex S. Jones, *Losing the News: The Future of the News that Feeds Democracy* (Oxford: Oxford University Press, 2009).

4 Doug Saunders, "Facebook's Threat to Democracy Is Worse than Cambridge Analytica," *Globe and Mail*, 22 March 2018.

5 D. Kellner, *Media Culture* (London: Routledge, 1995).

6 See, among others, Stephen Coleman, "New Media and Parliamentary Democracy," in *The Future of Parliament: Issues for a New Century*, ed. Philip Giddings (London: Palgrave Macmillan, 2005), 252.

7 Canada, "Number and Proportion of Foreign-Born Population in Canada, 1871 to 2036," Statistics Canada, n.d., https://www.statcan.gc.ca/eng/dai/btd/othervisuals/other006.

8 Andrew Heard, *Canadian Constitutional Conventions: The Marriage of Law and Politics* (Toronto: Oxford University Press, 1991); and Peter Aucoin, Mark D. Jarvis, and Lori Turnbull, *Democratizing the Constitution: Reforming Responsible Government* (Toronto: Edmond Montgomery Publications, 2011), 77.

9 Michael Kirby and Hugh Segal, *A House Undivided: Making Senate Independence Work* (Ottawa: Public Policy Forum, 2016).

10 See, among many others, Aucoin, Jarvis, and Turnbull, *Democratizing the Constitution*; Jeffrey Simpson, *The Friendly Dictatorship* (Toronto: McClelland Stewart, 2001); and Lawrence Martin, *Harperland: The Politics of Control* (Toronto: Penguin, 2011).

11 Samantha Wright Allen, "MPs Sick of State of Debate in Parliament, but Divided on How to Fix It: Samara Report," *Hill Times*, 26 September 2018.

12 Donald Shell, "The House of Lords: A Chamber of Scrutiny," in *The Future of Parliament: Issues for a New Century*, ed. Philip Giddings (London: Palgrave Macmillan, 2005), 113.

13 Patrick Diamond, *The End of Whitehall? Government by Permanent Campaign* (London: Palgrave Macmillan, 2018), 88.

14 Nevil Johnson, *Reshaping the British Constitution: Essays in Political Interpretation* (London: Palgrave Macmillan, 2004), 135.

15 "Electoral Reform," (Ottawa: Liberal Party of Canada, n.d.), https://www.liberal.ca/realchange/electoral-reform/.

16 For an excellent series of articles see Andrew Potter, Daniel Weinstock, and Peter Loewen, eds, *Should We Change How We Vote: Evaluating Canada's Electoral System* (Montreal: McGill-Queen's University Press, 2017).

17 See, among others, Henry Milner ed., *Steps Toward Making Every Vote Count: Electoral System Reform in Canada and Its Provinces* (Toronto: University of Toronto Press, 1999).

18 Canada, "Elections: Current and Past Elections," Elections Canada, n.d., http://www.elections.ca/content.aspx?section=ele&document=index&lang=e.

19 Aucoin, Jarvis, and Turnbull, *Democratizing the Constitution*, 6.

20 I am thinking here of Paul Martin, Stephen Harper, and Justin Trudeau, who gave the reform of Parliament an important place in their electoral reforms.

21 Philip Giddings, "Purpose and Prospects," in *The Future of Parliament: Issues for a New Century*, ed. Philip Giddings (London: Palgrave Macmillan, 2005), 259.

22 Aucoin, Jarvis, and Turnbull, *Democratizing the Constitution*, 221–3.

23 See C.E.S. Franks, "Omnibus Bills Subvert Our Legislative Process," *Globe and Mail*, 14 July 2010.

24 Bill Curry, "Opposition MPs Cry Foul over Liberals' Tabling of 300-Page Bill," *Globe and Mail*, 11 April 2017.

25 Senator Lowell Murray, "Power, Responsibility, and Agency in Canadian Government," in *Governing: Essays in Honour of Donald J. Savoie*, ed.

James Bickerton and B. Guy Peters (Montreal: McGill-Queen's University Press, 2013), 26.

26 Paul Thomas, "Some Quick, Brief Thoughts on Reform to the Supply Process" (mimeo, University of Manitoba, 7 April 2012).

27 William P. Cross and André Blais, *Politics at the Centre: The Selection and Removal of Party Leaders in Anglo Parliamentary Democracies* (Oxford: Oxford University Press, 2012).

28 Christopher Moore, "Keeping Party Leaders Honest: Canadians Do It Differently from Most – and Quite Possibly Not as Well," *Literary Review of Canada* 20, no. 5 (2012).

29 Quoted in ibid.

30 Kirby and Segal, *A House Undivided.*

31 André Pratte, "Why Regional Representation Is the Wrong Basis for Senate Reform," *Globe and Mail,* 26 September 2016.

32 The one contribution that stands out is Patrice Dutil's *Prime Ministerial Power in Canada: Its Origins Under Macdonald, Laurier and Borden* (Vancouver: UBC Press, 2017). Dutil makes an excellent contribution to the debate by leveraging a historical perspective to map out how government from the centre took shape.

33 Murray, "Power, Responsibility, and Agency in Canadian Government," 47.

34 Johnson, *Reshaping the British Constitution,* 85.

35 For an excellent book on the blame game, see Christopher Hood, *The Blame Game: Spin, Bureaucracy, and Self-Preservation in Government* (Princeton: Princeton University Press, 2011).

36 Johnson, *Reshaping the British Constitution,* 83–5.

37 See, for example, Carl Dahlström, B. Guy Peters, and Jon Pierre, *Steering from the Centre: Strengthening Political Control in Western Democracies* (Toronto: University of Toronto Press, 2011).

38 See, for example, Aaron Wherry, "How Justin Trudeau Plans to Deliver on Deliverology," CBC *News,* 27 August 2016, https://www.cbc.ca/news/politics/wherry-trudeau-deliverology-1.3735890.

39 Canada, *Canada's Public Service in 2017 – Part III* (Ottawa: Policy Horizon, n.d.), 29.

40 Kathryn May, "Tag, You're It: Auditor General Passes 'Broken' PS Culture to Politicians to Fix," *iPolitics,* 20 June 2018, https://ipolitics.ca/2018/06/20/tag-youre-it-auditor-general-passes-broken-ps-culture-to-politicians-to-fix/.

41 See, for example, Canada, *Twenty-Fourth Annual Report to the Prime Minister on the Public Service of Canada* (Ottawa: Privy Council Office, 31 March 2017).

42 Ralph Heintzman, "Can the Federal Public Service Fix Its Culture Problem?" *Globe and Mail*, 22 June 2018.

43 Canada, *Canada's Public Service in 2017 – Part III.*

44 Peter Aucoin, "New Political Governance in Westminster Systems: Impartial Public Administration and Management Performance at Risk," *Governance* 25, no. 2 (2012): 177–99.

45 Deputy ministers met in 2015 in Ottawa to discuss the problem. See Dean Beeby, "Top Bureaucrats Met to Resist Partisanship Imposed on Public Service," CBC *News*, 2 November 2015.

46 See, for example, Diamond, *The End of Whitehall?*

47 Andrea Lawlor, Alex Marland, and Thierry Giasson, "Emerging Voices, Evolving Concerns," in *Political Elites in Canada: Power and Influence in Instantaneous Times*, ed. Alex Marland, Thierry Giasson, and Andrea Lawlor (Vancouver: UBC Press, 2018), 276.

48 Donald J. Savoie, *Whatever Happened to the Music Teacher?*, 127.

49 Peter Aucoin and Mark D. Jarvis, *Modernizing Government Accountability: A Framework for Reform* (Ottawa: Canada School of Public Service, 2005), 82.

50 Canada, Commission of Inquiry into the Sponsorship Program and Advertising Activities, *Restoring Accountability: Recommendations* (Ottawa: Her Majesty the Queen in Right of Canada, 2006), 150–1.

51 Heintzman, "Can the Federal Public Service Fix Its Culture Problem?"

52 See, for example, Ralph Heintzman, "Establishing the Boundaries of the Public Service: Toward a New Moral Contract," the Vanier Lecture, Institute of Public Administration in Canada, 2007, 97.

53 "Treasury Hopes Senior Cuts Will Boost Employee Morale," *Ottawa Citizen*, 18 April 1989, A3

54 Ibid.

55 Savoie, *Breaking the Bargain*, 225.

56 Canada, GC Info Base, n.d., www.GCInfoBase.ca.

57 "But Was It Time Theft?" *Globe and Mail*, 9 September 2010, A3.

58 Kathryn May, "Top Bureaucrat Says Parliament Should Look at Changing PS Rules for Firing," *iPolitics*, 20 June 2018, https://ipolitics. ca/2018/06/20/top-bureaucrat-says-parliament-should-look-at-changing-ps-rules-for-firing/.

59 Canada, *Canada's Public Service in 2017 – Part III*, 27–8.
60 Kathryn May, "Union Still Furious over Clerk's Proposal to Make Firing Public Servants Easier," *iPolitics*, 8 August 2018, https://ipolitics. ca/2018/08/08/union-still-furious-over-clerks-proposal-to-make-firing-public-servants-easier/.
61 Savoie, *Whatever Happened to the Music Teacher?*, 216.
62 Barbara Wake Carroll and David Siegel, *Service in the Field: The World of Front-Line Public Servants* (Montreal: McGill-Queen's University Press, 1999), 119.
63 Aucoin, Jarvis, and Turnbull, *Democratizing the Constitution*, 248.

Index

and transfer payments, 133; and J. Trudeau's Cabinet, 174; war efforts and, 148–9, 171–2

opposition: and access to information legislation, 298; and blame game, 295; and budget, 198; and "gotcha" headlines, 193; and government spending accountability, 198; and media, 198; and officers of Parliament, 194, 195, 295

Ornstein, Michael, 132–3

Osborne, David, 268

Ouellet, André, 222

Owen, Taylor, 247

Oxford Internet Institute, 251

Paine, Thomas, 23, 35–6, 37; *Common Sense*, 36; *Rights of Man*, 26, 36

Palmerston, Lord, 290

Paltiel, Khayyam, 78

Paquin, Stéphane, 14

Parliament: Bagehot on, 33–4, 66; Bill of Rights and, 41; Charter of Rights and Freedoms and, 309, 340; courts vs, 66; Crown and, 5; decline of, 187; executive dominance over, 177; French language in, 129; governing from centre vs, 352; and government accountability, 191; and government spending, 186, 187, 189; history of, 30; as mattering, 176; media vs, 352; ministers as responsible to, 219; and monarchy, 30–1, 32–4; as observer vs participant, 112–13; officers of, 193–7; omnibus bills, 355–6; as permanent body, 31; press gallery, 241, 243–4; prime ministers

and, 354–5; prime ministers and changes to, 331; public opinion of, 313, 333; and Quebec Resolutions, 57; and representative democracy, 353; role, 177; scrutiny of legislation, 355–6; and Senate reform, 208; strengthening role of, 352, 354–5; supremacy of, 95, 110, 308, 340, 352; Supreme Court and, 95

Parliamentary Budget Office/officer, 196–7, 282, 283, 411n87

Parrish, Carolyn, 183

parties, political: in 1867, 78, 96, 181; and brand ambassadors, 252–3; brokerage model, 160; Canadian union and, 43; candidate nominations, 159; career vs novice politicians and, 158; and citizen engagement in politics, 168–9; Crown and, 66; and education of citizens, 163; evolution of, 95–7; fear of alienation of important societal segments, 169; and federal-provincial programs, 124; federal spending regardless of, 123; first-past-post voting system and, 170–1; and geography, 161; and House of Commons confidence, 169; ideological polarization in Britain, 185; and ideology, 160; immigration and, 127; increased definition overtime, 110, 181–2; judges and, 307, 311; leaders' power to reject candidates, 355; linguistic cleavages and, 161; lobbyists and, 320; loss of brand to leaders, 175; loyalty to, 182–3; membership, 8, 157, 164; and